S0-BJA-984

# STAND OUT

## Evidence-Based Learning for College and Career Readiness

**5**

THIRD EDITION

# LESSON PLANNER

STACI JOHNSON

ROB JENKINS

NATIONAL
GEOGRAPHIC
LEARNING

CENGAGE
Learning·

Australia • Brazil • Mexico • Singapore • United Kingdom • United States

**Stand Out 5: Evidence-Based Learning for College and Career Readiness, Third Edition**
**Staci Johnson and Rob Jenkins**
**Lesson Planner**

Publisher: Sherrise Roehr

Executive Editor: Sarah Kenney

Development Editor: Lewis Thompson

Editorial Project Manager: Jason A. Velázquez

Director of Global Marketing: Ian Martin

Executive Marketing Manager: Ben Rivera

Product Marketing Manager: Dalia Bravo

Director of Content and Media Production:
   Michael Burggren

Production Manager: Daisy Sosa

Media Researcher: Leila Hishmeh

Senior Print Buyer: Mary Beth Hennebury

Cover and Interior Designer:
   Brenda Carmichael

Composition: Lumina Datamatics, Inc.

Cover Image: Seth Joel/Getty Images

Bottom Images: Jay B Sauceda/Getty Images;
   Tripod/Getty Images; Portra Images/Getty
   Images; Portra Images/Getty Images; Mark
   Edward Atkinson/Tracey Lee/Getty Images;
   Hero Images/Getty Images; Jade/Getty
   Images; James Porter/Getty Images; LWA/
   Larry Williams/Getty Images; Dimitri Otis/
   Getty Images

© 2017 National Geographic Learning, a part of Cengage Learning

ALL RIGHTS RESERVED. No part of this work covered by the copyright herein may be reproduced or distributed in any form or by any means, except as permitted by U.S. copyright law, without the prior written permission of the copyright owner.

"National Geographic" "National Geographic Society" and the Yellow Border Design are registered trademarks of the National Geographic Society
® Marcas Registradas

For product information and technology assistance, contact us at
**Cengage Learning Customer & Sales Support, 1-800-354-9706**

For permission to use material from this text or product,
submit all requests online at **cengage.com/permissions**

Further permissions questions can be emailed to
**permissionrequest@cengage.com**

Student Book
ISBN 13: 978-1-305-65565-2

**National Geographic Learning/Cengage Learning**
20 Channel Center Street
Boston, MA 02210
USA

Cengage Learning is a leading provider of customized learning solutions with office locations around the globe, including Singapore, the United Kingdom, Australia, Mexico, Brazil, and Japan. Locate your local office at:
**international.cengage.com/region**

Cengage Learning products are represented in Canada by Nelson Education, Ltd.

Visit National Geographic Learning online at **NGL.Cengage.com**
Visit our corporate website at **www.cengage.com**

Printed in the United States of America
Print Number: 01   Print Year: 2016

# ACKNOWLEDGMENTS

Ellen Albano
*Mcfatter Technical College, Davie, FL*

Esther Anaya-Garcia
*Glendale Community College, Glendale, AZ*

Carol Bellamy
*Prince George's Community College, Largo, MD*

Gail Bier
*Atlantic Technical College, Coconut Creek, FL*

Kathryn Black
*Myrtle Beach Family Learning Center, Myrtle Beach, SC*

Claudia Brantley
*College of Southern Nevada, Las Vegas, NV*

Dr. Joan-Yvette Campbell
*Lindsey Hopkins Technical College, Miami, FL*

Maria Carmen Iglesias
*Miami Senior Adult Educational Center, Miami, FL*

Lee Chen
*Palomar College, San Marcos, CA*

Casey Cahill
*Atlantic Technical College, Coconut Creek, FL*

Maria Dillehay
*Burien Job Training and Education Center, Goodwill, Seattle, WA*

Irene Fjaerestad
*Olympic College, Bremerton, WA*

Eleanor Forfang-Brockman
*Tarrant County College, Fort Worth, Texas*

Jesse Galdamez
*San Bernardino Adult School, San Bernardino, CA*

Anna Garoz
*Lindsey Hopkins Technical Education Center, Miami, FL*

Maria Gutierrez
*Miami Sunset Adult, Miami, FL*

Noel Hernandez
*Palm Beach County Public Schools, Palm Beach County, FL*

Kathleen Hiscock
*Portland Adult Education, Portland, ME*

Frantz Jean-Louis
*The English Center, Miami, FL*

Annette Johnson
*Sheridan Technical College, Hollywood, FL*

Ginger Karaway
*Gateway Technical College, Kenosha, WI*

Judy Martin-Hall
*Indian River State College, Fort Pierce, FL*

Toni Molinaro
*Dixie Hollins Adult Education Center, St Petersburg, FL*

Tracey Person
*Cape Cod Community College, Hyannis, MA*

Celina Paula
*Miami-Dade County Public Schools, Miami, FL*

Veronica Pavon-Baker
*Miami Beach Adult, Miami, FL*

Ileana Perez
*Robert Morgan Technical College, Miami, FL*

Neeta Rancourt
*Atlantic Technical College, Coconut Creek, FL*

Brenda Roland
*Joliet Junior College, Joliet, IL*

Hidelisa Sampson
*Las Vegas Urban League, Las Vegas, NV*

Lisa Schick
*James Madison University, Harrisonburg, VA*

Rob Sheppard
*Quincy Asian Resources, Quincy, MA*

Sydney Silver
*Burien Job Training and Education Center, Goodwill, Seattle, WA*

Teresa Tamarit
*Miami Senior Adult Educational Center, Miami, FL*

Cristina Urena
*Atlantic Technical College, Fort Lauderdale, FL*

Pamela Jo Wilson
*Palm Beach County Public Schools, Palm Beach County, FL*

# ABOUT THE AUTHORS

## Staci Johnson

Ever since I can remember, I've been fascinated with other cultures and languages. I love to travel and every place I go, the first thing I want to do is meet the people, learn their language, and understand their culture. Becoming an ESL teacher was a perfect way to turn what I love to do into my profession. There's nothing more incredible than the exchange of teaching and learning from one another that goes on in an ESL classroom. And there's nothing more rewarding than helping a student succeed.

## Rob Jenkins

I love teaching. I love to see the expressions on my students' faces when the light goes on and their eyes show such sincere joy of learning. I knew the first time I stepped into an ESL classroom that this is where I needed to be and I have never questioned that resolution. I have worked in business, sales, and publishing, and I've found challenge in all, but nothing can compare to the satisfaction of reaching people in such a personal way.

Along with the inclusion of National Geographic content, the third edition of **Stand Out** boasts several innovations. In response to initiatives regarding the development of more complexity with reading and encouraging students to interact more with reading texts, we are proud to introduce new rich reading sections that allow students to discuss topics relevant to a global society. We have also introduced new National Geographic videos that complement the life-skill videos **Stand Out** introduced in the second edition and which are now integrated into the student books. We don't stop there; **Stand Out** has even more activities that require critical and creative thinking that serve to maximize learning and prepare students for the future. The third edition also has online workbooks. **Stand Out** was the first mainstream ESL textbook for adults to introduce a lesson plan format, hundreds of customizable worksheets, and project-based instruction. The third edition expands on these features in its mission to provide rich learning opportunities that can be exploited in different ways. We believe that with the innovative approach that made **Stand Out** a leader from its inception, the many new features, and the new look, programs, teachers, and students will find great success!

## Stand Out Mission Statement:

Our goal is to give students challenging opportunities to be successful in their language-learning experience so they develop confidence and become independent lifelong learners.

# TO THE TEACHER

## ABOUT THE SERIES

The **Stand Out** series is designed to facilitate *active* learning within life-skill settings that lead students to career and academic pathways. Each student book and its supplemental components in the six-level series expose students to competency areas most useful and essential for newcomers with careful treatment of level-appropriate but challenging materials. Students grow academically by developing essential literacy and critical-thinking skills that will help them find personal success in a changing and dynamic world.

## THE STAND OUT PHILOSOPHY

### Integrated Skills

In each of the five lessons of every unit, skills are introduced as they might be in real language use. They are in context and not separated into different sections of the unit. We believe that for real communication to occur, the classroom should mirror real life as much as possible.

### Objective Driven Activities

Every lesson in **Stand Out** is driven by a performance objective. These objectives have been carefully selected to ensure they are measurable, accessible to students at their particular level, and relevant to students and their lives. Good objectives lead to effective learning. Effective objectives also lead to appropriate self, student, and program assessment which is increasingly required by state and federal mandates.

### Lesson Plan Sequencing

**Stand Out** follows an established sequence of activities that provides students with the tools they need to have in order to practice and apply the skills required in the objective. A pioneer in Adult Education for introducing the Madeline Hunter WIPPEA lesson plan model into textbooks, **Stand Out** continues to provide a clear and easy-to-follow system for presenting and developing English language skills. The WIPPEA model follows six steps:

- **W**arm up and Review
- **I**ntroduction
- **P**resentation
- **P**ractice
- **E**valuation
- **A**pplication

### Learning and Acquisition

In **Stand Out**, the recycling of skills is emphasized. Students must learn and practice the same skills multiple times in various contexts to actually acquire them. Practicing a skill one time is rarely sufficient for acquisition and rarely addresses diverse student needs and learning styles.

### Critical Thinking

Critical thinking has been defined in various ways and sometimes so broadly that any activity could be classified to meet the criteria. To be clear and to draw attention to the strong critical thinking activities in **Stand Out,** we define these activities as *tasks that require learners to think deeper than the superficial vocabulary and meaning.* Activities such as ranking, making predictions, analyzing, or solving problems demand that students think beyond the surface. Critical thinking is highlighted throughout so the instructor can be confident that effective learning is going on.

### Learner-Centered, Cooperative, and Communicative Activities

**Stand Out** provides ample opportunities for students to develop interpersonal skills and to practice new vocabulary through graphic organizers and charts like Venn diagrams, graphs, classifying charts, and mind maps. The lesson planners provide learner-centered approaches in every lesson. Students are asked to rank items, make decisions, and negotiate amongst other things.

Dialogues are used to prepare students for these activities in the low levels and fewer dialogues are used at the higher levels where students have already acquired the vocabulary and rudimentary conversation skills.

Activities should provide opportunities for students to speak in near authentic settings so they have confidence to perform outside the classroom. This does not mean that dialogues and other mechanical activities are not used to prepare students for cooperative activities, but these mechanical activities do not foster conversation. They merely provide the first tools students need to go beyond mimicry.

### Assessment

Instructors and students should have a clear understanding of what is being taught and what is expected. In **Stand Out**, objectives are clearly stated so that target skills can be effectively assessed throughout.

Formative assessments are essential. Pre- and post-assessments can be given for units or sections of the book through ExamView®—a program that makes developing tests easy and effective. These tests can be created to appear like standardized tests, which are important for funding and to help students prepare.

Finally, *learner logs* allow students to self-assess, document progress, and identify areas that might require additional attention.

## SUPPLEMENTAL COMPONENTS

The **Stand Out** series is a comprehensive tool for all student needs. There is no need to look any further than the resources offered.

### Stand Out Lesson Planners

The lesson planners go beyond merely describing activities in the student book by providing teacher support, ideas, and guidance for the entire class period.

- **Standards correlations** for **CCRS, CASAS,** and **SCANS** are identified for each lesson.
- **Pacing Guides** help with planning by giving instructors suggested durations for each activity and a selection of activities for different class lengths.
- **Teacher Tips** provide point-of-use pedagogical comments and best practices.
- **At-A-Glance Lesson Openers** provide the instructor with everything that will be taught in a particular lesson. Elements include the agenda, the goal, grammar, pronunciation, academic strategies, critical thinking elements, correlations to standards, and resources.
- **Suggested Activities** go beyond what is shown in the text providing teachers with ideas that will stimulate them to come up with their own.
- **Listening Scripts** are integrated into the unit pages for easy access.

### Stand Out Workbook

The workbook in the third edition takes the popular **Stand Out Grammar Challenge** and expands it to include vocabulary building, life-skill development, and grammar practice associated directly with each lesson in the student book.

### Stand Out Online Workbook

One of the most important innovations in the third edition of **Stand Out** is the online workbook. This workbook provides unique activities that are closely related to the student book and gives students opportunities to have access to audio and video.

The online workbook provides opportunities for students to practice and improve digital literacy skills essential for 21st century learners. These skills are essential for standardized computer and online testing. Scores in these tests will improve when students can concentrate on the content and not so much on the technology.

### Activity Bank

The activity bank is an online feature that provides several hundred multilevel worksheets per level to enhance the already rich materials available through **Stand Out**.

### DVD Program

The **Stand Out Lifeskills Video Program** continues to be available with eight episodes per level; however, now the worksheets are part of the student books with additional help in the lesson planners.

New to the third edition of **Stand Out** are two National Geographic videos per level. Each video is accompanied by four pages of instruction and activities with support in the lesson planners.

### ExamView®

ExamView® is a program that provides customizable test banks and allows instructors to make lesson, unit, and program tests quickly.

## STANDARDS AND CORRELATIONS

**Stand Out** is the pioneer in establishing a foundation of standards within each unit and through every objective. The standards movement in the United States is as dominant today as it was when **Stand Out** was first published. Schools and programs must be aware of ongoing local and federal initiatives and make attempts to meet ever-changing requirements.

In the first edition of **Stand Out**, we identified direct correlations to SCANS, EFF, and CASAS standards. *The Secretary's Commission on Achieving Necessary Skills,* or SCANS, and *Equipped for the Future,* or EFF, standards are still important and are identified in every lesson of **Stand Out**. These skills include the basic skills, interpersonal skills, and problem-solving skills necessary to be successful in the workplace, in school, and in the community. **Stand Out** was also developed with a thorough understanding of objectives established by the *Comprehensive Adult Student Assessment Systems* or CASAS. Many programs have experienced great success with their CASAS scores using **Stand Out**, and these objectives continue to be reflected in the third edition.

Today, a new emphasis on critical thinking and complexity has swept the nation. Students are expected to think for themselves more now than ever before. They must also interact with reading texts at a higher level. These new standards and expectations are highly visible in the third edition and include *College and Career Readiness Standards.*

**Stand Out** offers a complete set of correlations online for all standards to demonstrate how closely we align with state and federal guidelines.

# IMPORTANT INNOVATIONS IN THE THIRD EDITION

### New Look

Although the third edition of **Stand Out** boasts the same lesson plan format and task-based activities that made it one of the most popular books in adult education, it now has an updated look with the addition of National Geographic content, which will capture the attention of the instructor and every student.

### Critical Thinking

With the advent of new federal and state initiatives, teachers need to be confident that students will use critical thinking skills when learning. This has always been a goal in **Stand Out**, but now those opportunities are highlighted in each lesson.

### College and Career Readiness Skills

These skills are also identified by critical thinking strategies and academic-related activities, which are found throughout **Stand Out**. New to the third edition is a special reading section in each unit that challenges students and encourages them to develop reading strategies within a rich National Geographic environment.

### Stand Out Workbook

The print workbook is now more extensive and complete with vocabulary, life skills, and grammar activities to round out any program. Many instructors might find these pages ideal for homework, but they of course can be used for additional practice within the classroom.

### Media and Online Support

Media and online support includes audio, video, online workbooks, presentation tools, multi-level worksheets, ExamView®, and standards correlations.

# CONTENTS

| Numeracy/Academic Skills | CCRS | SCANS | CASAS |
|---|---|---|---|
| • Pronunciation: Enunciate clearly<br>• Develop research skills and ideas<br>• Take notes<br>• Focused listening<br>• Prepare and deliver an oral presentation<br>• Write a personal message | RI1, RI4, RI7, W2, W6, W7, W8, W9, SL1, SL2, SL3 | **Many SCANS skills are incorporated in this unit with an emphasis on:**<br>• Listening<br>• Speaking<br>• Social<br>• Visualization<br>• Cultural diversity | **1:** 0.1.1, 0.1.2, 0.1.4, 7.2.1<br>**2:** 0.2.1, 0.2.4<br>**3:** 0.2.3<br>**RE:** 7.44 |
| • Reading<br>• Interpret meanings of words in context<br>• Develop categories<br>• Write a paragraph<br>• Focused listening<br>• Take notes from lecture/oral sources<br>• Interpret bar graphs<br>• Research online | RI1, RI2, RI3, RI4, RI7, RI10, W2, W4, W7, W8, SL1, SL2, SL3, L1 | **Many SCANS skills are incorporated in this unit with an emphasis on:**<br>• Writing<br>• Social<br>• Negotiation<br>• Leadership<br>• Self-esteem<br>• Self-management<br>• Responsibility<br>• Decision making | **VB:** 7.4.5<br>**1:** 7.4.2, 7.4.9<br>**2:** 4.1.9, 7.4.2<br>**3:** 7.4.2<br>**4:** 7.1.1, 7.1.2, 7.1.3, 7.4.2<br>**5:** 7.1.3<br>**RV:** 7.2.1<br>**RE:** 4.9.3, 7.2.1, 7.4.4, 7.4.5, 7.4.6<br>**TP:** 4.8.1, 4.8.5, 4.8.6 |
| • Interpret meaning of idioms in context<br>• Focused listening<br>• Analyze and evaluate readings and budgets<br>• Outline readings<br>• Summarize reading passages and other sources of information<br>• Make calculations<br>• Create a budget | RI1, RI2, RI3, RI4, RI5, RI7, RI10, W2, W4, W5, W7, W8, SL1, SL2, SL3, SL6, L1, L2, L5 | **Many SCANS skills are incorporated in this unit with an emphasis on:**<br>• Mathematics<br>• Social<br>• Self-management<br>• Responsibility<br>• Problem-solving<br>• Decision making | **VB:** 7.4.5<br>**1:** 1.5.1, 4.1.4, 2.5.5<br>**2:** 1.6.2<br>**3:** 7.4.2<br>**4:** 1.3.2, 7.4.2<br>**5:** 1.6.2, 7.4.2<br>**RV:** 7.2.1<br>**RE:** 4.9.3, 7.2.1, 7.4.4, 7.4.5, 7.4.6<br>**TP:** 4.8.1, 4.8.5, 4.8.6 |

# CONTENTS

| Numeracy/ Academic Skills | CCRS | SCANS | CASAS |
|---|---|---|---|
| • Organize sentences effectively to convey meaning<br>• Focused listening<br>• Read and interpret information<br>• Scan for details<br>• Outline prior to writing<br>• Write two paragraph essay<br>• Research through interview and on the computer<br>• Make calculations<br>• Interpret a chart | RI1, RI4, RI7, RI10, W2, W4, W5, W6, W7, W8, SL1, SL2, SL3, SL4, SL6, L3 | **Many SCANS skills are incorporated in this unit with an emphasis on:**<br>• Mathematics<br>• Reading<br>• Writing<br>• Listening<br>• Negotiation<br>• Decision making | **VB:** 7.4.5<br>**1:** 1.9.5<br>**2:** 1.9.6<br>**3:** 1.9.8<br>**4:** 1.9.3<br>**5:** 1.9.2<br>**RV:** 7.2.1<br>**RE:** 4.9.3, 7.2.1, 7.4.4, 7.4.5, 7.4.6<br>**TP:** 4.8.1, 4.8.5, 4.8.6 |
| • Understand and use parts of speech related to root words<br>• Focused listening<br>• Summarize reading passages<br>• Scan for details<br>• Skim for general ideas<br>• Prepare and deliver an oral presentation<br>• Research online | RI1, RI2, RI3, RI4, RI7, RI10, W2, W7, W8, SL1, SL2, SL3, SL4, SL6, L1, L3 | **Many SCANS skills are incorporated in this unit with an emphasis on:**<br>• Problem-solving<br>• Self-management<br>• Reading<br>• Mathematics<br>• Creative thinking<br>• Responsibility<br>• Visualization | **VB:** 7.4.5<br>**1:** 2.1.8<br>**2:** 1.4.3<br>**3:** 1.4.5<br>**4:** 1.4.6<br>**5:** 1.4.7, 1.4.8<br>**RV:** 7.2.1<br>**RE:** 4.9.3, 7.2.1, 7.4.4, 7.4.5, 7.4.6<br>**TP:** 4.8.1, 4.8.5, 4.8.6 |
| • Analyze and use root words and related parts of speech<br>• Focused listening<br>• Make calculations<br>• Interview others<br>• Understand bar graphs<br>• Read a spread sheet<br>• Brainstorm<br>• Use reference materials including a computer | RI1, RI2, RI3, RI4, RI7, RI10, W2, W3, W4, W5, W7, W8, SL1, SL2, SL4, SL5 SL6, L1, L2, L5 | **Many SCANS skills are incorporated in this unit with an emphasis on:**<br>• Mathematics<br>• Reading<br>• Self-esteem<br>• Self-management<br>• Responsibility<br>• Problem-solving<br>• Visualization<br>• Decision making | **VB:** 7.4.5<br>**1:** 3.5.8, 3.5.9<br>**2:** 3.2.3, 3.2.4<br>**3:** 3.2.3, 3.4.5<br>**4:** 3.2.3<br>**5:** 3.4.3<br>**RV:** 7.2.1<br>**RE:** 4.9.3, 7.2.1, 7.4.4, 7.4.5, 7.4.6<br>**TP:** 4.8.1, 4.8.5, 4.8.6 |

# CONTENTS

**Appendices**

For other national and state specific standards, please visit:
**www.NGL.Cengage.com/SO3**

| Numeracy/ Academic Skills | CCRS | SCANS | CASAS |
|---|---|---|---|
| • Understand and use synonyms<br>• Use reference materials<br>• Research online<br>• Use a computer to study<br>• Take notes<br>• Scan for main ideas and details<br>• Brainstorm and construct arguments | RI1, RI2, RI3, RI4, RI7, RI8, W1, W2, W4, W5, W6, W7, W8, W9, SL1, SL2, SL4, SL5, SL6, L1 | **Many SCANS skills are incorporated in this unit with an emphasis on:**<br>• Social interaction<br>• Negotiation<br>• Self-management<br>• Decision making<br>• Writing | **VB:** 7.4.5<br>**1:** 1.2.4, 1.2.3, 1.2.5, 6.4.1, 6.4.3, 7.4.4<br>**2:** 1.3.1, 1.3.3<br>**3:** 1.6.3, 1.6.4, 1.7.1<br>**4:** 1.3.3<br>**5:** 1.6.3<br>**RV:** 7.2.1<br>**RE:** 4.9.3, 7.2.1, 7.4.4, 7.4.5, 7.4.6<br>**TP:** 4.8.1, 4.8.5, 4.8.6 |
| • Interpret visual representations<br>• Understand root words and suffixes<br>• Analyze and evaluate<br>• Understand and write directions and reports<br>• Focused listening<br>• Summarize reading passages | RI1, RI2, RI3, RI4, RI7, RI10, W2, W4, W5, W8, W9, SL1, SL2, L1 | **Many SCANS skills are incorporated in this unit with an emphasis on:**<br>• Social<br>• Problem-solving<br>• Visualization<br>• Creative thinking<br>• Negotiation<br>• Teamwork<br>• Leadership<br>• Reading | **VB:** 4.5.1, 7.4.5<br>**1:** 4.4.8, 4.5.1, 4.5.4, 4.5.6<br>**2:** 4.5.7<br>**3:** 4.5.3, 4.7.2<br>**4:** 4.8.1, 4.8.5, 4.8.6<br>**5:** 4.6.4<br>**RV:** 7.2.1<br>**RE:** 4.9.3, 7.2.1, 7.4.4, 7.4.5, 7.4.6<br>**TP:** 4.8.1, 4.8.5, 4.8.6 |
| • Interpret meanings of words in context<br>• Focused listening<br>• Scan for details<br>• Skim for general ideas<br>• Identify and paraphrase information<br>• Analyze and evaluate<br>• Interview others<br>• Write a paragraph<br>• Use transitional expressions in writing<br>• Create visual representation to brainstorm<br>• Write a speech | RI1, RI2, RI3, RI4, RI5, RI8, RI10, W1, W3, W4, W5, SL1, SL2, SL3, SL4, SL6, L5 | **Many SCANS skills are incorporated in this unit with an emphasis on:**<br>• Reading<br>• Speaking<br>• Responsibility<br>• Cultural diversity<br>• Decision making | **VB:** 7.4.5<br>**1:** 1.5.1, 5.3.6<br>**2:** 1.6.2, 5.2.2, 5.3.2, 5.7.1,<br>**3:** 5.6.2 , 5.3.8, 7.4.2<br>**4:** 1.3.2, 5.3.7, 5.7.1, 7.4.2<br>**5:** 5.1.6, 5.7.1, 7.4.2<br>**R:** 7.2.1<br>**RE:** 4.9.3, 7.2.1, 7.4.4, 7.4.5, 7.4.6<br>**IP:** 4.8.1, 4.8.5, 4.8.6 |

# INTRODUCING
# STAND OUT, Third Edition!

**Stand Out** is a six-level, standards-based ESL series for adult education with a proven track record of successful results. The new edition of **Stand Out** continues to provide students with the foundations and tools needed to achieve success in life, college, and career.

## *Stand Out* now integrates real-world content from National Geographic

UNIT **1**
**Balancing Your Life**

**UNIT OUTCOMES**
- Analyze and create schedules
- Identify goals and obstacles and suggest solutions
- Write about a personal goal
- Analyze study habits
- Manage time

**Look at the photo and answer the questions.**
1. What do you think the people are doing?
2. What activities do you do every day?
3. What do you want to do in the future?

Construction workers on beams at the top of the Stratosphere Tower in Las Vegas.

- **Stand Out** now integrates high-interest, real-world content from National Geographic which enhances its proven approach to lesson planning and instruction. A stunning National Geographic image at the beginning of each unit introduces the theme and engages learners in meaningful conversations right from the start.

# *Stand Out* supports college and career readiness

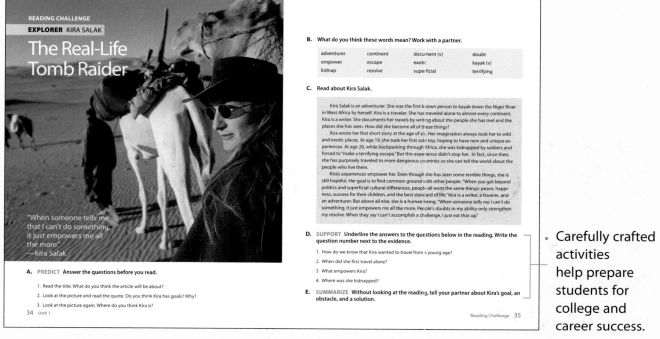

**READING CHALLENGE**
**EXPLORER** KIRA SALAK

## The Real-Life Tomb Raider

*"When someone tells me that I can't do something, it just empowers me all the more."*
—Kira Salak

**A.** **PREDICT** Answer the questions before you read.

1. Read the title. What do you think the article will be about?
2. Look at the picture and read the quote. Do you think Kira has goals? Why?
3. Look at the picture again. Where do you think Kira is?

34 Unit 1

**B.** What do you think these words mean? Work with a partner.

| | | | |
|---|---|---|---|
| adventurer | continent | document (v) | doubt |
| empower | escape | exotic | kayak (v) |
| kidnap | resolve | superficial | terrifying |

**C.** Read about Kira Salak.

Kira Salak is an adventurer. She was the first known person to kayak down the Niger River in West Africa by herself. Kira is a traveler. She has traveled alone to almost every continent. Kira is a writer. She documents her travels by writing about the people she has met and the places she has seen. How did she become all of these things?

Kira wrote her first short story at the age of six. Her imagination always took her to wild and exotic places. At age 19, she took her first solo trip, hoping to have new and unique experiences. At age 20, while backpacking through Africa, she was kidnapped by soldiers and forced to "make a terrifying escape." But this experience didn't stop her. In fact, since then, she has purposely traveled to more dangerous countries so she can tell the world about the people who live there.

Kira's experiences empower her. Even though she has seen some terrible things, she is still hopeful. Her goal is to find common ground with other people. "When you get beyond politics and superficial cultural differences, people all want the same things: peace, happiness, success for their children, and the best standard of life." Kira is a writer, a traveler, and an adventurer. But above all else, she is a human being. "When someone tells me I can't do something, it just empowers me all the more. People's doubts in my ability only strengthen my resolve. When they say I can't accomplish a challenge, I just eat that up."

**D.** **SUPPORT** Underline the answers to the questions below in the reading. Write the question number next to the evidence.

1. How do we know that Kira wanted to travel from a young age?
2. When did she first travel alone?
3. What empowers Kira?
4. Where was she kidnapped?

**E.** **SUMMARIZE** Without looking at the reading, tell your partner about Kira's goal, an obstacle, and a solution.

Reading Challenge 35

- Carefully crafted activities help prepare students for college and career success.

- **NEW Reading Challenge** in every unit features a fascinating story about a **National Geographic explorer** to immerse learners in authentic content.

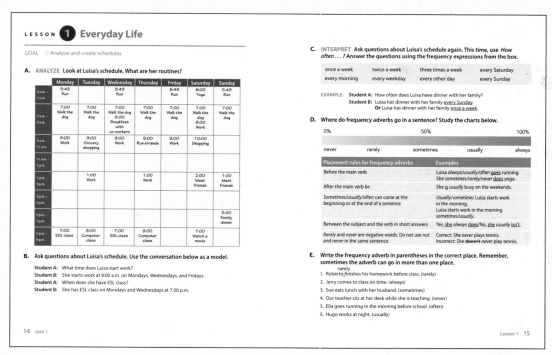

**LESSON 1 Everyday Life**

GOAL ■ Analyze and create schedules

**A.** **ANALYZE** Look at Luisa's schedule. What are her routines?

| | Monday | Tuesday | Wednesday | Thursday | Friday | Saturday | Sunday |
|---|---|---|---|---|---|---|---|
| 5 a.m.–7 a.m. | 5:45 Run | | 5:45 Run | | 5:45 Run | 6:00 Yoga | 5:45 Run |
| 7 a.m.–9 a.m. | 7:00 Walk the dog | 7:00 Walk the dog | 7:00 Walk the dog 8:00 Breakfast with co-workers | 7:00 Walk the dog | 7:00 Walk the dog | 7:00 Walk the dog 8:00 Work | 7:00 Walk the dog |
| 9 a.m.–11 a.m. | 9:00 Work | 9:00 Grocery shopping | 9:00 Work | 9:00 Run errands | 9:00 Work | 10:00 Shopping | |
| 11 a.m.–1 p.m. | | | | | | | |
| 1 p.m.–3 p.m. | | 1:00 Work | | 1:00 Work | | 2:00 Meet friends | 1:00 Meet friends |
| 3 p.m.–5 p.m. | | | | | | | |
| 5 p.m.–7 p.m. | | | | | | | 5:00 Family dinner |
| 7 p.m.– | 7:00 ESL class | 8:00 Computer class | 7:00 ESL class | 8:00 Computer class | 7:00 Watch a movie | | |

**B.** Ask questions about Luisa's schedule. Use the conversation below as a model.

Student A: What time does Luisa start work?
Student B: She starts work at 9:00 a.m. on Mondays, Wednesdays, and Fridays.
Student A: When does she have ESL class?
Student B: She has ESL class on Mondays and Wednesdays at 7:00 p.m.

14 Unit 1

**C.** **INTERPRET** Ask questions about Luisa's schedule again. This time, use *How often . . . ?* Answer the questions using the frequency expressions from the box.

| | | | |
|---|---|---|---|
| once a week | twice a week | three times a week | every Saturday |
| every morning | every weekday | every other day | every Sunday |

EXAMPLE: Student A: How often does Luisa have dinner with her family?
Student B: Luisa has dinner with her family *every Sunday*.
Or Luisa has dinner with her family *once a week*.

**D.** Where do frequency adverbs go in a sentence? Study the charts below.

| 0% | | 50% | | 100% |
|---|---|---|---|---|
| never | rarely | sometimes | usually | always |

| Placement rules for frequency adverbs | Examples |
|---|---|
| Before the main verb | Luisa *always/usually/often* goes running. She *sometimes/rarely/never* does yoga. |
| After the main verb *be* | She *is* usually busy on the weekends. |
| *Sometimes/usually/often* can come at the beginning or at the end of a sentence | *Usually/sometimes* Luisa starts work in the morning. Luisa starts work in the morning *sometimes/usually*. |
| Between the subject and the verb in short answers | Yes, she always does/No, she usually isn't. |
| *Rarely* and *never* are negative words. Do not use *not* and *never* in the same sentence. | Correct: She *never* plays tennis. Incorrect: She doesn't *never* play tennis. |

**E.** Write the frequency adverb in parentheses in the correct place. Remember, sometimes the adverb can go in more than one place.

*rarely*
1. Roberto finishes his homework before class. (rarely)
2. Jerry comes to class on time. (always)
3. Sue eats lunch with her husband. (sometimes)
4. Our teacher sits at her desk while she is teaching. (never)
5. Elia goes running in the morning before school. (often)
6. Hugo works at night. (usually)

Lesson 1 15

- **EXPANDED Critical Thinking Activities** challenge learners to evaluate, analyze, and synthesize information to prepare them for the workplace and academic life.

- **NEW Video Challenge** showcases **National Geographic footage and explorers**, providing learners with the opportunity to synthesize what they have learned in prior units through the use of authentic content.

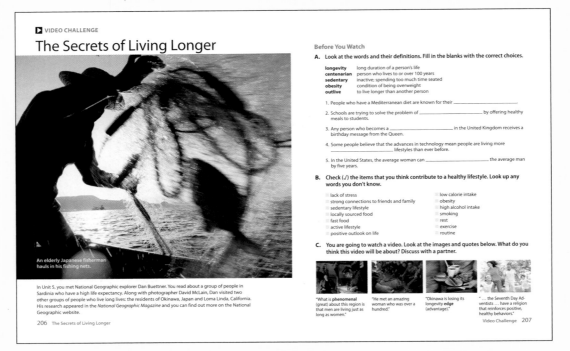

▶ VIDEO CHALLENGE

## The Secrets of Living Longer

An elderly Japanese fisherman hauls in his fishing nets.

In Unit 5, you met National Geographic explorer Dan Buettner. You read about a group of people in Sardinia who have a high life expectancy. Along with photographer David McLain, Dan visited two other groups of people who live long lives: the residents of Okinawa, Japan and Loma Linda, California. His research appeared in the *National Geographic Magazine* and you can find out more on the National Geographic website.

206   The Secrets of Living Longer

**Before You Watch**

**A. Look at the words and their definitions. Fill in the blanks with the correct choices.**

| | |
|---|---|
| **longevity** | long duration of a person's life |
| **centenarian** | person who lives to or over 100 years |
| **sedentary** | inactive; spending too much time seated |
| **obesity** | condition of being overweight |
| **outlive** | to live longer than another person |

1. People who have a Mediterranean diet are known for their _____

2. Schools are trying to solve the problem of _____ by offering healthy meals to students.

3. Any person who becomes a _____ in the United Kingdom receives a birthday message from the Queen.

4. Some people believe that the advances in technology mean people are living more _____ lifestyles than ever before.

5. In the United States, the average woman can _____ the average man by five years.

**B. Check (✓) the items that you think contribute to a healthy lifestyle. Look up any words you don't know.**

- lack of stress
- strong connections to friends and family
- sedentary lifestyle
- locally sourced food
- fast food
- active lifestyle
- positive outlook on life
- low calorie intake
- obesity
- high alcohol intake
- smoking
- rest
- exercise
- routine

**C. You are going to watch a video. Look at the images and quotes below. What do you think this video will be about? Discuss with a partner.**

"What is **phenomenal** (great) about this region is that men are living just as long as women."

"He met an amazing woman who was over a hundred."

"Okinawa is losing its longevity **edge** (advantage)."

" … the Seventh Day Adventists … have a religion that reinforces positive, healthy behaviors."

Video Challenge   207

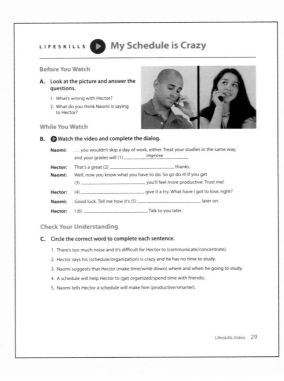

LIFESKILLS   ▶ **My Schedule is Crazy**

**Before You Watch**

**A. Look at the picture and answer the questions.**

1. What's wrong with Hector?
2. What do you think Naomi is saying to Hector?

**While You Watch**

**B. ▶ Watch the video and complete the dialog.**

**Naomi:** . . . you wouldn't skip a day of work, either. Treat your studies in the same way, and your grades will (1) __improve__

**Hector:** That's a great (2) _____, thanks.

**Naomi:** Well, now you know what you have to do. So go do it! If you get (3) _____ you'll feel more productive. Trust me!

**Hector:** (4) _____ give it a try. What have I got to lose, right?

**Naomi:** Good luck. Tell me how it's (5) _____ later on.

**Hector:** I (6) _____ Talk to you later.

**Check Your Understanding**

**C. Circle the correct word to complete each sentence.**

1. There's too much noise and it's difficult for Hector to (communicate/concentrate).
2. Hector says his (schedule/organization) is crazy and he has no time to study.
3. Naomi suggests that Hector (make time/write down) where and when he going to study.
4. A schedule will help Hector to (get organized/spend time with friends).
5. Naomi tells Hector a schedule will make him (productive/smarter).

Lifeskills Video   29

- The **Lifeskills Video** is a dramatic video series integrated into each unit of the student book that helps students learn natural spoken English and apply it to their everyday activities.

Pages shown are from **Stand Out**, Third Edition Level 3

- **NEW Online Workbook** engages students and supports the classroom by providing a wide variety of auto-graded interactive activities, an audio program, video from National Geographic, and pronunciation activities.

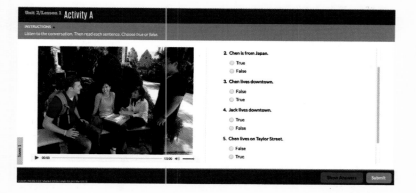

- **UPDATED Lesson Planner** includes correlations to **College and Career Readiness Standards (CCRS), CASAS, SCANS,** and references to **EL Civics** competencies to help instructors achieve the required standards.

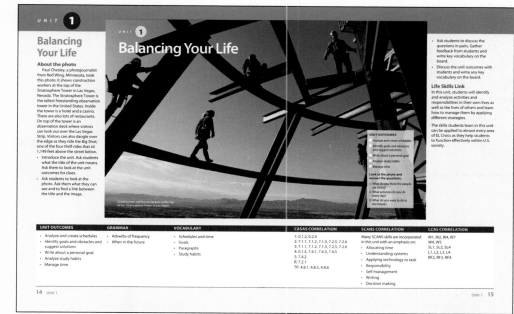

- **Teacher support  Stand Out** continues to provide a wide variety of user-friendly tools and interactive activities that help teachers prepare students for success while keeping them engaged and motivated.

## *Stand Out* supports teachers and learners

### LEARNER COMPONENTS

- Student Book
- Online Workbook powered by My**ELT**
- Print Workbook

### TEACHER COMPONENTS

- Lesson Planner
- Classroom DVD
- Assessment CD-ROM
- Teacher's companion site with Multilevel Worksheets

# Welcome

### Life Skills Link

Greet students with *Welcome!* Select random students to introduce yourself to. Give your name, and then ask his or her name. Respond with, *It's a pleasure to meet you, I'm pleased to meet you,* or *It's good to meet you.* After modeling these responses, introduce students to each other. Have them answer with *It's nice to meet you* or other reply.

Explain that asking about pastimes helps to drive conversation and that remarking on hobbies shows a polite interest in new friends. Demonstrate if possible; for example, if you notice that a student has a book of fiction, say, *I see you like to read! What kind of books do you like to read?* Urge students to respond in full sentences.

In this unit, students will learn and practice common public speaking behaviors, such as making and responding to introductions and discussing personal interests. They will also learn how to use technology to communicate, sending personal messages by e-mail.

The skills students learn in this unit can be applied to almost every area of EL Civics as they help students to function effectively within U.S. society.

### Workplace Link

All lessons and units in *Stand Out* include basic communication skills and interpersonal skills important for the workplace. They are not individually identified. Other workplace skills are indicated. They include *collecting and organizing information, making decisions and solving problems,* and *combining ideas and information.*

# Welcome

**UNIT OUTCOMES**
- Get to know people
- Talk about personal interests
- Write a personal message

### INSTRUCTOR'S NOTES

_____

_____

_____

_____

_____

## UNIT OUTCOMES

- Get to know people
- Talk about personal interests
- Write a personal message

## GRAMMAR

- Information questions
- Verb tense review
- Simple present
- Present perfect
- Punctuation review

## VOCABULARY

- Expressions of introduction
- Personal interests/hobbies: *emotional, creative, mental, physical, cook, do crossword puzzles, do yoga, draw, knit, lift weights, paint, play, soccer, play video games, read, run, swim, take pictures, watch movies, write*
- Personal letter writing: *dear*

## EL CIVICS

- Family
- Greetings
- Names

## CASAS

Many SCANS skills are incorporated in this unit with an emphasis on:

- Listening
- Speaking
- Sociability
- Visualization
- Cultural diversity

## SCANS

Lesson 1: 0.1.1, 0.1.2, 0.1.4, 7.2.1
Lesson 2: 0.2.1, 0.2.4
Lesson 3: 0.2.3
Research: 7.44

## CCRS

RI1, RI4, RI7, W2, W6, W7, W8, W9, SL1, SL2, SL3

# LESSON ① Classroom community

GOAL ▇ Get to know people

WORKPLACE CONNECTION
Exercise B: Interact appropriately with team members.
Exercise C: Collect and organize information; Complete tasks as assigned.

🎧 **A.** **COMPARE** **Read and listen to the conversation between Liam and Rani. Do you know people like them?** Answers will vary.

CD
TR 1

**B.** **Introduce yourself to four classmates. Ask them where they are from and why they are studying English.**

**C.** **Who are the four classmates you met? Complete the table below.** Answers will vary. Sample answers given.

| Name | Country | Why are you studying English? |
|---|---|---|
| Hamdi Mohamed | Somalia | He wants to be a doctor. |
| | | |
| | | |
| | | |

## AT-A-GLANCE PREP

**Goal:** Get to know people
**Pronunciation:** Enunciation
**Academic Strategy:** Public speaking
**Vocabulary:** Introductions

### Agenda

- Meet your classmates.
- Make introductions and respond to introductions.
- Introduce your classmates to one another.
- Introduce your classmates to the class.

### Resources

**Multilevel Worksheet:** Pre-Unit, Lesson 1, Worksheet 1
**Workbook:** Pre-Unit, Lesson 1
**Audio:** CD Tracks 1–3
**Stand Out Assessment CD-ROM with ExamView®**

### Pacing

- 1.5 hour classes
- 2.5 hour classes
- 3+ hour classes

## STANDARDS CORRELATIONS

*CCRS:* W2, SL1, SL2, SL3
*CASAS:* 0.1.4, 7.2.1
*SCANS:* **Information** Acquire and evaluate information, organize and maintain information, interpret and communicate information
**Interpersonal** Participate as a member of a team, teach others, work with cultural diversity
**Systems** Monitor and correct performance
**Basic Skills** Reading, writing, listening, speaking
**Thinking Skills** Think creatively, make decisions
**Personal Qualities** Sociability
*EFF:* **Communication** Read with understanding, convey ideas in writing, speak so others can understand, listen actively, observe critically
**Decision Making** Plan
**Interpersonal** Cooperate with others

## Preassessment *(optional)* ■■■

Use the Stand Out Assessment CD-ROM with ExamView® to create a pretest for the Pre-Unit.

## Warm-up and Review 5–10 mins. ■■■

As students enter your class for the first time, introduce yourself by giving them your name, saying *Nice to meet you* and shaking their hands.

## Introduction 10–20 mins. ■■■

Ask students to take out a piece of paper and number it from 1 to 4 for dictation. (To learn more about dictations, see the Best Practice on the next page.)

Dictation:

1. Liam is from France and would like to be a graphic designer.
2. Rani is from India and came here when her kids were in high school.
3. Haru just finished high school and needs to improve his writing skills.
4. Kimla came here four years ago and wants to study nursing.

State the goal: *Today, you will be getting to know your classmates.*

## Presentation 1 10–15 mins. ■■■

**A. COMPARE Read and listen to the conversation between Liam and Rani. Do you know people like them?**

Ask students if they know anyone who has come to the United States to study for a career. Ask if they know anyone who has lived here for many years, but is just now starting to study English.

> ## LISTENING SCRIPT 🎧
> *The listening script matches the conversation in Exercise A.*  CD TR 1

Ask a few volunteers to practice introducing themselves to you.

## Practice 1 10–15 mins. ■■■

**B. Introduce yourself to four classmates. Ask them where they are from and why they are studying English.**

## Evaluation 1 5–10 mins. ■■■

**C. Who are the four classmates you met? Complete the table below.**

Tell students that if they need to, they can talk to the classmates they met again to get the information correct.

**BEST PRACTICE**

## Dictation (*listen–repeat–write method*)

The purpose of dictation is for students to improve their active listening skills. In most real-world conversations, students will only hear things one time, but they should be able to get the general meaning from the phrases they catch and understand.

Dictation instructions for advanced-level students:

1. Tell students they will only be hearing each statement or question ONE time.
2. Tell them to listen FIRST with their pencils down and/or eyes closed.
3. Once they have heard the statement, tell them to say it quietly to themselves or in their heads.
4. Once they have listened to the statement and repeated it to themselves, tell them to write it down.

Dictation instructions for the teacher:

1. Read each statement once, giving students enough time to write it down. Do not repeat.
2. Once all of the statements have been read and written, read each one again, more quickly this time, just giving students enough time to make small corrections.
3. Ask students to share their dictation with a person sitting next to them and fill in what they missed or make corrections.
4. Ask volunteers to come to the board and write each statement.
5. Tell students they can come to the board and correct any mistakes they see.
6. When the class agrees that the dictation is correct, read the statements on the board yourself and indicate which statements are indeed correct and which ones still contain errors. Allow volunteers to come to the board and make corrections. Go through this process until everything on the board is correct.

**Note:** Students who are not familiar with this style of dictation will find it difficult at first, but, as the course progresses, they will be proud of how much their active listening skills have improved.

## Presentation 2                    5–10 mins.

**D. Read and listen to the conversation between Liam, Rani, and Haru. What does Liam say to introduce Haru to Rani?**

> LISTENING SCRIPT
> *The listening script matches the conversation in Exercise D.*
> CD TR 2

**E. Study the expressions below. Any response can be used for an introduction.**

Discuss the expressions with students. Discuss which ones are formal and which ones are informal. Then, read each expression out loud and have students practice repeating it after you with correct intonation.

## Practice 2                    10–15 mins.

(Shorter classes can practice making introductions with their family and friends at home.)

**F. Work with a partner. Introduce him or her to four people in your class. Make sure you include the person's name, country, and why he or she is studying English in your introduction.**

Help facilitate this activity by making sure that everyone is included. Explain to students that everyone's task is to meet one person and then introduce that person to four of their classmates. Tell students they must write down the names of the people they interacted with. They should have five recorded names by the end of the exercise.

Have students ask each other, *Have we been introduced?* when they first pair up. Then, have students ask, *Have you been introduced?* each time they present their partners to another person. Write both questions on the board as a model.

## Evaluation 2

Observe students' interaction. Help students locate partners if necessary.

**D.** Read and listen to the conversation between Liam, Rani, and Haru. What does Liam say to introduce Haru to Rani?

CD TR 2

**E.** Study the expressions below. Any response can be used for an introduction.

| Introduction | Response |
|---|---|
| I'd like to introduce you to _____. | (It's) A pleasure to meet you. |
| I'd like you to meet _____. | (It's) A pleasure meeting you. |
| This is (friend's name) _____. | (I'm) Pleased to meet you. |
| Do you know _____? | (It's) Nice to meet you. |
| Have you met _____? | (It's) Good to meet you. |

**F.** Work with a partner. Introduce him or her to four people in your class. Make sure you include the person's name, country, and why he or she is studying English in your introduction.

WORKPLACE CONNECTION
Exercise H: Interpret and communicate information.
Exercise I: Interact appropriately with team members.

**G. Read and listen to Haru as he introduces Kimla to the class.**

CD
TR 3

**H. Choose two people who you have met in class today. Write introductions for them below. Use Haru's introduction in Exercise G as an example.** Answers will vary.

Name of classmate: _____

Information about classmate: _____

_____

_____

_____

Name of classmate: _____

Information about classmate: _____

_____

_____

_____

**I. APPLY Choose one of the people from Exercise H to introduce to the class.**

## Presentation 3     5–10 mins. ■■■

**G. Read and listen to Haru as he introduces Kimla to the class.**

> **LISTENING SCRIPT**    🎧
> CD
> TR 3
> *The listening script matches the conversation in Exercise G.*

## Practice 3     10–15 mins. ■

(Shorter classes can do Exercise H for homework. If students are doing the exercise for homework, assign each student a different person to write about so that each student in the class gets introduced at least once.)

**H. Choose two people who you have met in class today. Write introductions for them below. Use Haru's introduction in Exercise G as an example.**

Help students choose the person they will write introductions for so that each student in the class is being written about at least once.

## Evaluation 3     5–10 mins. ■

Walk around the classroom and help students. Make sure they include the appropriate information. When students have finished, they can practice reading their introductions to you. Help them with their enunciation.

> ### PRONUNCIATION
>
> ### Enunciation
>
> It is important for ESL/EFL students to clearly articulate words and phrases when they are having conversations or giving speeches. Help students improve their enunciation by having them speak slowly and clearly. If you have time to work individually with students, point out which words, letters, or sounds they should work on.

## Application     15–25 mins. ■■■

(Shorter classes who did not do Exercise H in class can choose someone they met at this class meeting and introduce the person to the class.)

**I. APPLY Choose one of the people from Exercise H to introduce to the class.**

Have each student stand in the front of the classroom or near the person he or she is introducing. Students may choose to read the introduction they wrote in their books or do it off the top of their heads.

> ### MULTILEVEL WORKSHEET
>
> Pre-Unit, Lesson 1, Worksheet 1: Introductions (listening)

**Refer students to *Stand Out 5 Workbook,* Pre-Unit, Lesson 1 for more practice with introductions.**

**Go to the *Activity Bank* online for suggestions on promoting digital literacy and using the Internet to enhance this lesson.**

### INSTRUCTOR'S NOTES

_____

_____

_____

_____

_____

_____

_____

_____

_____

_____

_____

_____

_____

_____

_____

_____

_____

**Goal:** Talk about personal interests
**Pronunciation:** Enunciation
**Vocabulary:** Personal interests

## Agenda

- Discuss personal interests.
- Ask about personal interests.

## Resources

**Multilevel Worksheets:** Pre-Unit, Lesson 2, Worksheets 1–2
**Workbook:** Pre-Unit, Lesson 2
**Audio:** CD Track 4

## Pacing

- 1.5 hour classes
- 2.5 hour classes
- 3+ hour classes

## STANDARDS CORRELATIONS

*CCRS:* RI7, W8, SL1, SL2, SL3
*CASAS:* 0.2.4
*SCANS:* **Information** Acquire and evaluate information, interpret and communicate information
**Interpersonal** Participate as a member of a team, work with cultural diversity
**Systems** Monitor and correct performance
**Basic Skills** Reading, writing, listening, speaking
**Thinking Skills** Think creatively, make decisions
**Personal Qualities** Responsibility, sociability, self-management
*EFF:* **Communication** Read with understanding, convey ideas in writing, speak so others can understand, listen actively
**Interpersonal** Cooperate with others

## Warm-up and Review          5–10 mins. ■■■

Ask volunteers to introduce some of their classmates. They may take out what they wrote in the previous lesson or just include the things they remember in their introductions.

## Enunciation

Throughout the book there will be opportunities for students to give a presentation or speak out loud to the class. Teach them how important it is to speak clearly so they can be understood. Encourage students to speak slowly and clearly. As practice, have each student stand up and read a sentence or two out loud. Have students focus on speaking clearly while they are reading the sentences. This is a simple exercise, but it will give students an idea of how they sound to others as well as give timid students more opportunities to practice their speech.

## Introduction          10–20 mins. ■■■

**Note:** See the Best Practice on page 4a for a method to use while giving students a dictation.

Dictation:

1. Jason's hobbies are watching movies and playing soccer.
2. In her free time, Jenni likes to play the piano and write in her journal.
3. Kevin's personal interests are photography and digital video editing.
4. John and Maggie like to cook and throw parties.

State the goal: *Today, we will talk about our personal interests.*

## Presentation 1          5 mins. ■■■

**A. INFER** Look at the pictures of Haru, Rani, and Kimla. What do you think their personal interests are?

## Practice 1          10–15 mins. ■■■

**B.** Listen to the conversation between Haru, Rani, and Kimla. Answer the questions below.

**Note:** The listening script is on page 7a.

## Evaluation 1          5 mins. ■■■

**C.** Share your answers with a partner.

After students review with their partner, go over the answers as a class.

# LESSON ② What are your hobbies?

GOAL ■ Talk about personal interests

WORKPLACE CONNECTION
Exercise A: Interpret and communicate information.
Exercise B: Complete tasks as assigned.
Exercise C: Interact appropriately with team members.

**A. INFER** Look at the pictures of Haru, Rani, and Kimla. What do you think their personal interests are?

_playing video games_

_taking photographs_

_reading_

**🎧 B.** Listen to the conversation between Haru, Rani, and Kimla. Answer the questions below.

CD
TR 4

1. What kind of video games does Haru like to play?
   _adventure/problem solving_

2. What are three types of reading Kimla likes to do?
   _fiction, biographies, newspaper/magazine_

3. What type of photography does Rani like?
   _nature photography_

4. What doesn't Haru like to do?
   _reading_

5. How late does Kimla stay up reading?
   _until 2 in the morning_

6. What gift did Rani's son give her?
   _an SLR digital camera_

**C.** Share your answers with a partner.

WORKPLACE CONNECTION
Exercise E: Combine ideas and information; Interact appropriately with team members.
Exercise F: Complete tasks as assigned.

**D.** **People have many different types of interests. Look at the three categories of interests below. Can you think of some examples for each category?** Answers will vary.

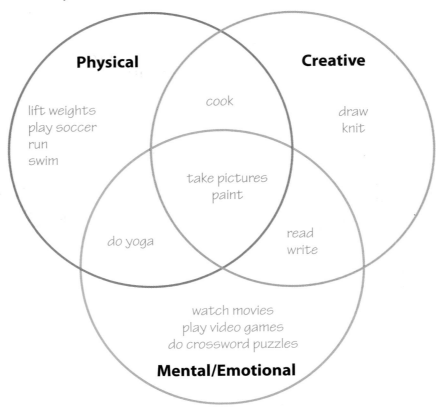

**E.** **CATEGORIZE** **Working with a small group, put each of the activities below into the circle you think is most appropriate. Some activities may belong in more than one circle.** Answers may vary.

| | | |
|---|---|---|
| cook | lift weights | run |
| do crossword puzzles | paint | swim |
| do yoga | play soccer | take pictures |
| draw | play video games | watch movies |
| knit | read | write |

**F.** **Think about your own personal interests. Write them in the appropriate categories below.** Answers will vary.

Physical: _____

Creative: _____

Mental/Emotional: _____

## LISTENING SCRIPT

CD
TR 4

**Haru:** *So, Mrs. Morgan wants us to talk about our personal interests. What do you think she means by "personal interests?"*

**Rani:** *I think she means, "What do we like to do when we are not at school or not working?"*

**Kimla:** *I think you're right, Rani. When I'm not working or at school, I like to read. Not schoolbooks, but fiction and biographies, newspapers, magazines— anything I can get my hands on. Sometimes, I'm up until two in the morning, just reading.*

**Haru:** *Wow, that's impressive! I hate reading, which made it pretty hard to get through my last year of high school. I like to play video games. Just like you can read for hours, I can sit and stare at a TV screen for hours, playing games. My favorite kinds of games are adventure where you have to solve problems to get to the next level.*

**Rani:** *I know I've said it before, but you remind me so much of my son. He likes video games, too. Although now that he has a family, he doesn't get to play them as much anymore. In my free time, I like to take pictures. My son and his wife gave me a new SLR digital camera and it takes such amazing pictures! My favorite type of photography is nature photography, so I'm outdoors a lot.*

**Kimla:** *That's great, Rani. The three of us have such varied interests. It's so fun to hear about what other people do when they aren't at school.*

## Presentation 2          5–10 mins. ■■■

**D. People have many different types of interests. Look at the three categories of interests below. Can you think of some examples for each category?**

Write the terms *Physical, Creative,* and *Mental/ Emotional* on the board. Ask students to give you some examples of activities that could go in each of these categories without looking in their books. Write their ideas on the board.

## Practice 2          10–15 mins. ■■

(Shorter classes can do these exercises for homework.)

**E. CATEGORIZE Working with a small group, put each of the activities below into the circle you think is most appropriate. Some activities may belong in more than one circle.**

Draw a three-circle Venn diagram and show how interests that cross over into two or three category terms can be placed where the circles intersect.

Pre-Unit, Lesson 2, Worksheet 1: List of Personal Interests

## Evaluation 2          10–15 mins. ■■

Ask volunteers to come to the board and write the activities under each category head that you wrote in the presentation. Then, see if the class can come up with more examples for each category.

**F. Think about your own personal interests. Write them in the appropriate categories below.**

Have students complete this exercise by themselves.

## INSTRUCTOR'S NOTES

_____

_____

_____

_____

_____

_____

_____

_____

_____

_____

_____

_____

_____

_____

_____

_____

_____

## Presentation 3

5–10 mins. ■■■

### G. How would you ask people about their personal interests? Study the phrases below.

Go over the expressions with the class. Have them repeat after you and practice their intonation. Ask students to think back to Rani and Kimla. Ask them to imagine that they are writing a conversation in which the two women will discuss their personal interests. As a class, write a conversation on the board.

## Practice 3

10–15 mins. ■

(Shorter classes can do this exercise for homework. Students can either create an imaginary person to have a conversation with or use a friend or family member.)

### H. COMPOSE Work with a partner. Write a conversation in which you discuss your personal interests.

## Evaluation 3

10–15 mins. ■

Observe and help as necessary. Have volunteer partners read their conversation in front of the class. Help students understand what a native English speaker would say in these situations.

## Application

10–20 mins. ■■■

### I. In a small group, discuss your personal interests. When you have finished, share what you have learned about each other with the rest of the class.

Suggestion: Put students in small groups by having them number or count off. (See the Best Practice on this page.) This technique will ensure that students who may have never met before get to work together. When the groups have finished their discussions, ask for each group to share what they learned about its members.

### BEST PRACTICE

## Group work

The ability to work together in groups is important for students at this level. Group size should be limited to five; four is usually the ideal number of students for maximum participation. A variety of grouping strategies are suggested below. The type of strategy you use to group students should depend on the type of task they are doing.

1.  Allow students to self-select groups. Students sometimes perform well with friends or people they feel comfortable with.
2.  Arrange groups according to students' language level. Sometimes proficient students will excel when working in groups with other proficient students. Likewise, less proficient students won't feel intimidated by working with more proficient students and, consequently, will take more risks.
3.  Arrange students in cross- or diverse-ability groups. More proficient students often enjoy helping less proficient students, and you'll have several mentors in the class instead of just one teacher.
4.  Group students by having them "number off." Using this technique, students count one to four (or more depending on the desired number of groups). Students then go to the group of students that shares their "number." This grouping method ensures that students get to know students other than their friends.
5.  To encourage the use of English, avoid putting students in homogeneous language groups whenever possible.

### MULTILEVEL WORKSHEET

Pre-Unit, Lesson 2, Worksheet 2: Personal Interests Conversations (listening)

**Refer students to *Stand Out 5 Workbook,* Pre-Unit, Lesson 2 for more practice with conversation strategies.**

**Go to the *Activity Bank* online for suggestions on promoting digital literacy and using the Internet to enhance this lesson.**

WORKPLACE CONNECTION
Exercise H: Interact appropriately with team members; Collect and organize information.
Exercise I: Interact appropriately with team members.

**G.** **How would you ask people about their personal interests? Study the phrases below.**

> What do you like to do in your free time?
> What are your hobbies?
> What are your interests outside of school/work?

**H.** **COMPOSE** **Work with a partner. Write a conversation in which you discuss your personal interests.** Answers will vary. Sample answers given.

Student A: Hi. My name is Hamdi.

Student B: Hi, Hamdi. My name is Peter.

Student A: Nice to meet you.

Student B: You, too. Why are you taking this class?

Student A: I'm studying English now to take biology next year.

Student B: Why biology?

Student A: I'd like to be a doctor one day.

Student B: Good for you! What are your hobbies?

Student A: Well, I volunteer at a hospital on Saturdays.

Student B: I volunteer, too. I work in a free food kitchen.

Student A: That's a nice thing to do. What do you do in your free time?

Student B: I like to run for exercise. I also play chess.

Student A: Me, too! I love playing chess.

Student B: Maybe we can have a game after class one day.

**I.** **In a small group, discuss your personal interests. When you have finished, share what you have learned about each other with the rest of the class.**

# LESSON ③ Dear friend

GOAL ■ Write a personal message

WORKPLACE CONNECTION
Exercise B: Complete tasks as assigned.
Exercise C: Interpret and communicate information.

## A. Read the e-mail that Liam wrote to his family.

| | |
|---|---|
| ⇨ Send now | 💾 Draft 🗑 Trash ✎ Attachment ✐ Signature |

From: liam@ma1l.com

To: liamsdad@ma1l.com

Cc:

Subject: Living in the United States

Dear Mom and Dad,

Sorry it's been so long since my last e-mail. I've been so busy with work and school that I haven't had time to do anything else. I'm really enjoying being here in the United States. I've made a lot of great friends at my job and at school, and I'm really starting to feel like I belong here.

I think I told Dad when we spoke on the phone that I got a promotion at work. Instead of being a sales associate, I am now a sales manager. The added responsibility makes me a little nervous, but I think the bigger paycheck will make that go away! ☺

I just started a new English class, and my teacher, Mrs. Morgan, is great. She's pretty tough, but I think I'll learn a lot in her class. I'm hoping that by the end of this semester, my English will be good enough to start taking some graphic design classes. I've been practicing using my computer as much as I can in my free time, but I'm starting to need some professional guidance on how I can improve my design skills.

I hope you are both doing well! I really miss you and hope you can find some time to come out and visit. Mom, I really think you'd like it here.

Love,
Liam

## B. This is a personal e-mail, not a formal e-mail. How can you tell that this e-mail is personal?

Liam writes informally about personal activities and his emotions, and signs it using "Love."

## C. INFER What do you think the following expressions mean? Answers may vary. Sample answers are given.

1. feel like I belong _I am a part of something._

2. pretty tough _a little difficult_

3. added responsibility _more duties_

4. professional guidance _pay someone for advice_

## AT-A-GLANCE PREP

**Goal:** Write a personal message
**Grammar:** Error correction
**Academic Strategy:** Personal writing
**Vocabulary:** *feel like I belong, added responsibility, pretty tough, professional guidance*

### Agenda

- [ ] Read Liam's e-mail.
- [ ] Practice vocabulary.
- [ ] Discuss writing personal messages.
- [ ] Read Liam's thank-you note.
- [ ] Read Rani's e-mail.
- [ ] Write a personal e-mail.

### Resources

**Multilevel Worksheet:** Pre-Unit, Lesson 3, Worksheet 1
**Workbook:** Pre-Unit, Lesson 3
**Suggested Realia:** Personal e-mails

### Pacing

- ■ 1.5 hour classes
- ■ 2.5 hour classes
- ■ 3+ hour classes

## STANDARDS CORRELATIONS

*CCRS:* RI1, RI4, W2, W6
*CASAS:* 0.2.3
*SCANS:* **Information** Acquire and evaluate information, use computers to process information *(optional)*
**Interpersonal** Participate as a member of a team, teach others, negotiate to arrive at a decision, work with cultural diversity
**Systems** Monitor and correct performance
**Technology** Apply technology to a task *(optional)*
**Basic Skills** Reading, writing
**Thinking Skills** Think creatively, make decisions
**Personal Qualities** Responsibility, sociability, self-management
*EFF:* **Communication** Read with understanding, convey ideas in writing
**Decision Making** Plan
**Interpersonal** Cooperate with others
**Lifelong Learning** Use information and communications technology *(optional)*

## Warm-up and Review    5–10 mins. ■■■

Have students get in different small groups from the ones they were in during the previous class meeting and discuss their personal interests.

## Introduction    5–10 mins. ■■■

**Note:** For more information on dictations, see the Best Practice on page 4a.

Dictation:

1. I've met a lot of great friends at school and I'm really starting to feel like I belong here.
2. It was so thoughtful of you to remember us on our special day.
3. Both of our sons are married now with families of their own.
4. I really miss you and hope you can find some time to come out and visit.

State the goal: *Today, you will be reading and writing personal e-mails.*

## Presentation 1    10–15 mins. ■■■

**A. Read the e-mail that Liam wrote to his family.**

Read Liam's e-mail as a class. You can read the e-mail out loud to the class or you can call on students to read the different paragraphs.

**B. This is a personal e-mail, not a formal e-mail. How can you tell that this e-mail is personal?**

Discuss the different aspects of the e-mail that make it personal, such as the informal greeting, the fact that there is no return address, and the informal language used throughout.

## Practice 1    10–15 mins. ■■■

**C. INFER What do you think the following expressions mean?**

Have students work in small groups to come up with the meanings for these expressions.

## Evaluation 1    5–15 mins. ■■■

Go over the answers as a class. For added practice, have students write sentences using these expressions. More specifically, have them write sentences they might use in a personal e-mail to a friend or family member.

## Presentation 2

5–10 mins. ■■■

D. **A personal message is a message that you write to a family member, a friend, or someone who you already know. Personal messages usually contain personal information and are written informally. Think of some people that you might write a personal message to. Who are they?**

As a class, make a list of people that personal messages could be written to.

## Practice 2

10–15 mins. ■■

(Shorter classes can do this exercise for homework.)

E. **There are many reasons for writing a personal message. Work in a small group to come up with a short list.**

## Evaluation 2

10–15 mins. ■■

As a class, create a list on the board from all the different groups' responses.

## Presentation 3

5–10 mins. ■■■

Circle *thank-you note* from the list on the board if your students came up with it in Evaluation 2. If they did not think of it before, add it to the list now. Ask students when they might write thank-you notes.

## Practice 3

15–20 mins. ■

(Shorter classes can do this exercise for homework.)

F. **DETERMINE** **Read Liam's thank-you note. There are nine mistakes. Find the mistakes and correct them.**

## Evaluation 3

5–10 mins. ■

Go over the answers as a class.

G. **Rewrite Liam's note on a separate piece of paper. Correct the mistakes.**

**Refer students to *Stand Out 5 Workbook,* Pre-Unit, Lesson 3 for more practice with editing.**

**Go to the *Activity Bank* online for suggestions on promoting digital literacy and using the Internet to enhance this lesson.**

WORKPLACE CONNECTION
Exercise D: Combine ideas and information.
Exercise E: Interact appropriately with team members.
Exercise F: Complete tasks as assigned.

**D.** A personal message is a message that you write to a family member, a friend, or someone who you already know. Personal messages usually contain personal information and are written informally. Think of some people that you might write a personal message to. Who are they?

_family members and friends_

**E.** There are many reasons for writing a personal message. Work in a small group to come up with a short list. _Answers will vary. Sample answers are given._

1. _to thank someone for a gift, a dinner, or a favor_

2. _to ask about someone's health_

3. _to say you were thinking about/miss someone_

4. _to make plans to get together in the future_

**F.** **DETERMINE** Read Liam's thank-you note. There are nine mistakes. Find the mistakes and correct them.

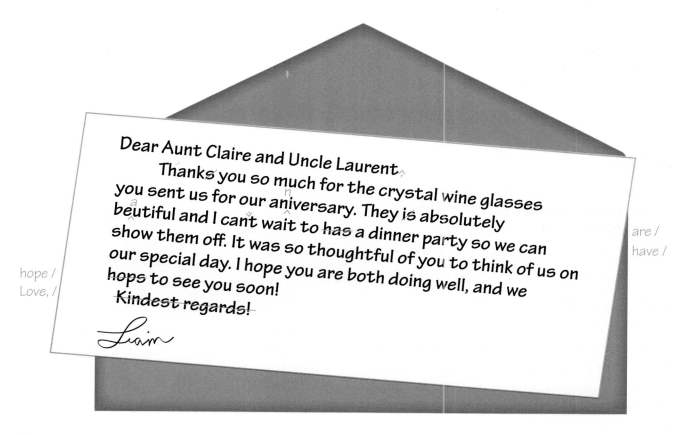

Dear Aunt Claire and Uncle Laurent,
Thanks you so much for the crystal wine glasses you sent us for our aniversary. They is absolutely beutiful and I cant wait to has a dinner party so we can show them off. It was so thoughtful of you to think of us on our special day. I hope you are both doing well, and we hops to see you soon!
Kindest regards!
Liam

are /
have /

hope /
Love, /

**G.** Rewrite Liam's note on a separate piece of paper. Correct the mistakes.

WORKPLACE CONNECTION
Exercise H: Complete tasks as assigned.
Exercise I: Interact appropriately with team members.

**H.** **Mrs. Morgan asked her class to choose someone they had just met in class and send them an e-mail. Read the e-mail that Rani wrote to Kimla.**

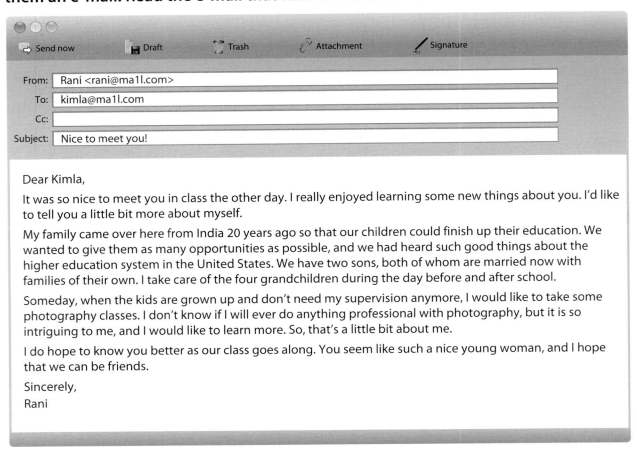

| ⊝ ⊚ ⊚ | | | | |
|---|---|---|---|---|
| ⇨ Send now | 🖫 Draft | 🗑 Trash | ✑ Attachment | ✎ Signature |

From: Rani <rani@ma1l.com>

To: kimla@ma1l.com

Cc:

Subject: Nice to meet you!

Dear Kimla,

It was so nice to meet you in class the other day. I really enjoyed learning some new things about you. I'd like to tell you a little bit more about myself.

My family came over here from India 20 years ago so that our children could finish up their education. We wanted to give them as many opportunities as possible, and we had heard such good things about the higher education system in the United States. We have two sons, both of whom are married now with families of their own. I take care of the four grandchildren during the day before and after school.

Someday, when the kids are grown up and don't need my supervision anymore, I would like to take some photography classes. I don't know if I will ever do anything professional with photography, but it is so intriguing to me, and I would like to learn more. So, that's a little bit about me.

I do hope to know you better as our class goes along. You seem like such a nice young woman, and I hope that we can be friends.

Sincerely,

Rani

**I.** **COMPOSE** **Choose one of the classmates you recently met and write him or her a personal message about yourself on a separate piece of paper.** Answers will vary.

**Nowadays, keeping in touch is easier than ever.**

## Application

10–20 mins. ■■■

**H. Mrs. Morgan asked her class to choose someone they had just met in class and send them an e-mail. Read the e-mail that Rani wrote to Kimla.**

Have students read the e-mail quietly to themselves and then discuss it as a class.

**I. COMPOSE Choose one of the classmates you recently met and write him or her a personal message about yourself on a separate piece of paper.**

**Optional Computer Activity:** If students have e-mail accounts, these messages can be written online and transmitted electronically.

### BEST PRACTICE

## Technology in the classroom

If you have access to computers, set up e-mail accounts for all the students in your class so they communicate with you as well as with one another. There are a number of free e-mail services offered on the Web, including Google™, Yahoo™, and MSN Hotmail™.

Suggestion: Print out the online form that students will have to fill out to apply for a free e-mail account. Help them fill out all the information correctly before they submit the form online. It is a good idea for students to come up with a variety of user names in advance since the ones they choose may have already been taken by other e-mail users. Discuss with them the importance of safe but easy to remember passwords.

### MULTILEVEL WORKSHEET

Pre-Unit, Lesson 3, Worksheet 1: Personal Letters

### BEST PRACTICE

## Correcting errors

For certain activities, it is not important to correct student errors. Since the purpose of this message is to communicate something personal, error correction is not necessary as long as the letter's meaning can be understood by the reader.

### INSTRUCTOR'S NOTES

# Balancing Your Life

### About the Photo

This photo was taken by Chinese photographer Jianan Yu. It shows a student napping at his desk during a lunch break. The photo illustrates the amount of studying students do for the national university entrance exam, known as the *gaokao*. The competition for university entrance is fierce, not just because of the Chinese population, but also the pressure exerted on students by their parents. For most students, the time leading up to the exam is extremely stressful.

- Introduce the unit by reading the title out loud.
- Have students look at the photo and ask a volunteer to read the caption to the class.
- Ask students how the photo relates to the title.
- Ask students to look at the photo again and answer the questions.
- Go over the unit outcomes.

UNIT **1**

# Balancing Your Life

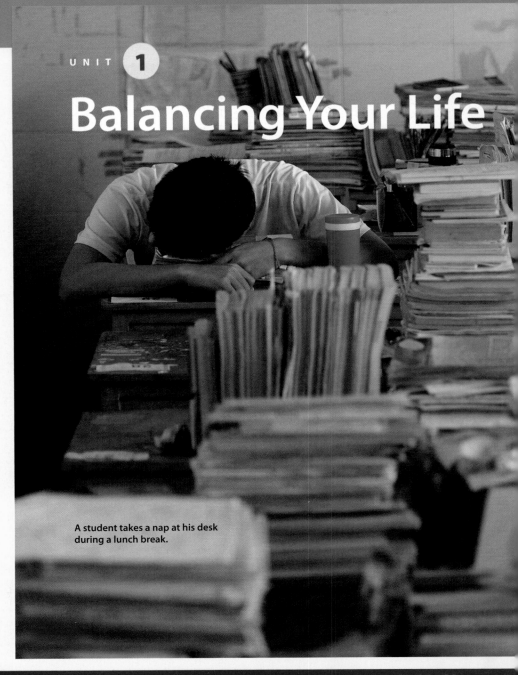

A student takes a nap at his desk during a lunch break.

| UNIT OUTCOMES | GRAMMAR | VOCABULARY | EL CIVICS |
|---|---|---|---|
| • Identify learning styles<br>• Identify career paths<br>• Balance your life<br>• Identify and prioritize goals<br>• Motivate yourself | • Review of simple verb tenses: present, past, future<br>• Future perfect<br>• Gerunds<br>• Superlative adjectives<br>• Future with *will* | • Learning style: *visual, auditory, tactile, kinesthetic*<br>• Career path: *evaluate progress, inspire, monitor progress*<br>• Motivation: *earning power, pursue, educational attainment*<br>• Goal setting: *achieve, balance, long-term, motivate, prioritize*<br>• Multiple intelligences: *auditory, bodily, rhythmic, interpersonal*<br>• Careers: *architect, engineer, interior designer, mechanic, journalist, lawyer, politician, teacher, translator, writer, accountant, computer programmer, doctor, researcher, scientist, actor, athlete, dancer,* (more) | The skills students learn in this unit can be applied to the following EL Civics competency areas:<br>• Employment<br>• Communication<br>• Families |

## Life Skills Link

In this unit, students will learn and practice organizational and planning activities, such as setting goals, managing priorities, and identifying career paths. They will also learn how to compare different careers by plotting income potentials on a bar graph.

The skills students learn in this unit can be applied to almost every area of EL Civics as they help students to function effectively within U.S. society.

## Workplace Link

All lessons and units in *Stand Out* include basic communication skills and interpersonal skills important for the workplace. They are not individually identified. Other workplace skills are indicated. They include *collecting and organizing information, making decisions and solving problems,* and *combining ideas and information.*

**UNIT OUTCOMES**

- ☐ Identify learning styles
- ☐ Identify career paths
- ☐ Balance your life
- ☐ Identify and prioritize goals
- ☐ Motivate yourself

**Look at the photo and answer the questions.**

1. Why do you think this student is taking a nap?
2. What job do you think this student wants in the future?

| CASAS | SCANS | CCRS |
|---|---|---|
| Vocabulary Builder: 7.4.5 <br> Lesson 1: 7.4.2, 7.4.9 <br> Lesson 2: 4.1.9, 7.4.2 <br> Lesson 3: 7.4.2 <br> Lesson 4: 7.1.1, 7.1.2, 7.1.3, 7.4.2 <br> Lesson 5: 7.1.3 <br> Review: 7.2.1 <br> Reaserch: 4.9.3, 7.2.1, 7.4.4, 7.4.5, 7.4.6 <br> Team Project: 4.8.1, 4.8.5, 4.8.6 | Many SCANS skills are incorporated in this unit with an emphasis on: <br><ul><li>Writing</li><li>Social</li><li>Negotiation</li><li>Leadership</li><li>Self-esteem</li><li>Self-management</li><li>Responsibility</li><li>Decision making</li></ul> | RI1, RI2, RI3, RI4, RI7, RI10, W2, W4, W7, W8, SL1, SL2, SL3, L1 |

# Vocabulary Builder

**A.** Look at the pictures and read the information. What can you learn about the students?

**Name:** Carl
**Learning style:** visual
**Career path:** graphic designer
**Motivation:** financial

**Name:** Gloria
**Learning style:** visual
**Career path:** photographer
**Motivation:** joy

**Name:** Akira
**Learning style:** tactile/kinesthetic
**Career path:** computer programmer
**Motivation:** fun

**Name:** Abir
**Learning style:** auditory
**Career path:** registered nurse
**Motivation:** time with family

**B.** What do you think each expression means? Write your own thoughts.

Answers will vary. Suggested answers are given.

1. learning style: _a person's best way of learning_

2. career path: _the education and training experiences leading toward fulfillment of employment goals_

3. motivation: _an idea, goal, or emotion that inspires a person_

**Goal:** Introduce new vocabulary
**Academic Strategies:** Categorizing vocabulary, using a dictionary
**Vocabulary:** See lessons

### Agenda

- Read about students in *Stand Out 5*.
- Categorize vocabulary.
- Find out what you know.
- Use a dictionary.

### Resources

**Dictionaries:** It is recommended that each student in class have an ESL learner's dictionary or that dictionaries be made available in the classroom for students to use. Dictionaries that will be referred to in this book are the *Heinle's Newbury House Dictionary of American English* and the *Collins Cobuild Intermediate* or *Advanced Dictionary of American English*.

### Pacing

- 1.5 hour classes
- 2.5 hour classes
- 3+ hour classes

## STANDARDS CORRELATIONS

*CCRS:* RI1, RI4, RI7

*CASAS:* 7.4.5

*SCANS:* **Information** Acquire and evaluate information, organize and maintain information

**Interpersonal** Participate as a member of a team, negotiate to arrive at a decision, work with cultural diversity

**Systems** Understand systems, monitor and correct performance

**Basic Skills** Reading, writing, listening, speaking

**Thinking Skills** Think creatively, make decisions, see things in the mind's eye

**Personal Qualities** Responsibility, sociability, self-management

*EFF:* **Communication** Read with understanding, convey ideas in writing, speak so others can understand, listen actively

**Decision Making** Use math to solve problems and communicate, solve problems and make decisions, plan

**Interpersonal** Cooperate with others

**Lifelong Learning** Take responsibility for learning, reflect and evaluate, learn through research

## Academic Feature: Vocabulary Builder

Each unit in *Stand Out 5* will begin with a vocabulary-building section. The purpose of this two-page section is to introduce students to many of the words they will be using in the unit lessons. Students will have a chance to see how much they already know, and they will get exposure to the new vocabulary found in the unit.

**Note:** All of the exercises on these two pages should be done in class, no matter the class length. Longer classes can do this lesson and then move onto Lesson 1 during the same class meeting; shorter classes may have to devote one whole class meeting to this lesson.

### Introduction                    5–10 mins. ■■■

State the goal: *Today, we will be identifying and working with the vocabulary you will learn in this unit.*

### Presentation 1                  10–15 mins. ■■■

**A. Look at the pictures and read the information. What can you learn about the students?**

### Practice 1                      10–15 mins. ■■■

**B. What do you think each expression means? Write your own thoughts.**

Have students complete this exercise by themselves.

### Evaluation 1                    5–10 mins. ■■■

Go over students' ideas as a class. Help students arrive at the correct definition.

## INSTRUCTOR'S NOTES

_____

_____

_____

_____

_____

_____

_____

_____

## Presentation 2 ■■■

**C. INFER** Below are groups of words that you will be working with in this unit. Make your best guess as to which topic in the box goes with each group. Topics can be used more than once.

Have students work with a partner to come up with topics for each group. Then, go over the answers as a class.

### PRONUNCIATION

## Vocabulary

When teaching students new vocabulary, pronounce each word for them several times and ask them to repeat it. Often, students may have heard the words you are introducing but have never seen them spelled out. By pronouncing a word for students, you allow students to make a connection between the word's spelling and its sound. It is also important that students learn the correct pronunciation of new words so they feel comfortable using their new vocabulary inside and outside of the classroom.

## Practice 2 10–15 mins. ■■

**D.** Circle every word in Exercise C that you are familiar with.

**E.** Choose two new words from Exercise C that you would like to know the meanings of. Use a dictionary and write the word, part of speech, definition, example sentence, and any related words on a separate piece of paper.

Go over the example with students. Make sure they understand each part of the definition. Discuss what makes a good example sentence. (Answer: An example sentence helps to define or illustrate the targeted word.)

## Evaluation 2 10–15 mins. ■■
Ask volunteers to write some of their definitions on the board.

### INSTRUCTOR'S NOTES

WORKPLACE CONNECTION
Exercise C: Collect and organize information.
Exercises D, E: Complete tasks as assigned.

**C.   INFER** Below are groups of words that you will be working with in this unit. Make your best guess as to which topic in the box goes with each group. Topics can be used more than once.

| career path | learning style | multiple intelligences |
|---|---|---|
| goal setting | motivation | |

1. _____learning styles_____

   auditory

   tactile/kinesthetic

   visual

2. _____motivation_____

   earning power

   pursue

   educational attainment

3. _____multiple intelligences_____

   musical/rhythmic

   interpersonal

   intrapersonal

   logical/mathematical

4. _____multiple intelligences_____

   naturalistic

   visual/spatial

   verbal/linguistic

   bodily/kinesthetic

5. _____goal setting_____

   achieve

   balance

   long-term

   motivate

   prioritize

   short-term

6. _____career path_____

   be flexible

   evaluate progress

   inspire

   monitor progress

   positive outlook

   support

**D.   Circle every word in Exercise C that you are familiar with.**

**E.   Choose two new words from Exercise C that you would like to know the meanings of. Use a dictionary and write the word, part of speech, definition, example sentence, and any related words on a separate piece of paper.** Answers will vary.

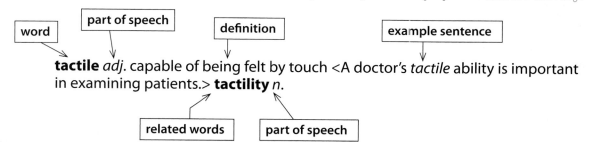

**tactile** *adj.* capable of being felt by touch <A doctor's *tactile* ability is important in examining patients.> **tactility** *n.*

# LESSON ① Learning styles

GOAL ▪ Identify learning styles

WORKPLACE CONNECTION
Exercise A: Complete tasks as assigned.
Exercises B, C: Collect and organize information.

**A. EVALUATE Check (✓) how you learn new skills. Do you . . .** Answers will vary.

☐ learn through seeing?     ☐ learn through listening?     ☐ learn through moving, doing, and touching?

🎧 **B. Listen to a lecturer talk about three learning styles and take notes. Write down any key words you hear to describe each learning style.**

CD
TR 5

| Visual | Auditory | Tactile/Kinesthetic |
|---|---|---|
| seeing | listening | moving |
| body language | lectures | doing, touching |
| facial expressions | discussions | explore surroundings |
| sit in front of class | listening to others | touching things |
| think in pictures | listen to tone, pitch, speed | moving |
| learn best using visuals | interpret meaning | trouble sitting still |
| take detailed notes | read text aloud | hands-on approach |

**C. Indicate the learning style next to each activity. Write *V* for *Visual*, *A* for *Auditory*, and *T/K* for *Tactile/Kinesthetic*.**

1. touching objects __T/K__

2. watching a video __V__

3. looking at a diagram __V__

4. reading a textbook __V__

5. doing a science experiment __T/K__

6. listening to a lecture __A__

7. participating in a discussion __A__

**D. EVALUATE Check (✓) the learning style you think best describes you.** Answers will vary.

_____ visual     _____ auditory     _____ tactile/kinesthetic

**Goal:** Identify learning styles

**Academic Strategies:** Active listening, note taking, active reading, finding main ideas

**Vocabulary:** *multiple intelligences, visual, auditory, tactile, kinesthetic, spatial, verbal, linguistic, logical, bodily, rhythmic, interpersonal, intrapersonal, naturalistic*

## Agenda

- ☐ Discover learning styles.
- ☐ Take notes.
- ☐ Study multiple intelligences.
- ☐ Find the main idea.
- ☐ Conduct a class poll.

## Resources

**Multilevel Worksheets:** Unit 1, Lesson 1, Worksheets 1–3

**Workbook:** Unit 1, Lesson 1

**Audio:** CD Track 5

**Stand Out Assessment CD-ROM with ExamView®**

## Pacing

- ■ 1.5 hour classes
- ■ 2.5 hour classes
- ■ 3+ hour classes

## STANDARDS CORRELATIONS

*CCRS:* RI1, RI2, RI4, W7, SL2, SL3

*CASAS:* 7.4.2, 7.4.9

*SCANS:* **Information** Acquire and evaluate information, organize and maintain information, interpret and communicate information

**Interpersonal** Participate as a member of a team, work with cultural diversity

**Systems** Understand systems, monitor and correct performance

**Technology** Apply technology to a task *(optional)*

**Basic Skills** Reading, writing, listening, speaking

**Thinking Skills** Think creatively, make decisions, see things in the mind's eye

**Personal Qualities** Responsibility, sociability

*EFF:* **Communication** Read with understanding, speak so others can understand, listen actively, observe critically

**Decision Making** Solve problems and make decisions, plan

**Interpersonal** Cooperate with others, advocate and influence, resolve conflict and negotiate, guide others

**Lifelong Learning** Take responsibility for learning, reflect and evaluate

## Pre-assessment (*optional*)　■■■

Use the Stand Out Assessment CD-ROM with ExamView® to create a pre-test for Unit 1.

## Warm-up and Review　　5–10 mins. ■■■

Ask students to call out new terms they learned in the previous unit. Make a list on the board. Have students make a checklist of the student book goals in their notebooks. The checklist should list the goals as well as the page numbers where students can find information to accomplish these goals. Show students how they can keep track on a daily or weekly basis.

## Introduction　　　10–15 mins. ■■■

As you may have noticed in the Pre-Unit, every Introduction section will begin with dictation. Dictation will help improve students' active listening skills and teach them to correct their errors. It is also motivating and will help get students to class on time if you begin the class with it.

Dictation: 1. Kevin learns best when he writes things down and memorizes them. 2. My sister likes to close her eyes and listen to the teacher talking. 3. His math teacher gives students small objects to practice addition and subtraction. 4. I like to see everything written on the board so I can study it.

State the goal: *Today, you will identify your own learning style and learn about multiple intelligences.*

## A.  Check (✓) how you learn new skills. Do you . . .

Have students check their learning styles individually. Take a class poll to find out how many students learn in each of the three ways. Write your findings on the board.

## Presentation 1　　　　10–15 mins. ■■■

Write *Visual, Auditory,* and *Tactile/Kinesthetic* as headings on the board. Prepare students for the listening exercise by going over the chart about learning styles. Discuss the three headings and ask students what they think the words mean.

## B.  Listen to a lecturer talk about the three learning styles and take notes. Write down any key words you hear to describe each learning style.

**Note:** The listening script is on page 17a.

## Note taking

Tell students that when someone is talking in an academic or training class, they should write down any important words they hear that will help them remember the information later. Refer to the Best Practice below for more information on note taking.

## LISTENING SCRIPT

*Do you learn best through seeing? Then you are a visual learner. Visual learners learn from body language and facial expressions. They like to sit in the front of the classroom so they can see clearly. They tend to think in pictures and learn best by looking at visuals, such as diagrams, pictures, overheads, videos, and handouts. Visual learners like to take detailed notes to help learn information.*

*Do you learn best by listening? Then you are an auditory learner. Auditory learners learn best by listening to lectures, participating in discussions, and listening to what others say. They also listen to tone of voice, pitch, and speed to interpret hidden meanings. Auditory learners learn best if they read texts out loud.*

*Do you like to learn by moving, doing, and touching? Then you are a tactile, or kinesthetic, learner. Kinesthetic learners like to actively explore their surroundings by touching things and moving. They have trouble sitting still for long periods of time. They learn best through a hands-on approach.*

## BEST PRACTICE

## Note taking

Taking notes is an important academic skill that students should practice as often as they can. Explain to students that they should focus on writing down the key words and phrases of a lecture—not all of the incidental words and phrases—so that they can recall the important ideas when they look back at their notes. Using Exercise B on page 16, show students how, in the first column, the words *seeing, body language,* and *facial expressions* are written as notes, not complete sentences.

To demonstrate note taking, you can:

1. Have a student tell you a story and, as he or she is talking, take notes on the board.
2. Use one of the recordings from the book and, as it is playing, show students on the board how you would take notes.

Have students share their notes with a classmate sitting next to them. Then, ask volunteers to come up to the board and write notes under one of three column headings.

### Practice 1                                5–10 mins. ■■■

C. **Indicate the learning style next to each activity. Write *V* for *Visual*, *A* for *Auditory*, and *T/K* for *Tactile/Kinesthetic*.**

Have students complete this exercise in pairs.

### Evaluation 1                              5 mins. ■■■

Go over the answers as a class.

D. **EVALUATE  Check (✓) the learning style you think best describes you.**

Have students think about the way they like to learn and answer the question. Ask: *Has anyone changed answers since Exercise A? If so, explain why.*

**Note:** Standards Correlations box is on page 16a.

### Presentation 2                           5–10 mins. ■■■

E. **What does *intelligence* mean? Write your ideas on a separate piece of paper. Then, look up the definition in a dictionary and write it below.**

Have students come up with a definition.

Have students look *intelligence* up in the dictionary and compare their definition to the dictionary's definition. Discuss the meaning as a class, focusing students on the meaning required for the reading. Also, discuss the different definitions and other word forms.

### Practice 2                               15–20 mins. ■■

(Shorter classes can do these exercises for homework.)

Ask students what they think the term *multiple intelligences* means. Go over the directions to Exercise F, telling students not to worry about the meaning of every word. Tell them to focus their attention on the main ideas.

F. **DETERMINE  Read about multiple intelligences. Underline the main idea in each paragraph.**

**E.** What does *intelligence* mean? Write your ideas on a separate piece of paper. Then, look up the definition in a dictionary and write it below. Answers will vary. A sample answer is given.

**intelligence** *n.* the capacity to acquire and apply knowledge

**F.** **DETERMINE** Read about multiple intelligences. Underline the main idea in each paragraph.

According to psychologist Howard Gardner, there are eight different ways to show intellectual ability. These eight intelligences are described as visual/spatial, verbal/linguistic, logical/mathematical, bodily/kinesthetic, musical/rhythmic, interpersonal, intrapersonal, and naturalistic.

Visual/spatial learners tend to think in pictures. They like to look at maps, charts, pictures, and videos. They are good at such things as reading, writing, understanding charts and graphs, building, fixing, and designing.

Verbal/linguistic learners have the ability to use language. Unlike visual learners, they think in words. Verbal/linguistic learners are good at listening, speaking, writing, teaching, remembering information, and persuading others.

Logical/mathematical learners are good at using reason, logic, and numbers. These learners ask many questions and like experimenting. Logical/mathematical learners are good at problem solving, classifying information, figuring out relationships between abstract concepts, doing complex mathematical calculations, and working with geometric shapes.

Bodily/kinesthetic learners express themselves with their bodies through movement. By moving in the space around them, they can process and recall information. These learners are good at dancing, physical sports, acting, using body language, and expressing themselves with their bodies.

Musical/rhythmic learners have the ability to appreciate and produce music. These learners can immediately appreciate and evaluate the music they hear. Musical/rhythmic learners are good at singing, playing instruments, writing music, and remembering tunes they hear.

Learners with interpersonal intelligence are good at relating to others. They can see things from the point of view of others and they can sense people's feelings. They are good at communicating.

Intrapersonal intelligence, not to be confused with interpersonal intelligence, is the ability to be aware of one's own feelings. These learners are good at self-reflecting, and they try to understand their own hopes, dreams, strengths, and weaknesses.

Naturalistic intelligence has to do with understanding nature, that is, nurturing and relating information to one's surroundings. Naturalistic learners are sensitive to nature and have the ability to nurture and grow things.

WORKPLACE CONNECTION
Exercises G, H: Complete tasks as assigned.
Exercises I, J: Interact appropriately with team members.
Exercise J: Collect and organize information.

## G. INTERPRET  Match each type of intelligence to a main idea.

1. visual/spatial __d__
2. verbal/linguistic __c__
3. logical/mathematical __h__
4. bodily/kinesthetic __f__
5. musical/rhythmic __e__
6. interpersonal __g__
7. intrapersonal __b__
8. naturalistic __a__

a. nurture
b. be aware of one's feelings
c. use language
d. think in pictures
e. appreciate and produce music
f. express with movement
g. relate well to others
h. use reason, logic, and numbers

## H. EVALUATE  Which types of intelligence do you think are strongest in you? Write down your top three in order. *1* is the strongest. Answers will vary.

1. _____   2. _____   3. _____

## I. How do you think the terms *learning styles* and *multiple intelligences* are related? Discuss your ideas in a small group. Answers will vary. Sample answers are given. Learning style is how someone likes to learn. Multiple intelligences are the way in which someone best shows or uses his or her intelligence.

## J. Take a class poll on learning styles and multiple intelligences. Which learning styles and types of intelligence are most common among your classmates? Answers will vary.

Musicians have the ability to appreciate and produce music.

BEST PRACTICE

## Reading for understanding

At this level, students have a high level of comprehension, but there still may be many words that they do not know. Have students focus their attention on the concepts necessary to complete the instructions for each activity rather than trying to understand every word in the exercise. In most exercises in *Stand Out 5*, it is more important for students to read for understanding and meaning than to understand each word. Tell students that when they are at home and have already completed the exercise, they can spend time looking up individual words in a dictionary.

## Practice 2 *(continued)*

**G. INTERPRET  Match each type of intelligence to the main idea.**

## Evaluation 2                    10–15 mins. ■■
Go over the answers as a class.

**H. EVALUATE  Which types of intelligence do you think are strongest in you? Write down your top three in order. *1* is the strongest.**

## Presentation 3                  5–10 mins. ■■■
Write *learning styles* on the board and have students tell you what the three learning styles are. Then, write *multiple intelligences* on the board and have students help you list them. Put students into small groups and tell them they will be discussing the connection between learning styles and multiple intelligences.

## Practice 3                      15–20 mins. ■
(Shorter classes can do the following exercise in written form for homework.)

**I.  How do you think the terms *learning styles* and *multiple intelligences* are related? Discuss your ideas in a small group.**

## Evaluation 3                    5–10 mins. ■
Observe students as they discuss their ideas.

## Application                     10–20 mins. ■■■

**J.  Take a class poll on learning styles and multiple intelligences. Which learning styles and types of intelligence are most common among your classmates?**

### MULTILEVEL WORKSHEETS

Use the template on the Multilevel Worksheets CD for students to calculate percentages and create a bar graph for their poll results.

### INTERNET RESEARCH

The Internet activities in *Stand Out 5* help students learn more about the topics in most lessons. In this lesson, have students do an online search for *Learning Styles*. Ask them to find a quiz they can take to assess their own learning styles. They can print out results to present to a small group or the class.

### MULTILEVEL WORKSHEETS

Unit 1, Lesson 1, Worksheet 1: Learning Styles

Unit 1, Lesson 1, Worksheet 2: Multiple Intelligences (listening)

Unit 1, Lesson 1, Worksheet 3: Class Poll—Learning Styles and Multiples Intelligences

**Refer students to *Stand Out 5 Workbook*, Unit 1, Lesson 1 for practice with gerunds as objects of prepositions.**

**Go to the *Activity Bank* online for suggestions on promoting digital literacy and using the Internet to enhance this lesson.**

### INSTRUCTOR'S NOTES

_____

_____

_____

_____

_____

## AT-A-GLANCE PREP

**Goal:** Identify career paths

**Academic Strategies:** Active listening, note taking, analyzing a bar graph

**Vocabulary:** *careers, pursue, educational attainment, earning power, credential*

### Agenda

☐ Define *job* and *career*.

☐ Match intelligence types with related careers.

☐ Interpret information about earning power in a bar graph.

☐ Listen to a conversation about Sonya's career path.

☐ Choose your career path.

### Resources

**Multilevel Worksheets:** Unit 1, Lesson 2, Worksheets 1–2

**Workbook:** Unit 1, Lesson 2

**Audio:** CD Track 6

### Pacing

■ 1.5 hour classes    ■ 2.5 hour classes

■ 3+ hour classes

## STANDARDS CORRELATIONS

*CCRS:* RI4, RI7, SL1, SL2

*CASAS:* 4.1.9, 7.4.2

*SCANS:* **Information** Acquire and evaluate information, interpret and communicate information

**Interpersonal** Participate as a member of a team, negotiate to arrive at a decision, work with cultural diversity

**Systems** Monitor and correct performance

**Technology** Apply technology to a task *(optional)*

**Basic Skills** Reading, writing, listening, speaking

**Thinking Skills** Think creatively, make decisions

**Personal Qualities** Responsibility, sociability

*EFF:* **Communication** Read with understanding, speak so others can understand, listen actively, observe critically

**Decision Making** Solve problems and make decisions, plan

**Interpersonal** Cooperate with others

**Lifelong Learning** Reflect and evaluate, learn through research, use information and communications technology *(optional)*

## Warm-up and Review    5–10 mins.

Facilitate a class discussion to review the terms used to describe learning styles and multiple intelligences. Try to get as many students as possible to participate.

## Introduction    5–10 mins.

Refer to the Best Practice on dictation on page 4a.

Dictation:

1. If you have a degree, you can make more money.
2. Do you have a job or a career?
3. What steps do you need to take to become a nurse?
4. People with verbal intelligence make good teachers.

State the goal: *Today, we will talk about different careers and you will identify a career path for yourself.*

## Presentation 1    10–15 mins.

**A. What is the difference between a job and a career? Discuss the similarities and differences with a partner. Write your ideas in the table below.**

Write the words *job* and *career* on the board and ask students to write notes in their books about the differences between the two.

**B. Look up the words *job* and *career* in a dictionary. Write the definitions below.**

Before you define the words for students, have them look them up in the dictionary. Briefly discuss the eight intelligences that students learned in the previous lesson. Make sure they understand the meaning of each one before they go on to Exercise C.

## Practice 1    10–15 mins.

**C. DETERMINE Certain careers are associated with different intelligences. Look at the list of careers in the table and write which intelligence fits each category.**

Review the vocabulary words in the table as a class. Model correct pronunciation. Have students repeat each word after you. Ask students to complete this exercise with a partner. Have students take turns saying the words to their partners before they begin.

# LESSON  **2**  Career planning

WORKPLACE CONNECTION
Exercises A, C: Collect and organize information.
Exercise B: Complete tasks as assigned.

**A.** **What is the difference between a job and a career? Discuss the similarities and differences with a partner. Write your ideas in the table below.**

Answers will vary. Sample answers are given.

| Job | Career |
|---|---|
| A job can be a short- or a long-term task or set of tasks done for money. | A career usually is a personal choice preceded by education and training. |

**B.** **Look up the words *job* and *career* in a dictionary. Write the definitions below.**

**job** *n.* an activity performed in exchange for payment

**career** *n.* a chosen career or life work

**C.** **DETERMINE** **Certain careers are associated with different intelligences. Look at the list of careers in the table and write which intelligence fits each category.**

| logical/mathematical | bodily/kinesthetic | musical/rhythmic |
|---|---|---|
| interpersonal | visual/spatial | intrapersonal |
| naturalistic | verbal/linguistic | |

| Intelligence | Careers |
|---|---|
| visual/spatial | architect, engineer, interior designer, mechanic |
| verbal/linguistic | journalist, lawyer, politician, teacher, translator, writer |
| logical/mathematical | accountant, computer programmer, doctor, researcher, scientist |
| bodily/kinesthetic | actor, athlete, dancer, firefighter, physical education teacher |
| musical/rhythmic | composer, conductor, disc jockey, musician, singer |
| interpersonal | businessperson, counselor, politician, salesperson, social worker |
| intrapersonal | philosopher, psychologist, researcher, scientist, writer |
| naturalistic | conservationist, farmer, gardener, scientist |

WORKPLACE CONNECTION
Exercise D: Complete tasks as assigned.
Exercise E: Interact appropriately with team members.
Exercise F: Interpret and communicate information.

**D. DETERMINE** Look back at the three types of intelligence you think best describe your way of processing information on page 18. Using this information, choose two careers listed in Exercise C that you would be good at or interested in. Answers will vary.

_____     _____

**E.** In a small group, discuss the two careers you chose in Exercise D and make notes. What steps do you think you would need to take to pursue one of these careers? Think about the education and training. Make notes of these steps. Answers will vary. Sample answers are given.

1. investigate career     2. take career courses     3. get experience

**F.** In theory, the more education you have, the more money you can earn. Careers that require more education usually pay more. Look at the graph below. Which two things are compared?

\_\_\_\_\_ Median Income \_\_\_\_\_ and \_\_\_\_\_ Education for Both Sexes 18 and Over \_\_\_\_\_

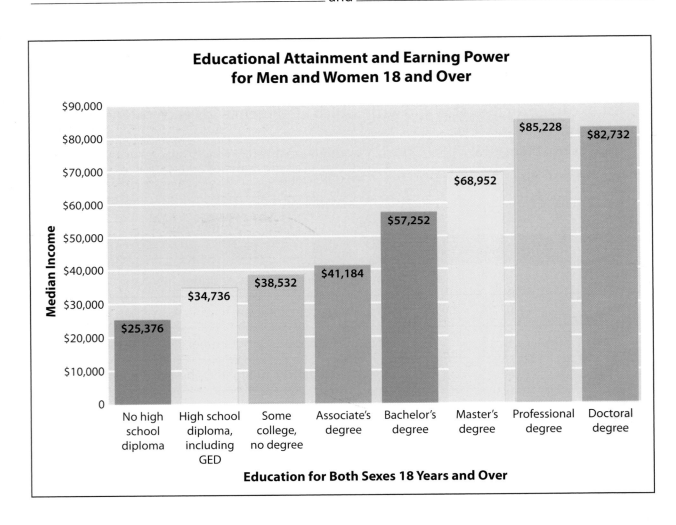

**Educational Attainment and Earning Power for Men and Women 18 and Over**

Median Income:
- No high school diploma: $25,376
- High school diploma, including GED: $34,736
- Some college, no degree: $38,532
- Associate's degree: $41,184
- Bachelor's degree: $57,252
- Master's degree: $68,952
- Professional degree: $85,228
- Doctoral degree: $82,732

**Education for Both Sexes 18 Years and Over**

## Evaluation 1

10–15 mins. ■■■

Go over the answers as a class.

**D. DETERMINE** Look back at the three types of intelligence you think best describe your way of processing information on page 18. Using this information, choose two careers listed in Exercise C that you would be good at or interested in.

**E.** In a small group, discuss the two careers you chose in Exercise D and make notes. What steps do you think you would need to take to pursue one of these careers? Think about the education and training. Make note of these steps.

To get students started, choose one of the careers that it seems unlikely for them to pick. Talk about what education or training might be needed for this career.

## Presentation 2

5–10 mins. ■■■

**F.** In theory, the more education you have, the more money you can earn. Careers that require more education usually pay more. Look at the graph below. Which two things are compared?

**Note:** Use the following listening script with Exercise H on pages 21/21a.

### LISTENING SCRIPT

CD TR 6

**Counselor:** *Hi, Sonya. How are you today?*
**Sonya:** *A bit tired. Taking care of the kids and going to school is keeping me quite busy!*
**Counselor:** *I'll bet. I remember those days. Even though you get tired sometimes, doing both of those things is so worthwhile.*
**Sonya:** *I know it is. I just have to keep reminding myself of that!*
**Counselor:** *Well, based on what we talked about in our last meeting, I would say your intelligences are most likely interpersonal as well as verbal and linguistic. Now, based on the list of careers we looked at, are there any that seem interesting to you?*
**Sonya:** *Actually, teacher kept jumping out at me. It showed up on the list for both of those intelligences. I have always loved working with children and helping them learn new things.*
**Counselor:** *Well, I think that sounds like a great career for you . . . elementary school teacher. Have you ever thought about doing that before?*
**Sonya:** *Not really. I never thought my English would be good enough to be a teacher. And I didn't think I could get into a school to earn a degree.*

**Counselor:** *Well, you are wrong on both counts. You have worked really hard and your English is getting better every day. And there are plenty of schools that would be happy to accept you as an education major.*
**Sonya:** *Will it be expensive?*
**Counselor:** *That all depends on what school you choose. But you can start at a city or community college to get your general education requirements done and then, you can transfer to a four-year school to finish up your degree and get your teaching credentials. That will definitely keep the costs down.*
**Sonya:** *How long will it take?*
**Counselor:** *Well, that all depends on you. If you can go to school full time, you could finish in four years. And I know you have little ones at home, so we can look around for some schools that offer some online classes, so you can study on your own time.*
**Sonya:** *I'll have to talk to my husband to see if he still needs me to work part time.*
**Counselor:** *If you have to, there's no reason you couldn't still work. It will just take you a little bit longer to get your degree.*
**Sonya:** *I wouldn't mind that. I don't want a full-time teaching job until both of my kids are in school anyway.*
**Counselor:** *That's smart. Your girls will appreciate having you home with them.*
**Sonya:** *So, what's the next step?*
**Counselor:** *Well, since you already have your high school diploma, let's start looking around at some local colleges where you can do your general education requirements. I'll put together a list for you and then we can do some research on what English level you need to be at before you can apply.*
**Sonya:** *Sounds great. Thank you so much for all your help!*

### INSTRUCTOR'S NOTES

_____

_____

_____

_____

_____

_____

_____

_____

_____

## Practice 2

10–15 mins. ■■

(Shorter classes can do this exercise for homework by practicing with someone at home or writing out sample conversations.)

The following exercise is a fun way to get students to study the information presented in the graph. Refer to the Best Practice on this page.

**G. With a partner, ask and answer the following questions. Use the information given in the graph in Exercise F to replace the underlined words and make new conversations.**

This activity should be fairly simple for students at this level so only do as much modeling as you think is necessary for them to be able to do it on their own. You may have them sit and talk with one partner or walk around the room and talk to a variety of people.

## Evaluation 2

■■

Observe students as they talk about the graph.

## Presentation 3

5 mins. ■■■

Have students read through Exercise H and ask them who they think each person is. Ask students what these women might be discussing. Then, focus students' attention on the information they will be listening for.

## Practice 3

15–20 mins. ■

**H. Listen to the conversation between a school counselor and Sonya. Take notes on the information you hear.**

**Note:** Refer to the Listening Script set on page 20a. Play the recording once.

### BEST PRACTICE

## Modeling

**Note:** Use this Best Practice with dialog exercises such as that found on page 21. In order to make sure that students understand how to do dialog practices, you may need to model the conversations for them before they work on their own. There are different levels of modeling, ranging from teacher-centered levels to student-centered levels:

1. Class to Class: Break the class up into two halves and have one half be Student A and the other

be Student B. Teacher can participate as a member of both halves.

2. Teacher to Student: Teacher takes the role of Student A; students collectively take the role of Student B.

3. Student to Student: Students work in pairs, switching roles.

## Evaluation 3

5–10 mins. ■

Go over the answers as a class. Once students have the correct answers written down, play the recording again.

## Application

10–20 mins. ■■■

**I. APPLY  Think about a career path you might like to take. Fill in the information below.**

If students do not know the answers, ask them how they might be able to find out the information. Some students in the class may know about different careers and can share their prior knowledge with the class. Your school may also have access to a school counselor who can give students more information.

### INTERNET RESEARCH

## Career research

If you have computers in your class, students may want to use the Internet to complete Exercise I. Have students research the careers they have chosen. Ask them: *How much money can you make? What are the education and experience requirements?*

### MULTILEVEL WORKSHEETS

Unit 1, Lesson 2, Worksheet 1: Choose the Career Path

Unit 1, Lesson 2, Worksheet 2: Conversations with Counselors (listening)

**Refer students to *Stand Out 5 Workbook,* Unit 1, Lesson 2 for practice with future conditional statements.**

**Go to the *Activity Bank* online for suggestions on promoting digital literacy and using the Internet to enhance this lesson.**

WORKPLACE CONNECTION
Exercise G: Interact appropriately with team members.
Exercises H, I: Complete tasks as assigned.

**G.** **With a partner, ask and answer the following questions. Use the information given in the graph in Exercise F to replace the underlined words and make new conversations.**

**Student A:** How much money can I make if I have <u>a master's degree</u>?

**Student B:** About <u>$69,000</u>.

**Student A:** If I want to make <u>over $70,000</u>, what level of education do I need?

**Student B:** You need <u>a doctoral or professional degree</u>.

**H.** **Listen to the conversation between a school counselor and Sonya. Take notes on the information you hear.**

CD TR6

1. Sonya's intelligences: _interpersonal, verbal, and linguistic_

2. Career she is interested in: _teaching_

3. Education she will need: _general education requirements, education degree, teaching credentials_

4. Time it will take to get her degree and credentials: _four years or longer_

5. What are some other things you learned about Sonya from this conversation?

   _She loves children. She likes helping them learn. She might have to work part time. Her English is good_

   _and getting better. She doesn't want to work full time until her children are grown._

   _____

**I.** **APPLY** **Think about a career path you might like to take. Fill in the information below.** Answers will vary.

1. Your intelligences: _____

2. Career you are interested in: _____

3. Education and/or training you will need: _____

4. Time it will take you to follow your career path: _____

# LESSON ③ Achieving balance

WORKPLACE CONNECTION
Exercise A: Complete tasks as assigned.
Exercises B, C, D: Combine ideas and information.
Exercise E: Interact appropriately with team members.

🎧 **A. Sonya has many roles. Listen and take notes.**

CD
TR 7

1. What are Sonya's roles?

| Review: *Be* | | | |
|---|---|---|---|
| **Subject** | **Past** | **Present** | **Future** |
| I | was | am | will be |
| You, We, They | were | are | will be |
| He, She, It | was | is | will be |

a wife _____ a student _____

a mother _____ a friend _____

a sister _____ a manager _____

2. What was Sonya's role? a secretary _____

3. What will Sonya's role be? an elementary school teacher _____

**B. IDENTIFY What are your roles? Write at least three statements.**

Answers will vary. Sample answers are given.

I am a brother, a son, a friend, and a student _____.

_____

_____

_____

**C. What were your roles? Write at least two statements.**

I was a grandson and a plumber _____.

_____

_____

**D. What will your roles be? Write at least two statements.**

I will be a husband, a father, and an engineer _____.

_____

_____

**E. COMPARE Share your responses with a partner. Are they similar or different?**

**Goal:** Balance your life
**Grammar:** Simple verb tenses
**Academic Strategy:** Active listening
**Vocabulary:** *balance*

## Agenda

- Find out who Sonya is.
- Describe yourself.
- Read Sonya's paragraph.
- Review simple verb tenses.
- Discuss balance in your life.

## Resources

**Multilevel Worksheets:** Unit 1, Lesson 3,
    Worksheets 1–3
**Workbook:** Unit 1, Lesson 3
**Audio:** CD Track 7

## Pacing

- 1.5 hour classes
- 2.5 hour classes
- 3+ hour classes

## STANDARDS CORRELATIONS

*CCRS:* RI1, RI2, W2, W4, SL2, L1
*CASAS:* 7.4.2
*SCANS:* **Information** Acquire and evaluate information, interpret and communicate information, use computers to process information *(optional)*
**Interpersonal** Participate as a member of a team, work with cultural diversity
**Systems** Monitor and correct performance
**Technology** Apply technology to a task *(optional)*
**Basic Skills** Reading, writing, listening, speaking
**Thinking Skills** Think creatively, make decisions, see things in the mind's eye
**Personal Qualities** Responsibility, sociability, self-management
*EFF:* **Communication** Read with understanding, convey ideas in writing, speak so others can understand, listen actively, observe critically
**Decision Making** Solve problems and make decisions, plan
**Interpersonal** Cooperate with others, advocate and influence, resolve conflict and negotiate, guide others
**Lifelong Learning** Take responsibility for learning, reflect and evaluate, use information and communications technology *(optional)*

## Warm-up and Review          5–10 mins. ■■■

Put students in small groups and have them discuss Exercise I from the previous lesson.

## Introduction          10–20 mins. ■■■

Refer to the Best Practice on page 4a for information on dictation.

Dictation:
1. If you want to be a teacher, you will need a college degree and a teaching credential.
2. Studying to be a teacher will take time away from your family.
3. Do you spend time with the people who are important to you?
4. If you could change your life somehow, what would you do?

State the goal: *Today, you will meet Sonya and see how she plans to balance her life. Then, you will write about balance in your own life.*

## Presentation 1          10–15 mins. ■■■

Suggest to students that a person can be perceived by others differently according to the role he or she fulfills. Write on the board, *Who is Sonya?* Ask students who they think she might be. Tell students they will be listening to Sonya describe herself. Play the recording.

**A. Sonya has many roles. Listen and take notes.**

After students have listened to the recording, go over the answers as a class.

> ## LISTENING SCRIPT          🎧 CD TR 7
>
> **Sonya:** *I am a wife. I am a mother. I am a sister. I am a student. I am a friend. I am a manager. I was a secretary. I will be an elementary school teacher.*

## Practice 1          10–15 mins. ■■■

Have students complete these exercises on their own.

**B. IDENTIFY  What are your roles? Write at least three statements.**

**C. What were your roles? Write at least two statements.**

**D. What will your roles be? Write at least two statements.**

## Evaluation 1          5 mins. ■■■

**E. COMPARE  Share your responses with a partner. Are they similar or different?**

## Presentation 2

**F. Read what Sonya wrote and answer the questions below the paragraph with a partner.**

Ask a volunteer to read Sonya's paragraph out loud. Have students answer the questions with a partner.

Answer Key for Exercise F. Answers will vary. Sample answers:

1. When Sonya was young, she spent a lot of time with her family, but now she works and studies a lot.
2. Her life isn't balanced right now because she wants to work less and she wants more time with her family.
3. She wants to find a job as a teacher, to make more money, and to work less.
4. Yes. If she makes all these changes, she will be happy because she will reach her goals.

**G. Review the simple tenses.**

Go over the review chart of simple tenses with the class. Based on your students' needs, spend as much or as little time as appropriate.

## Practice 2 10–15 mins. ■■

(Shorter classes can do this exercise for homework.)

**H. Complete each statement about yourself using the tense and verb in parentheses.**

## Evaluation 2 10–15 mins. ■■

Ask volunteers to write their sentences on the board. Review the grammar chart as a class.

**Refer students to *Stand Out 5 Workbook,* Unit 1, Lesson 3 for more practice with past, present, and future simple tenses.**

**Go to the *Activity Bank* online for suggestions on promoting digital literacy and using the Internet to enhance this lesson.**

---

### INSTRUCTOR'S NOTES

WORKPLACE CONNECTION
Exercise F: Interact appropriately with team members.
Exercise H: Complete tasks as assigned.

**F. Read what Sonya wrote and answer the questions below the paragraph with a partner.**

### Balance in My Life

When I was a little girl, I spent all my time playing with my two brothers. I just enjoyed doing whatever they were doing. Family was always very important to us. But as I grew older, I started working and studying more. It seemed like I was working all day, going to school every night, and studying whenever I had time. I didn't have any balance in my life. Now that I have my diploma, I don't study as much, but I still work a lot. I'm a manager at a restaurant, but I want to become an elementary school teacher. I am also a wife and a mother, and I want to spend more time with my family. I hope to find a job as a teacher where I can work fewer hours but still make enough money to help out. I will really enjoy being home with my family more and having more balance in my life.

1. How was Sonya's life different in the past from how it is now?
2. Is her life balanced right now? Why or why not?
3. What does she want to change in her life?
4. Do you think this change will make her happy? Why or why not?

*Answers are on Lesson Planner page 23a.*

**G. Review the simple tenses.**

| Review: Simple Tenses | | | | |
|---|---|---|---|---|
| **Subject** | **Past** | **Present** | **Future** | |
| He, She, It | studied | studies | will study | English every day. |
| We | put | put | will put | our studies first. |
| They | worked | work | will work | too many hours. |

*Sample answers are given.*

**H. Complete each statement about yourself using the tense and verb in parentheses.**

1. (*past*, spend) I spent time on the farm with my father _____.

2. (*present*, put) I put money in the bank every week _____.

3. (*future*, live) I will live in New York or Los Angeles _____.

WORKPLACE CONNECTION
Exercises I, J: Complete tasks as assigned.
Exercise K: Combine ideas and information.
Exercise L: Interact appropriately with team members.

**I.** **Think about balance in your life. What are some things that are important to you? What are your interests? What activities do you do regularly? Make a list.**
Answers will vary. Sample answers are given.

play soccer                    study                    cook good food

visit family                    play video games                    practice guitar

**J.** **EVALUATE** **Think about how you balanced your life in the past, how you balance it now, and what you want for the future. Answer the questions below.**
Answers will vary. Sample answers are below.

1. What was important to you in the past?

   My family and friends were important in the past.

2. What is important to you now?

   Studying and playing guitar are important now.

3. Do you spend enough time on the things that are important to you now? Why?

   No. Other responsibilities get in the way, or I don't manage my time wisely enough.

4. What changes would you like to make for the future?

   I want to get more exercise in the future.

**K.** **COMPOSE** **Using Sonya's paragraph in Exercise F as a writing model, write a paragraph on a piece of paper about balance in your life—past, present, and future.**
Answers will vary.

**L.** **Share your paragraph with a partner and ask for two suggestions about how to make your paragraph better. Write two suggestions for your partner's paragraph.**
Sample answers are below.

1. Write more details about the past.

2. Include more about my future hopes.

24   Unit 1

## Presentation 3      5–10 mins. ▪▪▪

**I. Think about balance in your life. What are some things that are important to you? What are your interests? What activities do you do regularly? Make a list.**

Talk students through this exercise. Have them call out some other ideas of what might be important to them.

## Practice 3      10–15 mins. ▪

(Shorter classes can do this exercise for homework.)

**J. EVALUATE Think about how you balanced your life in the past, how you balance it now, and what you want for the future. Answer the questions below.**

Go over the questions with students and then have them complete the exercise on their own.

## Evaluation 3      5–10 mins. ▪

Ask volunteers to share their responses with the class.

## Application      20–30 mins. ▪▪▪

(Shorter classes can do the following exercise for homework.)

**K. COMPOSE Using Sonya's paragraph in Exercise F as a writing model, write a paragraph on a piece of paper about balance in your life—past, present, and future.**

**L. Share your paragraph with a partner and ask for two suggestions about how to make your paragraph better. Write two suggestions for your partner's paragraph.**

Before you have students complete this exercise, give suggestions of the type of advice they can tell their partner. For example, *Maybe you could state this idea more clearly,* or *Maybe you could give more details about this idea.* (On the Multilevel Worksheets CD-ROM, there is a worksheet with a list of suggestions students might give.)

## BEST PRACTICE

### Pairing students for peer-editing

Peer-editing can be difficult because not all students have learned to critically analyze texts. Pairing students of similar levels works well when students are peer-editing. If you pair students of mixed levels, one student will end up getting more out of the activity than the other. There will be some pairs who are better at peer-editing than others. Spend your time helping the pairs who need it.

## MULTILEVEL WORKSHEETS

Unit 1, Lesson 3, Worksheet 1: Simple Verb Tenses

Unit 1, Lesson 3, Worksheet 2: Balance

Unit 1, Lesson 3, Worksheet 3: Suggestions to Improve Writing

## INSTRUCTOR'S NOTES

## AT-A-GLANCE PREP

**Goal:** Identify and prioritize goals
**Academic Strategy:** Goal setting
**Vocabulary:** *goal setting, big picture, long-term, short-term, prioritize, achieve, motivate*

### Agenda
◼ Read about a goal-setting workshop.
◼ Take notes on a lecture.
◼ Read about Sonya's goals.
◼ Set and prioritize goals.

### Resources
**Multilevel Worksheets:** Unit 1, Lesson 4, Worksheets 1–2
**Workbook:** Unit 1, Lesson 4
**Audio:** CD Track 8
**Suggested Realia:** Your own personal list of goals (if you have one) or things that motivate you (e.g., pictures).

### Pacing
◼ 1.5 hour classes　　◼ 2.5 hour classes
◼ 3+ hour classes

## STANDARDS CORRELATIONS

*CCRS:* RI4, RI7, SL1, SL2
*CASAS:* 7.1.3, 7.4.2
*SCANS:* **Information** Acquire and evaluate information, organize and maintain information, interpret and communicate information
**Interpersonal** Participate as a member of a team, work with cultural diversity
**Systems** Monitor and correct performance
**Basic Skills** Reading, writing, listening, speaking
**Thinking Skills** Think creatively, make decisions, see things in the mind's eye
**Personal Qualities** Responsibility, sociability, self-management
*EFF:* **Communication** Read with understanding, convey ideas in writing, listen actively, observe critically
**Decision Making** Plan
**Interpersonal** Cooperate with others, advocate and influence, resolve conflict and negotiate, guide others
**Lifelong Learning** Take responsibility for learning, reflect and evaluate

## Warm-up and Review　　5–10 mins. ◼◼◻

Have students take out their paragraphs from the previous lesson and share them with a small group.

## Introduction　　5–10 mins. ◼◼◻

**Note:** Refer to the Best Practice on dictation on page 4a to review purpose.

Dictation:

1. It is very important to set goals for your life.
2. There are many different types of goals you can set.
3. Setting and achieving goals will improve your self-confidence.
4. Have you ever set goals before?

State the goal: *Today, we will learn about goal setting and you will practice identifying and prioritizing your own goals.*

## Presentation 1　　10–15 mins. ◼◼◻

Use the dictation sentences as a springboard for a discussion about goals and goal setting. See what students already know and write their ideas on the board. Direct students' attention to the flier in their books. Discuss the flier and the idiomatic expressions found in it (examples: *big picture, get what you want out of life, make dreams a reality*).

## Practice 1　　10–15 mins. ◼◼◻

**A. Read the flier and answer the questions.**

Have students complete this exercise on their own.

## Evaluation 1　　10–15 mins. ◼◼◻

**B. In a small group, discuss your answers to the questions in Exercise A.**

Observe students' discussions.

# LESSON **4** Setting priorities

GOAL ■ Identify and prioritize goals

WORKPLACE CONNECTION
Exercise A: Interpret and communicate information.
Exercise B: Interact appropriately with team members.

**A.   Read the flier and answer the questions.**

**What is your BIG PICTURE?**
Get what you want out of life!

Attend this goal-setting workshop to learn how to set long- and short-term goals and make your dreams a reality.

Peterson Hall, Room 15
Wednesday, October 7th from 5 to 9 p.m.

RSVP: bigpic@set0urg0als.com

*Answers will vary. Sample answers are below.*

1. What do you think *big picture* means?

   my view of the future

2. What is *goal setting*?

   deciding specific things I want to accomplish

3. Would you attend the workshop? Why?

   Yes. I don't think about long-term goals enough.

4. Write three goals you have set for yourself in the past.

   a. Make money.          (No)

   b. Live in a big city.      (Yes)

   c. Get married.          (No)

5. Did you achieve your goals? Write *yes* or *no* next to each goal.

**B.   In a small group, discuss your answers to the questions in Exercise A.**

WORKPLACE CONNECTION
Exercise C: Interpret and communicate information.
Exercise D: Complete tasks as assigned.

**C. Listen to the lecture on goal setting and take notes about the following on a separate piece of paper:**

CD TR 8

- Goal setting  *a process to make me think about the future, helps motivate me, choose the direction I want to go, increase my self-confidence*

- First thing you should do  *create a big picture with short-term goals*

- Seven types of goals  *educational    career    financial    attitude family    physical    pleasure*

- Five tips for setting goals  *set realistic goals: don't be unrealistic    write down goals write goals as positive statements    be precise about goal times and dates prioritize: put goals in order of importance*

**D. CHOOSE Answer the following questions based on the notes you took. Circle the best answer.**

1. Which of the following is NOT true about goal setting?

   a. It will improve your self-confidence.

   b. It helps motivate you.

   c. It makes you think about your past.

   d. It helps you choose a direction for your life.

2  What are the seven types of goals?

   a. financial, physical, attitude, pleasure, education, mental, family

   b. physical, career, family, financial, attitude, personal, education

   c. education, career, technical, financial, physical, attitude, pleasure

   d. financial, physical, career, family, education, attitude, pleasure

3. Why is it important to prioritize your goals in a list?

   a. It will be easy to know when you have achieved a goal.

   b. It will help you focus your attention on the most important goals.

   c. It gives them life.

   d. It will improve your self-confidence.

## LISTENING SCRIPT

🎧
CD
TR 8

*Goal setting is a process that makes you think about your future and helps motivate you to make that future a reality. Setting goals helps you choose the direction you want your life to go in. As you set and achieve goals, your self-confidence will improve.*

*The first thing you should do is to create a big picture of where you want to be in a certain number of years. Once you have created your big picture, you can make smaller or short-term goals.*

*In this workshop, we'd like you to focus on seven different types of goals. First are educational goals. Is there anything special you want or need to learn? Or, is there any degree you need to get to pursue your career goals? Second are career goals. How far would you like to go in your career? Third are financial goals. How much money would you like to be earning? Fourth are attitude goals. Would you like to change the way you think or act? Fifth are family goals. Do you want to have a family, increase the size of your family, or improve some of your family relationships? Sixth are physical goals. Is there anything you'd like to do to improve your health? Would you like to enter a physical competition? And, finally, pleasure goals. Are there any hobbies you'd like to do? It is important to enjoy your life so make sure you think about goals for pleasure.*

*It is important to spend some time thinking about all these different goals and try to choose one goal in each category that best reflects what you want to do. Then you should prioritize these goals and focus on a small number of goals at one time.*

*So, how do you go about setting these goals? Here are five tips that should help you to set effective goals:*

1. *Set realistic goals. It is important to set a goal that you can actually achieve. It will lower your self-confidence if you set goals that are unrealistic.*
2. *Write down your goals. Writing your goals down gives them life. Try to put them in a place where you will see them every day.*
3. *Write each goal as a positive statement.*
4. *Be precise. When you set your goals, write down exact times, dates, etc. This way, it will be easy to see when you have achieved a goal.*
5. *Prioritize. When you have more than one goal, put them in order of importance. This will help you direct your attention to the most important goals and avoid feeling overwhelmed by having too much to do.*

*So, now that we have talked about types of goals and tips for setting these goals, should we get down to business?*

## Presentation 2

15–20 mins. ■■■

Prepare students for the listening activity by reviewing the outline for their notes in their books. Ask them to tell you what they will be listening for.

### C. Listen to the lecture on goal setting and take notes about the following on a separate piece of paper:

Review each item in the list. Then, play the listening a few times until you think students have been able to fill in most of the notes. Between listenings, have students share their answers with a partner to fill in things they may have missed. Have students complete Exercise D before you go over any of the notes.

## Practice 2

5 mins. ■■

(Shorter classes can do this exercise for homework.

### D. CHOOSE Answer the following questions based on the notes you took. Circle the best answer.

## Evaluation 2

10–15 mins. ■■

Go over the answers as a class. Go back to their notes and help students fill in what they may have missed or gotten wrong. You can do this using an overhead transparency or by playing the listening again.

### INSTRUCTOR'S NOTES

_____
_____
_____
_____
_____
_____
_____
_____
_____
_____

## Presentation 3 5–10 mins. ■■■

E. **Sonya attended the goal-setting workshop and created a list of goals that she now keeps on her refrigerator.**

As a class, talk about Sonya's *big picture* and her goals.

## Practice 3 5–10 mins. ■

(Shorter classes can do this exercise for homework.)

F. **Sonya's goals are prioritized (listed in order of importance). Do you think she put her goals in the right order? Discuss your ideas with a partner.**

## Evaluation 3 5–10 mins. ■

Ask pairs of students to report what they discussed.

## Application 10–20 mins. ■■■

G. **PRIORITIZE Think about where you would like to be ten years from now. Based on your thoughts, what are your long-term goals? Use the items below to help you clarify what your goals should be.**

### MULTILEVEL WORKSHEETS

Unit 1, Lesson 4, Worksheet 1: Goal-Setting (reading)

Unit 1, Lesson 4, Worksheet 2: Goal Chart

**Refer students to *Stand Out 5 Workbook,* Unit 1, Lesson 4 for practice with the past perfect.**

**Go to the *Activity Bank* online for suggestions on promoting digital literacy and using the Internet to enhance this lesson.**

### BEST PRACTICE

## Prioritizing

Explain to students that prioritizing is an important organizational skill. Prioritizing helps us avoid feeling overwhelmed or stressed and is a great tool for remembering important things. Point out that students are undoubtedly already familiar with setting priorities. Ask students if they have ever made a to-do list and discuss why. Have students make a to-do list for the next day and have them share it with a partner. Then, have volunteers write their to-do lists on the board to model prioritizing.

### INSTRUCTOR'S NOTES

_____

_____

_____

_____

_____

_____

_____

_____

_____

_____

_____

_____

_____

_____

_____

_____

_____

_____

WORKPLACE CONNECTION
Exercise F: Interact appropriately with team members.
Exercise G: Combine ideas and information; Complete tasks as assigned.

**E.** **Sonya attended the goal-setting workshop and created a list of goals that she now keeps on her refrigerator.**

I plan to be successful in my personal and professional life. I will be a highly educated elementary school teacher.

| SHORT-TERM GOALS | LONG-TERM GOALS |
|---|---|
| • spend more time with my children<br>• exercise to reduce stress<br>• enroll in community college | • get my bachelor's degree and teaching credentials<br>• become an elementary school teacher<br>• get a master's degree<br>• learn how to swim |

**F.** **Sonya's goals are prioritized (listed in order of importance). Do you think she put her goals in the right order? Discuss your ideas with a partner.** Answers will vary.

**G.** **PRIORITIZE** **Think about where you would like to be ten years from now. Based on your thoughts, what are your long-term goals? Use the items below to help you clarify what your goals should be.** Answers will vary. Sample answers are below.

1. Write one goal for each category.

   Education: get a Bachelor's degree in nursing

   Career: become a registered nurse

   Family: get married by the age of 30

   Financial: save money for a down payment

   Physical: lose 15 pounds

   Attitude: stay positive

   Pleasure: play on a soccer team

2. Number your three most important goals above in order of priority. Education, Career, and Physical

3. Based on these three long-term goals, what are some short-term goals you can set in order to help you reach the long-term ones?

   Short-term goals: get financial aid, work in a hospital, start running and lifting weights

4. Prioritize your short-term goals. Write them in order. See above.

# LESSON **5** Motivation

GOAL ■ Motivate yourself

WORKPLACE CONNECTION
Exercises B, D: Interact appropriately with team members.
Exercise C: Collect and organize information.

**A.** **What does *motivation* mean?** Answers will vary.

*motivation* (your own definition or one from a dictionary): ___to excite or encourage someone to act___

_____

**B.** **GENERATE How can you motivate yourself to reach your goals? Work with a small group and make a list.** Answers will vary.

stay positive                          take classes

choose short-term goals                stay active

do something you like                  talk to friends and family

make friends with similar people       get organized

**C.** **Listen to Mrs. Morgan's students talk about motivating themselves. Take notes about what each person says.**

CD TR 9

 Carl: gets support from family and friends

 Sonya: reads books and Internet articles

 Akira: keeps a goal chart in his room

 Gloria: has a positive attitude

 Abir: keeps a list of her goals in her planner

 Mario: sets small goals to achieve

**D.** **What idea for getting motivated does each person in Exercise C have? Share what you recall with a partner.**

28 Unit 1

**Goal:** Motivate yourself

**Grammar:** Future perfect

**Academic Strategies:** Active listening, note taking

**Vocabulary:** *motivation, support, inspire, refresh, evaluate, progress, monitor, be flexible, outlook*

### Agenda

☐ Take notes on motivation techniques.

☐ Complete a self-motivation checklist.

☐ Practice using the future perfect.

☐ Write goal statements and ideas to motivate yourself.

### Resources

**Multilevel Worksheets:** Unit 1, Lesson 5, Worksheets 1–2

**Workbook:** Unit 1, Lesson 5

**Audio:** CD Track 9

### Pacing

■ 1.5 hour classes    ■ 2.5 hour classes

■ 3+ hour classes

## STANDARDS CORRELATIONS

*CCRS:* RI4, W4, SL2, L1

*CASAS:* 7.1.3, 7.4.2

*SCANS:* **Resources** Allocate time

**Information** Acquire and evaluate information, organize and maintain information, interpret and communicate information

**Interpersonal** Participate as a member of a team, negotiate to arrive at a decision, work with cultural diversity

**Systems** Monitor and correct performance

**Basic Skills** Reading, writing, listening, speaking

**Thinking Skills** Think creatively, make decisions, see things in the mind's eye

**Personal Qualities** Responsibility, sociability, self-management

*EFF:* **Communication** Read with understanding, convey ideas in writing, speak so others can understand, listen actively, observe critically

**Decision Making** Solve problems and make decisions, plan

**Interpersonal** Cooperate with others

**Lifelong Learning** Take responsibility for learning, reflect and evaluate

## Warm-up and Review                    5–10 mins. ■■■

Have students take out the goals they wrote in the previous lesson in Exercise G. Have them share their short-term goals (items 3 and 4) and how they prioritized them with a small group.

## Introduction                    5–10 mins. ■■■

**Note:** Refer to the Best Practice on dictation on page 4a as needed.

Dictation:

1. I will already have become a teacher by the time my kids are in school.
2. When I turn 35, I will have been a graphic designer for five years.
3. I will have been accepted to college when I finish my last English class.
4. I will have been teaching English for 20 years when I retire.

State the goal: *Today, you will learn how to motivate yourself. You will write goal statements and make a commitment to motivate yourself.*

## Presentation 1                    10–15 mins. ■■■

### A. What does *motivation* mean?

Ask students to define *motivation*. Define the word as a class. Encourage students to refer to their dictionaries if they are stuck or need synonyms. Then, ask students the following questions and discuss as a class:

1. Are you motivated to achieve your goals?
2. Do you need someone to motivate you?
3. Can you motivate yourself?

### B. GENERATE How can you motivate yourself to reach your goals? Work with a small group and make a list.

When students have finished the exercise, have them share some of their ideas with the class by writing them on the board.

## Practice 1                    10–15 mins. ■■■

### C. Listen to Mrs. Morgan's students talk about motivating themselves. Take notes about what each person says.

**Note:** The listening script is on page 29a.

## Evaluation 1                    5 mins. ■■■

### D. What idea for getting motivated does each person in Exercise C have? Share what you recall with a partner.

Discuss the motivation strategies mentioned on the recording as a class.

## LISTENING SCRIPT

🎧 CD TR 9

**Carl:** *I told my friends and family about my goals so they could support me.*

**Sonya:** *I read books and look for articles on the Internet to inspire me.*

**Akira:** *I keep a chart up in my room of the goals I have reached and the ones I still need to reach. When I reach a goal, I put a sticker on the chart.*

**Gloria:** *I remind myself every morning to have a positive attitude. I tell myself, "I can do it!"*

**Abir:** *I made a list of all my goals and I keep it taped inside my planner, so I see it every day.*

**Mario:** *I set very small goals, so that I can get excited every time I achieve one.*

### Presentation 2                 10–15 mins. ■■■

**E.** **Below is a list of steps you can take to motivate yourself toward pursuing a goal. Check (✓) the steps you already do. Check (✓) the steps you would like to do.**

Go over each statement as a class. Have students put a check in the correct column once they understand each one.

**Suggestion:** Put up an overhead transparency and, as you go over each step, put a check in the correct column for yourself.

### Practice 2                 5–10 mins. ■■
(Shorter classes can do this exercise for homework.)

**F.** **COMPARE** **Share your list with a partner. Are there any steps that both of you would like to take? What are your differences?**

Students should be able to complete this exercise by themselves even if they don't completely understand the grammar, which will be presented in the next exercise. Play the listening from Exercise C again if students need a review of each person's motivation.

### Evaluation 2                 5 mins. ■■
Go over the answers as a class.

#### MULTILEVEL WORKSHEET

Unit 1, Lesson 5, Worksheet 1: Motivation Checklist/
Motivate Yourself

## INSTRUCTOR'S NOTES

WORKPLACE CONNECTION
Exercise E: Complete tasks as assigned.
Exercise F: Interact appropriately with team members.

**E.** Below is a list of steps you can take to motivate yourself toward pursuing a goal. Check (✓) the steps you already do. Check (✓) the steps you would like to do.

*Answers will vary.*

| I already do | I would like to do | Steps to motivate yourself toward pursuing a goal |
|---|---|---|
|  |  | 1. Write down your goals and put them in a place you will see them every day. |
|  |  | 2. Tell family and friends about your goals so they can support you. |
|  |  | 3. Tell yourself that you can do it. |
|  |  | 4. Keep a positive attitude. |
|  |  | 5. Be enthusiastic about your goals. |
|  |  | 6. When you slow down or don't have the energy to do anything, take small steps and continue moving forward. Don't stop. |
|  |  | 7. Evaluate your progress. Make a chart or do something to monitor progress. |
|  |  | 8. Don't be too fixed on one approach. Be flexible and make changes when needed. |
|  |  | 9. Read inspiring books. |
|  |  | 10. Take some time to refresh yourself. |
|  |  | 11. Exercise more to help your attitude. The better your health, the more positive your outlook. |
|  |  | 12. After you are motivated, motivate others. |

**F.** **COMPARE** Share your list with a partner. Are there any steps that both of you would like to take? What are your differences?

WORKPLACE CONNECTION
Exercise H: Complete tasks as assigned.
Exercises I, J: Combine ideas and information.

## G. Study the chart with your teacher.

| | | | Future Perfect Tense | |
|---|---|---|---|---|
| Subject | *will have* | Past participle | | Future event—Time expression |
| I | will have | become | a teacher | **by** the time my kids are in school. |
| He | will have | been | a graphic designer (for five years) | **when** he turns 35. |
| They | will have | found | a job | **by** 2017. |

We use the future perfect to talk about an activity that will be completed before another time or event in the future. ___|___ present ✗ future to be completed (perfect) ✗ future event with time expression ___

*Note:* The order of events is not important. If the future event with the time expression comes first, use a comma.

**Example:** *By the time my kids are in school, I will have become a teacher.*

## H. Mrs. Morgan's students wrote goal statements. Complete each statement with the correct form of the future perfect.

1. By the time I graduate from high school, I (do) _____ will have done _____ 500 hours of community service.

2. I (buy) _____ will have bought _____ a new house when I retire.

3. When I turn 60, I (travel) _____ will have traveled _____ to over 20 countries.

4. We (put) _____ will have put _____ three kids through college by 2020.

5. I (become) _____ will have become _____ a successful business owner by the time I turn 40.

6. By the time I finish getting my degree, I (apply) _____ will have applied _____ to three different graduate programs.

## I. Write three goal statements for yourself on a separate piece of paper. Use the future perfect tense. Answers will vary.

## J. DECIDE Now that you have written down your goals, what are you going to do to keep yourself motivated? Write down three ideas on a separate piece of paper.
Answers will vary.

## Presentation 3    5–10 mins. ■■■

### G. Study the chart with your teacher.

Let students read the chart by themselves before you present it. See how much of the target structure they can figure out on their own. This is now the third time they have been exposed to the future perfect in this lesson: the dictation, the statements in Exercise E, and the grammar chart. Once you have gone over the chart as a class, create a few more examples on the board to make sure everyone understands the use of the future perfect.

### BEST PRACTICE
## Grammar charts

At this level, students should be able to read and understand grammar charts by themselves. Chart reading is a skill that they will need as they continue on to higher levels and take other academic classes. Allow students to read each chart by themselves before you present the material to the class. Encourage students to ask questions and to create their own sentences to demonstrate the targeted grammar points.

## Practice 3    15–20 mins. ■
(Shorter classes can do this exercise for homework.)

### H. Mrs. Morgan's students wrote goal statements. Complete each statement with the correct form of the future perfect.

If students finish early, they can check their answers with a partner.

## Evaluation 3    5–10 mins. ■
Ask volunteers to come up and write the statements on the board. Ask the class to help you correct any mistakes.

### BEST PRACTICE
## Volunteers to the board

In the beginning of the course, you may have the same students volunteering to come to the board for each activity. As the course progresses, other students should begin to gain more confidence and volunteer as well. If, after a few weeks, some students are still not volunteering, select the students you wish to come to the board. If you think certain students may need help with the activity at the board, have them come up with a partner.

## Application    10–20 mins. ■■■

I. Write three goal statements for yourself on a separate piece of paper. Use the future perfect tense.

J. DECIDE Now that you have written down your goals, what are you going to do to keep yourself motivated? Write down three ideas on a separate piece of paper.

Remind students they can look back at the list in Exercise E for ideas. Ask volunteers to come to the front of the class and share what they wrote in Exercises I and J. Remind students that they will be more motivated if they share their goals and motivations!

### MULTILEVEL WORKSHEET

Unit 1, Lesson 5, Worksheet 2: Future Perfect Tense

**Refer students to *Stand Out 5 Workbook*, Unit 1, Lesson 5 for more practice with the future perfect tense.**

**Go to the *Activity Bank* online for suggestions on promoting digital literacy and using the Internet to enhance this lesson.**

**There are also two extension challenges— Extension Challenge 1 gives students practice with gerunds as direct objects, and Extension Challenge 2 gives students practice with the future perfect continuous (progressive) tense.**

**LIFESKILLS** ▶ # The presentation is due in two weeks

## Before You Watch

- Ask students if they have ever given a presentation before.
- Discuss student experiences as a class.

## A. Look at the picture and answer the questions.

- Ask students to look at the picture and answer the questions.
- Discuss the answers as a class.

## While You Watch

## B. Watch the video and complete the dialog.

- Tell students to watch the video and complete the dialog.
- Play the video and ask students to watch and listen carefully.
- Play the video again. Then, ask students to complete the dialog.
- Play the video once more and have students check their answers.

## Check Your Understanding

## C. Read the statements and write *True* or *False*.

- Have students read the statements.
- Ask students to write *True* or *False*.
- Discuss the answers as a class.

INSTRUCTOR'S NOTES

# LIFESKILLS ▶ The presentation is due in two weeks

## Before You Watch

**A.** Look at the picture and answer the questions.

1. What are Naomi, Hector, and Mateo doing? *They are working on a report.*

2. What is Naomi showing Hector and Mateo? *Naomi is showing them a bar graph.*

## While You Watch

**B.** ▶ Watch the video and complete the dialog.

**Naomi:** Come on, you guys. We have to do this (1) __presentation__ in two weeks. Two weeks! That's barely enough time.

**Hector:** OK, let's focus. The assignment was to do a presentation on jobs and (2) __careers__.

**Mateo:** The teacher gave a lecture about the relationship between education and (3) __income__. Remember? So, maybe we could do something about that.

**Naomi:** Good idea! Let's do a presentation showing how an advanced degree can increase your (4) __earning potential__.

**Hector:** I like it. There have got to be some good (5) __statistics__ on that.

**Mateo:** I think it would be good to show some of those statistics in the form of a graph or a (6) __graph__.

## Check Your Understanding

**C.** Read the statements and write *True* or *False*.

1. Naomi, Hector, and Mateo have three weeks to do their report.   __False__

2. Mateo takes notes while they talk.   *False*

3. Their report is about education and earning power.   *True*

4. Hector designs the bar graph.   *False*

5. Their chart shows that you earn more money if you have more education.   *True*

# Review

**A.** Indicate the learning style next to each activity. Write *V* for *Visual*, *A* for *Auditory*, and *T/K* for *Tactile/Kinesthetic* on the line.

1. analyzing a graph __V__

2. listening to a discussion __A__

3. listening to a lecture __A__

4. participating in a dance __T/K__

5. reading a journal article __V__

6. touching objects __T/K__

7. watching an online newscast __V__

**B.** Complete each statement with a phrase from the box.

| | |
|---|---|
| appreciates music | relates well to surroundings |
| expresses oneself with movement | thinks in pictures |
| is aware of one's own feelings | uses language |
| relates well to others | uses reason, logic, and numbers |

1. A naturalistic person _relates well to surroundings_.

2. Someone with interpersonal intelligence _relates well to others_.

3. A person who is kinesthetic _expresses oneself with movement_.

4. A logical/mathematical person _uses reason, logic, and numbers_.

5. A person with visual intelligence _thinks in pictures_.

6. Someone with intrapersonal intelligence _is aware of one's own feelings_.

7. A musical/rhythmic person _appreciates music_.

8. A verbal/linguistic person _uses language_.

**C.** Ask a classmate how they relate to the information below. Write his or her answers on the lines. Answers will vary.

1. Types of intelligence: _____

2. Career interests: _____

3. What is important to you now? _____

4. What changes would you like to make for your future? _____

WORKPLACE CONNECTION
Exercises A, B: Complete tasks as assigned.
Exercise C: Interact appropriately with team members; Collect and organize information.

## AT-A-GLANCE PREP

**Goals:** All unit goals
**Grammar:** All unit grammar
**Academic Strategy:** Reviewing
**Vocabulary:** All Unit 1 vocabulary

### Agenda

- Discuss unit goals.
- Complete the review.
- Use unit vocabulary.

### Resources

**Stand Out Assessment CD-ROM with ExamView®**

### Pacing

- ■ 1.5 hour classes  ■ 2.5 hour classes
- ■ 3+ hour classes

## STANDARDS CORRELATIONS

*CCRS:* RI4, W2, SL1, SL2, SL3
*CASAS:* 7.2.1
*SCANS:* **Resources** Allocate time
**Information** Acquire and evaluate information
**Interpersonal** Participate as a member of a team, teach others, negotiate to arrive at a decision, work with cultural diversity
**Systems** Monitor and correct performance
**Basic Skills** Reading, writing, arithmetic, listening, speaking
**Thinking Skills** Think creatively, make decisions, solve problems, see things in the mind's eye
**Personal Qualities** Responsibility, sociability, self-management
*EFF:* **Communication** Read with understanding, convey ideas in writing, speak so others can understand, listen actively, observe critically
**Interpersonal** Cooperate with others, guide others
**Lifelong Learning** Take responsibility for learning, reflect and evaluate

### Warm-up and Review          5–10 mins. ■■■

Review the future perfect tense with students by asking volunteers to come to the board and write their goal statements from Exercise I in the previous lesson.

### Introduction          5–10 mins. ■■■

Ask students as a class to try to recall all the goals of this unit without looking back in their books. The goals for this unit include identifying your learning style, identifying a career path, balancing your life, identifying and prioritizing goals, and motivating yourself. Write all the goals on the board from Unit 1. Show students the first page of the unit and reread the five goals together.

State the goal: *Today, we will be reviewing everything you have learned in this unit and preparing for the team project.*

### Presentation          10–15 mins. ■■■

This presentation will cover the first three pages of the review. Quickly go to the first page of each lesson. Discuss the goal of each. Ask simple questions to remind students of what they have learned.

**Note:** Since there is little presentation in the review, you can assign the review exercises that don't require collaboration with a partner or group for homework and go over them in class the following day.

### Practice          20–25 mins. ■■■

**Note:** There are two ways to do the review:

1. Go through the exercises one at a time and, as students complete each one, go over the answers.
2. Quickly go through the instructions of each exercise, let students complete all of the exercises at once, and then go over the answers.

A. **Indicate the learning style next to each activity. Write *V* for *Visual, A* for *Auditory,* and *T/K* for *Tactile/Kinesthetic* on the line. (Lesson 1)**

B. **Complete each statement with a phrase from the box. (Lesson 1)**

C. **Ask a classmate how they relate to the information below. Write his or her answers on the lines. (Lessons 2–3)**

### Evaluation          5–15 mins. ■■■

Go around the classroom and check on students' progress. Help individuals when needed. If you notice consistent errors among several students, interrupt the class and give a mini-lesson or review until students feel comfortable with the concept or point being examined.

## Practice

D. **Write a paragraph about your partner on a separate piece of paper using the information from Exercise C. (Lesson 3)**

E. **Remember what you learned about goal setting. Without looking back in the unit, write four tips for setting goals. (Lesson 4)**

F. **Walk around the classroom and ask your classmates for suggestions on how to motivate yourself. Write five ideas below. (Lesson 5)**

G. **Choose a verb from the box below and complete each goal statement with the correct form of the future perfect. (Lesson 5)**

## Evaluation

Go around the classroom and check on students' progress. Help individuals when needed. If you see consistent errors among several students, again, interrupt the class and give a mini-lesson or review to help students feel comfortable with the concept.

### BEST PRACTICE

## Recycling/Review

The review exercises, the research activity, and the team project are part of the recycling/review process. Students often need to be reintroduced to concepts to solidify what they have learned. Many concepts are studied but forgotten when students are engaged in learning other new concepts. This is because students learn but are not necessarily ready to acquire language concepts.

Therefore, it becomes very important to review material with students and to show them how to review it on their own. It is also important to recycle the new concepts in different contexts.

### INSTRUCTOR'S NOTES

Learner Log

| I can balance my life. | I can identify and prioritize goals. | I can motivate myself. |
|---|---|---|
| ☐ Yes ☐ No ☐ Maybe | ☐ Yes ☐ No ☐ Maybe | ☐ Yes ☐ No ☐ Maybe |

**D.** Write a paragraph about your partner on a separate piece of paper using the information from Exercise C.  Answers will vary.

**E.** Remember what you learned about goal setting. Without looking back in the unit, write four tips for setting goals.  Answers will vary. Sample answers are below.

1. Write goals as positive statements.

2. Prioritize (in order of importance).

3. Write goals where I can read them every day.

4. Tell friends my goals so they can support me.

**F.** Walk around the classroom and ask your classmates for suggestions on how to motivate yourself. Write five ideas below.  Answers will vary.

1. _____

2. _____

3. _____

4. _____

5. _____

**G.** Choose a verb from the box below and complete each goal statement with the correct form of the future perfect.

| buy and sell | raise | program |
|---|---|---|
| apply | compete | |

1. By the time I graduate from technical school, I __will have programmed__ over twenty computers.

2. She __will have bought and sold__ at least ten properties when she retires.

3. When he turns 65, he __will have raised__ two amazing children.

4. They __will have competed__ in their first triathlon by the year 2018.

5. By the time I get my master's degree, I __will have applied__ for forty jobs at companies all over the country.

WORKPLACE CONNECTION
Exercise D: Combine ideas and information.
Exercises E, G: Complete tasks as assigned.
Exercise F: Interact appropriately with team members, Collect and organize information.

Review  33

# Vocabulary Review

Use these words and phrases to help you complete all the exercises on this page. Some words may be used more than once.

| | | |
|---|---|---|
| achieve | evaluate | positive outlook |
| balance | inspire | prioritize |
| be flexible | long-term | pursue |
| earning power | monitor | short-term |
| educational attainment | motivate | support |

**A. Complete each sentence with the best verb. Note that some sentences can have more than one answer. Then, work with a partner and use the five questions for a discussion.** Answers may vary. Sample answers are given.

1. If you _____ prioritize _____ your goals, you can focus on the most important ones first.

2. Have you ever created a chart to _____ evaluate _____ your progress?

3. What career do you think you might _____ pursue _____?

4. How do you _____ motivate _____ yourself?

5. What goals have you wanted to _____ achieve _____ in the past?

6. Have you found family and friends to _____ inspire _____ you?

**B. Write sentences about goal setting with the following terms.** Answers will vary. Samples are given.

1. balance: It is important to maintain a balance of your goals.

2. be flexible: If you are flexible in your goal-setting, you will be happy.

3. positive outlook: Keep a positive outlook when working on goals.

4. achieve: Try to achieve both long- and short-term goals.

**C. Complete each sentence below.** Sample answers are given.

1. To improve your earning power, you should get a good education and some experience.
   _____.

2. If you want to achieve your goals, you must be organized, motivated, and flexible
   _____.

3. In order to best reach your long-term goals, you have to make a plan, get support, and prioritize
   your activities
   _____.

WORKPLACE CONNECTION
Exercises A, B, C: Complete tasks as assigned.

## Practice

### Vocabulary Review

**Use these words and phrases to help you complete all the exercises on this page. Some words may be used more than once.**

A. Complete each sentence with the best verb. Note that some sentences can have more than one answer. Then, work with a partner and use the five questions for a discussion.

B. Write sentences about goal setting with the following terms.

C. Complete each phrase below.

## Evaluation
5–15 mins. ■■■

Go around the classroom and check on students' progress. Help individuals when needed. If you see consistent errors among several students, interrupt the class and give a mini-lesson or review to help students feel comfortable with the concept.

## Assessment *(optional)*
■■■

Use the Stand Out Assessment CD-ROM with ExamView® to create a post-test for Unit 1.

## AT-A-GLANCE PREP

**Goal:** Research information about careers
**Academic Strategy:** Research

### Agenda

- Use key words to conduct online research.
- Use the Bureau of Labor Statistics' website to find information.

### Resources

**Web Site Addresses:** Bureau of Labor Statistics
http://www.bls.gov/home.htm
http://www.bls.gov/oco/
**Multilevel Worksheets:** *Occupational Outlook Handbook* (reprints of each section in PDF form)

### Pacing

- 1.5 hour classes
- 2.5 hour classes
- 3+ hour classes

## STANDARDS CORRELATIONS

*CCRS:* W7, W8
*CASAS:* 4.9.3, 7.2.1, 7.4.4, 7.4.5, 7.4.6
*SCANS:* **Information** Acquire and evaluate information, organize and maintain information, interpret and communicate information, use computers to process information *(optional)*
**Interpersonal** Participate as a member of a team, teach others, negotiate to arrive at a decision, work with cultural diversity
**Systems** Understand systems
**Technology** Select technology, apply technology to a task, maintain and troubleshoot technology *(optional)*
**Basic Skills** Reading, writing
**Thinking Skills** Creative thinking, decision making, seeing things in the mind's eye
**Personal Qualities** Responsibility, sociability, self-management
*EFF:* **Communication** Read with understanding, convey ideas in writing, observe critically
**Decision Making** Solve problems and make decisions, plan
**Lifelong Learning** Take responsibility for learning, reflect and evaluate, learn through research, use information and communications technology *(optional)*

## Academic Feature: Research Project

Each unit will have a research page where students are required to complete a task by conducting research. Options will be given for students to use the computer, or specifically, the Internet, as well as printed resource materials. Important resource materials for Unit 1 can be found on the Multilevel Worksheets CD-ROM.

## Introduction                                   5–10 mins.

Remind students about the research they did in the Pre-Unit. Ask students how they did this research. Ask them to help you brainstorm other ways to research. Make a list on the board. State the goal: *Today, you will research the career path you chose by using the Internet and printed material.*

## Presentation                                   10–15 mins.

**A. One of the fastest ways to research something is to search the Internet. For example, you might want to know how much money you can make at a certain career. What are some key words you could use to search for this information?**

As a class, talk about key words and how we use them to search for something on the Internet. If you have access to a computer connected to a projector, you can show students how to search.

## Practice                                       15–30 mins.

**B. Conduct an online search to find out the following information for the career path that you chose in Lesson 2, Exercise I.**

**C. The Bureau of Labor Statistics (bls.gov) publishes the *Occupational Outlook Handbook* every two years. This handbook gives information about hundreds of different types of jobs. In this handbook, you will find the following types of information: the training and education needed, earnings, expected job prospects, what workers do on the job, working conditions.**

Refer to the student book page for this list of topics.

## Evaluation                                     5–10 mins.

As a class, have each student tell you his or her career path and which topic he or she underlined.

## Application                                    10–30 mins.

**D. Find the *Occupational Outlook Handbook* online at bls.gov/ooh. Search for the information about your chosen career.**

RESEARCH PROJECT ✔ Get a new job

**A.** One of the fastest ways to research something is to search the Internet. For example, you might want to know how much money you can make at a certain career. What are some key words you could use to search for this information?

*Sample answers are given.*        *career, average salary, earnings, wages*

**B.** Conduct an online search to find out the following information for the career path that you chose in Lesson 2, Exercise I. *Answers will vary.*

Career title: _____

Training needed: _____

Education needed: _____

Possible earnings: _____

**C.** The Bureau of Labor Statistics (bls.gov) publishes the *Occupational Outlook Handbook* every two years. This handbook gives information about hundreds of different types of jobs. In this handbook, you will find the following types of information: the training and education needed, earnings, expected job prospects, what workers do on the job, and working conditions. *Answers will vary.*

The following topics are from the *Occupational Outlook Handbook*. Underline the topic you think would have information about your career.

Management, Business, and Financial Occupations

Engineers, Life and Physical Scientists, and Related Occupations

Arts, Design, Entertainment, Sports, and Media Occupations

Education and Community and Social Service Occupations

Computer and Mathematical Occupations

Legal and Social Science Occupations

Health Diagnosing and Treating Practitioners

Health Technologists, Technicians, and Healthcare Support Occupations

Service Occupations: Cleaning, Food, and Personal

Protective Service Occupations

Sales Occupations

Office and Administrative Support Occupations

Farming, Fishing, Forestry, and Transportation Occupations

Construction Trades and Related Occupations

Installation, Maintenance, and Repair Occupations

Production Occupations

**D.** Find the *Occupational Outlook Handbook* online at bls.gov/ooh. Search for the information about your chosen career.

# READING CHALLENGE

## About the Explorer

Trip Jennings is a filmmaker and a professional kayaker. Specializing in conservation, Trip spends his time working to protect rivers around the world. He is the head of a production company called Balance Media. The company focuses on telling stories through videography for environmental and social justice organizations. Trip is also on the advisory board of Adventurers and Scientists for Conservation (ASC), which brings adventurers and scientists together to share data collected from around the world.

## About the Photo

This photo was taken by portrait photographer Marco Grob. It shows how Trip would look after immediately after kayaking. As a professional kayaker, Trip has traveled down some of the most fast-moving stretches of shallow water in the world. On his travels, he has seen how the environment around these places where humans play has been destroyed. Through his filmmaking, he hopes to change the way people interact with the environment.

- Introduce the explorer, Trip Jennings. Have students look at the photo.
- Read the title and discuss with students what they think it means.
- Read the quote out loud. Have students guess what Trip Jennings' job is.

READING CHALLENGE

**EXPLORER** TRIP JENNINGS

# Protecting the Places We Play

"The real challenge we're faced with today is not just exploring or doing exciting new things. It's also honoring the world we live in and protecting wild lands, wild animals, and the places we play."
— Trip Jennings

**A. PREDICT** Trip Jennings is a filmmaker and a professional kayaker. What do you think these two things could have to do with one another?

*Answers will vary, but may include suggestions that extreme outdoor sports are a popular subject*
*for video storytelling.*

**B. INFER** Read the quote. What do you think he means by "honoring the world we live in"?

*Answers will vary, but may include the concept of treating the planet with respect, gratitude, or care.*

_____

_____

_____

_____

**CCRS FOR READING**

RI1, RI2, RI3, RI4, RI10

**C.   Read about Trip Jennings.**

Trip Jennings is a filmmaker who loves to kayak. Or should that be a professional kayaker who loves to make films? Watching kayaking videos as a child, he decided that he wanted to be the one behind the camera. For years, he kayaked and produced whitewater (fast-moving and shallow stretches of water) kayaking videos, documenting some of the most beautiful places in the world. But to get to those amazing places, he had to travel through places where the environment had been destroyed. This caused him to rethink the purpose of his filmmaking.

In addition to being an award-winning filmmaker, kayaker, and adventurer, Trip is a conservationist. He spends his time working to protect rivers around the world. He also documents fossil fuel extraction, mining, and energy export in North America. To help get his word out, he runs a video production company called Balance Media. The company focuses on telling stories through videography for environmental and social justice organizations. He is also on the advisory board of Adventurers and Scientists for Conservation (ASC), which brings adventurers and scientists together to share data collected from around the world.

With everything that Trip has going on, it is often hard to stay balanced. When asked what a normal day is like for him, this is what he said: "I spend a fair amount of my time wishing for normal days, trying to find balance. I'm out and about for around half the year, traveling, filming, and working on conservation projects. In 2011, that led me to the Democratic Republic of the Congo, Canada three times, Mexico, and a number of trips within the U.S. The rest of the year I spend editing, fund-raising, and planning—all of the office work that makes the fieldwork possible and useful. So, half the year I'm waking up at sunrise in the wilderness, getting dirty, carrying cameras into the backcountry, and documenting beauty and destruction. The other half, I'm waking up and walking to my Portland office to click and drag most of the day."

**D.   Answer the questions on a separate piece of paper.**

1. How does Trip work to "protect the wild lands, wild animals, and the places we play"?

2. Why do you think Trip decided to start making films about kayaking?

3. What caused his filmmaking purpose to change?

4. Think about Trip's "normal day." How is it is different from yours? Is it similar to yours in any way? How do you think he finds balance?

1. He uses videography to tell stories about the work of environmental and social justice organizations.
2. Answers will vary, but should contain a reference to the kayaking videos he saw as a child.
3. To get to kayaking spots, he had to travel through places that had been destroyed.
4. Answers will vary.

**A.   PREDICT   Trip Jennings is a filmmaker and a professional kayaker. What do you think these two things could have to do with one another?**

Tell students that Trip Jennings is a filmmaker and a professional kayaker. Ask students what these two things have in common with each other. Then, discuss as a class.

**B.   INFER   Read the quote. What do you think he means by "honoring the world we live in"?**

• Have students re-read the quote to themselves.

• Ask students what Trip means by "honoring the world we live in"?

• Have students discuss among themselves. Then, discuss as a class.

**C.   Read about Trip Jennings.**

Have students read about Trip Jennings.

**D.   Answer the questions on a separate piece of paper.**

## READING STRATEGIES

## Predicting

Predicting asks students what they think will happen in the reading. It is an important strategy because it taps into students' background knowledge and allows them to make connections between new information and what they already know. While reading, students can check and revise their predictions, thereby blending new knowledge with old knowledge.

# Personal Finance

### About the Photo

Karl Damon Parr took this photograph. It shows a man busking by playing a guitar in York, UK. Busking has become commonplace in busy towns and cities. It allows artistic people to showcase their talents and to be compensated for it. In addition to musical performers, people can encounter artists performing magic and circus routines as well as those who intricately apply makeup and adorn costumes to pose as human statues.

- Introduce the unit by reading the title out loud.
- Ask students to look at the photo and have a volunteer read the caption out loud. Then, ask students how they think the title is related to the photo.
- Have students look at the photo and answer the questions. Discuss as a class.
- Go over each unit outcome.

UNIT **2**

# Personal Finance

A man plays the guitar in front of a coffee shop in a town center.

| UNIT OUTCOMES | GRAMMAR | VOCABULARY | EL CIVICS |
|---|---|---|---|
| • Organize finances<br>• Reduce debt and save money<br>• Identify investment strategies<br>• Maintain good credit<br>• Protect against identity theft | • Future perfect<br>• Past perfect continuous<br>• *Need* and *want* plus infinitive statements<br>• Modal *should*<br>• Information questions<br>• Imperatives<br>• Present perfect<br>• Simple past | • Financial expressions: *budget cut, buy in bulk, capital gains, commit fraud, counterfeit checks, current income, delinquent accounts, false pretenses, unauthorized transactions, bankruptcy*<br>• Expenses: *mortgage, rent, home maintenance, fees, renters' insurance, gas, electric, water, telephone, cell phone, food, restaurants, medical, dental, auto expenses, tolls, fares, parking, clothes* | The skills students learn in this unit can be applied to the following EL Civics competency areas:<br>• Banking<br>• Communication<br>• Families |

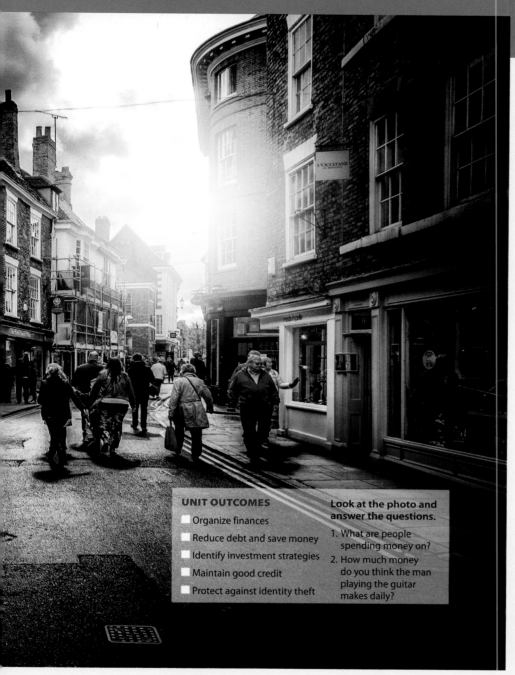

## Life Skills Link

In this unit, students will learn necessary strategies for creating and maintaining personal financial stability, such as how to reduce debt and save money, identify investment strategies, maintain good credit, and protect against identity theft.

The skills students learn in this unit can be applied to almost every area of EL Civics as they help students to function effectively within U.S. society.

### UNIT OUTCOMES

- ☐ Organize finances
- ☐ Reduce debt and save money
- ☐ Identify investment strategies
- ☐ Maintain good credit
- ☐ Protect against identity theft

**Look at the photo and answer the questions.**

1. What are people spending money on?
2. How much money do you think the man playing the guitar makes daily?

| CASAS | SCANS | CCRS |
|---|---|---|
| Vocabulary Builder: 7.4.5<br>Lesson 1: 1.5.1, 4.1.4, 2.5.5<br>Lesson 2: 1.6.2<br>Lesson 3: 7.4.2<br>Lesson 4: 1.3.2, 7.4.2<br>Lesson 5: 1.6.2, 7.4.2<br>Review: 7.2.1<br>Research: 4.9.3, 7.2.1, 7.4.4, 7.4.5, 7.4.6<br>Team Project: 4.8.1, 4.8.5, 4.8.6 | Many SCANS skills are incorporated in this unit with an emphasis on:<br>• Mathematics<br>• Social<br>• Self-management<br>• Responsibility<br>• Problem-solving<br>• Decision making | RI1, RI2, RI3, RI4, RI5, RI7, RI10, W2, W4, W5, W7, W8, SL1, SL2, SL3, SL6, L1, L2, L5 |

# Vocabulary Builder

**A.** **Kimla made a list of her financial goals. Read what she wrote.**

> 1. I need to stop *impulse buying* and pay off my credit cards.
> 2. I want to stop *living paycheck to paycheck* and save enough money for a down payment on a house.
> 3. I want to increase my *purchasing power* by putting $200 a month into an emergency savings account.
> 4. I want us to start *living within our means*, so I can start giving $100 a month to charity.

**B.** **INFER** **What does each italicized expression mean? Discuss them with your classmates.** impulse buying = buying without a plan; living paycheck to paycheck = not saving money; purchasing power = ability to buy; living within our means = not overspending a paycheck

**C.** **Some phrases have special meanings. Often, if you try to understand the meaning of the individual words, you can understand the phrase. Talk to your classmates to discover the meanings of the following expressions.** Answers will vary.

| | | |
|---|---|---|
| 1. reduce spending | 2. buy large amounts | 3. money earned as profit |
| 1. budget cut | 2. buy in bulk | 3. capital gains |
| 4. use false information intentionally | 5. fake checks | 6. money earned now |
| 4. commit fraud | 5. counterfeit checks | 6. current income |
| 7. overdue money owed | 8. untrue information | 9. illegal financial deal |
| 7. delinquent accounts | 8. false pretenses | 9. unauthorized transactions |

It's easier than ever to monitor your bank account, but be careful when making online transactions.

Secure payment

pay now

Credit Card allowed

## AT-A-GLANCE PREP

**Goal:** Introduce new vocabulary
**Academic Strategies:** Using context clues, using a dictionary
**Vocabulary:** See lessons

### Agenda

- Read about Kimla's financial goals.
- Define vocabulary expressions.
- Use context to discover meaning.

### Resources

**Dictionaries:** It is recommended that each student in class have an ESL learner's dictionary or that there be dictionaries available in the classroom for students to use. Dictionaries that will be referred to in this book are the *Heinle's Newbury House Dictionary of American English* and the *Collins Cobuild Intermediate* or *Advanced Dictionary of American English*.

### Pacing

- 1.5 hour classes
- 2.5 hour classes
- 3+ hour classes

## STANDARDS CORRELATIONS

*CCRS:* RI1, RI4, W4, SL1
*CASAS:* 7.4.5
*SCANS:* **Information** Acquire and evaluate information, organize and maintain information
**Interpersonal** Participate as a member of a team, negotiate to arrive at a decision, work with cultural diversity
**Systems** Understand systems, monitor and correct performance
**Basic Skills** Reading, writing, listening, speaking
**Thinking Skills** Think creatively, make decisions, see things in the mind's eye
**Personal Qualities** Responsibility, sociability, self-management
*EFF:* **Communication** Read with understanding, convey ideas in writing, speak so others can understand, listen actively
**Decision Making** Use math to solve problems and communicate, solve problems and make decisions, plan
**Interpersonal** Cooperate with others
**Lifelong Learning** Take responsibility for learning, reflect and evaluate, learn through research

## Academic Feature: Vocabulary Builder

Each unit will begin with a vocabulary-building section. The purpose of this two-page section is to introduce students to many of the words they will be using in the unit lessons. Students will have a chance to see how much they already know, and they will get exposure to the new vocabulary found in the unit.

**Note:** All of the exercises on these two pages should be done in class, no matter the class length. Longer classes can do this lesson and then move onto Lesson 1 during the same class meeting; shorter classes may have to devote one whole class meeting to this lesson.

### Introduction          5–10 mins. ■■■

State the goal: *Today, we will be identifying and working with the vocabulary you will study in this unit.*

### Presentation 1          10–15 mins. ■■■

**A. Kimla made a list of her financial goals. Read what she wrote.**

Read or ask a volunteer to read Kimla's goals out loud.

**B. INFER  What does each italicized expression mean? Discuss them with your classmates.**

As you discuss the vocabulary, talk about what each goal means.

### Practice 1          10–15 mins. ■■■

**C. Some phrases have special meanings. Often, if you try to understand the meaning of the individual words, you can understand the phrase. Talk to your classmates to discover the meanings of the following expressions.**

### Evaluation 1          5–15 mins. ■■■

Go over the answers as a class.

## INSTRUCTOR'S NOTES

_____

_____

_____

_____

_____

## Presentation 2
5–10 mins. ■■■
Show students how to find the meaning of a word by looking at an example sentence. You can use some of the expressions from Exercise A or even some of the examples in Exercise D.

### PRONUNCIATION

#### Vocabulary

When teaching students new vocabulary, pronounce each word for them several times and ask them to repeat it. Often, students may be familiar with the words you are introducing but have never seen them spelled out. By pronouncing the words for students, you allow students to make a connection between the words' spellings and their sounds. It is also important that students learn the correct pronunciation of new words so they feel comfortable using their new vocabulary inside and outside of the classroom.

## Practice 2
10–15 mins. ■■

**D. INFER Look at the following sentences. Try to figure out the meanings of the underlined words by reading them in context.**

## Evaluation 2
10–15 mins. ■■
Go over the answers as a class.

## Application
5–10 mins. ■■■

**E. Look back at Kimla's financial goals in Exercise A. Using some of the new vocabulary phrases, write four of your own financial goals.**

### BEST PRACTICE

#### Context clues

Context clues are hints in the text that help us understand the meaning of a particular word. Some examples of context clues may be the following:

- Synonyms — The director *committed fraud*; she stole money from the company's accounts.
- Antonyms — Ahmed is *quiet*, not like his classmates who talk all the time.
- Definitions — Do you have *current income* such as a salary.
- Comparisons — The best *decision* that I ever made was going to college.

### INSTRUCTOR'S NOTES

WORKPLACE CONNECTION
Exercise D: Combine ideas and information.
Exercise E: Complete tasks as assigned.

**D.  INFER  Look at the following sentences. Try to figure out the meanings of the underlined words by reading them in context.** *Answers may vary. Sample answers are given.*

1. The company declared <u>bankruptcy</u> when it ran out of money. *not enough money*

    *Bankruptcy* means *without money to pay creditors* .

2. I took out a loan at the bank and used my house as <u>collateral</u>. *something given to assure that the loaner won't lose money*

    *Collateral* means *property used as security for a loan* .

3. The thought of starting a business was <u>daunting</u>, but he decided to do it anyway.

    *Daunting* means *intimidating or discouraging* .

4. <u>Inflation</u> was so great that bread cost twice as much in June as it did in May.

    *Inflation* means *an increase in money so that prices rise beyond value* .

5. His <u>investment</u> in the stock market has made him a millionaire.

    *Investment* means *to commit money to gain money* .

6. The company has no <u>liquid</u> assets; therefore, it can't pay its bills.

    *Liquid* means *easily converted to cash money* .

7. She paid the <u>penalty</u> of a large fine for lying on her income tax returns.

    *Penalty* means *a punishment by law for a crime committed* .

8. He <u>periodically</u> reviews his budget and makes changes when necessary.

    *Periodically* means *at regular intervals of time or date* .

9. Putting money in the stock market might be <u>risky</u> because you could lose it.

    *Risky* means *exposure to danger or damage* .

**E.  Look back at Kimla's financial goals in Exercise A. Using some of the new vocabulary phrases, write four of your own financial goals.** *Answers may vary. Sample answers are given.*

1. *I want to cut my budget.*

2. *I need to stop living paycheck to paycheck.*

3. *I hope to increase my current income.*

4. *I will reduce my impulse buying.*

# LESSON ① Getting organized

GOAL ■ Organize finances

WORKPLACE CONNECTION
Exercises A, B: Complete tasks as assigned.
Exercise C: Interpret and communicate information.

**A.** **Look back at the goals you wrote in Exercise E on page 41. Rewrite the goals below, giving each one a time frame.** Answers will vary. Sample answers are given.

EXAMPLE: By the end of next year, I will have paid off my credit cards.

1. By the end of this week, I will have cut my budget.

2. By the end of this month, I will have stopped living paycheck to paycheck.

3. By six months from now, I will have increased my income.

4. By this time tomorrow, I will have stopped my impulse buying.

**B.** **EVALUATE** **Do you know how much money you spend? Many people are not certain of the exact amount it costs them to live. Often, people don't include the expenses that come up occasionally in their personal budgets. Think about how you spend your money. Answer the following questions on a separate piece of paper.**
Sample answers are given.

1. Did you go on a vacation last year? How much did it cost?  yes; $1,500

2. Do you know how much you spend during the holidays every year? How much?  about $1,000

3. How often do you get your hair cut? How much does it cost?  5 times/year; $150

4. How often do you pay car insurance premiums? How much is each premium?  monthly; $75

**C.** **Listen to a financial planner talking about how to organize personal finances. Write down the most important points.**

CD
TR 10

1. Go through all financial paperwork for the past year.

2. Write all categories in which I spend money.

3. Write down how much I spend in each category per month.

4. Add up how much per year is spent for each category.

5. Divide those numbers by 12 to get average monthly spending.

**D.** **Compare your notes in Exercise C with a partner. Add any important points you missed.**

## AT-A-GLANCE PREP

**Goal:** Organize finances
**Academic Strategies:** Note taking, making calculations
**Vocabulary:** *expense, fixed, variable, cut, live within one's means*

### Agenda

- Assess your expenses.
- Listen to a financial planner.
- Study Kimla and her husband's Money Out Worksheet.
- Make calculations.
- Discuss fixed and variable expenses.
- Create your own Money Out Worksheet.

### Resources

**Multilevel Worksheets:** Unit 2, Lesson 1, Worksheets 1–2
**Workbook:** Unit 2, Lesson 1
**Audio:** CD Track 10
**Stand Out Assessment CD-ROM with ExamView®**

### Pacing

- 1.5 hour classes
- 2.5 hour classes
- 3+ hour classes

## STANDARDS CORRELATIONS

*CCRS:* RI7, SL2
*CASAS:* 1.5.1
*SCANS:* **Resources** Allocate money
**Information** Acquire and evaluate information, organize and maintain information, interpret and communicate information, use computers to process information *(optional)*
**Interpersonal** Participate as a member of a team, negotiate to arrive at a decision, work with cultural diversity
**Systems** Understand systems, monitor and correct performance, improve and design systems
**Technology** Apply technology to a task *(optional)*
**Basic Skills** Reading, writing, arithmetic, listening, speaking
**Thinking Skills** Think creatively, make decisions, solve problems, see things in the mind's eye
**Personal Qualities** Responsibility, sociability, self-management
*EFF:* **Communication** Speak so others can understand, listen actively, observe critically
**Decision Making** Use math to solve problems and communicate, solve problems and make decisions, plan
**Interpersonal** Cooperate with others, resolve conflict and negotiate
**Lifelong Learning** Take responsibility for learning, reflect and evaluate, use information and communications technology *(optional)*

## Preassessment (*optional*) ■■■

Use the Stand Out Assessment CD-ROM with ExamView® to create a pre-test for Unit 2.

## Warm-up and Review    5–10 mins. ■■■

**A. Look back at the goals you wrote in Exercise E on page 41. Rewrite the goals below, giving each one a time frame.**

Have students do this exercise by themselves. While they are working, walk around the classroom and write down four student goals to use as dictation.

## Introduction    10–20 mins. ■■■

Dictation: Use the four sentences you collected during the Warm-up. State the goal: *Today, you will learn how to organize your finances.*

## Presentation 1    10–15 mins. ■■■

**B. EVALUATE Do you know how much money you spend? Many people are not certain of the exact amount it costs them to live. Often, people don't include the expenses that come up occasionally in their personal budgets. Think about how you spend your money. Answer the following questions on a separate piece of paper.**

Go over this exercise with students and have them write their own answers. When they have finished, ask them for some ideas on how they do or would organize the money they spend.

## Practice 1    10–15 mins. ■■■

**C. Listen to a financial planner talking about how to organize personal finances. Write down the most important points.**

Prepare students for this activity by telling them they will be listening for five different suggestions. Remind them that taking notes is just writing down the important ideas, not every single word they hear. Play the recording more than once if necessary.

**Note:** The listening script is on page 43a.

## Evaluation 1    5–10 mins. ■■■

**D. Compare your notes in Exercise C with a partner. Add any important points you missed.**

Go over the notes with the class.

**LISTENING SCRIPT** 🎧 CD TR 10

**Counselor:** *Let's get started. The first thing you need to do is go through all of your bank statements, credit card statements, receipts—basically all of the financial paperwork you have for the past year. Next, write down all of the categories in which you spend money. Then, figure out how much you spent in each category each month. Fourth, add up how much you spent each month to find out how much you spent per year in each category. Finally, total up all these annual numbers and divide the total by 12 to find out how much you spent each month on average. If you do all these things, you'll get a good idea of your annual or yearly expenses.*

**Presentation 2**          5–10 mins. ■■■

**E. ANALYZE** After meeting with a financial planner, Kimla and her husband looked at all of their bank statements, credit card statements, ATM records, and receipts. Look at the worksheet below that they created. What do they still need to calculate?

Talk about the worksheet as a class, using an overhead transparency if you can. Go over each expense, making sure students understand what each one is. Then, talk about how much money Kimla and her family spend monthly or annually.

Point out which calculations are missing. Make sure students know how to do multiplication and division, using the math box to practice.

**Practice 2**          10–15 mins. ■■

(Shorter classes can do this exercise for homework.)

**F. Calculate Kimla and her husband's annual and monthly totals.**

**Evaluation 2**          10–15 mins. ■■
Go over the answers as a class by asking volunteers to come up and write the correct numbers on the board or overhead transparency.

**MULTILEVEL WORKSHEET**

Unit 2, Lesson 1, Worksheet 1: Money Out

**G.** Together, Kimla and her husband make $70,000 annually before deductions. Answer the questions.

**BEST PRACTICE**

**Math**

Basic calculations are a life skill that students will need to be able to do on a daily basis. Advise students to do calculations on paper before they resort to using calculators. Observe their abilities and provide supplemental review of math skills as needed.

**INSTRUCTOR'S NOTES**

_____

_____

_____

_____

_____

_____

_____

_____

_____

_____

_____

_____

_____

_____

_____

_____

_____

_____

_____

_____

_____

_____

**E. ANALYZE** After meeting with a financial planner, Kimla and her husband looked at all of their bank statements, credit card statements, ATM records, and receipts. Look at the worksheet below that they created. What do they still need to calculate?

| MONEY OUT | | |
|---|---|---|
| | Annual | Monthly |
| Mortgage/Rent | $26,400 | $2,200 |
| Home maintenance fees | $3,000 | $250 |
| Renters' insurance | $1,200 | $100 |
| Gas/Electric | $2,700 | $225 |
| Water | $660 | $55 |
| Telephone/Cell phone | $1,560 | $130 |
| Food/Restaurants | $3,600 | $300 |
| Medical/Dental | $1,740 | $145 |
| Auto expenses | $2,880 | $240 |
| Tolls/Fares/Parking | $720 | $60 |
| Clothes/Shoes | $1,200 | $100 |
| Dry cleaning | $360 | $30 |
| Hair/Manicure/Facial | $900 | $75 |
| Kids' school | $1,800 | $150 |
| Training/Education | $300 | $25 |
| Income taxes | $2,100 | $175 |
| Internet | $600 | $50 |
| Credit cards/Loans | $10,200 | $850 |
| Subscriptions | $48 | $4 |
| Entertainment | $1,500 | $125 |
| Cable/Satellite | $1,800 | $150 |
| Vacations | $2,100 | $175 |
| Hobbies | $180 | $15 |
| Gifts | $800 | $66.66 |
| **TOTAL** | $68,348 | $5,695.66 |

Calculations

To calculate annual expenses, multiply monthly expenses by 12:

$$\begin{array}{cccc} 250 & 15 & 55 & 1300 \\ \times 12 & \times 12 & \times 12 & \times 12 \\ \hline 3000 & 180 & 660 & 15{,}600 \end{array}$$

To calculate monthly expenses, divide annual expenses by 12:

$3000 \div 12 = 250$    $180 \div 12 = 15$

$660 \div 12 = 55$    $15{,}600 \div 12 = 1300$

**F. Calculate Kimla and her husband's annual and monthly totals.** See chart.

**G. Together, Kimla and her husband make $70,000 annually before deductions. Answer the questions.**

1. How much do they have left over annually?

   $1,652

2. How much do they have left over each month?

   $137.67

3. Do you think Kimla and her husband live within their means? Why? Yes, but they should put money in a savings account.

WORKPLACE CONNECTION
Exercise H: Collect and organize information; Interact appropriately with team members.
Exercise J: Complete tasks as assigned; Combine ideas and information.

**H.** In the worksheet in Exercise E, some expenses are *fixed* (stay the same every month) and others are *variable* (change from month to month). With a partner, make a list of Kimla and her husband's fixed and variable expenses. *Answers may vary. Sample answers are below.*

| Fixed | Variable |
|---|---|
| mortgage/rent, loans, subscriptions, cable TV, computer | credit cards, loans, postage, vacations, entertainment, hobbies, gifts |

**I.** JUSTIFY  Look back at Kimla's financial goals on page 40. How much money does she want to start saving each month for emergencies and giving to charity? Does she have enough money in her budget for these items? If not, which expenses do you think Kimla and her husband can cut back on? *Sample answer: Cut back on restaurants, hobbies, and entertainment.*

**J.** Create a worksheet like the one in Exercise E, listing all the monthly and annual expenses you have. Next to each expense, write *f* for a fixed expense or *v* for a variable expense. Look at the worksheet below to get you started. *Answers will vary.*

| | Annual | Monthly |
|---|---|---|
| Mortgage/Rent (f) | | |
| Home maintenance fees (v) | | |
| Gas/Electric (v) | | |
| Water (v) | | |
| | | |
| | | |
| | | |
| | | |
| | | |

## Presentation 3      5–10 mins. ■■■

Write *Fixed Expenses* on the board. Ask students to help you define this term and talk about a few examples. Now write *Variable Expenses* on the board. Define this term and have students come up with examples.

## Practice 3      10–15 mins. ■

H. In the worksheet in Exercise E, some expenses are *fixed* (stay the same every month) and others are *variable* (change from month to month). With a partner, make a list of Kimla and her husband's fixed and variable expenses.

(Shorter classes can do Exercise H for homework and review at the next class meeting.)

## Evaluation 3      5–10 mins. ■

Ask volunteers to come to the board and add to the lists you started in the Presentation.

I. JUSTIFY Look back at Kimla's financial goals on page 40. How much money does she want to start saving each month for emergencies and giving to charity? Does she have enough money in her budget for these items? If not, which expenses do you think Kimla and her husband can cut back on?

## Application      10–20 mins. ■■■

J. Create a worksheet like the one in Exercise E, listing all the monthly and annual expenses you have. Next to each expense, write *f* for a fixed expense or *v* for a variable expense. Look at the worksheet below to get you started.

MULTILEVEL WORKSHEET

Unit 2, Lesson 1, Worksheet 2: Expense Sheets (template)

**Refer students to *Stand Out 5 Workbook*, Unit 2, Lesson 1 for practice with the future perfect versus the future perfect continuous (progressive).**

**Go to the *Activity Bank* online for suggestions on promoting digital literacy and using the Internet to enhance this lesson.**

INSTRUCTOR'S NOTES

**Goal:** Reduce debt and save money

**Grammar:** Past perfect progressive

**Academic Strategies:** Identifying purpose of reading, finding details, focused listening

**Vocabulary:** *paycheck to paycheck, up to your ears, settlements, purpose, impulse buying, bargains, generic, deductible, in full, buy in bulk*

## Agenda

☐ Read an ad about reducing debt.

☐ Read money-saving tips.

☐ Listen to a conversation about Kimla and Derek's spending habits.

☐ Practice using the past perfect progressive.

☐ Think about ways you can save money.

## Resources

**Multilevel Worksheets:** Unit 2, Lesson 2, Worksheets 1–3

**Workbook:** Unit 2, Lesson 2

**Audio:** CD Track 11

## Pacing

■ 1.5 hour classes   ■ 2.5 hour classes
■ 3+ hour classes

## STANDARDS CORRELATIONS

*CCRS:* RI1, RI5, RI7, RI10, SL2, L1

*CASAS:* 1.6.2

*SCANS:* **Information** Acquire and evaluate information, organize and maintain information, interpret and communicate information

**Interpersonal** Participate as a member of a team, negotiate to arrive at a decision, work with cultural diversity

**Systems** Monitor and correct performance

**Basic Skills** Reading, writing, listening, speaking

**Thinking Skills** Think creatively, make decisions

**Personal Qualities** Responsibility, sociability

*EFF:* **Communication** Read with understanding, convey ideas in writing, speak so others can understand, listen actively, observe critically

**Decision Making** Solve problems and make decisions, plan

**Interpersonal** Cooperate with others

**Lifelong Learning** Take responsibility for learning, reflect and evaluate, learn through research

## Warm-up and Review          5–10 mins. ■ ■ ■

Talk about the Money Out worksheets from the previous lesson. Ask students if they filled out their worksheets at home. Discuss the challenges with filling them out, such as difficulty finding records.

## Introduction          10–20 mins. ■ ■ ■

Dictation:

1. We try to live within our means every month.
2. They have been living paycheck to paycheck for the past year.
3. She doesn't know where her money goes every month.
4. He has decided to pay off all his debts by the end of next year.

State the goal: *Today, you will discover ways to reduce debt and save money.*

## Presentation 1          10–15 mins. ■ ■ ■

### A. Read the ad.

Let students read the ad silently. Then, ask a volunteer to read it out loud to the class. Ask students if they have any questions about the vocabulary. Try not to answer questions that students will have to answer in Exercise B.

### MULTILEVEL WORKSHEET

Unit 2, Lesson 2, Worksheet 1: Debt Ad Vocabulary

## Practice 1          10–15 mins. ■ ■ ■

### B. Answer the questions about the ad with a partner.

## Evaluation 1          5 mins. ■ ■ ■

Go over the answers as a class.

### INSTRUCTOR'S NOTES

_____

_____

_____

_____

# LESSON ② Managing money

GOAL ▪ Reduce debt and save money

WORKPLACE CONNECTION
Exercise B: Interact appropriately with team members;
Interpret and communicate information.

## A. Read the ad.

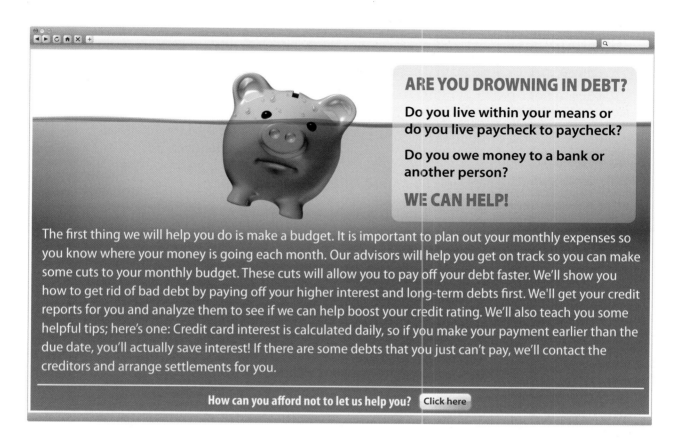

**ARE YOU DROWNING IN DEBT?**

Do you live within your means or do you live paycheck to paycheck?

Do you owe money to a bank or another person?

**WE CAN HELP!**

The first thing we will help you do is make a budget. It is important to plan out your monthly expenses so you know where your money is going each month. Our advisors will help you get on track so you can make some cuts to your monthly budget. These cuts will allow you to pay off your debt faster. We'll show you how to get rid of bad debt by paying off your higher interest and long-term debts first. We'll get your credit reports for you and analyze them to see if we can help boost your credit rating. We'll also teach you some helpful tips; here's one: Credit card interest is calculated daily, so if you make your payment earlier than the due date, you'll actually save interest! If there are some debts that you just can't pay, we'll contact the creditors and arrange settlements for you.

How can you afford not to let us help you? **Click here**

## B. Answer the questions about the ad with a partner. Answers will vary.

1. Who do you think wrote this ad? _a debt-reduction agency_

2. What is the purpose of this ad? _to help people in debt_

3. Would you click on the bottom of the ad? Why? _I would be concerned if their help might affect_ _my credit rating badly._

4. The ad mentions different ways to help people reduce debt. List four suggestions.

   a. _Make a budget._

   b. _Cut monthly budget._

   c. _Get rid of bad debt by paying off high-interest/long-term debt._

   d. _Get credit reports and analyze them._

## C. Read the tips on how to save money.

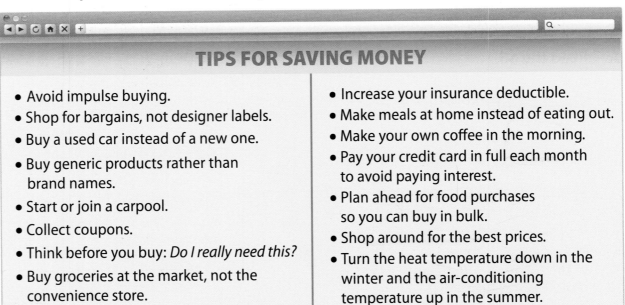

### TIPS FOR SAVING MONEY

- Avoid impulse buying.
- Shop for bargains, not designer labels.
- Buy a used car instead of a new one.
- Buy generic products rather than brand names.
- Start or join a carpool.
- Collect coupons.
- Think before you buy: *Do I really need this?*
- Buy groceries at the market, not the convenience store.

- Increase your insurance deductible.
- Make meals at home instead of eating out.
- Make your own coffee in the morning.
- Pay your credit card in full each month to avoid paying interest.
- Plan ahead for food purchases so you can buy in bulk.
- Shop around for the best prices.
- Turn the heat temperature down in the winter and the air-conditioning temperature up in the summer.

## D. Listen to Kimla and her husband, Derek, talk about saving money. Write *T* (*true*) or *F* (*false*) on the line before each statement.

CD TR 11

___T___ 1. Kimla buys designer clothes.

___T___ 2. Derek had been buying his coffee at a coffee shop.

___T___ 3. Kimla had been paying high interest on credit cards.

___F___ 4. Derek had been looking at new cars.

___T___ 5. Kimla turns off the air conditioner before she goes to bed.

___T___ 6. Derek called the insurance company to increase their deductible.

___F___ 7. Kimla has never bought generic products.

___T___ 8. Derek collects coupons.

## E. ANALYZE Do you already follow some of the tips in Exercise C? Circle the ones you are familiar with. Underline the ones you would like to follow in the future. Answers will vary.

## Presentation 2     5–10 mins. ■■□□

### C. Read the tips on how to save money.

Go over the tips as a class.

## Practice 2     10–15 mins. ■■□□

(Shorter classes can do this exercise for homework by using the script in the back of the book.)

> **MULTILEVEL WORKSHEET**
>
> Unit 2, Lesson 2, Worksheet 2: Saving Money (listening)

### D. Listen to Kimla and her husband, Derek, talk about saving money. Write *T* (*true*) or *F* (*false*) on the line before each statement.

Students may find this exercise difficult because of the grammar used in the conversation, but play it a few times for students and see if they can discover the speakers' general meaning.

---

### LISTENING SCRIPT

CD
TR 11

**Kimla:** *Derek, I really think we need to come up with some more ways to save money.*

**Derek:** *More? I thought we were doing really well with our money. I'm really proud of myself for making my own coffee instead of buying it at a coffee shop and clipping coupons.*

**Kimla:** *Yes, you are doing a great job. But weren't you supposed to buy a used car? I thought you were looking at used cars, but then you ended up buying a new one.*

**Derek:** *Well, what about you and your designer clothes?*

**Kimla:** *At least I started buying generic-name products and turning off the air conditioner before I go to bed.*

**Derek:** *Um, what about your designer clothes?*

**Kimla:** *I know, I know, I used to be so good at looking for bargains. But I just love the designer fashions. At least I was able to call the credit card companies and lower our interest rates, so we are no longer paying on high interest cards.*

**Derek:** *Yeah, that was a good move. And I called the insurance company to increase our deductible so our premiums would go down.*

**Kimla:** *I guess you're right, Derek. We are doing a pretty good job.*

**Derek:** *Yep, I agree.*

---

## Evaluation 2     10–15 mins. ■■□□

Go over the answers as a class.

### E. ANALYZE Do you already follow some of the tips in Exercise C? Circle the ones you are familiar with. Underline the ones you would like to follow in the future.

**INSTRUCTOR'S NOTES**

_____
_____
_____
_____
_____
_____
_____
_____
_____
_____
_____
_____
_____
_____
_____
_____
_____
_____
_____
_____
_____
_____
_____
_____

## Presentation 3 5–10 mins. ■■□

**F. Study the chart with your teacher.**

## Practice 3 15–20 mins. ■□
(Shorter classes can do this exercise for homework.)

**G. Think about your past behavior and how you have changed it to reduce debt and save money. Write four statements.**

## Evaluation 3 5–10 mins. ■□
Ask volunteers to write their statements on the board. As a class, evaluate them for content and grammatical accuracy.

## Application 10–20 mins. ■■■

**H. DECIDE Come up with three ways in which you are going to change your behavior to reduce debt and save money.**

### MULTILEVEL WORKSHEET

Unit 2, Lesson 2, Worksheet 3: Past Perfect Continuous

**Refer students to *Stand Out 5 Workbook,* Unit 2, Lesson 2 for more practice with the past perfect continuous.**

**Go to the *Activity Bank* online for suggestions on promoting digital literacy and using the Internet to enhance this lesson.**

### BEST PRACTICE

## Writing on the board

Having students write on the board is a common activity that doesn't usually require much preparation. However, providing a few tips can benefit students.

1. Always have students print, not write.
2. Ask students to watch out for spelling mistakes. If students are unsure of the spelling of a word, tell them not to be afraid to ask the class.
3. Ask students to try to write in straight lines in letters that aren't too big or small.

### INSTRUCTOR'S NOTES

**F.  Study the chart with your teacher.**

| Past Perfect Continuous Tense | | | | | |
|---|---|---|---|---|---|
| **First event in past** | | | | | **Second event in past** |
| Subject | *had* | *been* | Verb + *-ing* | | |
| Kimla | had | been | buying | designer clothes | before she started bargain shopping. |
| He | had | been | buying | coffee at a coffee shop | before he began making it at home. |
| They | had | been | paying | a lower deductible | before they called the insurance company. |

- We use the past perfect continuous to talk about an activity that was happening for a while before another event happened in the past. For the most recent event, we use the simple past tense.

- Remember to use a comma if you put the second event as the first part of the sentence. Example: Before she started bargain shopping, Kimla had been buying designer clothes.

**G.  Think about your past behavior and how you have changed it to reduce debt and save money. Write four statements.** Answers will vary.

EXAMPLE:  *I had been eating out for lunch every day before I started making my lunch at home.*

1. _____

2. _____

3. _____

4. _____

**H.  DECIDE  Come up with three ways in which you are going to change your behavior to reduce debt and save money.** Answers will vary.

EXAMPLE:  *Tomorrow, I will start making my lunch at home.*

1. _____

2. _____

3. _____

# LESSON ③ Investing wisely

WORKPLACE CONNECTION
Exercise A: Complete tasks as assigned.
Exercises C, D: Interact appropriately with team members;
Interpret and communicate information.

**A.** **In a small group, look at the following list of words and phrases. Which do you know? Find the meanings of those you don't know.**

| | | | | |
|---|---|---|---|---|
| capital gains | convert | inflation | liquid | net appreciation |
| penalty | risky | value | vehicle | purchasing power |

**B.** **COMPARE Look at your meaning for *vehicle*. Compare your definition with the definition below.**

*vehicle:* a way in which something is accomplished   *investment option or opportunity*

**C.** **PREDICT Based on the words and phrases you defined in Exercise A, what do you think the article below is about? Discuss your ideas with your classmates.**

**D.** **Read the article about investing money.**

Due to inflation, money is worth less and less each year, so by not investing your money, you are actually losing money. In order to prevent inflation from destroying the value of your money, you need to invest. Let's take a look at some basic kinds of investments.

An investment can make you money in three basic ways. First, an investment can earn *current income*. Current income is money that you receive periodically, for example, every month or every six months. An example of an investment that provides current income is a certificate of deposit (CD) because interest is paid to your account periodically. A second way that an investment can make money is through *capital growth*. This is when the amount of money you have invested grows in value over time. When you sell the investment, you get your money back plus any increase in value. Examples of capital growth investments are stocks and other assets that you own, such as your home. Finally, a third way that an investment can earn income is through a combination of current income and capital growth. Examples include rental property and stocks that pay dividends, that is, extra or bonus amounts of money.

There are many different ways to invest your money, but let's look at five of the most widely used investment vehicles.

Probably the most popular investment vehicle is the savings account, which offers low minimum deposits, liquidity (the ability to withdraw and deposit whenever you want), and insurance protection. Because

<table>
<tr><td>

## AT-A-GLANCE PREP

**Goal:** Identify investment strategies
**Academic Strategies:** Outlining, writing a summary
**Vocabulary:** *capital gains, convert, inflation, liquid, net appreciation, penalty, purchasing power, risky, value, vehicle, worth, prevent, destroy, investment, periodically, current income, CD, capital growth, stocks, bonds, earnings*

## Agenda

- Learn investment-related vocabulary.
- Read about and discuss investing money.
- Complete an outline.
- Write a summary.

## Resources

**Multilevel Worksheets:** Unit 2, Lesson 3, Worksheets 1–2
**Workbook:** Unit 2, Lesson 3
**Suggested Realia:** Money magazines (e.g., *Consumer Reports, Money, Fortune,* etc.)

## Pacing

- 1.5 hour classes
- 2.5 hour classes
- 3+ hour classes

## STANDARDS CORRELATIONS

*CCRS:* RI1, RI2, RI4
*CASAS:* 7.4.2
*SCANS:* **Information** Acquire and evaluate information, organize and maintain information, interpret and communicate information
**Interpersonal** Participate as a member of a team, teach others, work nwith cultural diversity
**Systems** Monitor and correct performance
**Basic Skills** Reading, writing, listening, speaking
**Thinking Skills** Think creatively, make decisions
**Personal Qualities** Responsibility, sociability, self-management
*EFF:* **Communication** Read with understanding, convey ideas in writing, speak so others can understand, listen actively
**Decision Making** Plan
**Interpersonal** Cooperate with others
**Lifelong Learning** Take responsibility for learning, reflect and evaluate, learn through research

</td><td>

### Warm-up and Review  10–20 mins.
In small groups, have students discuss ways to reduce debt and save money.

### Introduction  5–10 mins.
Dictation: 1. Young investors are interested in making money over time. 2. Older investors are more interested in earning current income. 3. Think carefully about how soon you will need to access your money. 4. Due to inflation, money is worth less and less every year.

State the goal: *Today, you will identify different ways to invest the money you are saving.*

### Presentation 1  10–15 mins.
Go over any vocabulary from the dictation that students don't understand. Some of these items will be included in Exercise A.

### Practice 1  10–15 mins.

**A. In a small group, look at the following list of words and phrases. Which do you know? Find the meanings of those you don't know.**

### Evaluation 1  5–15 mins.

**B. COMPARE Look at your meaning for *vehicle*. Compare your definition with the definition below.**

See if students can come up with more words that have more than one meaning but are spelled the same. Tell students these words are called *homonyms* (or more precisely, *homographs*, meaning they are spelled the same). Go over the meanings of all the words and phrases from Exercise A as a class.

### Presentation 2  10–20 mins.

**C. PREDICT Based on the words and phrases you defined in Exercise A, what do you think the article below is about? Discuss your ideas with your classmates.**

**D. Read the article about investing money.**

Ask students to read the article silently. Tell them that they can read it more than one time if necessary.

</td></tr>
</table>

## BEST PRACTICE

### Silent reading

Silent reading is a very important skill that should be fostered in the classroom and encouraged at home. The more silent reading activities you can provide in class, the better your students will master this skill. To encourage silent reading, you can start a small library of interesting things for students to read when they have finished an activity the rest of the class is still working on. Your library may include books, magazines, and newspapers. Alternatively, you can make it part of your daily routine to have all students spend 15 minutes per day doing silent reading.

### Practice 2

5–10 mins. ■■

**E. Discuss the following questions with a partner.**

When students have finished reading the article, have them find a partner and discuss the questions.

### Evaluation 2

10–15 mins. ■■

Go over the article as a class, making sure students understand the general ideas covered in the article.

#### MULTILEVEL WORKSHEETS

Unit 2, Lesson 3, Worksheet 1: Investing Vocabulary Practice

Unit 2, Lesson 3, Worksheet 2: "The Chicken or the Market?" (reading comprehension)

## BEST PRACTICE

### Group discussion

Students should be familiar with group discussion by now. However, to ensure full participation, ask each student to contribute a comment or two. If there are discussion questions, it might be a good idea to form groups based on the number of questions and assign each group member a question to read and answer first.

of these features, savings accounts pay relatively low interest rates. Another investment vehicle that is somewhat similar to a savings account in that it offers low interest rates and insurance protection is a certificate of deposit (CD). A CD requires that you put money in and leave it for a certain amount of time—three months, six months, a year, etc. Usually, the longer the amount of time you keep it in, the higher the interest. CDs are not perfectly liquid because early withdrawal of funds from a CD often results in a penalty. Another type of investment is a mutual fund where a number of investors put their money together to buy specific investments. Some mutual funds invest in stocks, some in bonds, and some in real estate. The mutual fund investor owns shares of the fund, not the actual stocks, bonds, or property purchased by the fund. Most likely, when a person thinks of investing, he or she probably thinks of the stock market. Ownership of a stock represents ownership of a *claim* on the net earnings of a company. Therefore, stock earnings depend on how well the company is doing. Stocks can be quickly converted to cash by selling them on the stock market, but because the price of stocks changes daily, there is no guarantee that you will get back the money that you paid for the stock. And finally, property or real estate is a popular investment because it can produce returns in two ways: current income and net appreciation (capital gains). You can receive current income if the property is used, such as in situations where tenants are renting it or if crops are grown on the land. Net appreciation occurs if the property increases in value during the time that you own it. A major disadvantage of real estate and rental property is that they are not very liquid; it takes time and resources to turn them into cash. It may take many months to sell a piece of property.

So, which investment will be best for you? Only you can decide. Think carefully about your financial situation, how much money you can or want to invest, and how soon you will need access to the money.

**E. Discuss the following questions with a partner.** Answers will vary.

1. Do you invest your money? If so, how do you invest it?

2. What investment vehicles would you like to try?

3. Would you say you are conservative with your money? Why or why not?

WORKPLACE CONNECTION
Exercises F, G: Complete tasks as assigned.
Exercise H: Interpret and communicate information.

**F.** **Use the ideas you have learned about investment strategies in this lesson to complete the sentences below. Each sentence may have more than one answer.**

*Answers may vary.*

1. If you don't invest your money, you will lose _____purchasing power_____ over time.

2. The _____price/value_____ of stocks is based on the earnings of the company.

3. Savings accounts and mutual funds are not very _____profitable_____.

4. My favorite investment _____strategy_____ is _____mutual funds_____ (your own idea).

5. It is not easy to _____turn/convert/liquidate_____ real estate into cash.

6. Savings accounts are very _____popular_____. You can get the cash whenever you need it.

**G.** **An outline is a way to organize the main ideas of something you have listened to or read. You can write notes or complete sentences in an outline, but do not directly copy the author's words. Based on the article in Exercise D, complete the outline below.**

I. Inflation

    A. *Money is worth less and less each year—by not investing, people lose money.*

II. Investments make you money.

    A. **Current income** (CDs)

    B. *Capital growth (real estate, stocks, etc.)*

    C. *A combination of current income and capital growth*

III. Popular investment types

    A. *Savings accounts*

    B. *Certificates of deposit (CDs)*

    C. **Stocks**

    D. *Mutual funds*

    E. *Real estate/Property*

**H.** **SUMMARIZE** **A summary is a brief statement of main ideas. On a separate piece of paper, write a one-paragraph summary of the article in Exercise D using the notes from your outline in Exercise G.** *Answers may vary.*

## Evaluation 2 *(continued)*

**F.  Use the ideas you have learned about investment strategies in this lesson to complete the sentences below. Each sentence may have more than one answer.**

Tell students they can use the vocabulary they worked with in Exercise A to complete these sentences.

## Presentation 3                5–10 mins. ■■□

Go over the answers as a class. Ask volunteers to come up with original sentences using the same words.

Write the word *outline* on the board and see if students can help you define it. Use the example in Exercise G to clarify the term. Ask students why outlining is an important skill.

## Practice 3                15–20 mins. ■□□

(Shorter classes can do this exercise for homework and review the next class day.)

**G.  An outline is a way to organize the main ideas of something you have listened to or read. You can write notes or complete sentences in an outline, but do not directly copy the author's words. Based on the article in Exercise D, complete the outline below.**

Show students how some of the outline has been filled in for them and have them complete the outline by themselves.

## Evaluation 3                5–10 mins. ■□□

Go over the answers as a class. Have students help you complete the outline on the board or on an overhead transparency.

## Application                10–20 mins. ■■■

**H.  SUMMARIZE  A summary is a brief statement of main ideas. On a separate piece of paper, write a one-paragraph summary of the article in Exercise D using the notes from your outline in Exercise G.**

Make sure students understand that a summary uses the main ideas of a text but omits the details.

Refer students to *Stand Out 5 Workbook,* Unit 2, Lesson 3 for practice with ability modals: *can* and *could*.

Go to the *Activity Bank* online for suggestions on promoting digital literacy and using the Internet to enhance this lesson.

### INSTRUCTOR'S NOTES

## AT-A-GLANCE PREP

**Goal:** Maintain good credit

**Academic Strategies:** Reading for understanding, outlining, summary writing

**Vocabulary:** *daunting, bankruptcy, mainstream, lender, omissions, delinquencies, liens, credit bureau, collateral, creditworthiness, overextended*

### Agenda

☐ Discuss credit.

☐ Read an online article.

☐ Give advice.

☐ Define new vocabulary.

☐ Create an outline and summary.

☐ List ways you can establish and maintain good credit.

### Resources

**Multilevel Worksheets:** Unit 2, Lesson 4, Worksheets 1–2

**Workbook:** Unit 2, Lesson 4

### Pacing

■ 1.5 hour classes    ■ 2.5 hour classes
■ 3+ hour classes

## STANDARDS CORRELATIONS

*CCRS:* RI1, RI2, RI4, RI10

*CASAS:* 1.3.2, 7.4.2

*SCANS:* **Information** Acquire and evaluate information, organize and maintain information, interpret and communicate information

**Interpersonal** Participate as a member of a team, teach others, exercise leadership, negotiate to arrive at a decision, work with cultural diversity

**Systems** Monitor and correct performance

**Technology** Apply technology to a task (*optional*)

**Basic Skills** Reading, writing, arithmetic, listening, speaking

**Thinking Skills** See things in the mind's eye

**Personal Qualities** Responsibility, sociability, self-management

*EFF:* **Communication** Read with understanding, convey ideas in writing

**Decision Making** Use math to solve problems and communicate, solve problems and make decisions, plan

**Interpersonal** Cooperate with others

**Lifelong Learning** Take responsibility for learning, reflect and evaluate, learn through research, use information and communications technology (*optional*)

## Warm-up and Review          5–10 mins. ■■■

Have students take out their summaries from the previous lesson. Ask a volunteer to come to the board and write down one new thing they learned about investing. Tell the next volunteer that he or she has to write something new that isn't already on the board. Continue to do this until no one has anything new to write.

## Introduction          5–10 mins. ■■■

Dictation:

1. Getting credit when you don't have any can be daunting.
2. Without a good credit history, it's hard to get new credit.
3. But without credit, it's tough to build a good credit history.
4. Every day, people take steps to establish and improve their image in the eyes of lenders.

State the goal: *Today, you will learn about credit and how to establish and maintain good credit.*

## Presentation 1          10–15 mins. ■■■

### A. In a small group, discuss the following questions.

These questions serve as a preview. The answers can be found in the article that students will read in Exercise B. See what students already know and try not to answer too many questions.

Exercise A answer key for the instructor:

1. money lent to a consumer instead of immediate payment; credit-worthiness
2. Good: Keep a bank account, pay bills on time, use credit wisely; Bad: Don't pay bills on time, max out credit cards, spend beyond your means
3. get a credit report
4. Read credit report for errors, contact the bank or creditor or credit bureau if there are errors, pay bills on time, add positive information to your report, establish credit and use it correctly.

## Practice 1          10–15 mins. ■■■

### B. Read the article below. As you read it, underline the main ideas.

Go over the directions with students, making sure they remember what a main idea is.

Before students start reading, review the information about the author of "The Four Keys to Great Credit" on page 52a.

# LESSON 4 Credit

WORKPLACE CONNECTION
Exercise A: Interact appropriately with team members.
Exercise B: Complete tasks as assigned.

**A. In a small group, discuss the following questions.** Answers will vary.

1. What is credit?

2. What makes credit good or bad?

3. How can you find out if you have good or bad credit?

4. If you have bad credit, how can you improve it?

*Refer to Lesson Planner page 51a for answers.*

**B. Read the article below. As you read it, underline the main ideas.**

### The Four Keys to Great Credit

**By Liz Pulliam Weston**

Your credit history can make or break you when trying to convince lenders you're a good risk. Here's how to build the best record you can—before you need it:

✓ Open checking and savings accounts. Having bank accounts establishes you as part of the financial mainstream. Lenders want to know you have a checking account available to pay bills, and a savings account indicates you're putting aside something for the future.

✓ Get your credit report—if you have one. Next, you need to find out how lenders view you. Most lenders base their decisions on credit reports, which are compiled by companies known as credit bureaus. You are entitled to a free credit report from each of the three major bureaus each year. Typically, a credit report includes identifying information about you, such as your name, address, social security number, and birth date. The report may also list any credit accounts or loans opened in your name, along with your payment history, account limits, and unpaid balances.

Fix any errors or omissions. Some credit reports include errors— accounts that don't belong to you or that include out-of-date or misleading information. You should read through each of your three reports and note anything that's incorrect. Negative information, such as late payments, delinquencies, liens, and judgments against you, should be dropped after seven years. Bankruptcies can stay on your report for up to ten years.

*(continued)*

Add positive information to your report. The more information you can provide about yourself, the more comfortable lenders may feel extending credit to you. Here's a list of items to consider:

- Are your employer and your job title listed?
- Is your address listed and correct?
- Is your social security number listed and correct?
- Is your telephone number listed and correct?
- Does your report include all the accounts you've paid on time?

✓ Establish credit. There are three common routes for establishing new credit:

1. Apply for department store and gasoline cards. These are usually easier to get than major bank credit cards.
2. Consider taking out a small personal loan from your local bank or credit union and paying the money back over time. The bank may require you to put up some collateral—such as the same amount you're borrowing, deposited into a savings account.
3. Apply for a secured credit card. These work something like the loan described above: You deposit a certain amount at a bank, and in return you're given a Visa or MasterCard with a credit limit roughly equal to the amount you deposited.

✓ Once you've got credit, use it right. Charge small amounts on each card—but never more than you can pay off each month. You need to use credit regularly to establish your credit history, but there's usually no advantage to paying interest on those charges. Once you've been approved for one card or loan, don't rush out and apply for several more. Applying for too much credit will hurt, rather than help, your score.

## C. ADVISE Imagine you are a financial advisor. Give your partner advice based on the following questions.

1. What can I do to establish good credit?

   You can apply for credit cards, take out small loans, apply for a secure card.

   _____

2. What should I look for in my credit report?

   You should look for errors or omissions, negative information.

   _____

3. How can I add positive information to my credit report?

   You can check that all job information and personal data is accurate.

   _____

Unit 2, Lesson 4, Worksheet 1: "The Four Keys to Great Credit" (Reading Comprehension)

This worksheet contains more in-depth work with the article in the Student Book.

**Optional Internet Activity:** The article in this lesson is from an online column found on the website money.msn.com. Liz Pulliam is a columnist who is available online to answer questions. In fact, students themselves can go online, find the article, and come up with a few questions to e-mail to Ms. Pullman. If she is no longer doing her online column when students go to the website, have them write questions to the new columnist.

## Evaluation 1                    10–15 mins. ■■■

Discuss the article as a class, helping students understand what the main ideas are. Try to refrain from going over too much vocabulary in depth since students will be doing this with a partner in Exercise D.

**C. ADVISE Imagine you are a financial advisor. Give your partner advice based on the following questions.**

Have students take turns playing the advisor and the person who needs advice.

## INSTRUCTOR'S NOTES

## Presentation 2

5–10 mins. ■■■

Ask students to look back at the article and call out some words they don't understand. Start to make a list on the board. Choose one of the words and have a student look it up in a dictionary and read the definition out loud. Make sure he or she chooses the definition as it relates to the article.

## Practice 2

15–20 mins. ■■

(Shorter classes can do this exercise for homework.)

**D. Go back through the article and underline six words or phrases you do not understand. Work with a partner and look in a dictionary to discover their meanings.**

## Evaluation 2

10–15 mins. ■■

Answer any questions students may have. Give them a chance to look the words up in a bilingual dictionary if they want to make sure they are confident about the meanings.

## Presentation 3

5–10 mins. ■■■

Help students begin an outline by asking them how many main sections are in the article. Have them tell you what the first two sections are.

## Practice 3

20–30 mins. ■

(Shorter classes can do this exercise for homework.)

**E. On a separate piece of paper, make an outline of the article. Then, write a summary.**

### MULTILEVEL WORKSHEET

Unit 2, Lesson 4, Worksheet 2: The Four Keys to Great Credit: Outline Template and Sample Outline

## Evaluation 3

5–10 mins. ■

Walk around the classroom and help students as they work. Remind them that everyone's outline and summary will not be exactly the same. If there's time, ask a few volunteers to share their summaries out loud.

## Application

10–20 mins. ■■■

**F. Having read the article, what are four things you need to do to help establish or maintain your credit?**

Refer students to *Stand Out 5 Workbook,* Unit 2, Lesson 4 for practice with advisability modals: *should* and *ought to.*

Go to the *Activity Bank* online for suggestions on promoting digital literacy and using the Internet to enhance this lesson.

### INSTRUCTOR'S NOTES

_____
_____
_____
_____
_____
_____
_____
_____
_____
_____
_____
_____
_____
_____
_____
_____
_____
_____
_____
_____
_____
_____

WORKPLACE CONNECTION
Exercise D: Complete tasks as assigned.
Exercise E: Collect and organize information; Combine ideas and information.

**D.** **Go back through the article and underline six words or phrases you do not understand. Work with a partner and look in a dictionary to discover their meanings.** Answers will vary.

1. _____

2. _____

3. _____

4. _____

5. _____

6. _____

**E.** **On a separate piece of paper, make an outline of the article. Then, write a summary.**
Answers will vary.

**F.** **Having read the article, what are four things you need to do to help establish or maintain your credit?**

1. Open a checking and savings account.
   _____

2. Fix errors and omissions in your credit report.
   _____

3. Add positive information to your report.
   _____

4. Establish credit.
   _____

LESSON **5** **Identity theft**

GOAL ■ Protect against identity theft

WORKPLACE CONNECTION
Exercise A: Complete tasks as assigned; Collect and organize information.
Exercises B, C: Interact appropriately with team members.

🎧 **A.** **Listen to each of the following people talk about their financial problems. What happened? Take notes on the lines below each photo.**

CD TR 12

1. charges from unfamiliar companies on credit card statement; stolen number from Internet

2. charged for calls not made; someone stole personal information and added a phone line

3. ATM card declined; all money stolen from account

**B.** **Have you ever had any problems similar to the ones in Exercise A? If so, what did you do about it? Tell your classmates.**

**C.** **INFER** **In a small group, discuss the following questions.** Answers may vary.

1. What is identity theft? When your financial and life information is stolen and used fraudulently.

2. What do you think the following terms mean: *dumpster diving, skimming, phishing,* and *pretexting*? Refer to listening script on page 55a for definitions.

3. What are some things a person who steals your identity might do? Come up with some ideas in addition to the three in Exercise A. Use your ID to take out loans or buy a car.

4. What can you do if someone steals your identity? Notify your credit card companies, notify the police, notify credit bureau, and check credit reports

Protect your PIN when using ATMs.

## AT-A-GLANCE PREP

**Goal:** Protect against identity theft
**Pronunciation:** Clear speech
**Academic Strategies:** Focused listening, identifying details, writing a summary, giving a presentation
**Vocabulary:** *commit fraud, good name, dumpster diving, rummage, skimming, phishing, spam, pop-up messages, reveal, divert, pretexting, false pretenses, delinquent accounts, counterfeit checks, unauthorized transactions, awareness*

### Agenda

- Listen to people discuss financial problems.
- Discuss identity theft.
- Listen to an interview about identity theft.
- Write a summary.
- Prepare a presentation.

### Resources

**Multilevel Worksheet:** Unit 2, Lesson 5, Worksheet 1
**Workbook:** Unit 2, Lesson 5
**Audio:** CD Tracks 12–13

### Pacing

- 1.5 hour classes
- 2.5 hour classes
- 3+ hour classes

## STANDARDS CORRELATIONS

*CCRS:* RI2, RI4, W2, W4, W5, SL1, SL2, SL3, SL6, L1, L2, L5
*CASAS:* 7.4.2
*SCANS:* **Resources** Allocate time, allocate materials and facility resources, allocate human resources
**Information** Acquire and evaluate information, organize and maintain information, interpret and communicate information
**Interpersonal** Participate as a member of a team, teach others, exercise leadership, negotiate to arrive at a decision, work with cultural diversity
**Systems** Monitor and correct performance
**Basic Skills** Reading, writing, listening, speaking
**Thinking Skills** Think creatively, make decisions, solve problems, see things in the mind's eye
**Personal Qualities** Responsibility, sociability, self-management
*EFF:* **Communication** Read with understanding, convey ideas in writing, speak so others can understand, listen actively, observe critically

**Decision Making** Solve problems and make decisions, plan
**Interpersonal** Cooperate with others, advocate and influence, resolve conflict and negotiate, guide others
**Lifelong Learning** Take responsibility for learning, reflect and evaluate, learn through research

### Warm-up and Review            5–10 mins. ■■■
Ask volunteers to come to the board and write ideas on how to establish and maintain good credit.

### Introduction            5–10 mins. ■■■
Read the following aloud: *Approximately nine million Americans have their identities stolen each year. You or someone you know may have experienced some form of identity theft.*

State the goal: *Today, you will learn how to protect yourself against identity theft.*

### Presentation 1            5 mins. ■■■
Write *identity theft* on the board and see if students can help you define the term. You will be discussing it again in Exercise C. Have students look at the pictures in Exercise A and guess what the problems are.

### Practice 1            10–15 mins. ■■■

**A.** **Listen to each of the following people talk about their financial problems. What happened? Take notes on the lines below each photo.**

### Evaluation 1            5–10 mins. ■■■
Go over the answers as a class.

**B.** **Have you ever had any problems similar to the ones in Exercise A? If so, what did you do about it? Tell your classmates.**

### Presentation 2            10–15 mins. ■■■

**C.** **INFER In a small group, discuss the following questions.**

Tell students that they will be listening to a representative from the Federal Trade Commission (FTC) who will answer all of these questions. If students don't know what the FTC is, review the FTC website description on page 56a.

**Note:** Listening script for Exercise A appear on page 55a.

## LISTENING SCRIPT

CD TR 12

**Man 1:** *I was looking over my credit card statement last night and I noticed some charges from unfamiliar companies. When I called the companies to see what the charges were for, I found out that they were companies that I had never done business with. Apparently, someone had gotten my credit card number off of the Internet and had been using it for months to make online purchases.*

**Man 2:** *My cell phone bill was really expensive this month. When I looked at it closer, I realized that I had been charged for a phone number that wasn't mine. When I called the phone company to dispute it, they said that I had indeed called and added a line to my account. I told them this wasn't true, and we discovered that someone had stolen my personal information and added a phone line to my account.*

**Woman:** *I was in the supermarket the other day. When I tried to pay for my groceries with my ATM card, it was declined due to insufficient funds. So, then I went to an ATM machine and tried to withdraw money. My card was declined again. I called my bank and found out that someone in another state had gotten a copy of my ATM card and had withdrawn all of the money in my account.*

## Practice 2

10–15 mins. ■■

**D. Listen to an interview with a member of the Federal Trade Commission (FTC). In each question below, one answer is NOT correct. Circle the incorrect answer.**

## LISTENING SCRIPT

CD TR 13

*Identity theft occurs when someone uses your personal identification information, such as your name, social security number, or credit card number without your permission to commit fraud or other crimes. The FTC estimates that as many as nine million Americans have their identities stolen each year. In fact, you or someone you know may have experienced some form of identity theft. Identity theft is serious. While some identity theft victims can resolve their problems quickly, others spend hundreds of dollars and many days repairing damage to their name and credit record.*

*How do thieves steal an identity? Identity theft starts with the misuse of your personal identification information, such as your name and social security number, credit card numbers, or other financial account information. Skilled identity thieves may use a variety of methods to get hold of your information, including: dumpster diving, skimming, and phishing. When thieves dumpster dive, they rummage through trash looking for bills or other paper with your personal information on it. When thieves employ the skimming method, they steal credit or debit card numbers by using a special storage device when processing your card. If thieves are phishing, they pretend to be financial institutions or companies and send spam or pop-up messages to get you*

*to reveal your personal information. Often thieves change your address by completing a change-of-address form and they then divert your billing statements to another location. Identity thieves also use forms of old-fashioned methods, such as stealing wallets and purses; mail, including bank and credit card statements; pre-approved credit offers; and new checks or tax information. They steal personnel records or bribe employees who have access to them. Thieves also use false pretenses to obtain your personal information from financial institutions, telephone companies, and other sources.*

*What do thieves do with a stolen identity? Once they have your personal information, identity thieves use it in a variety of ways.*

**Credit card fraud:** *They may open new credit card accounts in your name. When they use the cards and don't pay the bills, the delinquent accounts appear on your credit report. They may change the billing address on your credit card so that you no longer receive bills, and then run up charges on your account. Because your bills are now sent to a different address, it may be some time before you realize there's a problem.*

**Phone or utilities fraud:** *They may open a new phone or wireless account in your name, or run up charges on your existing account. They may use your name to get utility services like electricity, heating, or cable TV.*

**Bank/finance fraud:** *They may create counterfeit checks using your name or account number. They may open a bank account in your name and write bad checks. They may clone your ATM or debit card and make electronic withdrawals in your name, draining your accounts. They may take out a loan in your name.*

**Government documents fraud:** *They may get a driver's license or official ID card issued in your name, but with their picture. They may use your name and social security number to get government benefits. They may file a fraudulent tax return using your information.*

**Other fraud:** *They may get a job using your social security number. They may rent a house or get medical services using your name. They may give your personal information to police during an arrest. If they don't show up for their court date, a warrant for arrest is issued in your name.*

*How can you find out if your identity was stolen? The best way to find out is to monitor your accounts and bank statements each month, and check your credit report on a regular basis. If you check your credit report regularly, you may be able to limit the damage caused by identity theft.*

*What should you do if your identity is stolen? Filing a police report, checking your credit reports, notifying creditors, and disputing any unauthorized transactions are some of the steps you must take immediately to restore your good name.*

*What can you do to help fight identity theft? A great deal. Awareness is an effective weapon against many forms of identity theft. Be aware of how information is stolen and what you can do to protect yours, monitor your personal information to uncover any problems quickly, and know what to do when you suspect your identity has been stolen. You can also help fight identity theft by educating your friends, family, and members of your community.*

🎧 **D.** **Listen to an interview with a member of the Federal Trade Comission (FTC). In each question below, one answer is NOT correct. Circle the incorrect answer.**

CD
TR 13

1. What is identity theft?

   a. when someone uses your credit card number without permission to buy things

   b. when someone steals your name and social security number to commit crimes

   c. when someone commits fraud using your personal information

   (d.) when someone asks you for your personal information

2. What are some ways thieves steal your identity?

   a. dumpster diving

   (b.) changing your name

   c. stealing

   d. skimming

3. An example of bank fraud is . . .

   a. when someone takes out a loan in your name.

   (b.) when someone gets a driver's license in your name.

   c. when someone opens an account in your name.

   d. when someone creates counterfeit checks using your account number.

4. How can you find out if your identity has been stolen?

   (a.) cancel credit card accounts

   b. monitor bank accounts

   c. check credit reports

   d. check bank statements

5. What should you do if your identity has been stolen?

   a. notify creditors

   (b.) try to find the thief

   c. file a police report

   d. check credit reports

6. How can you help fight identity theft?

   (a.) donate money to the Federal Trade Commission

   b. be aware of how information is stolen

   c. monitor personal information

   d. educate friends and family about identity theft

**E.** **SUMMARIZE**  Using the information in Exercise D, work with a group to write a summary about identify theft.  Answers will vary.

_____

_____

_____

_____

_____

_____

_____

_____

_____

_____

_____

_____

**F.** In your group, use your summary to prepare a presentation that will educate your classmates about identity theft. Answer the questions below.  Answers will vary.

1. What information will you present to the class? _____

_____

_____

2. How will you present your information? (orally only, orally and visually, etc.)

_____

3. Who will present which part of the presentation? (Everyone in your group must participate.)

_____

_____

## Evaluation 2　　　　　10–15 mins. ■■☐

Go over the answers as a class.

## Presentation 3　　　　5–10 mins. ■■■

Prepare students to write their summaries by going over the information in Exercise D. Establish the main idea or purpose of the summary and identify the supporting details. Make an outline on the board.

## Practice 3　　　　　　5–7 mins. ■☐☐

(Shorter classes can do this exercise individually for homework.)

**E. SUMMARIZE** Using the information in Exercise D, work with a group to write a summary about identify theft.

## Evaluation 3　　　　　10–15 mins. ■☐☐

Walk around the classroom and help students as needed.

## Application　　　　　20–30 mins. ■■■

**F. In your group, use your summary to prepare a presentation that will educate your classmates about identity theft. Answer the questions below.**

Explain to students that they will be getting up in front of the class and giving a presentation on identity theft. Tell them to be creative and go beyond just standing up and reading their summaries. You might brainstorm with them on what they can do to make their presentations more interesting.

If time allows, have students practice their presentations with their group and then give the presentation to the class.

### MULTILEVEL WORKSHEET

Unit 2, Lesson 5, Worksheet 1: Identity Theft

**Statement from the FTC website:** The FTC deals with issues that touch the economic life of every American. It is the only federal agency with both consumer protection and competition jurisdiction in broad sectors of the economy. The FTC pursues vigorous and effective law enforcement; advances consumers' interests by sharing its expertise with federal and state legislatures and U.S. and international government agencies; develops policy and research tools through hearings, workshops, and conferences; and creates practical and plain-language educational programs for consumers and businesses in a global marketplace with constantly changing technologies.

**Refer students to *Stand Out 5 Workbook,* Unit 2, Challenge 5 for practice with uncertainty modals: *may, might,* and *could.***

**Go to the *Activity Bank* online for suggestions on promoting digital literacy and using the Internet to enhance this lesson.**

**There are also two extension challenges for review of material studied. Extension Challenge 1 practices the future continuous (progressive). Extension Challenge 2 practices uncertainty future modals: *should, ought to, may, might,* and *could.***

### INSTRUCTOR'S NOTES

_____

_____

_____

_____

_____

_____

_____

_____

_____

_____

_____

_____

_____

_____

## Before You Watch

- Read the video title out loud.
- Ask students what identity theft is.

### A. Look at the picture and answer the questions.

- Have students look at the picture. Then, ask them to answer the questions.
- Discuss the answers as a class.

## While You Watch

### B. Watch the video and complete the dialog.

- Ask students to watch the video and complete the dialog.
- Play the video and ask students to watch and listen carefully.
- Play the video again. Then, ask students to complete the dialog.
- Play the video once more and have students check their answers.

## Check Your Understanding

### C. Put the sentences in order to make a conversation.

- Have students read each statement in the conversation.
- Ask students to put the sentences in order to make a conversation.
- Have students practice the conversation with partners.
- Ask volunteers to read the conversation to the class.
- Have students check their answers as their classmates read.

| INSTRUCTOR'S NOTES |
| --- |

# LIFESKILLS ▶ It's called identity theft

## Before You Watch

**A. Look at the picture and answer the questions.**

1. Where are Mateo and Naomi? *Mateo and Naomi are at the diner where she works.*
2. What has happened to Mateo? *Mateo has lost his wallet.*

## While You Watch

**B. ▶ Watch the video and complete the dialog.**

**Mr. Sanchez:** ... such as your driver's (1) ___license___ or social security number?

**Mateo:** I keep my driver's license and my social (2) ___security___ card in my wallet.

**Mr. Sanchez:** That's all they needed. With that information, they can get into your bank account and take out all your money. They can even start a new account and take out a loan in

your name. It's called (3) ___identity theft___ theft.

**Mateo:** What (4) ___should___ I do?

**Mr. Sanchez:** Well, the first thing you need to do is (5) ___freeze___ your checking account. That will prevent the thieves from taking any more money out of your account.

## Check Your Understanding

**C. Put the sentences in order to make a conversation.**

a. __2__ **Customer:** I lost my wallet.

b. __3__ **Teller:** What was in it?

c. __6__ **Customer:** When can I get a new card?

d. __5__ **Teller:** We'd better freeze your account immediately.

e. __7__ **Teller:** It'll take about 10 days.

f. __4__ **Customer:** My ATM card and my driver's license.

g. __1__ **Teller:** What seems to be the problem?

# Review

**A.** Roger and Rupert are brothers who live together. Complete their worksheet below by filling in the missing amounts. Together, Roger and Rupert make $85,000 a year.

| MONEY OUT | | |
|---|---|---|
| | Annual | Monthly |
| Rent | $26,400 | $2,200 |
| Home maintenance fees | $1,800 | $150 |
| Renters' insurance | $1,200 | $100 |
| Gas/Electric | $2,640 | $220 |
| Water | $480 | $40 |
| Telephone/Cell phone | $1,440 | $120 |
| Food/Restaurants | $4,800 | $400 |
| Medical/Dental | $1,680 | $140 |
| Auto expenses | $10,680 | $890 |
| Clothes/Shoes | $1,125 | $93.75 |
| Hair/Manicure/Facial | $1,500 | $125 |
| Training/Education | $700 | $58.33 |
| Income taxes | $950 | $79.16 |
| Internet | $900 | $75 |
| Credit cards/Loans | $11,700 | $975 |
| Entertainment | $5,100 | $425 |
| Cable/Satellite TV | $1,680 | $140 |
| Vacations | $2,500 | $208.33 |
| Gifts | $795 | $66.25 |
| TOTAL | $78,070 | $6,505.83 |

1. How much do they have left over each year? $6,930

2. How much do they have left over each month? $577.50

3. Do you think Roger and Rupert live within their means? yes

4. What suggestions would you make for curbing their spending? Sample answers are given.
   a. reduce credit card use
   b. reduce entertainment
   c. reduce auto expenses
   d. reduce hair expenses

**B.** Write four tips for saving money.

1. make a budget
2. invest money in stocks
3. open a savings account
4. cut monthly expenses

**C.** Complete each statement with the past perfect continuous and the simple past.

1. Erika **had been buying** (buy) lunch every day before she **started** (start) making it at home.

2. Justin **had been charging** (charge) his credit cards to their maximum limits before he **cut** (cut) them up.

WORKPLACE CONNECTION
Exercises A, B, C: Complete tasks as assigned.
Exercise A: Perform basic computations.

**Goals:** All unit goals
**Grammar:** All unit grammar
**Academic Strategy:** Reviewing
**Vocabulary:** All Unit 2 vocabulary

## Agenda

- [ ] Discuss unit goals.
- [ ] Complete the review.
- [ ] Use unit vocabulary.

## Resources

**Stand Out Assessment CD-ROM with ExamView®**

## Pacing

- ■ 1.5 hour classes
- ■ 2.5 hour classes
- ■ 3+ hour classes

## STANDARDS CORRELATIONS

*CCRS:* RI4, RI7
*CASAS:* 7.2.1
*SCANS:* **Resources** Allocate time
**Information** Acquire and evaluate information
**Interpersonal** Participate as a member of a team, teach others, negotiate to arrive at a decision, work with cultural diversity
**Systems** Monitor and correct performance
**Basic Skills** Reading, writing, arithmetic, listening, speaking
**Thinking Skills** Think creatively, make decisions, solve problems, see things in the mind's eye
**Personal Qualities** Responsibility, sociability, self-management
*EFF:* **Communication** Read with understanding, convey ideas in writing, speak so others can understand, listen actively, observe critically
**Interpersonal** Cooperate with others, guide others
**Lifelong Learning** Take responsibility for learning, reflect and evaluate

## Warm-up and Review          5–10 mins. ■■■

Have students take out a piece of paper and write down the most important things they learned about identity theft in the previous lesson. Ask volunteers to read their ideas out loud.

## Introduction          5–10 mins. ■■■

Ask students as a class to try to recall all the goals of this unit without looking back in their books. The goals for this unit include organizing your finances, reducing debt and saving money, identifying

investment strategies, maintaining good credit, and protecting yourself against identity theft. Write all the goals on the board from Unit 2. Show students the first page of the unit and mention the five goals.

State the goal: *Today, we will be reviewing everything we have learned in this unit and preparing for the team project.*

## Presentation          10–15 mins. ■■■

This presentation will cover the first three pages of the review. Quickly go to the first page of each lesson. Discuss the goal of each. Ask simple questions to remind students of what they have learned.

**Note:** Since there is little presentation in the review, you can assign the review exercises that don't require collaboration with a partner or group for homework and go over them in class the following day.

## Practice          20–25 mins. ■■■

**Note:** There are two ways to do the review: 1. Go through the exercises one at a time and, as students complete each one, go over the answers. 2. Quickly go through the instructions of each exercise, let students complete all of the exercises at once, and then go over the answers.

A. **Roger and Rupert are brothers who live together. Complete their worksheet below by filling in the missing amounts. Together, Roger and Rupert make $85,000 a year. (Lesson 1)**

B. **Write four tips for saving money. (Lesson 2)**

C. **Complete each statement with the past perfect continuous and the simple past. (Lesson 2)**

Review the example with students.

## Evaluation          5–10 mins. ■■■

Go around the classroom and check on students' progress. Help individuals when needed. If you see consistent errors among several students, interrupt the class and give a mini-lesson or review to help students feel comfortable with the concept.

## Practice

25–30 mins. ■■■

D. Write four things you have learned about investing on a piece of paper. Share your ideas with a partner. Add two ideas that your partner came up with. (Lesson 3)

E. Answer the following questions by yourself or with a partner. (Lesson 4)

F. Read each scenario. Write what you think happened and what the person should do to fix the problem. (Lesson 5)

## Evaluation

5–10 mins. ■■■

Go around the room and check on student progress. Help individuals when needed. If you see consistent errors among several students, interrupt the class and give a mini-lesson/review to help students feel comfortable with the concept.

### BEST PRACTICE

## Recycling/Review

The review exercises, the research activity, and the team project are part of the recycling/review process. Students often need to be reintroduced to concepts to solidify what they have learned. Many concepts are learned and forgotten when students are engaged in learning other new concepts. This is because students learn but are not necessarily ready to acquire language concepts.

Therefore, it becomes very important to review material with students and to show them how to review it on their own. It is also important to recycle the new concepts in different contexts.

### INSTRUCTOR'S NOTES

**Learner Log**

| I can identify investment strategies. | I can maintain good credit. | I can protect against identity theft. |
|---|---|---|
| ☐ Yes ☐ No ☐ Maybe | ☐ Yes ☐ No ☐ Maybe | ☐ Yes ☐ No ☐ Maybe |

3. Before the Ingrams _____*bought*_____ (buy) a new car, they

_____*had been leasing*_____ (lease) a used one.

4. We _____*had been living*_____ (live) beyond our means before we

_____*organized*_____ (organize) our finances.

5. Before she _____*researched*_____ (research) insurance rates, she

_____*had been spending*_____ (spend) too much on auto insurance.

**D.** **Write four things you have learned about investing on a piece of paper. Share your ideas with a partner. Add two ideas that your partner came up with.** *Answers will vary.*

**E.** **Answer the following questions by yourself or with a partner.** *Answers will vary.*

1. What is credit? *Financial status.*

2. What can you do to establish good credit? *Open bank accounts and get credit reports.*

3. What makes credit good or bad? *Good: Paying on time; Bad: Paying late or not at all.*

4. How can you find out if you have good or bad credit? *Get copies of credit reports.*

5. If you have bad credit, how can you improve it? *Fix errors, pay on time, establish credit.*

6. What should you look for in your credit report? *Correct employers and personal information.*

7. How can you add positive information to your credit report? *Include all accounts and creditors paid on time.*

**F.** **Read each scenario. Write what you think happened and what the person should do to fix the problem.**

1. Marika tried to withdraw money from her current account, which had over $1,000 in it the last time she checked it, but the bank said she had insufficient funds.

What happened? *Someone got her ATM number and password.*

Solution: *She should contact her bank and the police.*

2. Marco noticed some unfamiliar charges on his credit card statement.

What happened? *Someone used his credit card to make a purchase.*

Solution: *Call creditor, file police report, check credit reports.*

3. The IRS contacted Frankie and said he never paid income tax on a second job, which he didn't have.

What happened? *Someone stole his social security card.*

Solution: *Contact the department of social security; contact employer where the fraud happened.*

WORKPLACE CONNECTION
Exercise D: Complete tasks as assigned.
Exercise E: Interact appropriately with team members.
Exercise F: Interpret and communicate information.

# Vocabulary Review

**A.** A *synonym* is a word that has the same meaning as another word. Look at each of the words below and choose a word from the box that is its synonym.

| | | |
|---|---|---|
| bargain | delinquent | fraud |
| convert | earnings | risk |
| counterfeit | expense | worth |
| debt | | |

1. income _____earnings_____
2. fake _____counterfeit_____
3. late _____delinquent_____
4. scam _____fraud_____
5. cost _____expense_____
6. good deal _____bargain_____
7. money due _____debt_____
8. liability _____risk_____
9. change _____convert_____
10. value _____worth_____

**B.** Look back in the unit and find three new terms you learned (different from the words in the box in Exercise A). Write a sentence using each of these terms.
*Answers will vary.*

1. _____
2. _____
3. _____

**C.** Complete each sentence with an appropriate word or phrase from this unit. In many cases, more than one word or expression will work. *Answers will vary.*

1. There are many ways in which people can steal your identity. Two of them are _____skimming_____ and _____pretexting_____.

2. A safe way to invest your money is by investing in _CDs and mutual funds_.

3. A riskier way to invest is by investing in _the stock market_.

4. One good way to establish credit is _pay bills on time_.

5. Another way is _get a credit card and pay it regularly_.

6. If your identity is stolen, you should _file a police report, check credit reports, notify creditors_.

WORKPLACE CONNECTION
Exercises A, B, C: Complete tasks as assigned.

## Practice

25–30 mins. ■■■

### Vocabulary Review

A. A *synonym* is a word that has the same meaning as another word. Look at each of the words below and choose a word from the box that is its synonym.

B. Look back in the unit and find three new terms you learned (different from the words in the box in Exercise A). Write a sentence using each of these terms.

C. Complete each sentence with an appropriate word or phrase from this unit. In many cases, more than one word or expression will work.

## Evaluation

5–10 mins. ■■■

Go around the classroom and check on students' progress. Help individuals when needed. If you see consistent errors among several students, interrupt the class and give a mini-lesson or review to help students feel comfortable with the concept.

## Assessment *(optional)*

■■■

Use the Stand Out Assessment CD-ROM with ExamView® to create a post-test for Unit 2.

## AT-A-GLANCE PREP

**Goal:** Research government agencies
**Academic Strategy:** Research
**Vocabulary:** *agency, FDIC, FTC, handbook*

### Agenda

- Visit the website of the FDIC.
- Visit the website of the FTC.
- Find useful consumer information at www.consumeraction.gov.

### Resources

**Suggested Realia:** Telephone book, Internet, *Consumer Action Handbook* (must be ordered online)
**Multilevel Worksheets:** Research: FTC and FDIC

### Pacing

■ 1.5 hour classes    ■ 2.5 hour classes
■ 3+ hour classes

## STANDARDS CORRELATIONS

*CCRS:* W7, W8
*CASAS:* 4.9.3, 7.2.1, 7.4.4, 7.4.5, 7.4.6
*SCANS:* **Information** Acquire and evaluate information, organize and maintain information, interpret and communicate information, use computers to process information (*optional*)
**Interpersonal** Participate as a member of a team, teach others, negotiate to arrive at a decision, work with cultural diversity
**Systems** Understand systems
**Technology** Select technology, apply technology to a task, maintain and troubleshoot technology (*optional*)
**Basic Skills** Reading, writing
**Thinking Skills** Think creatively, make decisions, see things in the mind's eye
**Personal Qualities** Responsibility, sociability, self-management
*EFF:* **Communication** Read with understanding, convey ideas in writing, observe critically
**Decision Making** Solve problems and make decisions, plan
**Lifelong Learning** Take responsibility for learning, reflect and evaluate, learn through research, use information and communications technology (*optional*)

## Academic Feature: Research Project

As in other units, students are required to complete a task by conducting research. Options will be given for students to use the Internet as well as printed resource materials. The printed resource materials can be found on the Multilevel Worksheets CD-ROM.

### Introduction                                    5–10 mins.

State the goal: *Today, you will learn how to get financial help if you ever have a consumer issue.*

### Presentation                                    10–15 mins.

**A. The two agencies below are run by the government and can give people financial assistance. Discuss the questions with your classmates and teacher.**

- FDIC (Federal Deposit Insurance Corporation) Consumers and Communities
- FTC (Federal Trade Commission) Consumer Protection

### Practice                                    10–15 mins.

**B. Visit the websites of the agencies in Exercise A to gather more information. Click on the topics you find interesting listed in the consumer section of each site. Write down what you find.**

**C. Another website that has very useful information for consumers is usa.gov/consumer-complaints. Go to the website and order a free copy of the *Consumer Action Handbook*.**

**A.** The two agencies below are run by the government and can give people financial assistance. Discuss the questions with your classmates and teacher.

- FDIC (Federal Deposit Insurance Corporation)
  Consumers and Communities

- FTC (Federal Trade Commission)
  Consumer Protection

1. What does the FDIC do? How can they help?

2. What does the FTC do? How can they help?

**B.** Visit the websites of the agencies in Exercise A to gather more information. Click on the topics you find interesting listed in the consumer section of each site. Write down what you find. Answers may vary.

1. fdic.gov: You can find information about consumer news and information, loans and mortgages, banking and money, financial education and literacy, identify theft and fraud, financial privacy, and community affairs.

2. ftc.gov: You can find information about autos, computers, Internet, credit and loans, diet and health, education and scholarships, job placement, and other consumer concerns.

**C.** Another website that has very useful information for consumers is usa.gov/consumer-complaints. Go to the website and order a free copy of the *Consumer Action Handbook*.

1. The Federal Deposit Insurance Corporation (FDIC) is an independent agency created by Congress that maintains stability and public confidence in the nation's financial system by insuring deposits, examining and supervising financial institutions, and managing receiverships. It can help us by protecting our money in the bank and protecting us from corruption in financial institutions. It is an excellent resource for any information about consumer financial concerns such as loans and consumer news stories.

2. The FTC deals with issues that touch the economic life of every American. It is the only federal agency with both consumer protection and competition jurisdiction in broad sectors of the economy. The FTC pursues vigorous and effective law enforcement; advances consumers' interests by sharing its expertise with federal and state legislatures and U.S. and international government agencies; develops policy and research tools through hearings, workshops, and conferences; and creates practical and plain-language educational programs for consumers and businesses in a global marketplace with constantly changing technologies. It is an excellent educational source for all consumers.

# READING CHALLENGE

## About the Explorer

Ashley Murray is wastewater engineer. She lives in Ghana where her company reuses human waste to make things such as fertilizer and fish food. By turning the waste into usable commodities, Ashley is able to make a profit. She puts the money she makes back into the community to improve sanitation in poor neighborhoods.

## About the Photo

The photo shows Ashley next to an open sewage system. Compared to developed countries, underdeveloped countries rarely treat wastewater because it is too costly for the government. Open sewage systems have the potential to cause huge environmental and health problems. Sometimes people can die from water-borne diseases. In order to stop this from happening, Ashley aims to treat the wastewater in the way developed countries would in order to improve the quality of life for people in underdeveloped countries.

- Introduce the explorer, Ashley Murray. Ask students to look at the picture.
- Read the title. Then, ask students what the title means.
- Have a volunteer read the quote out loud. Then, ask students how the quote is related to the title. Discuss as a class.

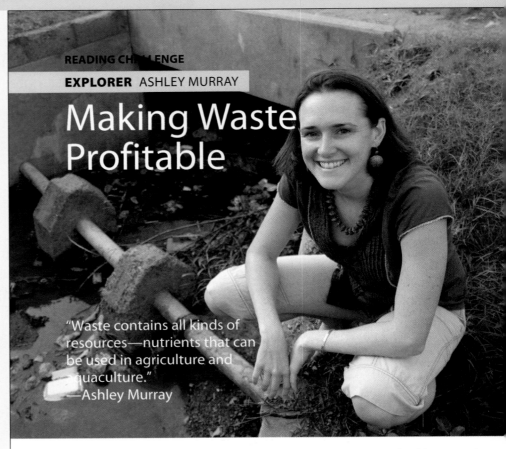

READING CHALLENGE

**EXPLORER** ASHLEY MURRAY

# Making Waste Profitable

"Waste contains all kinds of resources—nutrients that can be used in agriculture and aquaculture."
—Ashley Murray

**A. PREDICT** Read the title and look at the picture. What do you think Ashley Murray's job is? Answers will vary.

**B. Discuss the questions in a small group.** Answers will vary.

1. The article you are going to read is about wastewater. What is wastewater and where does the wastewater go in your community?
2. How can wastewater be reused?
3. Do you pay for the wastewater in your community to be reused?

62 Unit 2

## CCRS FOR READING

RI1, RI2, RI3, RI4, RI5, SL1, SL2

**C.  Read about Ashley Murray.**

What happens to the water that is flushed down our toilets, otherwise known as *wastewater*? In developed countries, the water is treated and can be reused. But in
1 underdeveloped countries, this treatment process is too costly for governments. Ashley Murray is a wastewater engineer who lives in Ghana. She believes, "Any surface water is an  1 open sewage stream. It's hard to overstate the enormous health and environmental impacts
1 of inadequate sanitation." There are over 2.5 billion people in the world with no access to basic sanitation. And "at any given time, half of the hospital beds in the world are filled with people suffering from water-related diseases." And millions of these people die! Ashley wants to solve this problem.

The biggest problem in countries where people have no access to basic sanitation is open sewage drains. This is because the water in those drains has a direct impact on people's health. But the underlying problem is that there is not enough money to do something
1 about it. Households in low-income areas don't have enough money to pay the fees required to treat the waste. And the governments in these countries have more pressing urban challenges than paying to treat the waste. Ashley had to figure out a way to make it an economic benefit for the government to treat and reuse the water.

Ashley set out to prove to the government of Ghana that "waste contains all kinds of resources—nutrients that can be used in agriculture and aquaculture," by starting a company called Waste Enterprises. This company reuses human waste, making things such as fertilizer  4
2 and fish food. It makes a profit from turning the waste into usable commodities and then
3 puts the profit back into the community to improve sanitation in poor neighborhoods.

Ashley's company is also working with researchers to find other uses for wastewater, such as a replacement for oil. She wants to prove that sanitation can be profitable and not a drain on the government's resources. But "the real goal is improving basic sanitation, health, and environmental conditions for some of the world's poorest populations." If she can do this, she hopes other companies will start doing the same, improving sanitation all around the world.

**D.  FIND EVIDENCE** For each question below, find the answer in the article, underline it, and write the question number next to it.

1. What are the problems with wastewater in developing countries?
2. How is Ashley trying to solve the financial problem?
3. How is she trying to solve the sanitation issue?
4. What can be made with wastewater?

**E.  Circle the words or phrases in the article that are new to you. Share with a partner and see if you can infer the meanings.** Answers will vary.

Reading Challenge   63

---

**READING STRATEGIES**

## Inferring Vocabulary

Inferring is a good strategy to use for understanding new vocabulary. When students see an unfamiliar word, they can use clues around the word to get the gist. Looking at how the word is used in the sentence will often tell its meaning. Also, sentences may include synonyms and antonyms which will clue the reader in on a word's meaning.

---

**A.  PREDICT Read the title and look at the picture. What do you think Ashley Murray's job is?**

- Have students look at the picture and the title again.
- Ask students what they think Ashley Murray's job is.
- Discuss students' predictions as a class.

**B.  Discuss the questions in a small group.**

**C.  Read about Ashley Murray.**

Have students read about Ashley Murray.

**D.  FIND EVIDENCE  For each question below, find the answer in the article, underline it, and write the question number next to it.**

- Ask students to find evidence.
- Tell students to read the questions below.
- Ask students to find the answers for each question in the article. Then, underline and write the number next to it.

**E.  Circle the words or phrases in the article that are new to you. Share with a partner and see if you can infer the meanings.**

Ask students to circle new words and phrases in the article. Then, have students share their marked articles and see if they can infer the meanings.

# Automotive Know-How

### About the Photo

Alexander Koerner took this photograph. It shows cars produced by the German carmaker Volkswagen being stored in a tower (silo) close to the factory where they were produced. The towers can be found at the *Autostadt* (Automobile City) in Wolfsburg, Germany. At the Autostadt, visitors can enjoy various attractions: They can go to the museum, watch a movie at one of the two cinemas, and take a tour of the factory. They can even pick up their new cars.

- Introduce the unit by reading the title out loud. Ask students what the title means.

- Have students look at the photo and answer the questions. Discuss answers as a class.

- Ask a volunteer to read the caption out loud. Ask students how it is related to the photo.

- Go over each unit outcome.

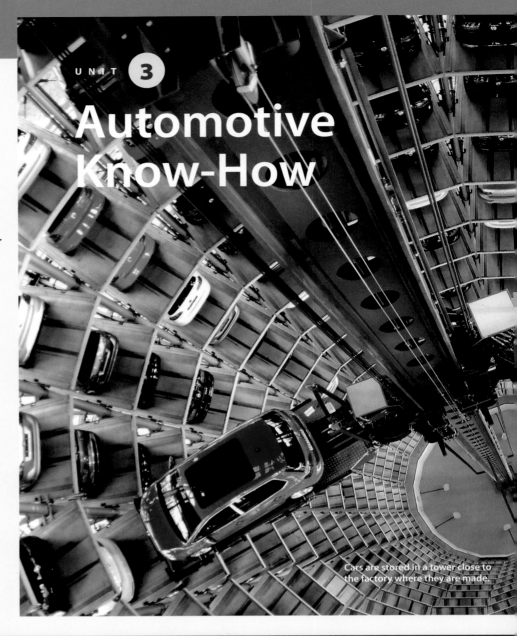

UNIT **3**

# Automotive Know-How

Cars are stored in a tower close to the factory where they are made.

| UNIT OUTCOMES | GRAMMAR | VOCABULARY | EL CIVICS |
|---|---|---|---|
| • Purchase a car<br>• Maintain and repair a car<br>• Interpret an auto insurance policy<br>• Compute mileage and gas consumption<br>• Follow the rules of the road | • Information questions<br>• Imperatives<br>• Compartive and superlative adjectives<br>• Modal with *must*<br>• Present perfect | • Vehicle names: *two-door coupe, four-door sedan, convertible, minivan, sport utility vehicle (SUV), sports car, station wagon, pickup truck, van*<br>• Automotive maintenance actions: *change, check, fill, inspect, perform, replace, top off, change, choose, commute, do, find, imagine, look at*<br>• Insurance terms: *accident coverage, make, premium, bodily injury, incident, model, uninsured motorist, collision, limits of liability, policy number, annual mileage, VIN, length of policy, policy premium*<br>• Vehicle parts: *air filter, alternator, battery, brake fluid reservoir, coolant reservoir, disc brake, distributor, exhaust manifold, fuel injection system* | The skills students learn in this unit can be applied to the following EL Civics competency areas:<br>• Car Insurance<br>• Department of Motor Vehicles<br>• Laws<br>• Signs<br>• Transportation |

## Life Skills Link

In this unit, students will immerse themselves in bumper-to-bumper knowledge of automobiles.
In addition to identifying parts of cars, both inside and out, students will learn about considerations when purchasing a car, financing and insurance, and responsible maintenance and safe operations of a motor vehicle. Special topics include gas and mileage, road signs, and safety belt usage.

## Workplace Link

All lessons and units in *Stand Out* include basic communication skills and interpersonal skills important for the workplace. They are not individually identified. Other workplace skills are indicated. They include *collecting and organizing information, making decisions and solving problems,* and *combining ideas and information.*

**UNIT OUTCOMES**

- Purchase a car
- Maintain and repair a car
- Interpret an auto insurance policy
- Compute mileage and gas consumption
- Follow the rules of the road

**Look at the photo and answer the questions.**

1. What different types of cars can you see?
2. Are the cars new or old? How can you tell?

| CASAS | SCANS | CCRS |
|---|---|---|
| Vocabulary Builder: 7.4.5 | Many SCANS skills are incorporated in this unit with an emphasis on: | RI1, RI4, RI7, RI10, W2, W4, W5, W6, W7, W8, SL1, SL2, SL3, SL4, SL6, L3 |
| Lesson 1: 1.9.5 | • Mathematics | |
| Lesson 2: 1.9.6 | • Reading | |
| Lesson 3: 1.9.8 | • Writing | |
| Lesson 4: 1.9.3 | • Listening | |
| Lesson 5: 1.9.2 | • Negotiation | |
| Review: 7.2.1 | • Decision making | |
| Research: 4.9.3, 7.2.1, 7.4.4, 7.4.5, 7.4.6 | | |
| Team Project: 4.8.1, 4.8.5, 4.8.6 | | |

# Vocabulary Builder

**A.** Look at the different types of cars below. Use the terms in Exercise B to label them.

four-door sedan

pickup truck

minivan

station wagon

SUV

convertible

sports car

van

two-door coupe

**B.** How would you describe each car? Write your ideas next to each term below.

Answers will vary.

1. two-door coupe: _only two doors but has a back seat_

2. four-door sedan: _four doors for front and back seats_

3. convertible: _the roof is flexible and can be fully opened_

4. minivan: _a van with many passenger seats and windows_

5. sport utility vehicle (SUV): _a vehicle for driving on rough terrain_

6. sports car: _a car with two doors usually built for speed and handling_

7. station wagon: _a sedan with space in rear for more goods_

8. pickup truck: _generally a two-seated truck with an open rear area_

9. van: _a large vehicle for transporting people or goods_

**Goal:** Introduce new vocabulary

**Academic Strategies:** Identifying and defining vocabulary, finding synonyms

**Vocabulary:** See lesson

## Agenda

- Describe different types of cars.
- Work with synonyms.

## Resources

**Dictionaries:** It is recommended that each student in class have an ESL learner's dictionary or that there be dictionaries available in the classroom for students to use. Dictionaries that will be referred to in this book are the *Heinle's Newbury House Dictionary of American English* and the *Collins Cobuild Intermediate* or *Advanced Dictionary of American English*.

## Pacing

- ■ 1.5 hour classes
- ■ 2.5 hour classes
- ■ 3+ hour classes

## STANDARDS CORRELATIONS

*CCRS:* RI4, SL1

*CASAS:* 7.4.5

*SCANS:* **Information** Acquire and evaluate information, organize and maintain information

**Interpersonal** Participate as a member of a team, negotiate to arrive at a decision, work with cultural diversity

**Systems** Understand systems, monitor and correct performance

**Basic Skills** Reading, writing, listening, speaking

**Thinking Skills** Think creatively, make decisions, see things in the mind's eye

**Personal Qualities** Responsibility, sociability, self-management

*EFF:* **Communication** Read with understanding, convey ideas in writing, speak so others can understand, listen actively

**Decision Making** Use math to solve problems and communicate, solve problems and make decisions, plan

**Interpersonal** Cooperate with others

**Lifelong Learning** Take responsibility for learning, reflect and evaluate, learn through research

## Academic Feature: Vocabulary Builder

Each unit will begin with a vocabulary-building section. The purpose of this two-page section is to introduce students to many of the words they will be using in the unit lessons. Students will have a chance to see how much they already know, and they will get exposure to the new vocabulary found in the unit.

**Note:** All of the exercises on these two pages should be done in class, no matter the class length. Longer classes can do this lesson and then move onto Lesson 1 during the same class meeting; shorter classes may have to devote one whole class meeting to this section.

### Introduction                    5–10 mins. ■■■

Ask how many students have a car. Find out how many students know how to drive. Ask a few students what kind of car they drive. (If you live in a community where most students don't drive cars, ask them if they had cars in their countries.)

State the goal: *Today, we will be identifying and working with the vocabulary you will learn in this unit.*

### Presentation 1                    5–10 mins. ■■■

**A. Look at the different types of cars below. Use the terms in Exercise B to label them.**

Have students take note of the size, shape, number of doors, and whether or not the vehicles have a roof. Then, go over the vocabulary words in Exercise B. Model the correct pronunciation for each word.

### Practice 1                    10–15 mins. ■■■

**B. How would you describe each car? Write your ideas next to each term below.**

### Evaluation 1                    5–10 mins. ■■■

Go over the answers as a class.

## Presentation 2          5 mins. ■■

Remind students what a *synonym* is. (*Two or more words having the same or nearly the same meaning.*) Ask them to give you some examples of synonyms.

## Practice 2          10–15 mins. ■■

C. **Below are some words and phrases that you will find in this unit. Replace each verb in bold with a synonym from the box. Some words can be used more than once.**

## Evaluation 2          10–15 mins. ■■

Go over the answers as a class.

## Presentation 3          5 mins. ■■■

D. **What do the following words have in common? Write the theme below.**

Read the list of words out loud and ask students to guess what the theme is.

### PRONUNCIATION

#### Vocabulary

When teaching students new vocabulary, pronounce each word for them several times and ask them to repeat it. Often, students may be familiar with the words you are introducing but have never seen them spelled out. By pronouncing the words for students, you allow students to make a connection between the words' spellings and their sounds. It is also important that students learn the correct pronunciation of new words so they feel comfortable using their new vocabulary inside and outside of the classroom.

## Practice 3          10–15 mins. ■

E. **FIND OUT  Check (✓) the terms you know in Exercise D. Circle the ones you don't know. Walk around the classroom and talk to your classmates. Find people who know the terms you have circled.**

## Evaluation 3

Walk around the classroom and observe students. It is not important for them to understand all of the words because they will be working with the words again in this unit.

### INSTRUCTOR'S NOTES

_____

_____

_____

_____

_____

_____

_____

_____

_____

_____

_____

_____

_____

_____

_____

_____

_____

_____

_____

_____

_____

_____

_____

_____

_____

_____

_____

_____

WORKPLACE CONNECTION
Exercises C, D: Complete tasks as assigned.
Exercise E: Interact appropriately with team members.

**C.** Below are some words and phrases that you will find in this unit. Replace each verb in bold with a synonym from the box. Some words can be used more than once.

| change | do | look at |
| choose | find | replace |
| commute | imagine | fill up |

1. _____Replace_____ **Change** your air filter.
2. _____Look at_____ **Check** your oil levels.
3. _____Commute_____ **Drive** during off-peak hours.
4. _____Look at_____ **Inspect** your brakes.
5. _____Find_____ **Look for** telecommuting opportunities.
6. _____Do_____ **Perform** an oil change.
7. _____Choose_____ **Pick** your lane and stick with it.
8. _____Imagine_____ **Pretend** you have a hybrid.
9. _____Change_____ **Replace** your wipers.
10. _____Fill up_____ **Top off** your washer fluid.

**D.** What do the following words have in common? Write the theme below.

Theme: _Information for car insurance_          Answers will vary.

| _____ accident | _____ coverage | _____ make | _____ premium |
| _____ bodily injury | _____ incident | _____ model | _____ uninsured motorist |
| _____ collision | _____ limits of liability | _____ policy | _____ VIN |

**E.** **FIND OUT** Check (✓) the terms you know in Exercise D. Circle the ones you don't know. Walk around the classroom and talk to your classmates. Find people who know the terms you have circled. Answers will vary.

GOAL ■ Purchase a car

WORKPLACE CONNECTION
Exercise A: Interact appropriately with team members.
Exercise B: Collect and organize information.

**A. In a group, discuss the following questions.** Answers will vary.

1. Which type of car do you have? (If you don't have a car, think of someone you know who does.)

2. What is the car like? (Ask about color, size, make, model, etc.)

3. How did you get the car?

4. How long have you had the car?

**B. Listen to an auto salesman who is trying to sell you a car. Take notes on what he says about the different types of cars.**

CD TR 14

| Vehicle | | Best for | Pros | Cons |
|---|---|---|---|---|
| sedan | | **most people** | secure trunk, easy entry, comfortable | ———— |
| 2-dr coupe | | single adults, childless couples | hatchback allows large items to be transported short distances | **backseats are hard to access** |
| station wagon | | **active family** | stable, good gas mileage, low insurance rates, large interiors | ———— |
| convertible | | two people | **great in good weather** | not great in bad weather |
| sports | | travel, weekend racing | cool, fun to drive | impractical for daily transport, need garage, expensive insurance |
| mini van | | families or cargo | handles like a car, good visibility | can't tow heavy loads |
| suv | | off-road usage | handles well | gas guzzler |
| pickup | | towing/hauling heavy loads | now offers more seating; tows heavy weights | doesn't handle well in snow/ice, low gas mileage |
| van | | transporting a lot of people | can carry up to 15 people, can tow heavy loads | ———— |

## AT-A-GLANCE PREP

**Goal:** Purchase a car
**Grammar:** Information questions
**Academic Strategies:** Focused listening, note taking
**Vocabulary:** *two-door coupe, four-door sedan, station wagon, convertible, sports car, minivan, SUV, pickup truck, van*

### Agenda

- Listen to a car salesman.
- Brainstorm ways to research different types of cars.
- Listen to ways Rachel researched cars.
- Create a car purchase plan.

### Resources

**Multilevel Worksheets:** Unit 3, Lesson 1, Worksheets 1–2
**Workbook:** Unit 3, Lesson 1
**Audio:** CD Tracks 14 and 15
**Suggested Realia:** Newspaper with ads for cars, copies of *Autotrader*-style journals
**Stand Out Assessment CD-ROM with ExamView®**

### Pacing

- 1.5 hour classes
- 2.5 hour classes
- 3+ hour classes

## STANDARDS CORRELATIONS

*CCRS:* W4, W7, W8, SL1, SL2
*CASAS:* 1.9.5
*SCANS:* **Information** Acquire and evaluate information, organize and maintain information, interpret and communicate information
**Interpersonal** Participate as a member of a team, negotiate to arrive at a decision, work with cultural diversity
**Systems** Monitor and correct performance
**Technology** Apply technology to a task *(optional)*
**Basic Skills** Reading, writing, listening, speaking
**Thinking Skills** Think creatively, make decisions
**Personal Qualities** Sociability, self-management
*EFF:* **Communication** Convey ideas in writing, speak so others can understand, listen actively
**Decision Making** Solve problems and make decisions, plan
**Interpersonal** Cooperate with others
**Lifelong Learning** Learn through research, use information and communications technology *(optional)*

## Pre-assessment *(optional)*

Use the Stand Out Assessment CD-ROM with ExamView® to create a pre-test for Unit 3.

## Warm-up and Review    5–10 mins.

Write *Transportation* on the board. As a class, brainstorm different types of transportation. Then, take a class poll to see how many people use each type of transportation the most.

## Introduction    5–10 mins.

Dictation:

1. If you want to go fast and have fun, you should drive a sports car.
2. Almost all of the families I know drive SUVs or minivans.
3. Her husband has to drive a pickup truck because of all the stuff he has to move back and forth.
4. When I was a child, my mom drove us around in a station wagon.

State the goal: *Today, we will learn more about different types of cars and create a purchase plan for buying a car.*

## Presentation 1    10–15 mins.

### A. In a group, discuss the following questions.

Have students go around in a circle and answer each question. Then, ask for some volunteers to report what they learned from their classmates.

Go over the chart in Exercise B with students and ask them what they will be listening for. Go over the examples in the chart and ask them to guess what they might fill in for some of the boxes: *What kind of person do you think a sports car would be best for? What are the advantages of a minivan?*

## Practice 1    10–15 mins.

### B. Listen to an auto salesman who is trying to sell you a car. Take notes on what he says about the different types of cars.

**Note:** The listening script is on page 69a.

## Evaluation 1    5 mins.

Go over the answers as a class. Evaluation 1 is continued on the next page.

## LISTENING SCRIPT

🎧
CD
TR 14

**Car Salesman:** Well, since you don't know what kind of car you are looking for, let me tell you about all the different types of vehicle on the market. Then, you can decide which one will be best for you.

First, let's talk about the **four-door sedans**. Sedans are a good choice for most automobile shoppers. The enclosed trunk offers security, while the rear doors allow easy entry for rear-seat passengers. Most luxury vehicles are four-door sedans because they're more comfortable than most other body styles. A smaller car is a **two-door coupe**. Coupes are usually driven by single adults or childless couples. Many two-door coupes have a hatchback instead of a trunk to allow large items to be carried for short distances. The rear seats are difficult to access, as the front doors must be used.

A larger car is a **station wagon**. An active family will want to look at minivans, sport-utility vehicles, or station wagons. In most of the world, station wagons remain the first choice for active families. Station wagons offer the most stability, the best gas mileage, the lowest insurance rates, as well as large interiors. You won't lose your all-wheel drive either, as Subaru, Volkswagen, Audi, Volvo, and Mercedes-Benz offer all-wheel drive on all of their wagons.

Now, Let's talk about a fun car—the **convertible**. Most convertibles are sports cars, meaning two seats, high-performance engines, and superior handling. However, GM, Ford, Mitsubishi, and Chrysler offer a few "normal" convertibles—regular production coupes with four seats and convertible tops, such as the Chevrolet Cavalier, Pontiac Sunfire, Ford Mustang, Dodge Avenger, Chrysler Conquest, and Mitsubishi Eclipse Spyder. Luxury convertibles are available from BMW, Mercedes-Benz, Saab, and Volvo. Convertibles are great when the weather's perfect, but their drawbacks are obvious.

Here are some even more fun (and more expensive) sports cars. **Sports cars** were originally European two-seat roadsters designed for both daily travel and weekend racing. The term sports sedan is a more recent term to describe a four-door vehicle that handles like a sports coupe or roadster. Recently, we've seen luxury cars advertised as luxury sports sedans. Sports cars are cool and fun to drive, though impractical for daily transportation. You'll need a garage to store them in and a second mortgage to pay for their insurance. But if you've got money to burn, go for it!

Then there's the **minivan**. If you're constantly carting kids or cargo, a minivan may be your best choice. Most new models offer an additional fourth door on the driver's side as well as comfortable seating for seven. Minivans drive and handle just like a car, with the bonus of better visibility due to a higher center of gravity and an upright driving position. Don't look for minivans to handle your boat- or trailer-towing duties, as front wheel drive vehicles have a very limited towing capacity.

One of the most popular cars out there right now is the **sport-utility vehicle** or **SUV**. Although SUVs were designed for off-road usage, 98% of them never leave the road, fortunately for our wilderness. If a wagon isn't for you, the car-like SUVs ride and handle significantly better than the rest.

Unfortunately, they guzzle a lot of gas so you may want to think twice before buying one.

My personal favorite is the **pickup truck**. More new pickup trucks are sold in this country than any other type of vehicle. The smaller models now offer quad, or crew-cab four-door versions, with seating for five adults. Full-size models offer extended cabs with smaller third and fourth doors, giving access to the rear seats. Standard rear-wheel drive versions don't handle well on snow or ice without a substantial amount of weight in the rear of the truck. When equipped with towing packages with eight- or ten-cylinder engines, these rear-wheel drive vehicles can tow large boats and trailers. Full-size, two-wheel, and four-wheel drive pickups get about 15 miles per gallon.

A little less common, but necessary if you're transporting a lot of people, is the **van**. If you transport large amounts of cargo or need room for more than seven adults, a full-size van is your only option. They're available with and without windows and in payload capacities of over one ton. Extended vans can seat up to 15 adult passengers. Towing packages with eight- or ten-cylinder engines will allow these rear-wheel-drive vehicles to tow large boats and trailers.

(Source: www.safecarguide.com, 2002–2003. All rights reserved.)

## Evaluation 1 *(continued)*

**C.** IMAGINE  **You are going to buy a new or used car. Look back at the table in Exercise B. Which type of car would be best for you? Why?**

## Presentation 2
10–15 mins. ■■■

**D.** GENERATE  **Now that you have an idea which car is best for you based on the salesman's descriptions, it is a good idea to do some research on your own. What are the best ways to find out more about the car you want to buy? In a group, brainstorm ways to research different car models.**

After students brainstorm in groups, have them call out some of their ideas and make a list on the board.

Prepare students for Exercise E by reading the instructions. Point out that they will probably hear some of the same ideas they have just brainstormed.

## Practice 2
10–15 mins. ■■

**E.** **Rachel has decided to buy a two-door coupe. Listen and write what she did to research buying her car.**

**Note:** The listening script is on page 70a.

WORKPLACE CONNECTION
Exercises C, E: Interpret and communicate information.
Exercise D: Interact appropriately with team members.

**C.** **IMAGINE** **You are going to buy a new or used car. Look back at the table in Exercise B. Which type of car would be best for you? Why?** Answers will vary.

_____

_____

**D.** **GENERATE** **Now that you have an idea which car is best for you based on the salesman's descriptions, it is a good idea to do some research on your own. What are the best ways to find out more about the car you want to buy? In a group, brainstorm ways to research different car models.** Answers will vary.

Talk to people who own the same car.

Drive one at a dealer's.

Look online for reviews of the car.

Buy a consumer magazine about the car.

Ask your mechanic about the car's reputation.

Go to the manufacturer's website.

Talk to a dealer.

Make a list of questions before you go.

_____

_____

_____

_____

**E.** **Rachel has decided to buy a two-door coupe. Listen and write what she did to research buying her car.**

CD
TR 15

1. made a list of all 2-door coupes for sale

2. called family and friends to discuss their cars

3. went to dealerships to test-drive cars

4. did Internet research for best prices

5. looked in the newspaper and Auto Trading booklet

6. test drove and brought her mechanic to look

WORKPLACE CONNECTION
Exercise F: Complete tasks as assigned; Collect and organize information; Interact appropriately with team members.
Exercise G: Combine ideas and information.

**F.** **To supplement your research, ask a variety of people for their opinions about cars. What are some questions you might ask? With a partner, create a list of questions.**

*Answers will vary.*

### Friends and family

1. What do you love about your car?

2. What do you dislike about your car?

3. What repairs have you made to the car?

### Car dealer

1. Which cars do you have in my price range?

2. Which cars get the best mileage?

3. Which cars handle well in snow?

### Mechanic

1. Which cars are reliable?

2. Which cars rarely come in for repairs?

3. Which cars last for many years?

### Loan officer

1. What are the best interest rates?

2. How much down payment do you expect?

3. How much is it to lease a car versus buying?

**G.** **CREATE** **Make a plan to purchase a car. Write the steps you will take in the plan below.**

*Answers will vary.*

Step 1: Make a list of cars and prices I like.

Step 2: Talk to my mechanic, my friends, and dealers.
Do research online and in newspapers.

Step 3: Test-drive and think about what I don't like.
Have mechanic check car out.

## LISTENING SCRIPT

CD
TR 15

**Rachel:** *So, I finally decided that I want a two-door coupe. I think it will be the most economical for me because I am usually just driving myself places. The first thing I did was make a list of all the two-door coupes for sale. Wow, there were a lot! Then, I called all my friends and family who own coupes and asked them which cars they had. I asked them what they liked and didn't like about their cars. Once I narrowed down my list, I went out to car dealerships two weekends in a row to test-drive cars. That really helped me decide which ones I liked. At that point, there were really only two cars that I liked. So, I went home and did some Internet research to find out where I could get the best prices. I also looked in the newspaper and the Auto Trading booklet to see what used cars might be available. I realized that I was going to get a lot more for my money if I bought a used car, and it seemed like the Auto Trading booklet had some pretty good deals. So, I called up a few people to test-drive their cars. I fell in love with one of them and brought my mechanic with me to take a look. He agreed that it was in great shape and a good price. Sold! I had my new car.*

## Evaluation 2                    10–15 mins. ■■

Have students compare the list on the board to the list in Exercise E. What are the similarities and differences? Ask them to put a check next to each step in Exercise E that they have done when looking for a car.

## Presentation 3                  5–10 mins. ■■■

Ask students who the different people Rachel talked to were. Make a list. The list should include friends, family, car salesmen, car owners, and mechanic. Ask them if there's anyone else she could have talked to. You might suggest a loan officer. Ask them to come up with some questions they might ask each of these people if they were going to buy a car. Write one or two examples on the board.

## Practice 3                      15–20 mins. ■

(Shorter classes can do this exercise for homework.)

**F.  To supplement your research, ask a variety of people for their opinions about cars. What are some questions you might ask? With a partner, create a list of questions.**

## Evaluation 3                    5–10 mins. ■

Go over the questions that students came up with.

**Refer students to *Stand Out 5 Workbook,* Unit 3, Lesson 1 for more practice with *yes/no* and information questions.**

**Go to the *Activity Bank* online for suggestions on promoting digital literacy and using the Internet to enhance this lesson.**

## Application                     10–20 mins. ■■■

**G.  CREATE  Make a plan to purchase a car. Write the steps you will take in the plan below.**

Tell students they will be creating a plan of how they would go about purchasing a car. Remind them that a plan will need to include the steps they will take, a possible timeline, and any other information they think is necessary to the plan.

(On the Multilevel Worksheets, there is a sample plan that you might want to show students as well as a blank template for them to fill in.)

### INTERNET RESEARCH (*optional*)

Have students go to an auto-trading website or do a search using the phrase *cars for sale.* Have them find some ads for cars they might like. Have students print out examples of ads that impress them and ads that provide little information.

### MULTILEVEL WORKSHEETS

Unit 3, Lesson 1, Worksheet 1: Car Ad Practice: Questions

Unit 3, Lesson 1, Worksheet 2: Car Buying Plan: Sample and Template

### INSTRUCTOR'S NOTES

_____

_____

_____

_____

_____

_____

_____

_____

## AT-A-GLANCE PREP

**Goals:** Maintain and repair a car
**Academic Strategies:** Reading, outlining, summary writing
**Vocabulary:** Car parts

### Agenda

☐ Identify car parts and their purpose.
☐ Learn how to maintain and repair your car.

### Resources

**Multilevel Worksheet:** Unit 3, Lesson 2, Worksheet 1
**Workbook:** Unit 3, Lesson 2

### Pacing

■ 1.5 hour classes   ■ 2.5 hour classes
■ 3+ hour classes

## STANDARDS CORRELATIONS

*CCRS:* RI1, RI4, RI7, RI10, W2, W4, W5, L3
*CASAS:* 1.9.6
*SCANS:* **Information** Acquire and evaluate information, organize and maintain information, interpret and communicate information
**Interpersonal** Participate as a member of a team, teach others, exercise leadership, negotiate to arrive at a decision, work with cultural diversity
**Systems** Understand systems, monitor and correct performance, improve and design systems
**Technology** Apply technology to a task *(optional)*
**Basic Skills** Reading, writing, speaking
**Thinking Skills** Think creatively, make decisions, see things in the mind's eye
**Personal Qualities** Sociability, self-management
*EFF:* **Communication** Read with understanding, convey ideas in writing
**Decision Making** Plan
**Interpersonal** Cooperate with others
**Lifelong Learning** Take responsibility for learning, learn through research, use information and communications technology *(optional)*

## Warm-up and Review    5–10 mins. ■■■

Have students take out their purchase plans from the previous lesson and share them with a partner. Ask volunteers to come to the front of the classroom and share their plans with the class.

## Introduction    5–10 mins. ■■■

Dictation:

1. Maintaining your car will extend its life.
2. Finding a good mechanic may take you a long time.
3. Learning how to repair your car can be rewarding.
4. The more you know about your car, the better off you will be.

State the goal: *Today, we will identify different auto parts and learn about auto maintenance and repair.*

## Presentation 1    10–15 mins. ■■■

A. **With help from your teacher, identify the auto parts below. Write the name of each part in the corresponding box.**

## Practice 1    10–15 mins. ■■■

B. **DEFINE What is the purpose of each auto part in Exercise A? Work with a partner and use a dictionary to define each part on a separate sheet of paper. Share your answers with other pairs.**

Tell students that their classmates can be a helpful resource, as well as the dictionary or Internet. If you have access to computers in your classroom, let students use the Internet as a resource. If students own cars, have them bring in their vehicle owner's manuals to share. Encourage students to compare location of car parts from the diagrams of their cars. Ask: *Are all parts located in the same place?*

## Evaluation 1    5 mins. ■■■

Go over the answers as a class.

**Note:** There is a teaching resource that describes car part functions on page 72a.

# LESSON ② Maintenance and repair

GOAL ■ Maintain and repair a car

WORKPLACE CONNECTION
Exercise A: Complete tasks as assigned.
Exercise B: Interact appropriately with team members.

**A.** With help from your teacher, identify the auto parts below. Write the name of each part in the corresponding box.

| | | |
|---|---|---|
| air filter | distributor | radiator |
| alternator | exhaust manifold | rear axle |
| battery | fuel injection system | rear suspension |
| brake fluid reservoir | muffler | timing belt |
| coolant reservoir | power steering reservoir | water pump |
| disc brake | | |

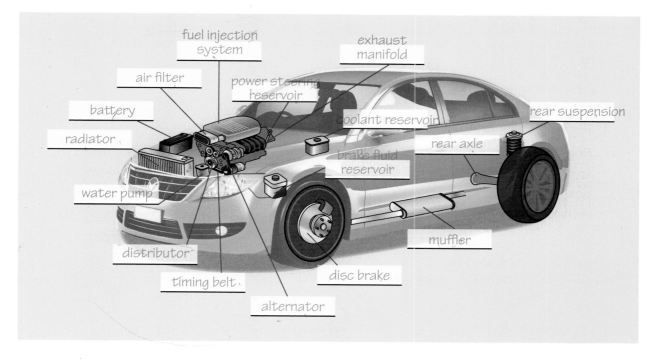

**B.** **DEFINE** What is the purpose of each auto part in Exercise A? Work with a partner and use a dictionary to define each part on a separate sheet of paper. Share your answers with other pairs. Answers will vary.

**C.** Now that you are more familiar with auto parts and their importance, read this excerpt from an auto maintenance and repair guide.

### How to Maintain Your Automobile

**Change your air filter.** A clogged air filter can affect your gas mileage as well as the performance of your engine. Change it on a regular basis.

**Check your oil levels.** Your engine needs a certain amount of oil to run properly, so it's important to check the oil levels regularly.

**Perform an oil change.** As your engine uses oil, the oil becomes dirty and should be changed at regular intervals.

**Perform a timing belt inspection.** A faulty timing belt can result in bent valves and other expensive engine damage. Check it at least every 10,000 miles, and replace it when the manufacturer recommends doing so.

**Replace your wipers.** Windshield wipers can wear out, and if they aren't working properly, they could impair your vision while on the road. Change them at least twice a year.

**Perform a radiator flush.** It's important to keep your radiator and cooling system clean.

**Check your power steering fluid.** Check your power steering fluid regularly to make sure your power steering doesn't fail.

**Inspect your brakes.** Protect yourself and your passengers by inspecting your brakes twice a year.

**Check and fill your coolant.** If your car is low on coolant, it will run hot, so make sure to check the coolant level in your radiator.

**Check and replace your spark plugs.** A faulty spark plug could cause poor gas mileage and/or a rough running engine and poor acceleration. Make sure to replace the spark plugs as recommended by your car's manual.

**Top off your washer fluid.** Make sure you have enough washer fluid so you can keep your windshield clean.

**Check your wheel bolts.** Check the tightness of your wheel bolts on a regular basis to make sure there is no danger of your wheels becoming loose.

**D.** **INTERPRET** With a partner, answer the following questions on a separate piece of paper.

1. What fluids need to be regularly checked? *oil, power steering fluid, coolant, and washer fluid*

2. Why is it important to replace windshield wipers? *Poorly performing wipers could impair driver vision on the road.*

3. Why is it bad to have a clogged air filter? *It will affect gas mileage and performance of the engine.*

4. Why should you inspect your timing belt? *A faulty belt can result in bent valves and other engine damage.*

5. Why should you check your wheel bolts? *Loose bolts might result in wheels becoming loose.*

6. What could happen if you don't have enough power steering fluid? *Power steering might fail.*

## Presentation 2

**C. Now that you are more familiar with auto parts and their importance, read this excerpt from an auto maintenance and repair guide.**

## Practice 2

10–15 mins. ■■

(Shorter classes can do these exercises for homework.)

**D. INTERPRET  With a partner, answer the following questions on a separate piece of paper.**

## Evaluation 2

5–10 mins. ■■

Go over the answers as a class.

### TEACHING RESOURCE

## Car parts

**Air cleaner/filter:** Air is drawn through it. Contains a filter that blocks dirt before it can enter the engine.

**Alternator:** Takes over from the battery when the engine is running. Recharges the battery and supplies power to all electrical components.

**Battery:** Supplies the initial electrical power that starts the engine.

**Carburetor:** Most new cars now have fuel injected engines. Older vehicles have carburetors. This gadget mixes air and fuel in the proper ratio for burning in the engine's combustion chambers.

**Coolant reservoir (tank):** Holds hot coolant (antifreeze) that overflows from the radiator and also draws it back into the radiator as it is needed.

**Distributor:** Distributes high voltage electricity to the spark plugs, one at a time.

**Exhaust manifold:** Set of pipes, one for each cylinder, that conducts exhaust away from cylinders.

**Fuel injection system:** Sprays controlled amount of fuel directly into either the intake manifold or combustion chambers, resulting in a very precise air-to-fuel ratio that improves fuel economy.

**Muffler:** The interior "baffles" and tubes quiet the explosive release of exhaust.

**Suspension system:** This system receives a great deal of punishment from the roads. This system consists of shock absorbers, struts, springs, motor mounts, tires, tie rods, ball joints, control arms, torsion bar, strut rods, the spindle, and axles.

**Power steering reservoir:** This reservoir contains fluid for your power steering system. Once the reservoir cap is unscrewed, the cap will consist of a dipstick. This will identify the fluid levels.

**Brake fluid reservoir:** The brake fluid level can be inspected by the plastic box or bottle by the firewall on the driver side.

**Disc brakes:** A metal disk that spins with the wheel that the brake pad uses to pressure against to stop.

**Oil dipstick:** The stick that's used to check the level of the motor oil.

**Rear axle:** A shaft that connects the power from the transmission to the wheels.

**Radiator:** The device that helps to remove heat from the cooling system as coolant passes through it.

**Timing belt:** The timing belt is a rubber belt that drives the engine's internal components. The timing belt is not easily visible and should be replaced at the indicated mileage and time, not on visual wear like a normal drive belt. If the timing belt breaks, the engine stops and costly internal engine damage can occur. The water pump on some vehicles is driven by the timing belt and should be replaced with the timing belt replacement.

(Source: www.mycargirl.com. Used by permission.)

### INSTRUCTOR'S NOTES

_____

_____

_____

_____

_____

_____

_____

_____

_____

_____

## Presentation 3

**E. Some people can perform their own maintenance while others need the help of trained professionals. Who will do your car repairs? If you need help, how will you find a reliable mechanic? Read the guide below.**

Have students read the guide silently to themselves. When they have finished, go over any questions they have.

## Practice 3

10–15 mins. ■

(Shorter classes can do this exercise for homework.)

Ask students to close their books. Then, read them the instructions for Exercise F.

**F. Take out a piece of paper and write the numbers *1* to *10*. Close your books and see how many suggestions from Exercise E you can remember. Write them down.**

## Evaluation 3

5–10 mins. ■

Let students open their books and see how many they got right.

## Application

10–25 mins. ■■■

**G. Make an outline for the guides in Exercises C and E.**

**H. SUMMARIZE Using your outlines, write a two-paragraph summary of what you have learned in this lesson. Remember to format your paragraph correctly.**

Have students share their paragraphs with a partner. Students should check that they understand each other's sentences and that the writing is clear.

### MULTILEVEL WORKSHEET

Unit 3, Lesson 2, Worksheet 1: Auto Maintenance and Repair

**Refer students to *Stand Out 5 Workbook,* Unit 3, Lesson 2 for more practice with information question words and answers.**

**Go to the *Activity Bank* online for suggestions on promoting digital literacy and using the Internet to enhance this lesson.**

## INSTRUCTOR'S NOTES

WORKPLACE CONNECTION
Exercises E, F: Complete tasks as assigned.
Exercise G: Collect and organize information.
Exercise H: Combine ideas and information.

**E.** Some people can perform their own maintenance while others need the help of trained professionals. Who will do your car repairs? If you need help, how will you find a reliable mechanic? Read the guide below.

### Guide to Getting Repairs Done

1. Ask a friend, relative, or coworker for recommendations when looking for a good auto shop or mechanic. Also, take time to find a local garage that you feel comfortable with.
2. Make a list of services you need performed or the symptoms your vehicle is experiencing so there is no misunderstanding.
3. Get more than one opinion about the repairs that need to be done.
4. Ask for a written estimate before the job is started.
5. Get more than one estimate and compare prices.
6. Ask about the warranty policy.
7. Have the mechanic show you what you need replaced and have him or her explain why you need to replace it.
8. Go for a test drive in your car before paying for the repairs. If something is not right with the repairs, make it understood that you are not happy. Do not pay the bill until the vehicle is repaired properly.
9. Pay with a credit card. Many credit cards offer consumer protection for fraud.
10. If you discover something is not fixed after you've paid and driven home, call the garage and explain the situation. Go back to the garage as soon as possible.

**F.** Take out a piece of paper and write the numbers *1* to *10*. Close your books and see how many suggestions from Exercise E you can remember. Write them down.

**G.** Make an outline for the guides in Exercises C and E.

**H.** SUMMARIZE Using your outlines, write a two-paragraph summary of what you have learned in this lesson. Remember to format your paragraphs correctly. Answers will vary.

Some people can perform their own maintenance, but it's important to have trained mechanics look at a car.

# LESSON ③ Car insurance

WORKPLACE CONNECTION
Exercises A, B: Interact appropriately with team members.
Exercise C: Complete tasks as assigned.

**A. Discuss these questions with your classmates.** Answers will vary.

1. Do you drive a car or ride a motorbike?
2. Do you have insurance?
3. Why is it important to have auto insurance?
4. Do you understand your insurance policy?
5. Is it against the law in your state to drive without insurance?

**B. Read what each person says about auto insurance policies. Discuss the meanings of the words in italics with a partner.**

"An insurance *policy* is a contract between you and the insurance company that states what the company will pay for in the event of an accident." — **Chalene**

"The insurance *premium* is the amount you pay for auto insurance for a certain period of time." — **Keona**

"*Coverage* is what is included in the insurance—what the company will pay for." — **Binata**

**C. Look at Chalene's policy and find each of the items below.**

### ★ Bright Star Insurance

| Name of Insured and Address: | Policy Number: |
|---|---|
| Chalene Johnson<br>24573 Thatch Street<br>Houston, TX 77042 | 05XX 52 870 1625 Q<br>**Policy Period:**<br>Effective Jan 13, 2017 to Jul 13, 2017 |

| Description of Vehicle(s)<br>Year and Make: 2015 Acurak<br>VIN: QXXPYR18924G23794 | Annual Mileage: 9,000<br>Premium for this Policy Period: $456.40 |
|---|---|

| Coverage | Limits of Liability | Six-Month Premium |
|---|---|---|
| A. Bodily Injury | Each Person $100,000; Each Accident $300,000 | 185.12 |
| B. Collision | Each Accident $50,000 | 170.81 |
| C. Comprehensive | Each Incident $25,000 | 44.83 |
| D. Uninsured Motor Vehicle Bodily Injury | Each Person $50,000; Each Accident $150,000 | 64.64 |
| E. Physical Damage | Deductible $1,000 | |
| | | **TOTAL** $465.40 |

1. Policy number: 05XX 52 870 1625 Q

2. VIN: QXXPYR18924G23794

3. Policy premium: $465.40

4. Annual mileage: 9,000

5. Deductible: $1,000

6. Make of vehicle: Acurak

## AT-A-GLANCE PREP

**Goal:** Interpret an auto insurance policy
**Grammar:** Information questions
**Vocabulary:** *policy, premium, coverage, liability, period, bodily injury, collision, comprehensive, uninsured, VIN*

### Agenda

☐ Learn about auto insurance policies.
☐ Read Chalene's insurance policy.
☐ Learn about different types of coverage.
☐ Interpret Keona's policy.

### Resources

**Multilevel Worksheet:** Unit 3, Lesson 3, Worksheet 1
**Workbook:** Unit 3, Lesson 3
**Suggested Realia:** Sample insurance policies

### Pacing

■ 1.5 hour classes   ■ 2.5 hour classes
■ 3+ hour classes

## STANDARDS CORRELATIONS

*CCRS:* RI1, RI4, RI7, L3
*CASAS:* 1.9.8
*SCANS:* **Information** Acquire and evaluate information, organize and maintain information, interpret and communicate information, use computers to process information
**Interpersonal** Participate as a member of a team, teach others, negotiate to arrive at a decision, work with cultural diversity
**Systems** Monitor and correct performance
**Basic Skills** Reading, writing, listening, speaking
**Thinking Skills** Decision making
**Personal Qualities** Responsibility, sociability, self-management
*EFF:* **Communication** Read with understanding, convey ideas in writing, speak so others can understand, listen actively
**Interpersonal** Cooperate with others, advocate and influence, resolve conflict and negotiate, guide others
**Lifelong Learning** Take responsibility for learning, reflect and evaluate

## Warm-up and Review     5–10 mins. ■■■

### A. Discuss these questions with your classmates.

Discuss the questions as a class. You might take a poll on questions 1, 2, and 4.

## Introduction     5–10 mins. ■■■

Dictation: Five tips to save money on auto insurance:

1. Make sure you get all the discounts you qualify for.
2. Keep your driver's record clean and up-to-date.
3. Adjust your coverage to assume more risk.
4. Drive a low-profile car equipped with certain money-saving safety features.
5. Shop around for a good, low-cost insurance provider.

State the goal: *Today, you will learn how to interpret an auto insurance policy.*

## Presentation 1     10–15 mins. ■■■

### B. Read what each person says about auto insurance policies. Discuss the meanings of the words in italics with a partner.

Talk about the policy as a class and answer any questions students might have.

## Practice 1     10–15 mins. ■■■

### C. Look at Chalene's policy and find each of the items below.

## Evaluation 1     5 mins. ■■■

Go over the answers as a class.

## INSTRUCTOR'S NOTES

_____

_____

_____

_____

_____

_____

_____

## Presentation 2                5–10 mins. ■■■

**D.** **There are different types of coverage listed on insurance policies. Match each type of coverage with what it covers. Write the corresponding letters on the lines.**

**BEST PRACTICE**

### Presentation: Access students' prior knowledge

Students are often already familiar with some of the information that is presented in *Stand Out 5*. When this is the case, you can rely on their prior knowledge and let them teach the class. There are several ways to elicit information from students:

**1.** Ask students to share what they know with a partner.
**2.** Have students write down what they already know.
**3.** Have students share what they know with the class orally or by coming to the board and writing.

Exercise D may resemble a practice exercise, but since it is in the presentation stage, it offers a chance for you to find out what students already know and teach them new concepts at the same time. For this matching exercise, see how much students can complete on their own before you give them the answers. Then, discuss each answer in detail to make sure students understand the different types of coverage.

Read the following scenarios to students and ask them what insurance coverage would apply.

**1.** *Imagine that you were driving to school this morning and someone stopped suddenly in front of you. You ran into their car. No one was hurt, but both cars were damaged. What coverage would apply?* (property damage liability—for the damage to the other car—and collision—for the damage to your car)
**2.** *Imagine that your car was parked in the school parking lot and when you got out of class to go home, you noticed that someone had smashed the passenger door in with their car. What coverage would apply?* (uninsured motorist's property damage)

## Practice 2                10–15 mins. ■■

**E.** **EVALUATE** **With a partner, read each scenario and decide which coverage would apply.**

(Shorter classes can do this exercise for homework.)

### Evaluation 2                10–15 mins. ■■
Go over the answers as a class.

**INSTRUCTOR'S NOTES**

_____
_____
_____
_____
_____
_____
_____
_____
_____
_____
_____
_____
_____
_____
_____
_____
_____
_____

WORKPLACE CONNECTION
Exercise D: Complete tasks as assigned.
Exercise E: Interact appropriately with team members.

**D.** **There are different types of coverage listed on insurance policies. Match each type of coverage with what it covers. Write the corresponding letters on the lines.**

| Coverage | What it covers |
|---|---|
| 1. bodily injury liability __a__ | a. other people's bodily injuries or death for which you are responsible |
| 2. property damage liability __b__ | b. damage to another vehicle or property |
| 3. collision __d__ | c. loss or damage to your vehicle or the vehicle you are driving for an incident other than collision (theft, fire, etc.) |
| 4. medical payments __e__ | d. damage to your vehicle due to an auto accident |
| 5. comprehensive __c__ | e. bodily injuries to you or your passengers caused by the accident |
| 6. uninsured motorist's bodily injury __f__ | f. bodily injury caused by another vehicle without insurance |
| 7. uninsured motorist's property damage __g__ | g. damage caused by another vehicle without insurance |

**E.** **EVALUATE** **With a partner, read each scenario and decide which coverage would apply.**

1. Chalene accidentally ran into a tree and damaged the front end of her car. Which type of

   coverage would apply? _____ collision _____

2. Binata was driving home from school when she hit another car. She had run through a red light, so the accident was her fault. There was no real damage to her car, but she hurt her back and had to go to the chiropractor. Also, there was significant damage to the car she hit.

   Which types of coverage would apply? _medical payments and property damage liability_

3. Keona and his friend Chalene were driving to work when a car hit them from behind. Then, the car drove off without giving them any information. Neither Keona nor Chalene was hurt, but there was damage to Keona's car. Which type of coverage would apply?

   _uninsured motorist's property damage_

4. Keona's car got stolen from the parking lot at a movie theater. Which type of coverage would

   apply? _____ comprehensive _____

WORKPLACE CONNECTION
Exercise F: Complete tasks as assigned.
Exercise G: Interpret and communicate information.

**F.** Look at Chalene's policy in Exercise C. Write a question for each answer.

EXAMPLE: Chalene Johnson: _Who is being insured through this policy?_

1. $170.81: _How much is collision coverage?_

2. $1,000: _What is the deductible?_

3. 05XX 52 870 1625 Q: _What is the policy number?_

4. 2015 Acurak: _What is the year and make of the vehicle?_

5. $465.40: _What is the premium for this policy period?_

6. 9,000: _What is the vehicle's annual mileage?_

**G.** Look at Keona's insurance policy and circle the correct answers.

### United Automobile Association • Dallas, TX

| STATE: TX | NAME AND ADDRESS OF INSURED: |
|---|---|
| POLICY NUMBER: QQP15 26 49L3798 1 | Keona lu |
| POLICY PERIOD: September 5, 2017 to March 5, 2018 | 54 Plover Plaza |
| VEHICLE(S): 2012 Fort Ficus, 2008 Chevnoret Tihoe | Galveston, TX 50472 |

| Limits of Liability | | 6-Month Premium |
|---|---|---|
| **LIABILITY** | | |
| Bodily Injury | Each Person $100,000; Each Accident $300,000 | 98.12 |
| Property Damage | Each Accident $50,000 | 69.07 |
| **UNINSURED MOTORISTS** | | |
| Bodily Injury | Each Person $100,000; Each Accident $300,000 | 27.00 |
| Property Damage | Each Accident $50,000 | 21.45 |
| **PHYSICAL DAMAGE** | | |
| Comprehensive Loss | Deductible $1,000 | 30.92 |
| Collision Loss | Deductible $1,000 | 96.41 |
| | | **TOTAL: $342.97** |

1. How many vehicles are covered by this policy?

   a. 1          (b. 2)          c. 3          d. 4

2. Where does the insured motorist live?

   a. Dallas     b. Lake Tahoe     (c. Galveston)     d. Houston

3. How much is United Automobile Association charging for liability?

   a. $98.12     b. $69.07     c. $21.45     (d. $167.19)

4. What is Keona's deductible for comprehensive loss?

   a. $96.41     b. $30.92     (c. $1,000)     d. $50,000

## Presentation 3
5–10 mins. ■■■

Have students turn back to the auto insurance policy on page 74. Ask them some questions about the policy: *What is the policy period? What vehicle is being insured? What is the six-month premium for collision coverage?* Then, ask volunteers to ask you a different question about the policy.

## Practice 3
10–15 mins. ■

(Shorter classes can do this exercise for homework.)

**F. Look at Chalene's policy in Exercise C. Write a question for each answer.**

Go over the instructions and example with students. Have them complete the exercise by themselves.

## Evaluation 3
10–15 mins. ■

When individual students have finished, have them share their answers with a partner. When everyone has finished, ask volunteers to come to the board and write their questions. It is very likely that students will have written different questions for the same answer. Show them how more than one question can be correct.

## Application
10–20 mins. ■■■

**G. Look at Keona's insurance policy and circle the correct answers.**

### MULTILEVEL WORKSHEET

Unit 3, Lesson 3, Worksheet 1: Auto Insurance Practice

**Refer students to *Stand Out 5 Workbook*, Unit 3, Lesson 3 for more practice with negative questions.**

**Go to the *Activity Bank* online for suggestions on promoting digital literacy and using the Internet to enhance this lesson.**

### INSTRUCTOR'S NOTES

# AT-A-GLANCE PREP

**Goal:** Compute mileage and gas consumption

**Academic Strategies:** Math calculations, focused listening, note taking

**Vocabulary:** *odometer, trip, MPG*

## Agenda

- Discuss ways to drive less.
- Keep track of gas and mileage.
- Calculate miles per gallon (MPG).
- Listen to maintenance tips that help reduce gas consumption.
- Discuss driving habits that save gas.
- Track your own mileage.

## Resources

**Multilevel Worksheets:** Unit 3, Lesson 4, Worksheets 1–3

**Workbook:** Unit 3, Lesson 4

**Audio:** CD Tracks 16–17

## Pacing

- ■ 1.5 hour classes
- ■ 2.5 hour classes
- ■ 3+ hour classes

## STANDARDS CORRELATIONS

*CCRS:* RI1, RI7, SL2

*CASAS:* 1.9.3

*SCANS:* **Information** Acquire and evaluate information

**Interpersonal** Participate as a member of a team, teach others, negotiate to arrive at a decision, work with cultural diversity

**Systems** Monitor and correct performance

**Basic Skills** Reading, writing, arithmetic, listening, speaking

**Thinking Skills** Think creatively, make decisions, solve problems, see things in the mind's eye

**Personal Qualities** Responsibility, sociability, self-management

*EFF:* **Communication** Read with understanding, convey ideas in writing, speak so others can understand, listen actively

**Decision Making** Use math to solve problems and communicate, solve problems and make decisions

**Interpersonal** Cooperate with others, resolve conflict and negotiate, guide others

**Lifelong Learning** Take responsibility for learning, reflect and evaluate

## Warm-up and Review      5–10 mins. ■■■

Put students in small groups and have them make a list of all the expenses associated with owning a car. Make it a game and tell them you want to see which group can come up with the longest list. When groups have finished, make a list of all their ideas on the board.

## Introduction      5–10 mins. ■■■

Dictation:

1. What is the best way to increase your miles per gallon? 2. Where is the cheapest place to buy gas? 3. What maintenance tips can help your fuel efficiency? 4. What driving tips can help you save money on gas?

If you have time, spend some discussion time on these questions. State the goal: *Today, you will learn how to compute mileage and gas consumption.*

## Presentation 1      10–15 mins. ■■■

A. **Read and listen to the conversation between Keona and Chalene.**

LISTENING SCRIPT

CD
TR 16

*The listening script matches the conversation in Exercise A.*

B. **SUGGEST Can you think of some other measures Keona and Chalene can take so they won't have to use their cars so much? Write your ideas below.**

Discuss students' ideas as a class.

## Practice 1      10–15 mins. ■■■

If necessary, help students come up with the calculation and do an example with them to get them started.

C. **Keona wanted to see his gas mileage, so he checked the display in his car. How do you think Keona might calculate his gas mileage in miles per gallon (MPG)? Create a formula and fill in the MPG column in the table.**

Go over the chart as a class, making sure students understand all the vocabulary.

## Evaluation 1      5 mins. ■■■

Go over the answers as a class.

# LESSON (4) Gas and mileage

GOAL  ▮ Compute mileage and gas consumption

WORKPLACE CONNECTION
Exercise B: Complete tasks as assigned;
Combine ideas and information.
Exercise C: Perform basic computations.

🎧 **A. Read and listen to the conversation between Keona and Chalene.**

CD
TR 16

**Keona:** I can't believe the price of gasoline! I've been spending almost $60 just to fill up my tank.

**Chalene:** Same here. I've been trying to figure out how I can use my car less, so I save some money on gas.

**Keona:** Any good ideas?

**Chalene:** Well, I'm going to start carpooling to school two days a week, which should help. And I'm trying to combine my errands, so I only go out once a week.

**Keona:** That sounds good. I think I'm going to look into public transportation. I have a long drive to work, so maybe I can figure out how to take the train into town. I'll have to drive to the station and park, but at least I won't be driving all the way to work.

**Chalene:** That's a great idea!

**B. SUGGEST** **Can you think of some other measures Keona and Chalene can take so they won't have to use their cars so much? Write your ideas below.**

Answers will vary.

walk to school and work, bicycle, suggest working electronically from home to employer

**C. Keona wanted to see his gas mileage, so he checked the display in his car. How do you think Keona might calculate his gas mileage in miles per gallon (MPG)? Create a formula and fill in the MPG column in the table.**

**Formula:** Example: 245 ÷ 13 = 18.85 MPG. Divide miles driven by gallons used.

| Date | Odometer | Trip | Gallons | MPG |
|------|----------|------|---------|-----|
| 8/7 | 12,200 | 245 miles | 13 | 18.85 |
| 8/15 | 12,475 | 275 | 14 | 19.64 |
| 8/24 | 12,760 | 285 | 15 | 19 |
| 9/1 | 13,020 | 260 | 14.5 | 17.93 |

WORKPLACE CONNECTION
Exercise D: Complete tasks as assigned.
Exercise E: Interpret and communicate information.
Exercise F: Perform basic computations.
Exercise G: Combine ideas and information.

**D. In order to improve your gas mileage, you can follow certain maintenance tips. Listen and write the five tips you hear below.**

CD TR 17

1. Get the engine tuned.

2. Keep tires properly inflated.

3. Check your air filter and replace it every 12,000 miles.

4. Use the right motor oil.

5. Don't carry junk in the trunk.

**E. How will each of the tips in Exercise D help? Listen again and write the reasons on the lines below.**

1. Improperly tuned engines hurt gas mileage.

2. Under inflated tires increase resistance and increase gas consumption.

3. If the air filter is clogged, car performance and fuel economy suffer.

4. The engine won't work as efficiently if the incorrect oil is used.

5. Reducing weight of the car increases mileage per gallon.

**F. Keona followed the tips. Look at his log below and calculate the MPG and cost per mile. Did his MPG improve?** Yes.

| Date | Odometer | Trip | Gallons | MPG | Cost per gallon | Cost per mile |
|------|----------|------|---------|-----|-----------------|---------------|
| 10/5 | 14,687 | 275 miles | 13 | 21 | $3.05 | $0.145 |
| 10/17 | 14,962 | 295 | 14 | 21 | $3.07 | $0.146 |
| 10/30 | 15,262 | 300 | 15 | 20 | $2.95 | $0.148 |
| 11/9 | 15,542 | 280 | 14.5 | 19 | $3.10 | $0.163 |

**G. ANALYZE Look at the cost per mile column in Exercise F. Which week was the cheapest? On a separate piece of paper, write ideas about how Keona can spend less per mile on gas.**

In terms of cost per mile, the week of 10/5 was cheapest.
Ideas: Drive more slowly to reduce gas consumption.
　　　Reduce length of trips if possible.

## Presentation 2                    5–10 mins. ■■■

Ask students if they know of any strategies to improve gas mileage. Brainstorm some ideas as a class.

## Practice 2                        10–15 mins. ■■

**D. In order to improve your gas mileage, you can follow certain maintenance tips. Listen and write the five tips you hear below.**

**E. How will each of the tips in Exercise D help? Listen again and write the reasons on the lines below.**

**F. Keona followed the tips. Look at his log below and calculate the MPG and cost per mile. Did his MPG improve?**

See if students can figure out how to calculate the cost per mile on their own.

**G. ANALYZE Look at the cost per mile column in Exercise F. Which week was the cheapest? On a separate piece of paper, write ideas about how Keona can spend less per mile on gas.**

Students can work in pairs or small groups to develop useful ideas for spending less on gas.

## Evaluation 2                      10–15 mins. ■■

As each exercise is completed, go over the answers as a class.

---

### BEST PRACTICE

## How to calculate gas consumption and mileage

Help students calculate gas consumption and mileage by providing the following formulas:

1. Trip Miles / Gallons = Mpg
2. Cost per gallon / Mpg = Cost per mile
3. Odometer = Original odometer reading + trips

---

### LISTENING SCRIPT
CD
TR 17

*Here are five tips that should help improve your gas mileage.*

1. *Get your engine tuned.*
   *An improperly tuned engine hurts gas mileage by an average of 4.1 percent, according to U.S. government studies. Most important to mileage is a properly working oxygen sensor, which helps keep your engine working efficiently.*

2. *Keep your tires properly inflated.*
   *Underinflated tires increase resistance and make it more difficult for the engine to move your car along the road. Check your tires every time you fill the tank. The U.S. Department of Energy estimates the average person can improve their gas mileage by 3.3 percent by inflating their tires regularly.*

3. *Check your air filter and replace it every 12,000 miles. Cars don't just run on gasoline. They actually run on gas and oxygen. If a clogged air filter restricts the flow of air, your performance and your fuel economy suffer. The U.S. Department of Energy estimates that you could save as much as 22 cents per gallon by replacing a bad air filter.*

4. *Use the right motor oil.*
   *Many people think it's OK to simply put any motor oil into their engine. While your motor will continue to work with a different grade of oil, it won't work quite as efficiently. You can save a couple of cents per gallon by using the exact oil recommended for your car.*

5. *Don't carry junk in your trunk.*
   *Get all those newspapers, cans, and other baggage out of your car and trunk. Reducing the weight of the car increases mileage over the course of a tank of gas.*

(Source: www.edmunds.com)

---

### INSTRUCTOR'S NOTES

_____

_____

_____

_____

_____

_____

## Presentation 3

5–10 mins. ■■■

Look at the first tip in Exercise H and ask students what they think it means and why it would help them save money on gas.

## Practice 3

15–20 mins. ■

**H.** Here are some tips on how to change your driving habits in order to save money on gas. In a small group, discuss each tip and figure out what it means.

**Note:** The entire article can be found on the Multilevel Worksheets.

1. **No more drag racing.** Gas is consumed more quickly during hard acceleration, so if you accelerate gradually from a green light, you stand to improve your mileage significantly.
2. **Look farther down the road.** Back off the accelerator if the traffic light two blocks away is red. Glide until you get the green and then accelerate moderately. This not only saves gas but also your brake pads.
3. **Pick your lane and stick with it.** Traffic studies have shown that changing lanes doesn't result in a significantly reduced travel time. It will lower your fuel consumption if you don't surge to switch lanes.
4. **Pretend you're a hybrid.** Most hybrids save gas by automatically shutting off at stoplights. Turn off your engine if you are stopped for a long period of time.
5. **Carpool with classmates or coworkers.** You can use the carpool lanes and share the driving expenses.
6. **Don't drive.** Use alternative forms of transportation such as public transportation, bicycles, or walking.
7. **Drive during off-peak hours.** Peak hours are when most people are going to or commuting from work. These are also known as "rush hours."
8. **Look for telecommuting opportunities.** Work at home using your commuter.

## Evaluation 3

5–10 mins. ■

Discuss the tips as a class.

## Application

10–20 mins. ■■■

**I.** Keona suggested that Chalene keep track of her gas consumption and mileage. Fill in the missing numbers in her chart below.

**J. CALCULATE**  Read about Binata and answer the questions.

### MULTILEVEL WORKSHEETS

Unit 3, Lesson 4, Worksheet 1: Gas/Mileage Chart (blank template)

Unit 3, Lesson 4, Worksheet 2: Compute Mileage and Gas

Unit 3, Lesson 4, Worksheet 3: How to Change Your Driving Habits to Save Gas

Refer students to *Stand Out 5 Workbook,* Unit 3, Lesson 4 for more practice with math language.

Go to the *Activity Bank* online for suggestions on promoting digital literacy and using the Internet to enhance this lesson.

### INSTRUCTOR'S NOTES

_____
_____
_____
_____
_____
_____
_____
_____
_____
_____
_____
_____

WORKPLACE CONNECTION
*Exercise H: Interact appropriately with team members.*
*Exercises I, J: Perform basic computations; Interpret and communicate information.*

**H.** **Here are some tips on how to change your driving habits in order to save money on gas. In a small group, discuss each tip and figure out what it means.** Answers may vary.

1. Drive the speed limit. *The harder a car's engine works, the more fuel it requires.*

2. Pick your lane and stick with it. *Erratic driving increases gas consumption.*

3. Carpool with classmates or coworkers. *Share rides to reduce expenses for all.*

4. Don't drive. *Share rides and take public transportation.*

5. Drive during off-peak hours. *Don't drive during heavy traffic.*

6. Look for telecommuting opportunities. *Work from home and avoid driving.*

**I.** **Keona suggested that Chalene keep track of her gas consumption and mileage. Fill in the missing numbers in her chart below.**

| Date | Odometer | Trip | Gallons | MPG | Cost per gallon | Cost per mile |
|------|----------|------|---------|-----|-----------------|---------------|
| 10/5 | 22,758 | 310 | 15 | 20.7 | $3.10 | 15 ¢ |
| 10/20 | 23,068 | 325 | 16 | 20.3 | $3.05 | 15 ¢ |
| 10/30 | 23,393 | 320 | 15.5 | 20.7 | $3.12 | 15 ¢ |
| 11/12 | 23,713 | 280 | 17 | 16.5 | $2.99 | 18 ¢ |
| 11/18 | 23,993 | 275 | 16.5 | 16.7 | $3.03 | 18 ¢ |
| AVERAGE | | 302 | 16 | 18.98 | $3.06 | approx. 16 ¢ |

**J.** **CALCULATE** **Read about Binata and answer the questions.**

1. Binata took a road trip from San Francisco, CA to Salt Lake City, UT. She filled her tank up with gas at $3.75 a gallon and she has an 18-gallon tank. She filled her tank up twice. How much did she spend on gas? $135

   ÷ 36

2. Binata drove 736 miles. How many miles did she get per gallon? 20.4

3. What was her cost per mile? 18 ¢

   Cost p.g. ÷ mpg

# LESSON **5** Traffic laws

GOAL ▪ Follow the rules of the road

WORKPLACE CONNECTION
Exercises A, B: Interact appropriately with team members.

## A. What does each of the following signs mean? Work with a partner.

two-way traffic

slippery when wet

railroad crossing

lane shifts to left

steep grade

no left turn

stoplight ahead

yield

no U-turns

divided highway ends

school crossing

merge

hospital

do not enter

bear right

full stop

## B. GENERATE Think about the traffic laws you are familiar with. In a small group, write a law for each item below. Answers may vary.

1. yellow light: You must slow down at a yellow light.

2. speed limit: You must obey the speed limit.

3. seat belts: Everyone in the car must wear a seat belt.

4. red light: You have to come to a full stop at a red light.

5. children: Watch carefully for children playing on crowded neighborhood streets.

6. pedestrians: Stop for pedestrians in a crosswalk.

7. stop sign: You must come to a full stop at a stop sign before proceeding.

8. police officer: You must obey the directions of a police officer.

9. school bus: Traffic behind and coming toward a school bus must stop when the bus has on flashing lights.

## AT-A-GLANCE PREP

**Goal:** Follow the rules of the road
**Academic Strategies:** Reading tables, interpreting facts
**Vocabulary:** *traffic signs, pedestrians, restrained, unrestrained, occupant, fatalities, arrested, narcotics*

## Agenda

☐ Discuss traffic signs and traffic laws.
☐ Interpret information related to seat belts and safety.
☐ Discuss alcohol-related laws and accidents.

## Resources

**Multilevel Worksheets:** Unit 3, Lesson 5, Worksheets 1–4
**Workbook:** Unit 3, Lesson 5
**Suggested Realia:** Driver handbooks or manuals from your state DMV

## Pacing

■ 1.5 hour classes    ■ 2.5 hour classes
■ 3+ hour classes

## STANDARDS CORRELATIONS

*CCRS:* RI1, RI7, SL1, SL2
*CASAS:* 1.9.2
*SCANS:* **Information** Acquire and evaluate information, organize and maintain information, interpret and communicate information, use computers to process information *(optional)*
**Interpersonal** Participate as a member of a team, teach others, negotiate to arrive at a decision, work with cultural diversity
**Systems** Understand systems, monitor and correct performance
**Technology** Apply technology to a task *(optional)*
**Basic Skills** Reading, writing, arithmetic, listening, speaking
**Thinking Skills** Think creatively, make decisions, solve problems, see things in the mind's eye
**Personal Qualities** Responsibility, sociability, self-management
*EFF:* **Communication** Read with understanding, convey ideas in writing, speak so others can understand, listen actively
**Decision Making** Use math to solve problems and communicate, solve problems and make decisions, plan
**Interpersonal** Cooperate with others, advocate and influence, resolve conflict and negotiate, guide others
**Lifelong Learning** Take responsibility for learning, reflect and evaluate, learn through research, use information and communications technology *(optional)*

## Warm-up and Review          5–10 mins. ■■■

Ask students to help you brainstorm a list of fuel-saving ideas. Write them on the board. Ask students who drive if any of them use these techniques. Ask them which one(s) they will start doing.

## Introduction          5–10 mins. ■■■

Dictation:

1. Driving a car comes with a lot of responsibility.
2. Following the rules of the road is very important.
3. What do you think is the most important traffic law?
4. Where can you go to find a list of traffic laws for your state?

State the goal: *Today, we will learn about the rules of the road and study some facts about seat-belt safety and alcohol-related accidents.*

## Presentation 1          10–15 mins. ■■■

**A. What does each of the following signs mean? Work with a partner.**

Since this is still the presentation stage, see what students already know and then talk about each sign as a class.

## Practice 1          10–15 mins. ■■■

**B. GENERATE Think about the traffic laws you are familiar with. In a small group, write a law for each item below.**

## Evaluation 1          5 mins. ■■■

Ask a volunteer from each group to come to the board and write one of the laws. Discuss the laws as a class.

## INSTRUCTOR'S NOTES

_____

_____

_____

_____

_____

## Presentation 2

5–10 mins. ■■■

**C. INTERPRET** The United States Department of Transportation has an organization called the National Highway Traffic Safety Administration (NHTSA) whose mission is to "save lives, prevent injuries, and reduce vehicle-related crashes." Read the data from a study the NHTSA conducted and answer the questions that follow.

Go over the chart as a class, asking questions to make sure students understand the data that are presented. Once students understand the data, have them answer the questions by themselves. Go over the answers as a class.

## Practice 2

10–15 mins. ■■

(Shorter classes can do this exercise for homework.)

**D. On a separate piece of paper, write each question above as a statement.**

Go over the example, making sure students understand what to do.

1. In 2007, 94.6% of drivers in California wore seat belts.
2. There was a −3.7% difference in seat belt use in Texas between 2012 and 2013.
3. In Massachusetts, 74.8% of people wore seat belts in 2013.
4. The difference in seat belt use in Alaska between 2012 and 2013 is −2%.
5. In Florida, 80.7% of drivers wore seat belts in 2006.

## Evaluation 2

10–15 mins. ■■

Ask volunteers to write the statements on the board. Evaluate them as a class.

## INSTRUCTOR'S NOTES

_____
_____
_____
_____
_____
_____
_____
_____
_____
_____
_____
_____
_____
_____
_____
_____
_____
_____
_____
_____
_____
_____
_____
_____
_____
_____
_____
_____
_____

WORKPLACE CONNECTION
Exercise C: Complete tasks as assigned; Interpret and communicate information.
Exercise D: Combine ideas and information.

**C.** **INTERPRET** The United States Department of Transportation has an organization called the National Highway Traffic Safety Administration (NHTSA) whose mission is to "save lives, prevent injuries, and reduce vehicle-related crashes." Read the data from a study the NHTSA conducted and answer the questions that follow.

| Seat Belt Use in the States, U.S. Territories, and Nationwide, 2006–2013 | | | | | | | | | |
|---|---|---|---|---|---|---|---|---|---|
| State or U.S. territory | 2006 | 2007 | 2008 | 2009 | 2010 | 2011 | 2012 | 2013 | 2012–2013 Change |
| AL | 82.9% | 82.3% | 86.1% | 90.0% | 91.4% | 88.0% | 89.5% | 97.3% | 7.8% |
| AK | 83.2% | 82.4% | 84.9% | 86.1% | 86.8% | 89.3% | 88.1% | 86.1% | -2.0% |
| CA | 93.4% | 94.6% | 95.7% | 95.3% | 96.2% | 96.6% | 95.5% | 97.4% | 1.9% |
| GA | 90.0% | 89.0% | 89.6% | 88.9% | 89.6% | 93.0% | 92.0% | 95.5% | 3.5% |
| FL | 80.7% | 79.1% | 81.7% | 85.2% | 87.4% | 88.1% | 87.4% | 87.2% | -0.2% |
| IL | 87.8% | 90.1% | 90.5% | 91.7% | 92.6% | 92.9% | 93.6% | 93.7% | 0.1% |
| MA | 66.9% | 68.7% | 66.8% | 73.6% | 73.7% | 73.2% | 72.7% | 74.8% | 2.1% |
| NY | 83.0% | 83.5% | 89.1% | 88.0% | 89.8% | 90.5% | 90.4% | 91.1% | 0.7% |
| TX | 90.4% | 91.8% | 91.2% | 92.9% | 93.8% | 93.7% | 94.0% | 90.3% | -3.7% |
| WA | 96.3% | 96.4% | 96.5% | 96.4% | 97.6% | 97.5% | 96.9% | 94.5% | -2.4% |

1. What percentage of drivers wore seat belts in California in 2007? ____94.6%____

2. Where was there a –3.7% difference in seat belt use between 2012 and 2013? _Texas_____

3. What percentage of people in Massachusetts wore seat belts in 2013? _74.8%_____

4. What is the percentage difference in seat belt use between 2012 and 2013 for drivers in Alaska?
   _–2%_____

5. What percentage of drivers wore seat belts in Florida in 2006? _80.7%_____

**D.** On a separate piece of paper, write each question above as a statement.

EXAMPLE: 94.6% of drivers in California wore seat belts in 2007.

WORKPLACE CONNECTION
Exercises E, G, H: Interact appropriately with team members.
Exercise F: Complete tasks as assigned.

**E.** **What are the driving laws regarding alcohol in your state? Discuss them with your class and write them below.** Answers will vary.

In Texas, the limit for blood alcohol concentration is .08. However, no traceable amount

of alcohol is permitted for people under 21 years of age.

**F.** **Read the facts on alcohol-related accidents. Check (✓) the ones that are the most surprising to you.** Answers will vary.

☐ Alcohol-related motor vehicle crashes kill someone every 31 minutes and non-fatally injure someone every two minutes.

☐ In 2013, 10,076 people were killed in alcohol-impaired driving crashes, accounting for nearly one-third (31%) of all traffic-related deaths in the United States.

☐ In 2010, over 1.4 million drivers were arrested for driving under the influence of alcohol or narcotics. That's one percent of the 112 million self-reported episodes of alcohol-impaired driving among U.S. adults each year.

☐ Drugs other than alcohol (e.g., marijuana and cocaine) are involved in about 18% of motor vehicle driver deaths. These other drugs are often used in combination with alcohol.

☐ Of the 200 child passengers ages 14 and younger who died in alcohol-impaired driving crashes in 2013, over half (121) were riding in the vehicle with the alcohol-impaired driver.

**G.** **With a partner, rewrite the facts above in your own words.**

EXAMPLE: Someone is killed every half an hour due to a car accident involving alcohol.

**H.** **DECIDE In a small group, make a list of five driving rules that you all think are the most important. Present your list to the class.** Answers will vary.

1. Example: Drivers must yield to pedestrians.

2. _____

3. _____

4. _____

5. _____

## Presentation 3

10–15 mins. ■■■

**E.  What are the driving laws regarding alcohol in your state? Discuss them with your class and write them below.**

**F.  Read the facts on alcohol-related accidents. Check (✓) the ones that are the most surprising to you.**

Read the facts as a class. Discuss which ones are the most surprising.

## Practice 3

10–15 mins. ■

(Shorter classes can do this exercise for homework.)

**G.  With a partner, rewrite the facts above in your own words.**

Go over the example with students, showing them how the fact was restated. Explain to them that the purpose of the exercise is to be able to clearly explain the facts to someone else, in which case, they must first understand the facts themselves.

## Evaluation 3

5–10 mins. ■

Call on different students to stand up and restate the facts.

## Application

10–20 mins. ■■■

**H.  DECIDE  In a small group, make a list of five driving rules that you all think are the most important. Present your list to the class.**

**Note:** There is a list of traffic or driving laws on the Multilevel Worksheets. To make this exercise easier, you can give students the list of laws and have them choose the five most important.

**Optional Computer Activity:** Go online to find the Department of Motor Vehicles (DMV) or the Registry of Motor Vehicles (RMV) for your state. Download a driver's handbook or manual.

### MULTILEVEL WORKSHEETS

Unit 3, Lesson 5, Worksheet 1: Sample Driving Tests

Unit 3, Lesson 5, Worksheet 2: Violation Scenarios (listening)

**Refer students to *Stand Out 5 Workbook,* Unit 3, Lesson 5 for more practice with writing questions.**

**Go to the *Activity Bank* online for suggestions on promoting digital literacy and using the Internet to enhance this lesson.**

### INSTRUCTOR'S NOTES

_____
_____
_____
_____
_____
_____
_____
_____
_____
_____
_____
_____
_____
_____
_____
_____
_____
_____
_____
_____
_____
_____
_____
_____

# LIFESKILLS ▶ I wish I had a car

## Before You Watch

- Read the title out loud. Then, ask students if they have ever said this.
- Ask students how many of them have a car.

### A. Look at the picture and answer the questions.

- Have students look at the picture. Then, have them answer the questions.
- Discuss the answers as a class.

## While You Watch

### B. Watch the video and complete the dialog.

- Ask students to watch the video and complete the dialog.
- Play the video and ask students to watch and listen carefully.
- Play the video again. Then, ask students to complete the dialog.
- Play the video once more and have students check their answers.

## Check Your Understanding

### C. Write a number next to each quote to show the correct order.

- Point out the quotes from the video and have students read each one.
- Ask students to write a number next to each quote to show the correct order.
- Show the video again so that students can check their answers.
- Go over answers as a class.

# LIFESKILLS  ▶ I wish I had a car

## Before You Watch

**A. Look at the picture and answer the questions.**

1. Where are Mateo, Hector, and Naomi?
   *Mateo, Hector, and Naomi are at the bus stop.*
2. Where are they going?
   *They are going to school.*

## While You Watch

**B. ▶ Watch the video and complete the dialog.**

**Naomi:** … I can't imagine what the insurance for a car like that would cost. But I guess you wouldn't pay that much for gas. Convertibles get good (1) ___mileage___ .

**Mateo:** Who cares about (2) ___insurance___ or mileage? The important thing is that you would look good.

**Hector:** Personally, I would rather have something more (3) ___practical___ , like that pickup.

**Mateo:** A (4) ___pickup___ ! Are you serious?

**Hector:** Think about it. If you got a pickup, you would have lots of (5) ___space___ in the back.

## Check Your Understanding

**C. Write a number next to each quote to show the correct order.**

a. __4__ "The mileage on an SUV is terrible."

b. __1__ "Convertibles get good mileage."

c. __3__ "A pickup? Are you serious?"

d. __2__ "Who cares about insurance or mileage?"

e. __5__ "I've heard hybrids barely use any gas."

# Review

**Learner Log**

I can purchase a car.  ▪Yes ▪No ▪Maybe
I can maintain and repair a car.  ▪Yes ▪No ▪Maybe
I can compute mileage and gas consumption.  ▪Yes ▪No ▪Maybe

**A.  List four different types of cars.**  *Answers will vary. Sample answers are given.*

1. _____ SUV _____
2. _____ minivan _____
3. _____ four-door sedan _____
4. _____ pickup truck _____

Which type of car is best for you? _____ sports car _____

**B.  Recall the auto maintenance tips you learned in Lesson 2. Write the correct verb from the box to complete each tip. You will need to use some of the verbs more than once.**

| change | check | fill | inspect | perform | replace | top off |
| --- | --- | --- | --- | --- | --- | --- |

*Answers will vary.*

1. _____ Perform _____ a radiator flush.
2. _____ Replace _____ your air filter. (Check/Inspect/Change)
3. _____ Fill _____ your washer fluid. (Check/Top off)
4. _____ Inspect _____ your wipers. (Change/Check/Replace)
5. _____ Fill _____ your power steering fluid. (Top off/Check)
6. _____ Check _____ your oil levels.
7. _____ Perform _____ an oil change.
8. _____ Perform _____ a timing belt inspection.
9. _____ Check _____ your brakes. (Inspect/Replace)
10. _____ Check _____ and _____ top off _____ your coolant.
11. _____ Check _____ your wheel bolts. (Inspect)

**C.  Help Gary calculate his gas mileage and how much he is spending on gas. With a partner, discuss five ways Gary can improve his gas mileage.**

| Date | Odometer | Trip | Gallons | MPG | Cost per gallon | Cost per mile |
| --- | --- | --- | --- | --- | --- | --- |
| 2/7 | 46,269 | 310 | 15 | 20.67 | $3.02 | $0.146 |
| 2/17 | 46,579 | 325 | 16 | 20.31 | $2.90 | $0.143 |
| 2/28 | 46,904 | 320 | 15.5 | 20.65 | $2.95 | $0.146 |
| 3/5 | 47,224 | 280 | 17 | 16.47 | $3.01 | $0.183 |
| AVERAGE | | 308.75 | 15.88 | 19.53 | $2.97 | $0.154 |

WORKPLACE CONNECTION
Exercises A, B: Complete tasks as assigned.
Exercise C: Perform basic computations.

**Goals:** All unit goals
**Grammar:** All unit grammar
**Academic Strategy:** Reviewing
**Vocabulary:** All Unit 3 vocabulary

## Agenda

☐ Discuss unit goals.
☐ Complete the review.
☐ Use unit vocabulary.

## Resources

**Stand Out Assessment CD-ROM with ExamView®**

## Pacing

■ 1.5 hour classes  ■ 2.5 hour classes
■ 3+ hour classes

## STANDARDS CORRELATIONS

*CCRS:* RI1, RI4, RI7

*CASAS:* 7.2.1

*SCANS:* **Resources** Allocate time

**Information** Acquire and evaluate information

**Interpersonal** Participate as a member of a team, teach others, negotiate to arrive at a decision, work with cultural diversity

**Systems** Monitor and correct performance

**Basic Skills** Reading, writing, arithmetic, listening, speaking

**Thinking Skills** Think creatively, make decisions, solve problems, see things in the mind's eye

**Personal Qualities** Responsibility, sociability, self-management

*EFF:* **Communication** Read with understanding, convey ideas in writing, speak so others can understand, listen actively, observe critically

**Interpersonal** Cooperate with others, guide others

**Lifelong Learning** Take responsibility for learning, reflect and evaluate

## Warm-up and Review     5–10 mins. ■■■

Have students take out their list of driving or traffic laws from the previous lesson. Ask a member from each group to write the list on the board. Ask the class to analyze what is written on the board to see what the lists have in common and how they differ.

## Introduction     5–10 mins. ■■■

Ask students as a class to try to recall all the goals of this unit without looking back in their books. The goals for this unit include purchasing a car,

maintaining and repairing your car, interpreting an auto insurance policy, computing mileage and gas consumption, and following the rules of the road. Write all the goals on the board from Unit 3. Show students the first page of the unit and mention the five goals. State the goal: *Today, we will be reviewing everything we have learned in this unit and preparing for the team project.*

## Presentation     10–15 mins. ■■■

This presentation will cover the three pages of the review. Quickly go to the first page of each lesson. Discuss the goal of each. Ask simple questions to remind students of what they have learned. **Note:** Since there is little presentation in the review, you can assign the review exercises that don't require collaboration with a partner or group for homework and go over them in class the following day.

## Practice     20–25 mins. ■■■

**Note:** There are two ways to do the review: 1. Go through the exercises one at a time and, as students complete each one, go over the answers. 2. Quickly go through the instructions of each exercise, let students complete all of the exercises at once, and then go over the answers.

**A.  List four different types of cars. (Lesson 1)**

**B.  Recall the auto maintenance tips you learned in Lesson 2. Write the correct verb from the box to complete each tip. You will need to use some of the verbs more than once. (Lesson 2)**

**C.  Help Gary calculate his gas mileage and how much he is spending on gas. With a partner, discuss five ways Gary can improve his gas mileage. (Lesson 4)**

Have students share results to help Gary improve his mileage.

## Evaluation     5–15 mins. ■■■

Go around the classroom and check on students' progress. Help individuals when needed. If you see consistent errors among several students, interrupt the class and give a mini-lesson or review to help students feel comfortable with the concept.

## Practice *(continued)*     25–30 mins. ■■■

**D. Read the insurance policy and answer the questions on a separate piece of paper. (Lesson 3)**

**E. On a separate piece of paper, write a summary about one of the topics below. (Lessons 1–5)**

Refer to the student book page for the topics.

## Evaluation *(continued)*     5–15 mins. ■■■

Go around the classroom and check on students' progress. Help individuals when needed. If you see consistent errors among several students, interrupt the class and give a mini-lesson or review to help students feel comfortable with the concept.

### BEST PRACTICE

## Recycling/Review

The review exercises, the research activity, and the team project are part of the recycling/review process. Students often need to be reintroduced to concepts to solidify what they have learned. Many concepts are learned and forgotten when students are engaged in learning other new concepts. This is because students learn but are not necessarily ready to acquire language concepts.

Therefore, it becomes very important to review material with students and to show them how to review it on their own. It is also important to recycle the new concepts in different contexts.

**INSTRUCTOR'S NOTES**

**D.  Read the insurance policy and answer the questions on a separate piece of paper.**

## DR DriveRite Automotive Insurance Co., Inc.

| Dung Nguyen<br>79563 Eastern Way<br>Ambrose, GA 31512 | Policy Number:<br>QPX2 80 56 45F5542 6<br>Policy Period:<br>2/10/15–2/09/16 | Vehicle: 2014 Folkswagin Passerine<br>VIN: ZXYI493807T984XXX<br>Annual Mileage: 12,500 |
|---|---|---|

| Type of Coverage | Cost of Coverage | Limits of Liability | |
|---|---|---|---|
| A. Medical | $182.50 | Each person $100,000<br>Each accident $300,000 | |
| B. Liability | $175.00 | Each person $100,000<br>Each accident $300,000 | |
| C. Collision | $98.26 | Each person $50,000<br>Each accident $50,000 | |
| D. Uninsured motorist | $135.00 | Each accident $150,000 | |
| E. Comprehensive | $76.45 | Each incident $25,000 | |

**Premium: $667.21**

1. Who is being insured through this insurance policy? *Dung Nguyen*

2. Where does the insured live? *Ambrose, GA*

3. How long is this policy in effect? *one year*

4. What is the total premium for the insured's policy? *$667.21*

5. How many miles does the insured drive per year? *12,500 miles*

6. Dung got in an accident last week, broke his leg, and damaged his car. Which types of coverage will pay for this? *medical, collision*

7. How much is the insurance company charging for comprehensive coverage? *$76.45*

8. If the insured's car gets stolen, how much will the insurance company pay to replace the car? *$25,000*

9. What is the most the insurance company will pay for the property damage in an accident? *$300,000*

10. How much will the insurance company pay for each person who is hurt in an accident caused by someone without insurance? *$150,000 per accident*

**E.  On a separate piece of paper, write a summary about one of the topics below.**

*Answers will vary.*

- Purchasing a car
- Maintaining a car
- Saving money on gas

- Keeping track of gas mileage
- Auto expenditures
- Rules of the road

WORKPLACE CONNECTION
Exercise D: Complete tasks as assigned.
Exercise E: Combine ideas and information.

Review  85

# Vocabulary Review

**A.** Write the name of each car part below. What does each part do? With a partner, take turns describing each part and its function.

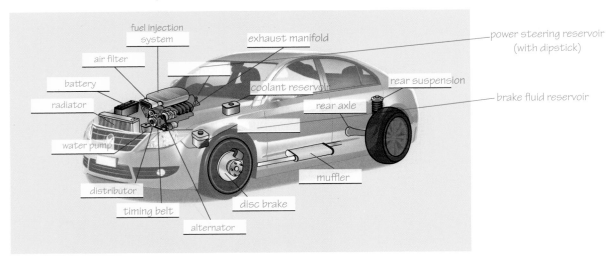

fuel injection system
exhaust manifold
power steering reservoir (with dipstick)
air filter
battery
coolant reservoir
rear suspension
radiator
rear axle
brake fluid reservoir
water pump
muffler
distributor
disc brake
timing belt
alternator

**B.** Write a defining sentence for each of the words below. Answers may vary.

1. coverage: _Coverage is what the insurance company will pay for._

2. premium: _The premium is the amount paid for car insurance._

3. collision: _A collision is an accident between two cars or a car and an object._

4. MPG: _MPG is miles per gallon._

5. odometer: _The odometer measures the number of miles traveled._

6. carpool: _Classmates or coworkers who carpool share rides to reduce expenses for all._

7. policy: _An insurance policy is a contract that states what the insurance company will pay for after an accident._

**C.** Read each phrase below and match it with a vocabulary word or phrase from the unit.

1. restrains driver and/or passengers in an accident: _seat belt_

2. identifies your vehicle: _VIN (Vehicle Identification Number)_

3. covers damage to another vehicle: _liability_

4. can get clogged and affect your gas mileage: _air, gas, and/or oil filters_

5. tells you how fast you can drive on any given road: _speed limit_

6. the different things an insurance company will pay for: _medical, collision, liability, comprehensive_

7. tells you how many miles you have driven: _odometer_

WORKPLACE CONNECTION
Exercises B, C: Complete tasks as assigned.

## Practice *(continued)*    25–30 mins. ■■■

### Vocabulary Review

**A. Write the name of each car part below. What does each part do? With a partner, take turns describing each part and its function.**

Students are not given the vocabulary for this exercise. See how many parts students can fill in themselves. Then, have them work with partners to fill in anything missing. Review as a class.

Have students draw diagrams if they are unfamiliar with the vocabulary. Encourage students more knowledgeable about cars to describe the various part functions.

**B. Write a defining sentence for each of the words below.**

Review the example with students.

**C. Read each phrase below and match it with a vocabulary word or phrase from the unit.**

Review the example with students.

## Evaluation *(continued)*    5–15 mins. ■■■

Go around the classroom and check on students' progress. Help individuals when needed. If you see consistent errors among several students, interrupt the class and give a mini-lesson or review to help students feel comfortable with the concept.

## Assessment *(optional)*    ■■■

Use the Stand Out Assessment CD-ROM with ExamView® to create a post-test for Unit 3.

WORKPLACE CONNECTION

*Combine ideas and information; Make decisions; Exercise leadership roles; Complete tasks as assigned; Interact appropriately with team members; Interpret and communicate information.*

## STANDARDS CORRELATIONS

*CCRS:* W2, W6, W8, SL1, SL3, SL4, SL6

*CASAS:* 4.8.1, 4.8.5, 4.8.6

*SCANS:* **Resources** Allocate time

**Information** Acquire and evaluate information, organize and maintain information, interpret and communicate information, use computers to process information

**Systems** Understand systems, improve and design systems

**Technology** Select technology, apply technology to exercise

**Basic Skills** Writing

**Thinking Skills** Think creatively, make decisions, solve problems, see things in the mind's eye, use reasoning

**Personal Qualities** Responsibility, self-esteem, self-management, integrity

*EFF:* **Communication** Read with understanding, convey ideas in writing, speak so others can understand, listen actively, observe critically

**Decision Making** Solve problems and make decisions, plan

**Interpersonal** Cooperate with others, advocate and influence, resolve conflict and negotiate, guide others

**Lifelong Learning** Take responsibility for learning, reflect and evaluate, learn through research, use information and communications technology *(optional)*

## TEAM PROJECT

### Create a class auto handbook

Each team will create a section of an auto handbook that will be compiled into one book at the end of the project. Sections could include different types of cars, how to buy a car, how to read an insurance policy, the rules of the road, how to keep track of gas and mileage, etc.

The team project is the final application for the unit. It gives students a chance to show that they have mastered all of the Unit 3 goals.

(Shorter classes can extend this project over two class meetings.)

### Stage 1
5 mins.

**COLLABORATE Form a team with four or five students. Choose positions for each member of your team.**

Have students decide who will lead each step as described on the student page. Provide well-defined directions on the board for how teams should

proceed. Explain that all the students do every step as a team. Teams shouldn't go to the next stage until the previous one is complete.

### Stage 2
10–15 mins.

**As a class, brainstorm a list of topics to go in your auto handbook. You might include maintenance tips, directions on reading an insurance policy, and rules of the road. Count the number of teams and narrow your list of topics down to that number. Each team must choose a single topic to work on.**

### Stage 3
20–30 mins.

**As a team, gather all the information for your group's section of the handbook.**

Students can use their books to find information or any other resources they have access to.

### Stage 4
10–15 mins.

**Decide how you would like to present your information. You can choose pictures, lists of facts, and graphs. Be creative!**

Ask students to try to be creative and make their section visually pleasing. (You might need to discuss what this means.)

### Stage 5
30–40 mins.

**Create your section of the handbook.**

**Optional Computer Activity:** Students may want to use the computer to design their section of the handbook.

### Stage 6
15–20 mins.

**Present your section of the handbook to the class.**

Help teams prepare for their presentations. Suggest that each team member choose a different part of the project to present.

### Stage 7
10–15 mins.

**Compile all the sections into one handbook.**

Choose one group or one student to compile all the sections into one book and design a creative cover.

**TEAM PROJECT** ✓ **Create a class auto handbook**

**With a team, you will create a section of an auto handbook. With the class, you will compile sections into a complete auto handbook.**

1. **COLLABORATE** Form a team with four or five students. Choose positions for each member of your team.

| Position | Job description | Student name |
|---|---|---|
| Student 1: Project Leader | Check that everyone speaks English. Check that everyone participates. | |
| Student 2: Secretary | Take notes on team's ideas. | |
| Student 3: Designer | Design layout of handbook section. | |
| Student 4: Spokesperson | Prepare team for presentation. | |
| Student 5: Assistant | Help secretary and designer with their work. | |

2. As a class, brainstorm a list of topics to include in your auto handbook. You might include maintenance tips, directions on reading an insurance policy, and rules of the road. Count the number of teams and narrow your list of topics down to that number. Each team must choose a single topic to work on.

3. As a team, gather all the information for your group's section of the handbook.

4. Decide how you would like to present your information. You can choose pictures, lists of facts, and graphs. Be creative!

5. Create your section of the handbook.

6. Present your section of the handbook to the class.

7. Compile all the sections into one handbook.

# READING CHALLENGE

## About the Explorer

Yu-Guo Guo is a chemist. His work with nanotechnology is changing the way the cars of the future are made. Yu-Guo has invented technology that will allow the batteries in electric vehicles to charge quicker than existing ones—even as quick as filling a car with gas! These advanced batteries recover more energy when cars stop, deliver more power when cars start, and enable vehicles to run longer. Yu-Guo believes this is important as more people switch to buying vehicles that are considerate of the environment.

## About the Photo

The photo shows Yu-Guo standing outside. The technology that he invented allows batteries to charge quicker and recover energy while in operation. He found a unique way to make an important part of this technology—lithium iron phosphate—less expensive and easier for manufacturers to work with. This has implications not only for manufacturers but also customers interested in buying electric vehicles.

- Introduce the explorer, Yu-Guo Guo.
- Read the title and ask students what it means.
- Read the quote out loud. Then, ask students what they think it means.
- Discuss as a class.

## CCRS FOR READING

RI1, RI4, RI10, SL1, SL2

READING CHALLENGE

**EXPLORER** YU-GUO GUO

# Fully Charged

"There is a serious need for sustainable energy sources to power electrical devices."
—Yu-Guo Guo

**A.** **PREDICT** Look at the title and read the quote. What job do you think Yu-Guo Guo has?

**B.** Batteries allow us to use things without having to plug them in. Make a list of things that use batteries. *Answers will vary.*

1. _____    2. _____
3. _____    4. _____
5. _____    6. _____
7. _____    8. _____

**C.** Discuss the following questions in a small group.

1. Do you drive a car? Why?
2. Do you think cars are bad for the environment? Why?

## READING STRATEGIES

### Inferring Word Meaning in Steps

Figuring out word meanings by educated guessing is called *inferring*. Inferring word meaning can be done in steps:

(1) Carefully read the sentence containing the unfamiliar word and ask yourself if the sentence makes sense.
(2) Read the sentence again and look for clues that point to the meaning.
(3) Go back and read the preceding sentence, looking for clues.
(4) If you have a guess about the word meaning, substitute it for the unfamiliar word and see if it makes any sense.
(5) Repeat the steps once again with a new guess.

**D.** Yu-Guo Guo is a chemist who has been working with nanotechnology to change the way cars are made. Read the interview.

**Q: Why is there a need for electric vehicles (EVs)?**
**Yu-Guo Guo:** There is a serious need for sustainable energy sources to power electrical devices, cars being one of them. Traditional sources, such as fossil fuels, cannot satisfy the growing demand, and the carbon emissions that cars give off raise great environmental concerns.

**Q: If that is the case, why don't more people drive EVs?**
**Yu-Guo Guo:** EVs are expensive because of the battery pack—the most important part of any EV. Batteries that are powerful enough to make cars go long distances are big and heavy, which makes an EV too costly for most consumers. On the other hand, using a smaller battery pack means the car couldn't go as far, making them undesirable for most drivers.

**Q: So is there a feasible solution?**
**Yu-Guo Guo:** The key to improving performance and lowering the battery cost is using nanoparticles that can quickly absorb and hold many lithium ions. This will improve the performance without causing deterioration in the electrode. In plain terms, this means that cars won't drain the energy storage capacity quickly. Compared with traditional lithium-ion batteries, this new high-power technology means batteries can be fully charged in just a few minutes, as quickly and easily as you fill your car with gas. These advanced batteries recover more energy when cars stop, deliver more power when cars start, and enable vehicles to run longer.

**Q: Why hasn't this been done before?**
**Yu-Guo Guo:** I invented the technology, so it hasn't been possible before. I found a unique way to make an important part of this technology—lithium iron phosphate—less expensive and easier for manufacturers to work with.

**Q: How soon will we start to see the EVs with the better, smaller battery packs?**
**Yu-Guo Guo:** Five years from now, the electric vehicle market should be well established. In cities, up to 10 percent of cars could be EVs.

**E.** Based on the interview, match each vocabulary expression to its correct meaning.

1. sustainable
2. lithium-ion battery
3. deterioration
4. nanoparticle
5. fossil fuels
6. undesirable

a. rechargeable power source
b. microscopic particle of matter
c. not wanted or wished for
d. fuel formed from the remains of living organisms
e. able to be maintained at a certain rate or level
f. process of becoming progressively worse

**F.** **INFER** Underline any words or phrases in the article that you don't understand and try to infer the meanings.

---

**A. PREDICT** Look at the title and read the quote. What job do you think Yu-Guo Guo has?

- Ask students why Yu-Guo Guo might be pictured standing in a forest.
- Ask students what a "serious need" suggests.
- Have students take turns offering examples of sustainable energy sources they have seen.

**B. Batteries allow us to use things without having to plug them in. Make a list of things that use batteries.**

- Tell students that batteries allow us to use things without having to plug them in.
- Ask students to think of the things they use batteries for and make a list.
- Have students share their lists with a partner.
- Ask volunteers to write some of their items on the board.

**C. Discuss the following questions in a small group.**

Have students discuss the questions in small groups.

**D. Yu-Guo Guo is a chemist who has been working with nanotechnology to change the way cars are made. Read the interview.**

Ask students to read the interview.

**E. Based on the interview, match each vocabulary expression to its correct meaning.**

Have students match each vocabulary expression to its correct meaning.

**F. INFER** Underline any words or phrases in the article that you don't understand and try to infer the meanings.

Ask students to make a list of words and phrases they don't understand and try to infer the meanings.

# UNIT 4

## Housing

### About the Photo

Architecture photographer Peter Stewart took this photo. It shows a close-up of a modern, designer apartment block in Shinonome, Tokyo. Over thirteen million people live in Tokyo, making it one of the most densely populated cities in the world. With many people living in city, the only way to accommodate them is to build tall and tightly crammed apartment buildings. Depending on the location of the apartments, some can cost as much as large houses in other parts of the world.

- Introduce the unit by reading the title out loud.
- Ask students to share with the class what type of housing they live in or have lived in.
- Have students look at the photo. Ask a volunteer to read the caption out loud.
- Have students answer the questions. Share and discuss answers as a class.
- Discuss with students what they do to prevent theft where they live.
- Go over each unit outcome.

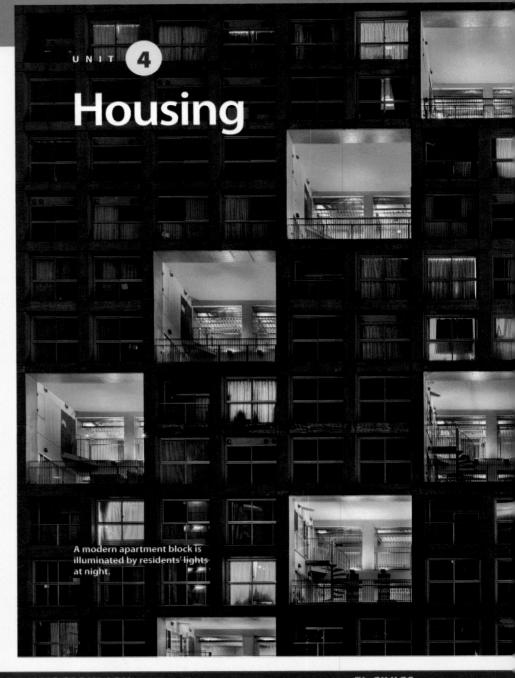

UNIT 4

## Housing

A modern apartment block is illuminated by residents' lights at night.

| UNIT OUTCOMES | GRAMMAR | VOCABULARY | EL CIVICS |
|---|---|---|---|
| • Communicate issues by phone<br>• Interpret rental agreements<br>• Identify tenant and landlord rights<br>• Get insurance<br>• Prevent theft | • Parts of speech: nouns, verbs, adjectives<br>• Noun forms<br>• Causative verbs<br>• Simple present<br>• Modals with *might* and *must*<br>• Information questions | • Housing: *abandon, dwelling, grounds, summon, premises, evident, responsible, exterior, seize, rental agreement, tenant, landlord, right,* (more)<br>• Home insurance: *prevention, installation, expiration, prolonged absence, replacement cost, sanitary regulations, structurally sound, time-consuming, litigate, terminate, vacate,* (more)<br>• Crime prevention: *burglarize, enticing, theft, break-in, burglary, crime, thief, disturbance, weapons* | The skills students learn in this unit can be applied to the following EL Civics competency areas:<br>• Communication – Business Communication<br>• Consumer Economics – Housing |

**90** Unit 4

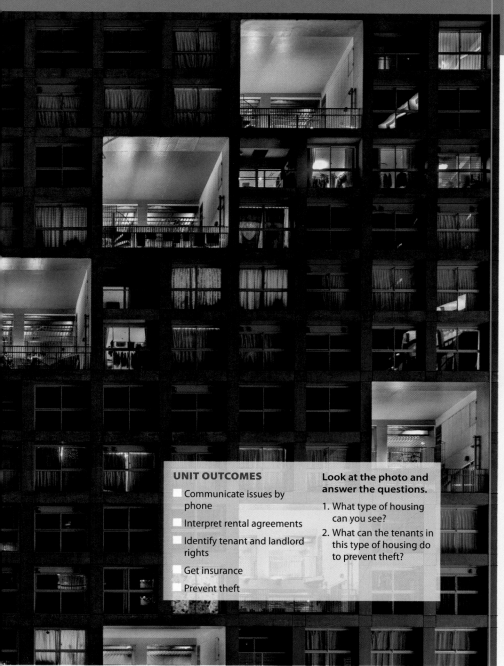

## Life Skills Link

In this unit, students are presented with an extended vocabulary of housing-related terms which will be immediately useful throughout the lessons, and in everyday life.

Students will learn about many topics pertaining both to renting and owning a home. The insurance, maintenance, and protection of homes against burglary are discussed in detail. Students will explore ways of establishing and preserving a balanced landlord-tenant relationship, and will learn about common legal mechanisms that protect both landlords and tenants, beginning with items included in a typical lease to the responsibilities of both parties when a tenant vacates rental housing.

## Workplace Link

All lessons and units in *Stand Out* include basic communication skills and interpersonal skills important for the workplace. They are not individually identified. Other workplace skills are indicated. They include *collecting and organizing information, making decisions and solving problems,* and *combining ideas and information.*

### UNIT OUTCOMES

- ☐ Communicate issues by phone
- ☐ Interpret rental agreements
- ☐ Identify tenant and landlord rights
- ☐ Get insurance
- ☐ Prevent theft

### Look at the photo and answer the questions.

1. What type of housing can you see?
2. What can the tenants in this type of housing do to prevent theft?

| CASAS | SCANS | CCRS |
|---|---|---|
| Vocabulary Builder: 7.4.5 | Many SCANS skills are incorporated in this unit with an emphasis on: | RI1, RI2, RI3, RI4, RI7, RI10, W2, W7, W8, SL1, SL2, SL3, SL4, SL6, L1, L3 |
| Lesson 1: 1.9.5 | • Problem-solving | |
| Lesson 2: 1.9.6 | • Self-management | |
| Lesson 3: 1.9.8 | • Reading | |
| Lesson 4: 1.9.3 | • Mathematics | |
| Lesson 5: 1.9.2 | • Creative thinking | |
| Review: 7.2.1 | • Responsibility | |
| Research: 4.9.3, 7.2.1, 7.4.4, 7.4.5, 7.4.6 | • Visualization | |
| Team Project: 4.8.1, 4.8.5, 4.8.6 | | |

# Vocabulary Builder

WORKPLACE CONNECTION
Exercises A, C: Complete tasks as assigned.
Exercise B: Collect and organize information.

**A. What do the following words have in common? Write the theme below.**

| | | | |
|---|---|---|---|
| abandon | dwelling | grounds | summon |
| burglarize | enticing | premises | theft |
| crime | evident | responsible | thief |
| disturbance | exterior | seize | weapons |

Theme: _Housing crime_

**B. CLASSIFY Put each word in the correct column according to its part of speech. Use a dictionary if you need help.**

| Noun | | Verb | Adjective |
|---|---|---|---|
| crime | theft | abandon | enticing |
| disturbance | thief | burglarize | evident |
| dwelling | weapons | seize | responsible |
| exterior | | summon | exterior |
| grounds | | | |
| premises | | | |

**C. Choose two words from each column in Exercise B. Write one sentence using each word.** Answers will vary. Sample answers are given.

1. _The dwelling was unoccupied._

2. _They abandoned the old building._

3. _The dark building was enticing to the criminals._

4. _____

5. _____

6. _____

**Goal:** Introduce new vocabulary
**Academic Strategies:** Identifying a vocabulary theme, using a dictionary
**Vocabulary:** See lesson

## Agenda

- Identify the unit theme.
- Identify words by part of speech.
- Write sentences.
- Match phrases to definitions.

## Resources

**Dictionaries:** It is recommended that each student in class have an ESL learner's dictionary or that there be dictionaries available in the classroom for students to use. Dictionaries that will be referred to in this book are the *Heinle's Newbury House Dictionary of American English* and the *Collins Cobuild Intermediate* or *Advanced Dictionary of American English*.

## Pacing

- 1.5 hour classes
- 2.5 hour classes
- 3+ hour classes

## STANDARDS CORRELATIONS

*CCRS:* RI4, L4

*CASAS:* 7.4.5

*SCANS:* **Information** Acquire and evaluate information, organize and maintain information

**Interpersonal** Participate as a member of a team, negotiate to arrive at a decision, work with cultural diversity

**Systems** Understand systems, monitor and correct performance

**Basic Skills** Reading, writing, listening, speaking

**Thinking Skills** Think creatively, make decisions, see things in the mind's eye

**Personal Qualities** Responsibility, sociability, self-management

*EFF:* **Communication** Read with understanding, convey ideas in writing, speak so others can understand, listen actively

**Decision Making** Use math to solve problems and communicate, solve problems and make decisions, plan

**Interpersonal** Cooperate with others

**Lifelong Learning** Take responsibility for learning, reflect and evaluate, learn through research

## Academic Feature: Vocabulary Builder

Each unit will begin with a vocabulary-building section. The purpose of this two-page section is to introduce students to many of the words they will be using in the unit lessons. Students will have a chance to see how much they already know, and they will get exposure to the new vocabulary found in the unit.

**Note:** All of the exercises on these two pages should be done in class, no matter the class length. Longer classes can do this lesson and then move onto Lesson 1 during the same class meeting; shorter classes may have to devote one whole class meeting to this section.

### Introduction                    5–10 mins. ■■■

State the goal: *Today, we will be identifying and working with the vocabulary you will learn in this unit.*

### Presentation 1                  10–15 mins. ■■■

**A. What do the following words have in common? Write the theme below.**

Pronounce each word for students and have them put a check next to each word that is familiar to them. As a class, discuss what some possible themes might be. The list leans heavily toward theft/burglary, so this topic is most likely what students will come up with.

**B. CLASSIFY Put each word in the correct column according to its part of speech. Use a dictionary if you need help.**

Make sure students know the difference between a noun, verb, and adjective, which, at this level, should be review. Do the first few items together and then have students complete the exercise on their own.

### Practice 1                      10–15 mins. ■■■

**C. Choose two words from each column in Exercise B. Write one sentence using each word.**

### Evaluation 1                    5–10 mins. ■■■

Ask volunteers to write their sentences on the board. Go over the sentences as a class, making sure that students used the words correctly, both in terms of structure and meaning.

## Vocabulary

When teaching students new vocabulary, pronounce each word for them several times and ask them to repeat it. Often, students may be familiar with the words you are introducing but have never seen them spelled out. By pronouncing the words for students, you allow students to make a connection between the words' spellings and their sounds. It is also important that students learn the correct pronunciation of new words so they feel comfortable using their new vocabulary inside and outside of the classroom.

## Presentation 2                    5–10 mins. ■■■

### D. Read.

Read this explanatory note about nouns out loud with students and discuss the concept of words having similar endings.

### ACADEMIC SKILL

## Word parts

Students will have a much broader vocabulary if they learn the meanings of common prefixes and suffixes:

pre-        before
over-       in excess; too much
-y          (adjective) the existence or condition of
-ness       (noun) the condition of
-ion, -sion, -tion    (nouns) the action or process of

## Practice 2                    15–20 mins. ■■

**E.  Change each verb below into its noun form. Then, define each new word on a separate piece of paper. Use a dictionary to check your spelling.**

**F.  DETERMINE  Without using a dictionary, match the phrases with their definitions.**

If students have difficulty with a phrase, ask them to identify which words they do understand in that particular phrase and then have them work with a partner to deduce the definition.

## Evaluation 2                    10–15 mins. ■■
Go over the answers as a class.

INSTRUCTOR'S NOTES

## D. Read.

You can often identify a word's part of speech just by looking at it. The following words are nouns. What do they have in common?

**prevention     installation     expiration**

The roots of these words are verbs: *prevent, install,* and *expire.* The suffix *-(a)tion* changes each verb into a noun. The noun form signifies the action or process of doing the action. For example, *prevention* signifies the action of preventing something.

## E. Change each verb below into its noun form. Then, define each new word on a separate piece of paper. Use a dictionary to check your spelling.

1. activate          *activation*
2. compensate        *compensation*
3. deteriorate       *deterioration*
4. estimate          *estimation*
5. litigate          *litigation*
6. possess           *possession*
7. terminate         *termination*
8. vacate            *vacation*

## F. DETERMINE  Without using a dictionary, match the phrases with their definitions.

_h_  1. fit for human occupancy          a. advance warning written in a business letter

_a_  2. formal written notice            b. estimate of how much one might pay for insurance

_e_  3. full compliance                  c. being gone for a long time; longer than expected

_f_  4. housing codes                    d. built well; building in good condition

_b_  5. insurance quote                  e. doing what one is required to do

_c_  6. prolonged absence                f. government regulations for building houses

_j_  7. replacement cost                 g. government rules regarding health and cleanliness

_g_  8. sanitary regulations             h. suitable for people to live in

_d_  9. structurally sound               i. taking up a lot of time

_i_  10. time-consuming                  j. cost of replacing something

# LESSON ①  I have a problem

GOAL ■ Communicate issues by phone

WORKPLACE CONNECTION
Exercise B: Complete tasks as assigned.

**A.** Read and listen to the phone conversation Ming Mei is having with her landlord. What is the problem? How is the landlord going to fix it?

| | |
|---|---|
| **Landlord:** | Hello? |
| **Ming Mei:** | Hi, Mr. Martin. This is Ming Mei from the apartment on Spring Street. |
| **Landlord:** | Oh, hi, Ming Mei. What's up? Is there a problem? |
| **Ming Mei:** | Well, after all the rain we had this weekend, the roof has started leaking. I think there may be a pool of water still on the roof because water is leaking through our ceiling even though the rain has stopped. |
| **Landlord:** | Oh, no. Has it damaged the carpet? |
| **Ming Mei:** | No, we caught it right away and put a bucket down to collect the drips. |
| **Landlord:** | Oh, great. Thanks for being on top of it. I'll have my handyman come over and look at the roof and your ceiling. Can you let him in around ten this morning? |
| **Ming Mei:** | I have to go to work, but I can get my sister to come over. |
| **Landlord:** | Great. Thanks for calling, Ming Mei. |
| **Ming Mei:** | Thank you, Mr. Martin. |

**B.** Practice the conversation with a partner. Switch roles.

**C.** Listen to the conversations between tenants and landlords. Take notes in the table below.

| | Problem | Solution |
|---|---|---|
| Conversation 1 | air-conditioning broken | install new unit; meanwhile give fans |
| Conversation 2 | broken door handle | send handyman |
| Conversation 3 | washing machine broken | tenant will fix and take cost off rent |

In a rented home, the landlord is responsible for maintenance.

**Goal:** Communicate issues by phone
**Grammar:** Causative verbs
**Pronunciation:** Clear speech on the phone
**Academic Strategy:** Focused listening
**Vocabulary:** *landlord, tenant, causative*

## Agenda

☐ Read about Ming Mei's problem.
☐ Practice conversations between tenants and landlords.
☐ Use causative verbs.
☐ Call your landlord.

## Resources

**Multilevel Worksheets:** Unit 4, Lesson 1,
    Worksheets 1–2
**Workbook:** Unit 4, Lesson 1
**Audio:** CD Tracks 18–21
**Stand Out Assessment CD-ROM with ExamView®**

## Pacing

■ 1.5 hour classes   ■ 2.5 hour classes
■ 3+ hour classes

## STANDARDS CORRELATIONS

*CCRS:* SL1, SL2, SL3, L1
*CASAS:* 2.1.8
*SCANS:* **Information** Acquire and evaluate information, organize and maintain information, interpret and communicate information
**Interpersonal** Participate as a member of a team, negotiate to arrive at a decision, work with cultural diversity
**Systems** Monitor and correct performance
**Basic Skills** Reading, writing, listening, speaking
**Thinking Skills** Think creatively, make decisions, solve problems
**Personal Qualities** Responsibility, sociability, self-management
*EFF:* **Communication** Read with understanding, convey ideas in writing, speak so others can understand, listen actively
**Decision Making** Solve problems and make decisions, plan
**Interpersonal** Cooperate with others
**Lifelong Learning** Take responsibility for learning, reflect and evaluate

## Pre-assessment *(optional)*   ■■■
Use the Stand Out Assessment CD-ROM with ExamView® to create a pre-test for Unit 4.

## Warm-up and Review   5–10 mins. ■■■
Ask students to take out a piece of paper and make a list of all the words and phrases they can remember

from the vocabulary-building section. When they have written down everything they can think of, have them talk to a partner and try to add one or two more words and phrases to their lists. Make a class list on the board.

## Introduction   5–10 mins. ■■■
**Note:** No dictation is in this lesson. If you would like to do dictation with your students, use the sentences from the grammar chart on page 95.

Ask students to raise their hands if they rent an apartment, house, or condo. Ask them who they pay rent to each month (landlord). Ask them to give you some reasons they might call their landlord. Make a list on the board.

State the goal: *Today, we will practice communicating issues by phone.*

## Presentation 1   5–10 mins. ■■■

A. **Read and listen to the phone conversation Ming Mei is having with her landlord. What is the problem? How is the landlord going to fix it?**

> ### LISTENING SCRIPT    CD TR 18
> *The listening script matches the conversation in Exercise A.*

## Practice 1   10–15 mins. ■■■

B. **Practice the conversation with a partner. Switch roles.**

### PRONUNCIATION

### Vocabulary

Have a small discussion about talking on the phone. Explain how important it is to speak clearly on the phone since you cannot use facial expressions or gestures to help convey your ideas.

C. **Listen to the conversations between tenants and landlords. Take notes in the table below.**

The listening script is on page 95a.

## Evaluation 1   5–10 mins. ■■■
Go over the answers as a class.

## LISTENING SCRIPT

CD
TR 19–21

**Conversation 1**
**Landlord:** *Hello?*
**Chris:** *Hi, Mrs. Kashyap. This is Chris from your apartment building on Jerome Avenue.*
**Landlord:** *Oh, hi, Chris. What can I do for you?*
**Chris:** *Well, I was hoping you might be able to get the air-conditioning fixed. It's been so hot this summer.*
**Landlord:** *I know. It seems like I'm hearing the same thing from all of my tenants. The issue is that the repairman can't find the parts for your unit because it is so old. So, I think I'm going to have to get a new unit installed, which could take me at least a month to do. In the meantime, I'm going to be dropping off some fans to all the tenants in your building. Would that be OK for now?*
**Chris:** *I guess so. When do you think you might come by?*
**Landlord:** *As soon as I can pick up those fans . . . before the end of the week. I'll call before I come.*
**Chris:** *OK. Thanks for your time, Mrs. Kashyap.*

**Conversation 2**
**Landlord:** *Hello?*
**Janice:** *Hi, Mrs. Sawyer. This is Janice from apartment 2B on Palo Verde.*
**Landlord:** *Oh, hi, Janice. How is everything going?*
**Janice:** *Pretty good. I was wondering if you might be able to fix the broken door handle on our bathroom. I know we talked about it when I moved in, but it's been over three months and it still isn't fixed.*
**Landlord:** *Oh, thank you for calling and reminding me, Janice. It completely slipped my mind. I'll send a handyman over first thing tomorrow.*
**Janice:** *Great, Mrs. Sawyer. Thanks!*

**Conversation 3**
**Landlord:** *Hello, is this Mr. Jessup?*
**Mr. Jessup:** *Sure is.*
**Landlord:** *Hi, it's Mr. Little. I'm returning your call from yesterday.*
**Mr. Jessup:** *Oh, yes, Mr. Little. Thanks for calling back. It seems that the washing machine in our building isn't working. My wife was trying to do some laundry a few days ago, and when she pulled the wet clothes out of the machine, they were still full of soap.*
**Landlord:** *Oh, dear. That doesn't sound right.*
**Mr. Jessup:** *Actually, I think I know what the problem is, but I wanted to talk to you first before I went ahead and fixed it myself.*
**Landlord:** *Of course. If you think you can fix it, go right ahead. I'll deduct whatever it costs you off next month's rent.*
**Mr. Jessup:** *Great. I'll try to fix it this afternoon, and I'll call you back to let you know if it's working again.*
**Landlord:** *Great, Mr. Jessup. Thanks for calling.*

## Presentation 2          5–10 mins. ■■■

**D. INTERPRET Look at the following statements from the conversation between Ming Mei and her landlord in Exercise A. Answer the questions.**

Do this exercise as a class. Focus first on the meaning of the sentence before you focus on the structure.

**E. We use causative verb structures when we want to indicate that the subject causes something to happen. Study the chart with your teacher.**

Go over the examples together and make sure students understand the structure. Causative verbs will be studied throughout this unit so just try to keep students focused on what is presented here.

## Practice 2          15–20 mins. ■■

(Shorter classes can do this exercise for homework.)

**F. Match the causative verb from Exercise E with its meaning. Two verbs have the same meaning.**

**Note:** Practice 2 is continued on the next page.

### INSTRUCTOR'S NOTES

_____
_____
_____
_____
_____
_____
_____
_____
_____

**D. INTERPRET** **Look at the following statements from the conversation between Ming Mei and her landlord in Exercise A. Answer the questions.**

*I'll have my handyman come over and look at the roof and your ceiling.*

1. Who is the subject of the sentence? *I (the landlord)*

2. Who is going to come over? *my handyman (the landlord's)*

*…I can get my sister to come over.*

3. Who is the subject of the sentence? *I (Ming Mei)*

4. Who is going to come over? *my sister (Ming Mei's)*

**E.** **We use causative verb structures when we want to indicate that the subject causes something to happen. Study the chart with your teacher.**

| Causative Verbs: *Get, Have, Help, Make, Let* | | | |
|---|---|---|---|
| **Subject** | **Verb** | **Noun/Pronoun** | **Infinitive (Omit *to* except with *get*.)** |
| He | will get | his handyman | to come. |
| She | had | her mom | wait for the repairperson. |
| The landlord | helped | me | move in. |
| Ming Mei | makes | her sister | pay half of the rent. |
| Mr. Martin | let | Ming Mei | skip one month's rent. |

**F.** **Match each causative verb from Exercise E with its meaning. Two verbs have the same meaning.**

_c_ 1. get          a. allow

_c_ 2. have          b. provide assistance

_b_ 3. help          c. delegate responsibility to someone

_a_ 4. let          d. require

_d_ 5. make

WORKPLACE CONNECTION
Exercises G, H: Complete tasks as assigned.
Exercise I: Complete tasks as assigned; Interact appropriately with team members.
Exercise J: Interact appropriately with team members.

**G.** **Unscramble the words and phrases to make causative statements. Then, write housing-related sentences of your own using the same verbs.** (Individual sentences will vary.)

1. them / had / their landlord / and leave a deposit / fill out an application

   Their landlord had them fill out an application and leave a deposit.

   _____

   My wife had me paint the children's bedroom.

   _____

2. to prospective renters / him / let / the apartment / show / his tenants

   His tenants let him show the apartment to prospective renters.

   _____

   (sample) My landlord let me fix the leak myself.

   _____

3. made / my parents / a condo / buy / me

   My parents made me buy a condo.

   _____

   (sample) I made the landlord fix the sink.

   _____

4. my boss / for me / will get / I / to write / a letter of reference

   I will get my boss to write a letter of reference for me.

   _____

   (sample) I will get my friends to help me move my furniture.

   _____

5. her husband / she / which house to rent / decide / will let

   She will let her husband decide which house to rent.

   _____

   (sample) I will let my roommate pay the utility bills.

   _____

6. find / my cousin / me / a new place to live / helped

   My cousin helped me find a new place to live.

   _____

   (sample) I helped them move out of the apartment.

   _____

**H.** **What should you do when you call your landlord? Read the sentences below and put them in the correct order (1–4).**

   _4_ Restate the solution for clarification.　　_3_ Ask for a solution.

   _2_ Clearly identify the problem.　　_1_ State your name and where you live.

**I.** **GENERATE** **What are some problems you might have with your home that would require you to call your landlord? Brainstorm a list on a separate piece of paper with a partner.** Sample answers: leaky roof, water in basement, insects or rodents, etc.

**J.** **With a partner, practice having phone conversations with a landlord. Follow the order of events from Exercise H and describe some of the problems you brainstormed in Exercise I.**

## Practice 2 (continued)

**G. Unscramble the words and phrases to make causative statements. Then, write housing-related sentences of your own using the same verb.**

Go over the example with students first, making sure they understand what they are supposed to do.

## Evaluation 2                    10–15 mins. ■■□

Go over the answers as a class. Ask volunteers to write their original sentences on the board.

## Presentation 3                  5–10 mins. ■■■

**H. What should you do when you call your landlord? Read the sentences below and put them in the correct order (1–4).**

Before you focus students' attention on the list in the book, see what sort of list they can come up with as a result of their own experiences.

## Practice 3                      5–15 mins. ■

(Shorter classes can do this exercise for homework.)

**I. GENERATE What are some problems you might have with your home that would require you to call your landlord? Brainstorm a list on a separate piece of paper with a partner.**

## Evaluation 3                    5–10 mins. ■

Make a comprehensive list on the board of everything the groups came up with.

## Application                     10–20 mins. ■■■

**J. With a partner, practice having phone conversations with a landlord. Follow the order of events from Exercise H and describe some of the problems you brainstormed in Exercise I.**

For this exercise, you can let students work with a partner and role-play a few conversations. Another option would be to divide the class in half and designate half landlords and the other half tenants. Choose one of the problems from the board and have each tenant go find a landlord to have a conversation with. Then, have them switch roles and

give them a different problem to discuss. Do this as many times as you want. To make it more realistic and to simulate a phone conversation, have students stand or sit back-to-back so they can't see one another while they are talking.

## MULTILEVEL WORKSHEETS

Unit 4, Lesson 1, Worksheet 1: Landlord/Tenant Conversations (listening)

Unit 4, Lesson 1, Worksheet 2: Causative Verbs

**Refer students to *Stand Out 5 Workbook,* Unit 4, Lesson 1 for more practice with causative verbs: *get, have, help, make,* and *let.***

**Go to the *Activity Bank* online for suggestions on promoting digital literacy and using the Internet to enhance this lesson.**

## INSTRUCTOR'S NOTES

_____  _____

_____  _____

_____  _____

_____  _____

_____  _____

_____  _____

_____  _____

_____  _____

_____  _____

_____  _____

_____  _____

_____  _____

## AT-A-GLANCE PREP

**Goal:** Interpret rental agreements
**Academic Strategies:** Determining meaning, summarizing
**Vocabulary:** Rental agreement vocabulary

### Agenda
▢ Interpret rental agreements.
▢ Summarize a rental agreement.

### Resources
**Multilevel Worksheets:** Unit 4, Lesson 2, Worksheets 1–2
**Workbook:** Unit 4, Lesson 2
**Suggested Realia:** Authentic rental agreements

### Pacing
■ 1.5 hour classes  ■ 2.5 hour classes
■ 3+ hour classes

## STANDARDS CORRELATIONS

*CCRS:* RI1, RI2, RI4, RI10, SL4, SL6, L3
*CASAS:* 1.4.3
*SCANS:* **Resources** Allocate time, allocate money, allocate materials and facility resources, allocate human resources
**Information** Acquire and evaluate information, organize and maintain information, interpret and communicate information
**Interpersonal** Participate as a member of a team, teach others, negotiate to arrive at a decision, work with cultural diversity
**Systems** Understand systems, monitor and correct performance
**Basic Skills** Reading, writing, listening, speaking
**Thinking Skills** Make decisions, see things in the mind's eye
**Personal Qualities** Responsibility, sociability, self-management
*EFF:* **Communication** Read with understanding, convey ideas in writing, speak so others can understand, listen actively, observe critically
**Decision Making** Solve problems and make decisions, plan
**Interpersonal** Cooperate with others, advocate and influence, resolve conflict and negotiate, guide others
**Lifelong Learning** Take responsibility for learning, reflect and evaluate

## Warm-up and Review          5–10 mins. ■■■

Repeat the application activity from the previous lesson regarding phone conversations.

## Introduction          10–20 mins. ■■■

Urge students to listen first! These sentences are difficult.

Dictation:

1. Security deposits will be deposited for the resident's benefit in a non-interest-bearing bank account.
2. Resident agrees to maintain the premises during the period of this agreement.
3. In the event repairs are needed beyond the competence of the resident, he or she is urged to arrange for professional assistance.
4. In the event that the smoke detector is missing or inoperative, the tenant must notify the landlord immediately.

State the goal: *Today, we will be interpreting a rental agreement.*

## Presentation 1          10–15 mins. ■■■

**A. Have you ever rented a property? If so, do you remember the information that was in your rental agreement? Make a list on a separate piece of paper.**

Do this exercise together as a class. Make a list of students' ideas on the board as they write in their books.

**B. Rental agreements are long and contain information to protect the tenant and the landlord. Much of the agreement is about money. Read the money-related section of a rental agreement.**

Have students read the text silently to themselves. Then, read it out loud to them or ask volunteers to read different sections.

## Practice 1          10–15 mins. ■■■

**C. ANALYZE In a group, interpret the money portion of the rental agreement. Underline words or phrases no one in your group understands and ask your teacher.**

## Evaluation 1          10–20 mins. ■■■

Go over the agreement as a class.

GOAL ◼ Interpret rental agreements

WORKPLACE CONNECTION
Exercise C: Interact appropriately with team members.

**A.** **Have you ever rented a property? If so, do you remember the information that was in your rental agreement? Make a list on a separate piece of paper.**

*Answers will vary.*

**B.** **Rental agreements are long and contain information to protect the tenant and the landlord. Much of the agreement is about money. Read the money-related section of a rental agreement.**

RENT: To pay as rental the sum of $ _____ per month, due and payable in advance from the first day of every month. Failure to pay rent when due will result in the Owner taking immediate legal action to evict the Resident from the premises and seize the security deposit.

LATE FEE: Rent received after the first of the month will be subject to a late fee of 10% plus $3.00 per day.

SECURITY DEPOSIT: Resident agrees to pay a deposit in the amount of $ _____ to secure Resident's pledge of full compliance with the terms of this agreement. The security deposit will be used at the end of the tenancy to compensate the Owner for any damages or unpaid rent or charges. Further damages will be repaired at Resident's expense with funds other than the deposit.

RETURN OF DEPOSIT: Security deposits will be deposited for the Resident's benefit in a non-interest-bearing bank account. Release of these deposits is subject to the provisions of State Statutes and as follows:

A. The full term of this agreement has been completed.

B. Formal written notice has been given.

C. No damage or deterioration to the premises, building(s), or grounds is evident.

D. The entire dwelling, appliances, closets, and cupboards are clean and left free of insects; the refrigerator is defrosted; all debris and rubbish has been removed from the property; and the carpets are cleaned and left odorless.

E. Any and all unpaid charges, pet charges, late charges, extra visitor charges, delinquent rents, utility charges, etc., have been paid in full.

F. All keys have been returned, including keys to any new locks installed while Resident was in possession.

G. A forwarding address has been left with the Owner.

Thirty days after termination of occupancy, the Owner will send the balance of the deposit to the address provided by the Resident, payable to the signatories hereto, or the Owner will impose a claim on the deposit and so notify the Resident by certified letter. If such written claim is not sent, the Owner relinquishes the right to make any further claim on the deposit and must return it to the Resident provided Resident has given the Owner notice of intent to vacate, abandon, and terminate this agreement prior to the expiration of its full term, at least seven days in advance.

**C.** **ANALYZE** **In a group, interpret the money portion of the rental agreement. Underline words or phrases no one in your group understands and ask your teacher.**

*Answers will vary.*

WORKPLACE CONNECTION
Exercise E: Interact appropriately with team members.
Exercise F: Combine ideas and information.

**D.** **Read the sections on maintenance and repairs.**

MAINTENANCE: Resident agrees to maintain the premises during the period of this agreement. This includes woodwork, floors, walls, furnishings and fixtures, appliances, windows, screen doors, lawns, landscaping, fences, plumbing, electrical, air-conditioning and heating, and mechanical systems. Tacks, nails, or other hangers nailed or screwed into the walls or ceilings will be removed at the termination of this agreement. Damage caused by rain, hail, or wind as a result of leaving windows or doors open, or damage caused by overflow of water, or stoppage of waste pipes, breakage of glass, damage to screens, deterioration of lawns and landscaping—whether caused by abuse or neglect—is the responsibility of the Resident.

RESIDENT'S OBLIGATIONS: The Resident agrees to meet all Resident's obligations including:

A. Taking affirmative action to ensure that nothing exists that might place the Owner in violation of applicable building, housing, and health codes.

B. Keeping the dwelling clean and sanitary; removing garbage and trash as they accumulate; maintaining plumbing in good working order to prevent stoppages and/or leakage of plumbing, fixtures, faucets, pipes, etc.

C. Operating all electrical, plumbing, sanitary, heating, ventilating, a/c, and other appliances in a reasonable and safe manner.

D. Assuring that property belonging to the Owner is safeguarded against damage, destruction, loss, removal, or theft.

REPAIRS: In the event repairs are needed beyond the competence of the Resident, he or she is urged to arrange for professional assistance. Residents are offered the discount as an incentive to make their own decisions on the property they live in. Therefore, as much as possible, the Resident should refrain from contacting the Owner except for emergencies or for repairs costing more than the discount since such involvement by the Owner will result in the loss of the discount. ANY REPAIR THAT WILL COST MORE THAN THE AMOUNT OF THE DISCOUNT MUST BE APPROVED BY THE OWNER OR THE TENANT WILL BE RESPONSIBLE FOR THE ENTIRE COST OF THAT REPAIR. Any improvement made by the tenant shall become the property of the Owner at the conclusion of this agreement.

**E.** **Divide into two groups and present. One group will present the responsibilities for maintenance, and the other group will present the responsibilities for repairs.**

**F.** **SUMMARIZE Make a summary of your section for the class.** Answers will vary.

## Presentation 2

5–10 mins. ■■■

### D. Read the sections on maintenance and repairs.

Have students read silently to themselves. Then, read it out loud or ask for volunteers to read different sections.

## Practice 2

10–15 mins. ■■

### E. Divide into two groups and present. One group will present the responsibilities for maintenance, and the other group will present the responsibilities for repairs.

As students are doing Exercise E, walk around the classroom and help them, making sure they clearly understand the key points. Ask them how they plan to present their information and give them some suggestions on how to make their presentation interesting. No single student should be responsible for explaining all the details.

## Evaluation 2

10–15 mins. ■■

### F. SUMMARIZE Make a summary of your section for the class.

Encourage students to ask questions of the "expert" teams.

### BEST PRACTICE

## Silent reading

Some teachers may argue that the time students spend on silent reading can be used for more productive classroom activities. They may choose to sacrifice silent reading for direct instruction. Research has shown that silent reading is beneficial to students, especially when used in combination with other activities before or after the reading. It also goes without saying that most reading in life is done outside of the classroom in some form of isolation, so it is a natural practice. Allowing students time to read on their own helps them improve both vocabulary and writing skills. Furthermore, it helps them connect with the text on a more personal level and builds a greater appreciation for reading.

### INSTRUCTOR'S NOTES

## Presentation 3

5–10 mins. ■■■

**G.** Based on what you have read so far, what do you think the rental agreement will say about each of the following items? Write your ideas.

Discuss each item as a class and encourage students to write notes in their books.

## Practice 3

5–10 mins. ■

(Shorter classes can do this exercise for homework.)

**H.** Read the information taken from the rental agreement about the topics in Exercise G. Write the correct topic on the line that follows each section.

## Evaluation 3

5–10 mins. ■

Go over the answers as a class. As you go over each answer, read the paragraph out loud and answer any questions students might have.

## Application

10–20 mins. ■■■

**I.** SUMMARIZE With a partner, go back through the sections of the rental agreement in this lesson. Make a list of all the topics. Then, on a separate piece of paper, write a statement about each topic, summarizing what the rental agreement says about it.

The following are the 12 topics in the rental agreement sections:

Rent
Late fee
Security deposit
Return of deposit
Appliances
Maintenance
Resident's obligations
Repairs

Phone service
Smoke detectors
Utilities
Lead-based paint

Unit 4, Lesson 2, Worksheet 1: Complete Rental Application

Unit 4, Lesson 2, Worksheet 2: Lease Agreement

**Refer students to *Stand Out 5 Workbook,* Unit 4, Lesson 2 for practice with perception verbs: *feel, hear, listen to, look at, notice, observe, see, smell,* and *watch.***

**Go to the *Activity Bank* online for suggestions on promoting digital literacy and using the Internet to enhance this lesson.**

## INSTRUCTOR'S NOTES

_____

_____

_____

_____

_____

_____

_____

_____

_____

_____

_____

_____

_____

_____

_____

_____

_____

WORKPLACE CONNECTION
Exercises G, H: Complete tasks as assigned.
Exercise I: Combine ideas and information; Interact appropriately with team members.

**G.** **Based on what you have read so far, what do you think the rental agreement will say about each of the following items? Write your ideas.** Answers will vary.

Lead-based paint: _____

Phone: _____

Smoke detectors: _____

Utilities: _____

**H.** **Read the information taken from the rental agreement about the topics in Exercise G. Write the correct topic on the line that follows each section.**

1. Resident agrees to install and maintain telephone service and agrees to furnish to the Owner the phone number, and any changes, within 3 days after installation.

   Phone _____

2. Smoke detectors have been installed in this residence. It's the Resident's responsibility to maintain appliances including testing periodically and replacing batteries as recommended by the manufacturer. In the event the detectors are missing or inoperative, the tenant has an affirmative duty to notify the landlord immediately.

   Smoke detectors _____

3. Resident shall be responsible for payments of all utilities, garbage, water and sewer charges, telephone, gas, or other bills incurred during his/her residency. He/She specifically authorizes the Owner to deduct amounts of unpaid bills from their deposits in the event they remain unpaid after the termination of this agreement.

   Utilities _____

4. Houses built before 1978 may contain lead-based paint. Lead from paint, paint chips, and dust can pose health hazards if not taken care of properly. Lead exposure is especially harmful to young children and pregnant women. Before renting pre-1978 housing, Owner must disclose the presence of known lead-based paint and lead-based paint hazards in the dwelling. Resident must also receive a federally approved pamphlet of lead-poisoning prevention.

   Lead-based paint _____

**I.** **SUMMARIZE** **With a partner, go back through the sections of the rental agreement in this lesson. Make a list of all the topics. Then, on a separate piece of paper, write a statement about each topic, summarizing what the rental agreement says about it.**

Refer to answers on Lesson Planner page 99a

# LESSON 3 Your rights

WORKPLACE CONNECTION
Exercises A, C: Interact appropriately with team members;
Interpret and communicate information.
Exercise B: Complete tasks as assigned.

**A. Discuss the following terms with a partner. Define them with your teacher.**

Answers will vary.

1. What is a *right*?

   a legal claim to something abstract or concrete

2. What is a *responsibility*?

   a duty of an individual or group to act in a certain way

**B. Tenants have rights and responsibilities, just as landlords do. Read the list below and indicate which responsibility belongs to each person: tenant (*T*) or landlord (*L*).**

1. __L__ Provide a clean apartment when the tenant moves in.

2. __L__ Maintain common areas (hallways, stairs, yards, entryways).

3. __T__ Give the landlord permission to enter the apartment at reasonable times and with advance notice to inspect it or to make any necessary repairs.

4. __T__ Keep noise at a level that will not disturb neighbors.

5. __T__ Keep the apartment and the surrounding area clean and in good condition.

6. __T__ Notify the landlord immediately if the apartment needs repair through no fault of the tenant.

7. __T__ Notify the landlord of any anticipated prolonged absence from the apartment so he or she can keep an eye on things.

8. __T__ Pay the rent on time.

9. __L__ Provide properly working plumbing and heating (both hot and cold running water).

10. __T__ Repair any damage occurring to the apartment through the fault of the tenant, tenant's family members, or tenant's guests. Notify landlord at once of major damage.

11. __L__ Provide well-lit hallways and entryways.

12. __T__ When moving out, give landlord proper advance notice. Be sure that the apartment is in the same condition as when the tenant moved in and return the key to the landlord promptly.

**C. RESTATE With a partner, restate each of the rights and responsibilities in Exercise B.**

Answers will vary.

EXAMPLE: "It is a landlord's responsibility to provide a clean apartment when the tenant moves in."

**Goal:** Identify tenant and landlord rights

**Grammar:** Causative verb *make*

**Academic Strategies:** Writing definitions, comparing and contrasting

**Vocabulary:** *right, responsibility, advance, notice, no fault, prolonged absence, fit for human occupancy, structurally sound, monetary damages, housing code, sanitary regulation*

## Agenda

▪ Discuss rights and responsibilities of landlords and tenants.

▪ Read about and discuss the implied warranty of habitability.

## Resources

**Multilevel Worksheet:** Unit 4, Lesson 3, Worksheet 1
**Workbook:** Unit 4, Lesson 3

## Pacing

■ 1.5 hour classes  ■ 2.5 hour classes
■ 3+ hour classes

---

### STANDARDS CORRELATIONS

*CCRS:* RI1, RI3, RI4, RI7, RI10, SL1, SL2, L1

*CASAS:* 1.4.5

*SCANS:* **Information** Acquire and evaluate information, interpret and communicate information

**Interpersonal** Participate as a member of a team, teach others, negotiate to arrive at a decision, work with cultural diversity

**Systems** Understand systems, monitor and correct performance

**Basic Skills** Reading, writing, listening, speaking

**Thinking Skills** Think creatively, make decisions, solve problems, see things in the mind's eye

**Personal Qualities** Responsibility, sociability, self-management

*EFF:* **Communication** Read with understanding, convey ideas in writing, speak so others can understand, listen actively, observe critically

**Decision Making** Solve problems and make decisions

**Interpersonal** Cooperate with others, resolve conflict and negotiate

**Lifelong Learning** Take responsibility for learning, reflect and evaluate

---

## Warm-up and Review          5–10 mins. ■■■

Ask students to call out things they learned about a rental agreement that they didn't know before. Discuss.

## Introduction          10–20 mins. ■■■

Dictation:

1. Provide a clean apartment when the tenant moves in.
2. Keep noise to a level that will not disturb neighbors.
3. Keep the apartment and the surrounding area clean and in good condition.
4. When moving out, give landlord proper advance notice.

State the goal: *Today, we will be identifying the rights and responsibilities of tenants and landlords.*

## Presentation 1          10–15 mins. ■■■

Write the words *Right* and *Responsibility* on the board. Discuss the meanings as a class. As you are discussing, ask for a student to look them up in a dictionary. See how close your discussion is to the dictionary definition.

**A. Discuss the following terms with a partner. Define them with your teacher.**

## Practice 1          10–15 mins. ■■■

**B. Tenants have rights and responsibilities, just as landlords do. Read the list below and indicate which responsibility belongs to each person: tenant (*T*) or landlord (*L*).**

## Evaluation 1          5 mins. ■■■

Go over the answers as a class.

**C. RESTATE With a partner, restate each of the rights and responsibilities in Exercise B.**

### INSTRUCTOR'S NOTES

_____

_____

_____

## Presentation 2

10–15 mins. ■■■

### D. Read about the implied warranty of habitability.

Have students read silently to themselves. Then, answer any questions they have.

## Practice 2

10–15 mins. ■■

### E. ANALYZE  In a small group, discuss the following questions.

Encourage students to rely on members of their own groups.

## Evaluation 2

10–15 mins. ■■

Walk around the classroom and listen to the groups. Although this exercise is difficult, try to have students work with their groups to struggle with answers. Intervene only if their comprehension needs to be redirected.

### BEST PRACTICE

## How to discuss in groups

Most students are already familiar with group work. However, when it comes to group discussion, it is always a good idea to establish some ground rules or provide students with tips. Teaching students how to discuss ensures that group discussions are *good* discussions.

- Ask students to be **active listeners**. This means that students should focus on the speaker. Explain that only the speaker is talking and listeners wait until they have an appropriate response to talk.
- Encourage students to be **active participants**. Clarify that this means that every student shares his or her feelings and opinions. Students give appropriate comments at the right times.
- Ask students to **support opinions with evidence**. Explain that viewpoints are always more credible and persuasive when backed up by concrete evidence.
- Tell students to **encourage others** in their group to ask questions and share. This ensures that everyone has a chance to get involved.
- Remind students to **be polite**. Point out that students can disagree, but it is always important to do it in a respectful way.

### INSTRUCTOR'S NOTES

## D. Read about the implied warranty of habitability.

The *implied warranty of habitability* states that a landlord must keep the property in a condition fit for human occupancy. In other words, it must be a safe place for human beings to live. Here are some questions a landlord might ask him or herself before renting a property: Are there any known hazards with the property? Do the fixtures work properly? Is the building structurally sound? Does the property have any recurring problems?

If a landlord does not comply with the *implied warranty of habitability*, a tenant can cancel the lease, leave the premises, take the costs of repairs out of the rent, or ask for monetary damages.

In determining whether a landlord has violated the *implied warranty of habitability*, courts will look at several factors:

1. Is the problem violating a housing code?
2. Is the problem violating a sanitary regulation?
3. Is the problem affecting a needed facility?
4. How long has the problem lasted?
5. How old is the building?
6. How much is the rent?
7. Has the tenant been ignoring the problem?
8. Is the tenant in any way responsible for the problem?

One or more of these factors will help the courts determine who is at fault and what the victim's rights may be.

## E. ANALYZE In a small group, discuss the following questions. Answers will vary.

1. If your landlord violated the implied warranty of habitability, what can you do?

   I would send my landlord a letter of complaint and save a copy. I would wait 30 days for a response

   before threatening legal action.

2. According to the list of questions that courts will ask, what are some situations in which you could take a landlord to court?

   A landlord might be taken to court if a problem violates a housing code or sanitary regulation,

   or if the problem affects a needed facility.

3. What are some situations when you couldn't take a landlord to court?

   If the tenant ignored the problem or was responsible for the problem.

WORKPLACE CONNECTION
Exercise F: Interact appropriately with team members.
Exercise G: Combine ideas and information.

**F. DETERMINE** With a partner, look at each picture below. Decide if it violates the *implied warranty of habitability*. Imagine that each of these situations has gone on for at least three weeks with no response from the landlord.

No

Yes

Yes

Yes

Yes

No

**G.** Imagine that you are a landlord. Use the rights and responsibilities in Exercise B to write statements using a causative verb structure. Answers will vary.

1. The law makes me provide a clean apartment for the tenant when he or she moves in.

2. The law makes me maintain common areas such as the hallway.

3. The law makes me provide a clean apartment free of bugs.

4. The law makes me provide and repair plumbing. (leaky sink)

5. The law makes me keep hallways well lit.

**H.** Imagine that you are a tenant. Use the rights and responsibilities in Exercise B to write statements using a causative verb structure. Answers will vary.

1. The law makes me pay the rent on time.

2. The law makes me keep a clean apartment.

3. The law makes me keep music at a reasonable level.

4. The law makes me inform the landlord of known problems. (broken elevator)

5. The law makes me give the landlord advance notice if I'm moving.

## Presentation 3    5–10 mins. ■■■

Have students look at the pictures in Exercise F. As a class, discuss what is happening in each picture.

## Practice 3    15–20 mins. ■

(Shorter classes can do this exercise for homework with or without a partner.)

**F.  DETERMINE  With a partner, look at each picture below. Decide if it violates the *implied warranty of habitability*. Imagine that each of these situations has gone on for at least three weeks with no response from the landlord.**

## Evaluation 3    5–10 mins. ■

Go over the answers as a class.

## Application    10–20 mins. ■■■

Go over the instructions and examples for Exercises G and H and then have students complete them on their own.

**G.  Imagine that you are a landlord. Use the rights and responsibilities in Exercise B to write statements using a causative verb structure.**

**H.  Imagine that you are a tenant. Use the rights and responsibilities in Exercise B to write statements using a causative verb structure.**

### MULTILEVEL WORKSHEET

Unit 4, Lesson 3, Worksheet 1: Noisy Neighbors

**Refer students to *Stand Out 5 Workbook*, Unit 4, Lesson 3 for practice with relative pronouns: *who, that, when,* and *where*.**

**Go to the *Activity Bank* online for suggestions on promoting digital literacy and using the Internet to enhance this lesson.**

### INSTRUCTOR'S NOTES

## AT-A-GLANCE PREP

**Goal:** Get insurance

**Academic Strategy:** Supporting ideas with examples

**Vocabulary:** *insurance quote, estimate, replacement cost, dwelling, square footage, exterior, covering*

### Agenda

- Learn about renter's insurance.
- Estimate value of personal property.
- Discuss differences between homeowner's and renter's insurance.
- Interview classmates about insurance.

### Resources

**Multilevel Worksheets:** Unit 4, Lesson 4, Worksheets 1–2

**Workbook:** Unit 4, Lesson 4

**Audio:** CD Track 22

**Suggested Realia:** Insurance policy, brochures from insurance companies

### Pacing

■ 1.5 hour classes ■ 2.5 hour classes
■ 3+ hour classes

## STANDARDS CORRELATIONS

*CCRS:* RI1, RI2, RI7, W7, W8, SL1, SL2, SL3

*CASAS:* 1.4.6

*SCANS:* **Information** Acquire and evaluate information, organize and maintain information, interpret and communicate information

**Interpersonal** Participate as a member of a team, teach others, negotiate to arrive at a decision, work with cultural diversity

**Systems** Monitor and correct performance

**Basic Skills** Reading, writing, arithmetic, listening, speaking

**Thinking Skills** Make decisions

**Personal Qualities** Responsibility, sociability, self-management

*EFF:* **Communication** Read with understanding, convey ideas in writing, speak so others can understand, listen actively

**Decision Making** Solve problems and make decisions, plan

**Interpersonal** Cooperate with others

**Lifelong Learning** Take responsibility for learning, reflect and evaluate

## Warm-up and Review　　　5–10 mins. ■■■

Have students work in small groups to make a list of their rights and responsibilities as tenants.

## Introduction　　　10–20 mins. ■■■

Dictation:

1. What type of insurance policy do you need?
2. How can you find an insurance company?
3. How much personal property coverage do you need?
4. How much can you spend per month on insurance?

State the goal: *Today, you will learn about renter's and homeowner's insurance and how to make sure you are covered.*

## Presentation 1　　　10–15 mins. ■■■

**A. Discuss the terms of the insurance quote below. Then, listen to Makela and Bryce talk about it.**

The listening script is on page 104a.

**B. Discuss the following questions with your classmates.**

You can have students do this in small groups or discuss as a class.

## Practice 1　　　10–15 mins. ■■■

**C. EVALUATE What is the value of your personal property? Write the estimated replacement costs below.**

Explain what it means to estimate and give students a few examples.

## Evaluation 1　　　5 mins. ■■■

After students have completed Exercise C independently, have them compare the cost of their personal property with Makela and Bryce's estimated quote. Ask students to estimate if their replacement costs would be more or less. Would their own premiums be more or less? Have volunteers offer answers, but assure students that financial information need not be shared with the class. Bring in copies of your own insurance policies and premium information if possible.

GOAL ■ Get insurance

WORKPLACE CONNECTION
Exercise B: Interact appropriately with team members.
Exercise C: Perform basic computations.

**A.** **Discuss the terms of the insurance quote below. Then, listen to Makela and Bryce talk about it.**

CD
TR 22

| Renter's Insurance Quote | |
|---|---|
| Value of personal property | $29,000 |
| Deductible | $250 |
| Liability | $100,000 |
| Medical payments | $1,000 |
| Annual premium | $220.08 |
| Monthly payment | $18.34 |

**B.** **Discuss the following questions with your classmates.**

1. Do you have insurance for your property? Why or why not?  Answers will vary.

2. What is a deductible? What is Makela's deductible?  money a person pays against a claim ($250)

3. What is the liability insurance for?  if Makela causes damage or physical harm to anyone

4. What are the medical payments for?  if someone gets hurt at the apartment

5. How much will Makela pay for one year of renter's insurance?  $220.08/year (12 × $18.34)

**C.** **EVALUATE** **What is the value of your personal property? Write the estimated replacement costs below.**

| Personal property | Typical replacement cost | Your estimated replacement cost |
|---|---|---|
| Personal computer, accessories, and software | $1,500--$4,000 | Answers will vary. |
| TV and stereo equipment (home and portable) | $500–$4,000 | |
| Music and movie collection | $500–$2,000 | |
| Furniture and household items | $5,000--$15,000 | |
| Clothing and shoes | $2,000--$4,000 | |
| Sporting goods | $500–$2,000 | |
| Camera and video equipment | $200–$1,000 | |
| Jewelry and watches | $1,000 | |
| Other (luggage, tools, etc.) | $1,000--$3,000 | |
| Total estimated replacement costs | $12,200–$36,000 | |

WORKPLACE CONNECTION
Exercise E: Complete tasks as assigned.
Exercise F: Perform basic computations.

**D. CONTRAST** Landlords should carry insurance for the structures they rent to others. How do you think homeowner's insurance is different from renter's insurance?

*Homeowner's insurance covers the whole building, covers more liability, and costs more.*

**E.** Read the Hahns' homeowner's insurance policy below. Then, answer the questions that follow.

## State One Insurance

**Name/Address of Insured:** Steve and Rosemary Hahn
7930 Inca Way
Kansas City, MO 64108

| Deductible: $2,500 | Annual Premium: $1,077.93 |
|---|---|
| **Coverage Type** | **Amount of Coverage** |
| Dwelling | $401,000 |
| Personal Property | $300,750 |
| Loss of Use | $80,200 |
| Personal Liability—Each Occurrence | $100,000 |
| Medical Payments to Others—Each Person | $1,000 |

1. How much will the insurance company pay to rebuild the house? *$401,000*

2. How much will the insurance company pay to replace personal belongings? *$300,750*

3. How much will the family have to pay before the insurance company pays? *$2,500*

4. What is the monthly premium? *$89.83*

**F.** To get homeowner's insurance, the insurance company needs information about your building. Read about the Hahns' home. Then, fill in the information about your home.

| Building feature | Hahns' home | My home |
|---|---|---|
| Year built | 1986 | *Answers will vary.* |
| Total square footage | 2,378 sq. ft. | |
| Number of stories | 2 | |
| Exterior wall construction material | stucco on frame | |
| Roof type | clay tile | |
| Garage or carport | attached garage: 2-car | |
| Wall partitions construction materials | drywall | |
| Wall/Floor covering materials | paint/wood and tile | |
| Number of kitchens/bathrooms | 1/3 | |
| Type of air/heat | central air/gas | |

## LISTENING SCRIPT

🎧 CD TR 22

**Makela:** *Hey, Bryce, do you have renter's insurance?*

**Bryce:** *No. I keep thinking I need to get it, but I just haven't looked into it yet.*

**Makela:** *Well, I just called my insurance company and got a quote. Will you take a look at it and tell me what you think?*

**Bryce:** *How did they come up with this premium?*

**Makela:** *They asked a bunch of questions about the value of my personal belongings. Then, they came up with the dollar amount of what it would cost to replace all my stuff.*

**Bryce:** *What are the medical payments for?*

**Makela:** *In case someone gets hurt while they are at my apartment.*

**Bryce:** *And what about the liability?*

**Makela:** *Liability covers me if I cause any damage or physical harm to anyone. I think this is required as part of the insurance.*

**Bryce:** *Well, $18 a month sounds pretty reasonable to me. Would it cover your belongings if someone stole them?*

**Makela:** *Yep. It also covers disasters like fires or a flood. I think I'm going to sign up today. You should call, too, Bryce.*

**Bryce:** *I think I will.*

## Presentation 2
5–10 mins. ■■■

**D. CONTRAST  Landlords should carry insurance for the structures they rent to others. How do you think homeowner's insurance is different from renter's insurance?**

Discuss the differences.

## Practice 2
10–15 mins. ■■■

(Shorter classes can do these exercises for homework.)

**E.  Read the Hahns' homeowner's insurance policy below. Then, answer the questions that follow.**

You can have students answer these questions by themselves or with a partner.

**F.  To get homeowner's insurance, the insurance company needs information about your building. Read about the Hahns' home. Then, fill in the information about your home.**

Go over this list with students. Make sure they understand the different topics.

## Evaluation 2
10–15 mins. ■■

Discuss the answers to Exercise E and answer any questions students might have about Exercise F.

## Presentation 3

5–10 mins. ■■■

Model questions and answers for students. Ask a volunteer to stand up. Walk up to the volunteer and say, *Are you a renter or a homeowner?* After he or she answers, say, *Do you have insurance?* After these two questions have been answered, decide which set of questions from Exercise G you will ask based on whether the person has insurance. Explain to students what you just did and model with a few more students if necessary.

### G. Do you have insurance? Answer the questions that apply to you.

Go over the questions with students and have them decide which set of questions to answer depending whether they carry insurance or not. Have students write answers in their books as you are reviewing the questions together.

## Practice 3

15–20 mins. ■

(Shorter classes can do this exercise for homework by interviewing friends or coworkers.)

### H. Using the questions in Exercise G, interview three classmates and take notes.

## Evaluation 3

5–10 mins. ■

Walk around the classroom and observe students as they interview each other.

## Application

10–20 mins. ■■■

### I. PLAN On a separate piece of paper, write a statement about what you are going to do to protect your home and personal property.

Go over the example statements with students. When students have finished, ask them to stand up and read their statements to the class. You might even tell students you are going to ask them next week if they did what they said they were going to do.

### MULTILEVEL WORKSHEETS

Unit 4, Lesson 4, Worksheet 1: Renter's Insurance

Unit 4, Lesson 4, Worksheet 2: Homeowner's Insurance

Refer students to *Stand Out 5 Workbook*, Unit 4, Lesson 4 for practice with passive voice verbs.

Go to the *Activity Bank* online for suggestions on promoting digital literacy and using the Internet to enhance this lesson.

### INSTRUCTOR'S NOTES

WORKPLACE CONNECTION
Exercise G: Complete tasks as assigned.
Exercise H: Interact appropriately with team members.
Exercise I: Combine ideas and information.

**G.** **Do you have insurance? Answer the questions that apply to you.** Answers will vary.

### I have insurance.

1. What type of policy do you have? (homeowner's, renter's) _____

2. How long have you had your policy? _____

3. What is your monthly premium? _____

4. How often do you review your policy in case changes need to be made?

_____

### I don't have insurance.

1. What type of policy do you need? (homeowner's, renter's) _____

2. How can you find an insurance company? _____

_____

3. How much personal property coverage do you need? _____

_____

4. How much can you spend per month on insurance? ($50, $100, $150) _____

**H.** **Using the questions in Exercise G, interview three classmates and take notes.**

Answers will vary.

Name: _____ Insurance (yes/no) Type: _____

Notes: _____

Name: _____ Insurance (yes/no) Type: _____

Notes: _____

Name: _____ Insurance (yes/no) Type: _____

Notes: _____

**I.** **PLAN** **On a separate piece of paper, write a statement about what you are going to do to protect your home and personal property.** Answers will vary.

EXAMPLE: *I need renter's insurance for my personal property. This week, I'm going to go online and get quotes from three insurance companies.*

# LESSON 5  Protecting your home

GOAL ■ Prevent theft

WORKPLACE CONNECTION
Exercise A: Complete tasks as assigned.
Exercise B: Interact appropriately with team members.

**A. Use a dictionary to define the two sets of words below. Include the part of speech for each word. Then, answer the questions that follow.** Answers may vary. Sample answers are given.

burglar: n. a house breaker, a thief

burglarize/burgle: v. to commit burglary, to break in and steal

burglary: n. the crime of breaking in with intent to commit a felony

theft: n. the act of stealing

thief: n. a person who steals property

thieve: v. to steal, to take by theft

1. What is the difference between the two sets of words? The first group includes

   thieving inside a house or property; the second is stealing in general.

2. There are three pairs of synonyms in the groups of words above. Write them on a separate piece of paper.

**B. PREDICT  You are about to read a newsletter on how to protect your home from being burglarized. What do you think it will say about the following items? Brainstorm with a group.** Answers will vary.

| Light | Time | Noise |
|---|---|---|
| Keep lights on outside at night. | Leave your house at different times. | Play a radio or TV when you're not home. |

Security lights help to deter burglars.

**Goal:** Prevent theft
**Academic Strategy:** Comparing and contrasting
**Vocabulary:** *burglar, burglarize, burglary, burgle, theft, thief, thieving, crime, enticing, weapons, activate, time-consuming, disturbance, summon*

## Agenda

☐ Define words related to theft.
☐ Read a newsletter about theft prevention.
☐ Listen to a police officer.
☐ Make a flier.

## Resources

**Multilevel Worksheet:** Unit 4, Lesson 5, Worksheet 1
**Workbook:** Unit 4, Lesson 5
**Audio:** CD Tracks 23–24

## Pacing

☐ 1.5 hour classes     ☐ 2.5 hour classes
☐ 3+ hour classes

## STANDARDS CORRELATIONS

*CCRS:* RI4, RI7, SL2, SL3
*CASAS:* 1.4.8
*SCANS:* **Information** Acquire and evaluate information, organize and maintain information, interpret and communicate information, use computers to process information *(optional)*
**Interpersonal** Participate as a member of a team, negotiate to arrive at a decision, work with cultural diversity
**Systems** Monitor and correct performance
**Technology** Apply technology to a task *(optional)*
**Basic Skills** Reading, writing, listening
**Thinking Skills** Think creatively, make decisions, see things in the mind's eye
**Personal Qualities** Responsibility, sociability, self-management
*EFF:* **Communication** Read with understanding, convey ideas in writing, listen actively, observe critically
**Decision Making** Plan
**Interpersonal** Cooperate with others, advocate and influence, guide others
**Lifelong Learning** Take responsibility for learning, reflect and evaluate, learn through research, use information and communications technology *(optional)*

## Warm-up and Review        5–10 mins. ■■■

Ask students if they followed through with the statements they made in the previous lesson. For those who haven't, ask them when they are going to.

## Introduction        5–10 mins. ■■■

Dictation:

1. If you don't own your home, seriously consider buying a renter's policy.
2. Your landlord will generally not be responsible for your possessions.
3. Most rental policies are available at competitive rates.
4. These policies also offer important protection against losses due to fire or storm damage.

State the goal: *Today, you will learn how to prevent theft in your home.*

## Presentation 1        5 mins. ■■■

Write the words *thief* and *burglar* on the board. Ask students if they can help you define them. Ask them what the difference between the two words is. (Don't give them any answers. Just find out what they know.)

## Practice 1        15–20 mins. ■■■

**A. Use a dictionary to define the two sets of words below. Include the part of speech for each word. Then, answer the questions that follow.**

## Evaluation 1        5 mins. ■■■

Go over the answers as a class.

## Presentation 2        5–10 mins. ■■■

Copy the chart from Exercise B on the board. Go over the instructions and come up with one example for each column as a class. Then, put students in groups to complete the exercise.

**B. PREDICT You are about to read a newsletter on how to protect your home from being burglarized. What do you think it will say about the following items? Brainstorm with a group.**

## Practice 2

(Shorter classes can do these exercises for homework.)

**C. Read the newsletter.**

**D. COMPARE  Look at the ideas you brainstormed in Exercise B and the tips from the newsletter. Are there any tips you didn't think of? List them in the table.**

Go over the concept of comparing and contrasting with students. Show them how to look at the list they made in Exercise B and compare it to what they read.

### ACADEMIC STRATEGY

#### Compare and contrast

Have students compare items to see what is the same about them and contrast items to find out what is different. In this activity, students will be looking at the list that they brainstormed and comparing it to the text, looking for similarities and differences. They will write the things they missed— the differences—in their new list.

### Evaluation 2

10–15 mins. ■■■

Make a comprehensive list of all the tips on the board. See if students can come up with any more. Add any additional ideas to the list.

### MULTILEVEL WORKSHEET

Unit 4, Lesson 5, Worksheet 1: Theft Prevention: Compare and Contrast

### BEST PRACTICE

#### Brainstorming points to consider

- Set a time limit for brainstorming depending on the topic. At the end of the session, ask a volunteer to summarize group ideas.
- Guide brainstorming without giving input on student ideas.
- Remind students to discuss, but not fight. Point out that all ideas are worthy of consideration.

### INSTRUCTOR'S NOTES

## C. Read the newsletter.

# Theft Prevention Newsletter

### Burglary Prevention

Each year in the United States, there are more than five million home burglaries. Nine out of ten of these crimes are preventable. The risk of being burglarized can be greatly reduced by taking simple steps to make your home more difficult to enter and less enticing to would-be burglars. **Remember the greatest weapons in the fight to prevent burglaries are light, time, and noise.**

### Light

- ○ Make sure that exterior lights are mounted out of reach so that burglars can't easily unscrew bulbs.
- ○ Consider buying motion-sensitive lights, which are now available at relatively low prices.
- ○ Use a variable light timer to activate lights inside your home.
- ○ Trim trees and shrubs near doors and windows so burglars can't hide in the shadows.

### Time

Make it time-consuming for a burglar to break into your home by ...
- ○ installing deadbolt locks on all exterior doors.
- ○ installing double key locks in doors that contain glass. This will keep a burglar from being able to open the door simply by breaking the glass and reaching through.
    *(Note: So that everyone in the house can get out in the event of a fire, be sure to keep the key in a designated place.)*
- ○ placing additional locks on all windows and patio doors.

### Noise

- ○ Get a dog. You don't need a large attack dog; even a small dog creates a disturbance that burglars would prefer to avoid. Remember to license and vaccinate it.
- ○ Consider having someone care for your dogs in your home while you're away instead of boarding them.
- ○ If you can afford it, install an alarm system that will alert neighbors of a burglar's presence. Most systems can even summon local police directly.

## D. COMPARE Look at the ideas you brainstormed in Exercise B and the tips from the newsletter. Are there any tips you didn't think of? List them in the table.

| Light | Time | Noise |
|---|---|---|
| • Outside lights should be hard to reach.<br>• Buy motion-sensitive lights.<br>• Use a variable light timer inside.<br>• Trim trees and shrubs. | • Install deadbolt locks.<br>• Install double key locks in doors with glass.<br>• Place locks on windows and patio doors. | • Get a dog.<br>• Keep dogs at home during vacation.<br>• Install an alarm system. |

WORKPLACE CONNECTION
Exercises E, F: Complete tasks as assigned; Interpret and communicate information.
Exercise G: Combine ideas and information.

**E.** Listen to the police officer talk about other tips to prevent a break in. Write the tips below.

CD TR 23

1. Look at your home like a burglar (easy ways to enter, etc.).

2. Keep guns, electronic devices, artwork hidden from windows.

3. Lock up tools.

4. Organize a Neighborhood Watch; tell each other about vacations.

5. While on vacation, have someone pick up mail and newspapers.

6. Post number clearly on house.

**F.** Sometimes all your efforts will not stop a determined burglar. It is wise to take some precautions that will help you get your property back should a criminal successfully break into your home. Listen to the police officer and take notes.

CD TR 24

1. Make a list of your belongings.

2. Keep copies of list and receipts in a safe place.

3. Photograph or videotape your possessions.

4. Engrave your valuables to prove ownership.

5. Be sure to have the right coverage for special items.

6. Renters should buy coverage for possessions.

**G. CREATE** Make a flier to post in your community. Include the most important tips you learned about how to prevent theft in your home.

Some communities form Neighborhood Watch groups to look out for each other.

NEIGHBORHOOD WATCH

PROGRAM IN FORCE

We report all Suspicious Persons & Activities to our Enforcement Agency

## Presentation 3
5–10 mins. ■■■

Go over the instructions for Exercises E and F and ask students what they will be listening for. See if they can come up with some ideas of what they might hear.

## Practice 3
15–20 mins. ■

(Shorter classes can read the script and do these exercises for homework.)

**E.** **Listen to the police officer talk about other tips to prevent a break in. Write the tips below.**

> ### LISTENING SCRIPT
>
> CD TR 23
>
> - *Think like a burglar. "Case" your home the way a burglar would and look for easy ways to enter your home.*
> - *Be sure valuables such as guns, electronic devices, and artwork are not visible from the street.*
> - *Be sure to lock up ladders and tools, which could be used to break into your home.*
> - *Work together with your neighbors. Organize a Neighborhood Watch and let your neighbors know when you will be away for an extended period.*
> - *While on vacation, have someone pick up your newspapers and mail, so that they do not accumulate and alert burglars to your absence.*
> - *Display your house number conspicuously and have it well illuminated. This will help police and emergency personnel find your home quickly.*
>
> (*Source:* http://www.jcsd.org/burglary_prevention.htm)

**F.** **Sometimes all your efforts will not stop a determined burglar. It is wise to take some precautions that will help you get your property back should a criminal successfully break into your home. Listen to the police officer and take notes.**

> ### LISTENING SCRIPT
>
> CD TR 24
>
> - *Make a list of your belongings. (Be sure to keep receipts, especially for expensive items like stereos and computers.) Be sure to update this list periodically.*
> - *Keep copies of your inventory list and receipts in a safe-deposit box or with a friend. (This is also important in the event of a house fire.)*
> - *Photographing and/or videotaping your possessions is a convenient way to keep a record of what you own.*
> - *Engrave your valuables with an identification mark to deter burglary and to prove ownership should the article be stolen and recovered by the police.*
> - *Be sure you have the right coverage. You may need to purchase additional coverage to protect special items like expensive jewelry or rare antiques.*
> - *If you don't own your home, seriously consider buying a renter's policy. Your landlord will generally not be responsible for your possessions. Rental coverages are available at competitive rates and these policies also offer important protection against liability and losses due to fire or storm damage.*
>
> (*Source:* http://www.jcsd.org/burglary_prevention.htm)

## Evaluation 3
5–10 mins. ■

Go over the answers as a class. Either play the recordings again or allow students to look at the script in the back of their books to see if they got the answers right.

## Application
10–20 mins. ■■■

**G.** **CREATE** **Make a flier to post in your community. Include the most important tips you learned about how to prevent theft in your home.**

**Optional Computer Activity:** Have students create their fliers on a computer.

**Refer students to *Stand Out 5 Workbook,* Unit 4, Lesson 5 for practice with the future passive voice.**

**Go to the *Activity Bank* online for suggestions on promoting digital literacy and using the Internet to enhance this lesson.**

## Before You Watch

- Read the title of the video out loud. Then, ask students what a handyman is.
- Ask students what they do when something is broken in their home.

### A. Look at the picture and answer the questions.

- Ask students to look at the picture. Then, have them answer the questions.
- Discuss answers as a class.

## While You Watch

### B. Watch the video and complete the dialog.

- Ask students to watch the video and complete the dialog.
- Play the video and ask students to watch and listen carefully.
- Play the video again. Then, have students complete the dialog.
- Play the video once more and ask students to check their answers.

## Check Your Understanding

### C. Write a number next to each quote to show the correct order.

- Ask students to read what each person says below.
- Have students write the number next to each quote to show the correct order.
- Ask volunteers to share their answers with the class. Then, have students practice the conversation with a partner.

**INSTRUCTOR'S NOTES**

▶ # I'll have my handyman fix it

## Before You Watch

**A. Look at the picture and answer the questions.**

1. What problem do Hector, Mateo, and Naomi have?
*They have water dripping from the ceiling.*
2. Who is the man in the blue shirt?
*The man in the blue shirt is the landlord.*

## While You Watch

**B. ▶ Watch the video and complete the dialog.**

**Hector:** Yeah, the ceiling is still (1) _dripping_ even though the rain has stopped.

**Landlord:** I see. Has the water (2) _damaged_ the floor?

**Naomi:** No, we caught it right away and put a bucket down to collect all the (3) _drips_.

**Hector:** But we can't keep emptying out this (4) _bucket_ day and night. And, the damage to the ceiling is getting worse.

**Mateo:** That's right. And we can't be (5) _responsible_ for any damage if the water spills over.

**Landlord:** I'll have my (6) _handyman_ come by tomorrow morning. Can one of you be here to let him in?

## Check Your Understanding

**C. Write a number next to each quote to show the correct order.**

a. _3_ **Landlord:** I'll have it repaired tomorrow.

b. _6_ **Tenant:** Thank you. I appreciate it.

c. _1_ **Landlord:** I got your message. What's the matter?

d. _4_ **Tenant:** Can you fix it sooner than that? It's very cold.

e. _5_ **Landlord:** In that case, I'll fix it today.

f. _2_ **Tenant:** My heater stopped working yesterday.

g. _7_ **Landlord:** You're welcome. Sorry for the inconvenience.

# Review

## Learner Log

I can communicate issues by phone.　　I can interpret rental agreements.
☐ Yes ☐ No ☐ Maybe　　　　　　　　☐ Yes ☐ No ☐ Maybe

**A.** With a partner, practice conversations between a tenant and a landlord. Practice both face-to-face and phone conversations. Use the scenarios below.

1. leaky faucet
2. broken window
3. can't pay rent on time
4. noisy neighbors

**B.** Using the words provided below, write complete sentences using the causative verb structure. You may choose the verb tense to use. Answers will vary. Sample answers are given.

1. she / make / her sister / move

   She made her sister move out of her apartment.

2. I / get / her / meet

   I got her to meet me at the apartment.

3. they / have / their friends / wait

   They had their friends wait at the bus stop.

4. Elliot / help / his father / repair

   Elliot helped his father repair the sink.

5. my father / make / me / pay

   My father makes me pay him $20 per month for the loan.

6. his landlord / let / him / fix

   His landlord lets him fix most simple repairs.

**C.** Make a list of topics that can be found in a rental agreement. After each topic, write a typical statement that might be found in such an agreement. Answers will vary.

1. Rent: The rent must be paid on the first day of each month.

2. Appliances: The owner assumes no responsibility for their operation.

3. Late fee: Rent received late will be subject to a 5% late fee.

4. Return of deposit: Security deposits will be held in an interest-bearing bank account.

5. Smoke detectors: Tenant must notify landlord immediately if detectors are missing or inoperative.

6. Lead-based point: Owner must reveal the presence of known lead-based paint on the property.

WORKPLACE CONNECTION
Exercise A: Interact appropriately with team members.
Exercises B, C: Complete tasks as assigned.

**Goals:** All unit goals
**Grammar:** All unit grammar
**Academic Strategy:** Reviewing
**Vocabulary:** All Unit 4 vocabulary

## Agenda

- Discuss unit goals.
- Complete the review.
- Use unit vocabulary.

## Resources

**Stand Out Assessment CD-ROM with ExamView®**

## Pacing

- 1.5 hour classes
- 2.5 hour classes
- 3+ hour classes

## STANDARDS CORRELATIONS

*CCRS:* RI1, RI2, RI4, RI7, L1

*CASAS:* 7.2.1

*SCANS:* **Resources** Allocate time

**Information** Acquire and evaluate information

**Interpersonal** Participate as a member of a team, teach others, negotiate to arrive at a decision, work with cultural diversity

**Systems** Monitor and correct performance

**Basic Skills** Reading, writing, arithmetic, listening, speaking

**Thinking Skills** Think creatively, make decisions, solve problems, see things in the mind's eye

**Personal Qualities** Responsibility, sociability, self-management

*EFF:* **Communication** Read with understanding, convey ideas in writing, speak so others can understand, listen actively, observe critically

**Interpersonal** Cooperate with others, guide others

**Lifelong Learning** Take responsibility for learning, reflect and evaluate

## Introduction
5–10 mins. ■■■

Ask students as a class to try to recall all the goals of this unit without looking back in their books. The goals for this unit include communicating issues by phone, interpreting rental agreements, identifying tenant and landlord rights, getting insurance, and preventing theft. Write all the goals on the board from Unit 4. Show students the first page of the unit and mention the five goals.

State the goal: *Today, we will be reviewing everything we have learned in this unit and preparing for the team project.*

## Presentation
10–15 mins. ■■■

This presentation will cover the three pages of the review. Quickly go to the first page of each lesson. Discuss the goal of each. Ask simple questions to remind students of what they have learned.

**Note:** Since there is little presentation in the review, you can assign the review exercises that don't require collaboration with a partner or group for homework and go over them in class the following day.

## Practice
20–25 mins. ■■■

**Note:** There are two ways to do the review:

1. Go through the exercises one at a time and, as students complete each one, go over the answers.
2. Quickly go through the instructions of each exercise, let students complete all of the exercises at once, and then go over the answers.

A. **With a partner, practice conversations between a tenant and a landlord. Practice both face-to-face and phone conversations. Use the scenarios below. (Lesson 1)**

B. **Using the words provided below, write complete sentences using the causative verb structure. You may choose the verb tense to use. (Lesson 1)**

C. **Make a list of topics that can be found in a rental agreement. After each topic, write a typical statement that might be found in such an agreement. (Lesson 2)**

## Practice *(continued)*  25–30 mins. ■■■

**D.** Identify one right for tenants and one right for landlords. (Lesson 3)

**E.** Read the insurance policy and answer the questions. (Lesson 4)

## Evaluation  5–15 mins. ■■■

Go around the classroom and check on students' progress. Help individuals when needed. If you see consistent errors among several students, interrupt the class and give a mini-lesson or review to help students feel comfortable with the concept.

**BEST PRACTICE**

### Recycling/Review

The review exercises, the research activity, and the team project are part of the recycling/review process. Students often need to be reintroduced to concepts to solidify what they have learned. Many concepts are learned and forgotten when students are engaged in learning other new concepts. This is because students learn but are not necessarily ready to acquire language concepts.

Therefore, it becomes very important to review material with students and to show them how to review it on their own. It is also important to recycle the new concepts in different contexts.

## Practice *(continued)*  25–30 mins. ■■■

**F.** Write *T* (true) or *F* (false) in front of each theft prevention tip. (Lesson 5)

**INSTRUCTOR'S NOTES**

Learner Log

I can identify tenant and landlord rights.
■ Yes  ■ No  ■ Maybe

I can get insurance.
■ Yes  ■ No  ■ Maybe

I can prevent theft.
■ Yes  ■ No  ■ Maybe

**D.  Identify one right for tenants and one right for landlords.**

1. A tenant has the right to _a clean apartment upon moving in / S/he has the right to clean, well-lit hallways._
   _S/he has the right to a returned security deposit if the apartment is in good order._
2. A landlord has the right to _enter an apartment at reasonable times_.
   _S/he has the right to receive the rent on time._

**E.  Read the insurance policy and answer the questions.** _S/he has the right to receive advance notice of tenant moving._

# Insurance Policy

| Deductible: $2,250.00 | Annual Premium: $989.45 |
|---|---|
| Coverage Type | Amount of Coverage |
| Dwelling | $330,000 |
| Loss of Use | $80,200 |
| Medical Payments to Others—Each Person | $1,000 |
| Personal Liability—Each Occurrence | $100,000 |
| Personal Property | $200,000 |

1. Is this a homeowner's or renter's policy? _homeowner's_

   How do you know? _It includes cost of the dwelling._

2. How much will the insurance company pay to rebuild the house? _$330,000_

3. What is the annual premium? _$989.45_

4. How much will the insurance company pay to replace personal belongings? _$200,000_

**F.  Write T (true) or F (false) in front of each theft prevention tip.**

_F_ 1. Place your valuables in easy-to-see locations.

_T_ 2. Lock up anything that could be used to break into your home.

_T_ 3. Install an alarm system.

_F_ 4. Make sure you turn off all the lights when you leave your home.

_F_ 5. Install double key locks on all your windows.

_T_ 6. Let your neighbors know when you will be out of town.

WORKPLACE CONNECTION
Exercises D, E, F: Complete tasks as assigned.

# Vocabulary Review

**A.** **Complete each question with a word or phrase from this unit. There may be more than one correct answer.** *Answers will vary.*

1. Are you a tenant or a _____landlord_____?

2. How much _____coverage_____ do you have for your personal property?

3. Do you have _____renter's_____ or _____homeowner's_____ insurance?

4. What is your monthly _____rent_____?

5. Do you have an _____alarm_____ installed in your house?

6. What would your landlord do if there were a _____burglary_____ in your building?

**B.** **With a partner, ask and answer the questions in Exercise A.**

**C.** **Without using a dictionary, define the following words. Include the part of speech.**
*Answers will vary.*

1. dwelling: _n. a place to live_

2. policy: _n. a statement of the legal rules_

3. right: _n. a legal privilege_

4. burglary: _n. act of theft from a house_

5. responsibility: _n. an obligation or duty_

6. prevent: _v. to stop from happening_

7. vacate: _v. to leave_

8. premium: _n. the money to be paid by owner before insurance begins to compensate loss_

**D.** **With a partner, write a conversation using as many of the words from Exercise C as you can include.** *Conversations will vary.*

Student A: _____

Student B: _____

Student A: _____

Student B: _____

Student A: _____

Student B: _____

Student A: _____

Student B: _____

WORKPLACE CONNECTION
Exercises A, C: Complete tasks as assigned.
Exercises B, D: Interact appropriately with team members.

**Vocabulary Review**

A.  Complete each question with a word or phrase from this unit. There may be more than one correct answer.

B.  With a partner, ask and answer the questions in Exercise A.

C.  Without using a dictionary, define the following words. Include the part of speech.

Refer to the student book page for the words.

D.  With a partner, write a conversation using as many of the words from Exercise C as you can include.

**Evaluation** *(continued)*       5–15 mins. ■■■

Go around the classroom and check on students' progress. Help individuals when needed. If you see consistent errors among several students, interrupt the class and give a mini-lesson or review to help students feel comfortable with the concept.

Have students perform the conversation they wrote for Exercise D.

**Assessment** *(optional)*       ■■■

Use the Stand Out Assessment CD-ROM with ExamView® to create a post-test for Unit 4.

## STANDARDS CORRELATIONS

*CCRS:* W2, W8, SL1, SL2, SL4, SL5 SL6

*CASAS:* 4.8.1, 4.8.5, 4.8.6

*SCANS:* **Resources** Allocate time

**Information** Acquire and evaluate information, organize and maintain information, interpret and communicate information, use computers to process information

**Systems** Understand systems, improve and design systems

**Technology** Select technology, apply technology to exercise

**Basic Skills** Writing

**Thinking Skills** Think creatively, make decisions, solve problems, see things in the mind's eye, use reasoning

**Personal Qualities** Responsibility, self-esteem, self-management, integrity

*EFF:* **Communication** Read with understanding, convey ideas in writing, speak so others can understand, listen actively, observe critically

**Decision Making** Solve problems and make decisions, plan

**Interpersonal** Cooperate with others, advocate and influence, resolve conflict and negotiate, guide others

**Lifelong Learning** Take responsibility for learning, reflect and evaluate, learn through research, use information and communications technology (*optional*)

## TEAM PROJECT

### Make a presentation related to housing issues

Each team will prepare a presentation for the class based on one of the topics from the unit. The presentation should include information from the unit as well as from additional research.

The team project is the final application for the unit. It gives students a chance to show that they have mastered all of the Unit 4 goals.

(Shorter classes can extend this project over two class meetings.)

### Stage 1                    5–10 mins.

**COLLABORATE** Form a team with four or five students. Decide which topic your team will work on. (Each team should choose a different topic from the list above.)

Make sure each team chooses a different topic.

### Stage 2                    15–20 mins.

**Choose positions for each member of your team.**

Have students decide who will lead each step as described on the student page. Provide well-defined directions on the board for how teams should proceed. Explain that all the students do every step as a team. Teams shouldn't go to the next stage until the previous one is complete.

### Stage 3                    15–20 mins.

**Gather the information for your presentation.**

Tell students to use what they learned in class and to conduct additional research.

### Stage 4                    15–20 mins.

**Decide how to present your information to the class. For example, you may want to use charts, role plays, or games.**

As a class, brainstorm different methods of presentation. Try to make the list exhaustive so that every team doesn't use the same exact presentation format. Briefly discuss how some presentation methods lend themselves better to some material. Encourage the teams to use at least two different presentation methods in their presentations.

### Stage 5                    20–30 mins.

**Create any materials needed for your presentation.**

**Optional Computer Activity:** Students may want to use the computer to create presentation materials.

### Stage 6                    15–20 mins.

**Rehearse your presentation.**

Remind students that each team member must be involved in the presentation.

### Stage 7                    15–20 mins.

**Give your presentation to the class.**

## Presentation Topics

- Communication with a landlord or tenant

- Rental agreements

- Tenant and landlord rights

- Renter's or homeowner's insurance

- Theft prevention

1. **COLLABORATE** Form a team with four or five students. Decide which topic your team will work on. (Each team should choose a different topic from the list above.)

2. Choose positions for each member of your team.

| Position | Job description | Student name |
|---|---|---|
| Student 1: Project Leader | Check that everyone speaks English. Check that everyone participates. | |
| Student 2: Project Secretary | Take notes on your team's ideas. | |
| Student 3: Coordinator | Divide presentation into parts. Assign each team member one part of the presentation. | |
| Student 4: Director | Organize a different method of presentation for each part. | |
| Student 5: Advisor | Give feedback on the presentation as each team member rehearses his/her part. | |

3. Gather the information for your presentation.

4. Decide how to present your information to the class. For example, you may want to use charts, role plays, or games.

5. Create any materials needed for your presentation.

6. Rehearse your presentation.

7. Give your presentation to the class.

# READING CHALLENGE

## About the Explorer

Constance Adams is a space architect. In the 1990s, Constance worked with NASA (National Aeronautics and Space Administration) on a concept for a transit habitat for the very first human mission to Mars. It was called TransHab (Transit Habitat). Constance came up with an inflatable design that folds up for launch and expands to a three-level home once in space. Big enough for six crew members, it also includes removable pieces that can be used for walls and furniture.

## About the Photo

The photo shows Constance sitting in the International Space Station (ISS) mockup facility holding a NestEgg—a birdhouse that uses space-rated materials. The TransHab project was eventually scrapped, but Constance has been trying to apply her ideas to earth-based projects, such as the NestEgg. While the product keeps birds safe and sheltered from the elements, the materials used to manufacture it are fully biodegradable, meaning that they reduce the possible negative impact on the environment.

- Introduce the explorer, Constance Adams.
- Read the title out loud. Have students look at the picture of Constance.
- Ask students what they think the title means. Share ideas as a class.
- Have a volunteer read the quote out loud. Then, ask students how the title is related to the quote.
- Discuss as a class.

READING CHALLENGE

EXPLORER  CONSTANCE ADAMS

## Out of This World

"We need to understand how our planet and all the little systems inside of it can coexist without causing too much strain. I'd like to find a way to bring it all back home again."
—Constance Adams

**A. PREDICT** Answer the questions about the small picture.

1. What type of housing do you think this is?
2. What makes it different from typical housing?
3. How is it the same?

**B. Match the following words to their correct meanings.**

1. coexist
2. fluctuation
3. inflatable
4. launch
5. requirements
6. strain
7. terrestrial
8. withstand

a. irregular rising and falling of something
b. remain undamaged or unaffected by
c. things that are needed or wanted
d. live at the same time or in the same place
e. ability to be filled with air
f. relating to the earth
g. excessive demand on the strength of something
h. send into outer space

114   Unit 4

## CCRS FOR READING

RI1, RI2, RI4, RI10

**C.** Read about Constance Adams.

What if your job was to design a house for space? Well, this was one of the first projects that NASA gave to Constance Adams, a space architect. Space housing cannot be like housing you would find on Earth. There are certain requirements: It would have to "withstand phenomenal strain, radiation, up to 500 degrees of temperature fluctuation, and orbital debris moving faster than a high-speed bullet—with an inflatable shell." And one more thing: It can only be 14 feet in diameter for a launch, but once it gets to space, it needs to expand to three times that size.

In the 1990s, NASA (National Aeronautics and Space Administration) started working on a concept for a transit habitat for the very first human mission to Mars. It was called TransHab (Transit Habitat). Aerospace company Lockheed Martin hired Constance, who studied sociology at Harvard University and a master's degree at Yale in the late 1990s. She was employed by them to support NASA's Mars exploration research efforts in Houston, Texas, at the Johnson Space Center. This is where she started working on the design for TransHab.

Adams came up with an inflatable design that folds up for launch and expands to a three-level home once in space. Big enough for six crew members, it also includes removable pieces that can be used for walls and furniture. Her design was also supposed to include a common room, gymnasium, and a shower. In order to make her design work, she had to research innovative ideas from other areas, such as engineering, industrial design, and sociology. Unfortunately, this project never made it past the design phase.

Even though the TransHab never came to be, Constance isn't giving up. "Someday I'd like to apply these principles to terrestrial projects," she says. "We need to understand how our planet and all the little systems inside of it can coexist without causing too much strain. I'd like to find a way to bring it all back home again."

**D.** COMPARE  On a separate piece of paper, draw the Venn diagram and complete it with the similarities and differences in housing.

**Space Housing**
- Protect against extreme temperatures
- Protect against radiation
- Inflatable shell
- Withstand cosmic debris

**Both**
- Furniture
- Shower
- Common room
- Withstand strain

**Earth Housing**
- Window screens
- Porches
- Swimming pools
- Pet doors

**A.** PREDICT  Answer the questions about the small picture.

- Ask students to look at the small picture.
- Have students read and answer the questions independently.
- Ask students to share their answers with a partner.
- Discuss answers as a class.

**B.** Match the following words to their correct meanings.

Ask students to match the words to their correct meanings.

**C.** Read about Constance Adams.

Have students read about Constance Adams.

**D.** COMPARE  On a separate piece of paper, draw the Venn diagram and complete it with the similarities and differences in housing.

Ask students to draw a Venn diagram on a separate piece of paper. Tell them to complete it with a partner.

## READING STRATEGIES

# Venn Diagrams

Students are sometimes required to organize information they have read into a Venn diagram. This method helps students visualize the similarities and differences between concepts. When the circles in the diagram overlap, students can see shared features or characteristics. In order to complete a Venn diagram, students need to take note of the section headings. Then, students should reread the text looking for the information. Once they have located the correct information, they can complete the Venn diagram.

## About the Photo

This photo shows the Huli men of Papua New Guinea. There are over 90,000 Huli speakers in Papua New Guinea, but the language is in danger of extinction because of the dependency on English in specific regions of the country. Huli is not the only language in danger of extinction, and the Enduring Voices Project is making an effort to preserve them for future generations. David Harrison, Greg Anderson, and Chris Ranier created the project with the National Geographic Society in order to be able to provide a record of thousands of languages they predict may go extinct over the next 50 years. Given the opportunities learning a second language presents people with, fewer people are using native languages to communicate.

▶ VIDEO CHALLENGE

# Enduring Voices

There are over 90,000 Huli speakers in Papua New Guinea, but the language is in danger of extinction because of the dependency on English.

Nowadays people learn a different language so that they can have greater opportunities in life; however, this can have a negative impact on small cultures because fewer people are using native languages. This means that the languages are in danger of becoming extinct. But there is hope: The Enduring Voices Project.

116    Enduring Voices

## BEST PRACTICES

There are many ways to use video in the classroom. Students should rarely watch a video without some kind of task. You might introduce comprehension questions before they watch so they know what they are looking for. Below are a few techniques that you may try for variety beyond the comprehension checks and other ideas already presented in this lesson.

**Freeze Frame:** Pause the video during viewing and use it like a picture dictionary, identifying and expanding on the vocabulary.

**Silent Viewing:** Show the video in segments without sound so students can guess at the story line. This helps them to understand that listening is more than just the words people say.

**Before You Watch**

**WORD FOCUS**

An *extinct language* is one that doesn't have any speakers.

A *dead language* is a one that is only used in special situations, but is not spoken every day.

**A.** Interview five classmates. Ask where they are from and what language(s) they speak. Answers will vary.

**B.** Read the words and definitions. Then, complete each sentence by choosing the correct word.

| | | | |
|---|---|---|---|
| **disappearing** | going away; dying | **enduring** | lasting forever |
| **extinct** | dead and gone | **elders** | older people |
| **endangered** | not safe or protected | | |

1. Many languages are _____. In fifty years, half of the languages in the world will be gone.
   a. elders       b. enduring       ⓒ disappearing

2. Only the _____ speak the native language. The young people all speak Spanish.
   ⓐ elders       b. enduring       c. endangered

3. The Klallam language is _____. The last known speaker died in 2014.
   a. enduring       b. disappearing       ⓒ extinct

4. The Huli language is _____ because fewer people are speaking it.
   ⓐ endangered       b. extinct       c. elders

5. Korean is a(n) _____ language. It is 2,600 years old and has over 65 million speakers.
   a. extinct       ⓑ enduring       c. disappearing

**C.** The video you are going to watch is about disappearing languages. How do you think a language can disappear? Discuss as a class.

**D.** Look at the list of languages. Circle one language that you think is *dead* and discuss as a class.

| | | | |
|---|---|---|---|
| English | French | Russian | (Latin) |
| Spanish | Italian | Portuguese | Korean |
| Mandarin Chinese | Arabic | Japanese | Vietnamese |

Video Challenge   117

**Before You Watch**

**A. Interview five classmates. Ask where they are from and what language(s) they speak.**

Explain to students that some countries have more than one official language. Other countries have school systems that require students to learn one or more languages besides their own. Have multilingual students share the reason why.

**B. Read the words and definitions. Then, complete each sentence by choosing the correct word.**

**C. The video you are going to watch is about disappearing languages. How do you think a language can disappear? Discuss as a class.**

Ask students if any languages in their native countries are spoken less frequently than in the past. Ask them if they can imagine future generations completely losing a language in favor of a more globally popular one.

**D. Look at the list of languages. Circle one language that you think is *dead* and discuss as a class.**

**Prediction Techniques:** Show portions of the video and ask students to predict what will come next.

**Listening without Viewing:** This helps students create their own image of what is happening. After a discussion, allow students to watch the video and the sound together.

**Back-to-Back:** In pairs, one student faces the video and the other faces away. Play the video without sound and ask the student viewing to report to the student who is facing away what is happening.

**Summary Strips:** Create strips of sentences that describe the events. Have students watch the video and then put the strips in the correct order, or ask students to predict the story line before watching and then check their answers. The Activity Bank has summary strips for each video in *Stand Out*.

# ▶ VIDEO CHALLENGE

## While You Watch

**A. Watch the video. Which countries do the researchers visit to study disappearing languages? Circle the correct answers.**

If any students are from Australia or India, ask if they would have been able to identify the countries from just the visual clues.

**B. Put the events in order. Number the items from 1 to 6.**

**C. Watch the video again. What equipment is included in the Special Language Technology Kit. Circle the equipment and write a paragraph about why it is used.**

Suggest to students that supplying this equipment to people in these areas would have been much more difficult a decade or more ago than it is today. Ask the students if the can come up with reasons why. See if anyone points out the greater availability and lower cost today.

---

**While You Watch**

**A. Watch the video. Which countries do the researchers visit to study disappearing languages? Circle the correct answers.**

| Bhutan | Italy | Spain |
|---|---|---|
| United States | (India) | Korea |
| (Australia) | Myanmar | China |

**B. Put the events in order. Number the items from 1 to 6.**

1. __3__ The team goes to India.
2. __1__ The team goes to Australia.
3. __6__ The woman teaches the team the word for *shoulder*.
4. __5__ The man invites the team into his house.
5. __4__ The equipment doesn't work.
6. __2__ The man teaches the team the word for *father*.

**C. Watch the video again. What equipment is included in the Special Language Technology Kit. Circle the equipment and write a paragraph about why it is used.**

| | |
|---|---|
| (laptop computer) | books on languages |
| maps | (basic recording equipment) |
| (video camera) | cell phone |
| CD | TV |
| radio | digital music player |

_____

_____

_____

_____

_____

118   Enduring Voices

---

## VIDEO STRATEGIES

### Sequencing Events

Ask students to take notes while they are watching the video and pay particular attention to the events as they occur. Later, have students review their notes and identify a central theme. Similar to a reading, the theme of the video is the main event. All of the other events are details related to this theme, presented in a certain order. Students' notes will generally show this order. Sequencing events allows students to recall specific details. It also helps them to understand the central theme of the video.

**A. Complete the video summary with the words from the box.**

| elders | photographer | disappear | endangered | extinct | speaker |
|---|---|---|---|---|---|

David Harrison and Greg Anderson study _____*endangered*_____ languages. Chris Ranier is a _____*photographer*_____. The three men created the Enduring Voices Project for the National Geographic Society. They want to protect languages. When we lose a language, we lose information about the speakers' culture. The men want people to know that more than half of the world's 7,000 known languages may _____*disappear*_____ in the next 50 years. They interview a man in northern Australia. This man may be the last _____*speaker*_____ of a language most people thought was _____*extinct*_____.

After Australia, the team travels to northeastern India. People speak many different languages there. Many of them are in danger of being lost forever. They interview the _____*elders*_____ in a village. They record their language because many younger people do not speak it. If young people do not speak a language, it does not survive.

**B. Read each sentence and choose *T* if a sentence is true and *F* if a sentence is false.**

1. There are 2,000 known languages in the world.     T   Ⓕ
2. Every two days, a language completely disappears.     T   Ⓕ
3. In the northeast of India, there are many endangered languages.     Ⓣ   F
4. A language can't survive if young people don't speak it.     Ⓣ   F

**C. Complete the table by writing answers to the questions. Discuss the questions in small groups.**

| Enduring Voices Project | |
|---|---|
| What do the researchers want to do? | How do they do it? |
| The researchers record as much of endangered languages as possible. | identify endangered languages<br>interview people who still speak the language<br>train local people to use Language Technology Kits |

## After You Watch

**A. Complete the video summary with the words from the box.**

- Suggest to students that words often contain roots, such as *danger* in the word *endangered*, that can help reveal the meaning of a word.
- Remind students that the context in which a word is used will frequently make word selection more obvious.

**B. Read each sentence and choose *T* if a sentence is true and *F* if a sentence is false.**

**C. Complete the table by writing answers to the questions. Discuss the questions in small groups.**

Students may want to write their recollections of the video on a piece of paper first, before filling in the chart. Groups may elect one student to write out ideas, or all students may record their answers individually and compare notes afterward.

# Health

### About the Photo

Underwater photographer Petra Van Borm took this photo. It shows a boy swimming in a pool to train for a triathlon. A triathlon is a three-stage competition in which competitors swim, cycle, and run. A bicycle can be seen in the photograph. The Olympic triathlon consists of a 1.5km swim, a 40km bike ride, and a 10km run. For some, this may look very difficult, but there are some athletes who participate in Ironman triathlons. The distances in this particular format are double that of the Olympic "short course."

- Introduce the unit by reading the title out loud.
- Ask students to look at the photo and have a volunteer read the caption to the class. Then, ask students how the title is related to the person in the photo.
- Have students look at the photo again and discuss the answers to the questions as a class.
- Go over each unit outcome.

UNIT **5**

Health

A boy swims in a pool to train for a triathlon.

| UNIT OUTCOMES | GRAMMAR | VOCABULARY | EL CIVICS |
|---|---|---|---|
| • Identify practices that promote mental and physical well-being<br>• Ask about medical bills<br>• Interpret health insurance information<br>• Identify addictions<br>• Interpret procedures for first aid | • Parts of speech: nouns, verbs, adjectives, adverbs<br>• Independent and dependent clauses<br>• Adverb clauses of concession<br>• Information questions<br>• Complete sentences<br>• Gerunds<br>• Conditional with *could* | • Health and well-being: *affecting, impairment, withdrawal, addiction, poisoning,* (more)<br>• Addiction: *psychological, physiological, dependence, substance, process, withdrawal, detoxification, addict,* (more)<br>• First-aid kit: *adhesive bandages, adhesive cloth tape, antibiotic ointment, antiseptic wipes, aspirin, cold compress, compress dressing,* (more) | The skills students learn in this unit can be applied to the following El Civics competency area:<br>• Health—Emergencie<br>• Health—Pharmacy<br>• Health—Health Care<br>• Health—Foods<br>• Recreation<br>• Common Activities |

**UNIT OUTCOMES**

- Identify practices that promote mental and physical well-being
- Ask about medical bills
- Interpret health insurance information
- Identify addictions
- Interpret procedures for first aid

**Look at the photo and answer the questions.**

1. How does swimming promote physical and mental well-being?
2. What other activities promote physical and mental well-being?

## Life Skills Link

In this unit, students are presented with an extended vocabulary of words relating to health and health care that will be immediately useful in each of the lessons as well as in everyday life.

Students will learn about concepts and practices of wellness, including both physical and mental health considerations. Diet, exercise, stress, and addiction are discussed. Additionally, students are exposed to common practices, forms, and terminology they are likely to encounter in the areas of health insurance and medical billing. A section on first aid provides students with basic procedures to employ in a medical emergency.

## Workplace Link

All lessons and units in *Stand Out* include basic communication skills and interpersonal skills important for the workplace. They are not individually identified. Other workplace skills are indicated. They include *collecting and organizing information, making decisions and solving problems*, and *combining ideas and information*.

| CASAS | SCANS | CCRS |
|---|---|---|
| Vocabulary Builder: 7.4.5<br>Lesson 1: 3.5.8, 3.5.9<br>Lesson 2: 3.2.3, 3.2.4<br>Lesson 3: 3.2.3, 3.4.5<br>Lesson 4: 3.2.3<br>Lesson 5: 3.4.3<br>Review: 7.2.1<br>Team Project: 4.8.1, 4.8.5, 4.8.6 | Many SCANS skills are incorporated in this unit with an emphasis on:<br>• Mathematics<br>• Reading<br>• Self-esteem<br>• Self-management<br>• Responsibility<br>• Problem-solving<br>• Visualization<br>• Decision making | RI1, RI2, RI3, RI4, RI7, RI10, W2, W3, W4, W5, W7, W8, SL1, SL2, SL4, SL5 SL6, L1, L2, L5 |

# Vocabulary Builder

**A.** A *word family* is a group of words with the same root. The words all have similar meanings but are used as different parts of speech. Look at the example below.

| Noun(s) | Verb | Adjective |
|---|---|---|
| survival, survivor | survive | surviving |

- There were no *survivors* of the car accident.

- If cancer is detected early, there is a good chance of *survival*.

- Drugs that dissolve blood clots can help people *survive* heart attacks.

- The *surviving* passengers from the plane crash tried to find help.

**B. CATEGORIZE** Put the words into the correct columns. Then, use a dictionary to find the other forms of each word family. *Note:* Not every word family has every part of speech. Answers will vary.

| affecting | withdrawal | poisoning | depressed | tolerance |
|---|---|---|---|---|
| impairment | addiction | meditate | insured | treat |

| Noun | Verb | Adjective | Adverb |
|---|---|---|---|
| affect, affection | affect | affecting, affective, affected | affectively |
| addiction | addict | addicted/addictive | addictedly |
| depression | depress | depressed/depressive | depressedly |
| impairment | impair | impaired | impairedly |
| insurance | insure | insured | |
| meditation | meditate | meditative | meditatively |
| poisoning | poison | poisoned/poisonous | |
| tolerance | tolerate | tolerable/tolerant | tolerably |
| treatment | treat | treated | |
| withdrawal | withdraw | withdrawn | |

## AT-A-GLANCE PREP

**Goal:** Introduce new vocabulary
**Academic Strategies:** Identifying parts of speech, using a dictionary, understanding word families
**Vocabulary:** See lesson

### Agenda

☐ Understand word families.
☐ Learn health expressions.

### Resources

**Dictionaries:** It is recommended that each student in class have an ESL learner's dictionary or that there be dictionaries available in the classroom for students to use. Dictionaries that will be referred to in this book are *Heinle's Newbury House Dictionary of American English* and the *Collins Cobuild Intermediate* or *Advanced Dictionary of American English.*

### Pacing

■ 1.5 hour classes    ■ 2.5 hour classes
■ 3+ hour classes

## STANDARDS CORRELATIONS

*CCRS:* RI4, L3
*CASAS:* 7.4.5
*SCANS:* **Information** Acquire and evaluate information, organize and maintain information
**Interpersonal** Participate as a member of a team, negotiate to arrive at a decision, work with cultural diversity
**Systems** Understand systems, monitor and correct performance
**Basic Skills** Reading, writing, listening, speaking
**Thinking Skills** Think creatively, make decisions, see things in the mind's eye
**Personal Qualities** Responsibility, sociability, self-management
*EFF:* **Communication** Read with understanding, convey ideas in writing, speak so others can understand, listen actively
**Decision Making** Use math to solve problems and communicate, solve problems and make decisions, plan
**Interpersonal** Cooperate with others
**Lifelong Learning** Take responsibility for learning, reflect and evaluate, learn through research

## Academic Feature: Vocabulary Builder

Each unit will begin with a vocabulary-building section. The purpose of this two-page section is to introduce students to many of the words they will be using in the unit lessons. Students will have a chance to see how much they already know, and they will get exposure to the new vocabulary found in the unit.

**Note:** All of the exercises on these two pages should be done in class, no matter the class length. Longer classes can do this lesson and then move onto Lesson 1 during the same class meeting; shorter classes may have to devote one whole class meeting to this section.

### Introduction                    5–10 mins. ■■■

State the goal: *Today, we will be identifying and working with the vocabulary you will learn in this unit.*

### Presentation 1                    5 mins. ■■■

**A.** A *word family* is a group of words with the same root. The words all have similar meanings but are used as different parts of speech. Look at the example below.

### Practice 1                    10–15 mins. ■■■

**B. CATEGORIZE** Put the words into the correct columns. Then, use a dictionary to find the other forms of each word family. *Note:* Not every word family has every part of speech.

Tell students that the parts of speech for the word entries might be in their abbreviated forms; for example, n. - noun, v. - verb, adj. - adjective, adv. - adverb, etc.

### Evaluation 1                    5 mins. ■■■

Go over the answers as a class.

## INSTRUCTOR'S NOTES

_____

_____

_____

_____

_____

_____

_____

## Vocabulary

When teaching students new vocabulary, pronounce each word for them several times and ask them to repeat it. Often, students may be familiar with the words you are introducing but have never seen them spelled out. By pronouncing the words for students, you allow students to make a connection between the words' spellings and their sounds. It is also important that students learn the correct pronunciation of new words so they feel comfortable using their new vocabulary inside and outside of the classroom.

### Practice 1 (continued)    5–10 mins. ■■■

C. **Choose one of the word families from Exercise B that has all four parts of speech. Write a sentence using each word form. Use the example sentences in Exercise A as a model.**

### Evaluation 1 (continued)    10–15 mins. ■■■

Ask volunteers to write their group of sentences on the board. Analyze the sentences for meaning and grammar.

### Presentation 2    10–15 mins. ■■■

D. **INFER Each expression below is related to health. What do you think each one means? Write your ideas on the lines.**

Have students write their ideas in their books and then go over the meanings as a class.

### Practice 2    10–15 mins. ■■

E. **Look at the following questions. Answer the ones you feel comfortable answering.**

### Evaluation 2    10–15 mins. ■■

Ask volunteers to share their answers.

**C.** **Choose one of the word families from Exercise B that has all four parts of speech. Write a sentence using each word form. Use the example sentences in Exercise A as a model.**

*Answers will vary.*

1. Addictions are difficult to cure.

2. Addictions to drugs and alcohol are difficult to stop.

3. The nicotine in cigarettes is addicting.

4. People can behave addictively around caffeine.

**D.** **INFER Each expression below is related to health. What do you think each one means? Write your ideas on the lines.**

*Answers will vary.*

1. mental health: the wellness of brain function

2. out of shape: your body doesn't function or look like it should

3. self-esteem: how you think about yourself

4. at risk: in danger

**E.** **Look at the following questions. Answer the ones you feel comfortable answering.**

*Answers will vary.*

1. What are the major health care issues facing your community? Which health care issues can be categorized as mental health issues?

   addiction, drug-resistant bacteria, mental health: depression

2. Do you consider yourself in good shape? Why?

   No, because I need to make my heart and body stronger.

3. Think about people who have high self-esteem. What are their traits? What are the traits of people with low self-esteem?

   high self-esteem: take care of themselves, positive

   low: negative attitude, don't try to change

4. Do you know your family's health history? If so, what health problems have some of your family members faced?

   yes; heart disease and cancer

# LESSON (1) Mind and body

WORKPLACE CONNECTION
Exercise A: Interact appropriately with team members.
Exercise B: Complete tasks as assigned.
Exercise C: Combine ideas and information.

GOAL ▊ Identify practices that promote mental and physical well-being

**A. Discuss the following questions in a small group.** Answers will vary.

1. Do you exercise? If so, what type of exercise do you do and how often?  yes; walking

2. Do you eat well? On a scale of one to ten (*ten* being the healthiest), how healthy are the foods you eat?  no; probably a five

3. How could you make your diet healthier?  add more vegetables; eat less candy

4. How much water do you drink each day?  four tall glasses

5. Do you have a lot of stress in your life? How do you relieve stress?  yes; by talking with friends and walking regularly

**B. Listen to the following people talk about how they relieve stress. Take notes.**
Answers will vary.

CD
TR 25

| **Cooper** | **Stephanie** | **Fletcher and Katie** |
|---|---|---|
| Reason for stress: | Reason for stress: | Reason for stress: |
| commission-based pay | worrying about money | taking care of mother/ works long hours |
| How he relieves stress: | How she relieves stress: | How they relieve stress: |
| meditation | running | talking to each other |
|  |  | walking at night |

**C. EVALUATE Do you identify with any of these people? If yes, in what ways? If not, why not?** Answers will vary.

Yes, I like to meditate and walk. I am taking care of a sick parent.

**Goal:** Identify practices that promote mental and physical well-being

**Academic Strategies:** Focused listening, note taking, writing

**Vocabulary:** *mental health, stress, depressed, survive, liveable, out of shape, affecting, self-esteem, obese, at risk, diabetes, prognosis, meditate, blood pressure, overworked*

## Agenda

◻ Discuss your health habits.

◻ Listen to ways people handle stress.

◻ Read and give health-related advice.

◻ Read a health-related article.

◻ Create a newsletter.

## Resources

**Multilevel Worksheets:** Unit 5, Lesson 1, Worksheets 1–3

**Workbook:** Unit 5, Lesson 1

**Audio:** CD Track 25

**Suggested Realia:** newspapers, advice columns

**Stand Out Assessment CD-ROM with ExamView®**

## Pacing

◼ 1.5 hour classes ◼ 2.5 hour classes
◼ 3+ hour classes

## STANDARDS CORRELATIONS

*CCRS:* RI1, RI2, W2, W3, W4, W5, W7, W8, SL1, SL2, L1, L2, L5

*CASAS:* 3.5.8, 3.5.9

*SCANS:* **Resources** Allocate time, allocate money, allocate materials and facility resources, allocate human resources

**Information** Acquire and evaluate information, organize and maintain information, interpret and communicate information, use computers to process information (*optional*)

**Interpersonal** Participate as a member of a team, teach others, exercise leadership, negotiate to arrive at a decision, work with cultural diversity

**Systems** Monitor and correct performance

**Technology** Select technology, apply technology to a task (*optional*)

**Basic Skills** Reading, writing, arithmetic, listening, speaking

**Thinking Skills** Think creatively, make decisions, solve problems, see things in the mind's eye

**Personal Qualities** Responsibility, sociability, self-management

*EFF:* **Communication** Read with understanding, convey ideas in writing, speak so others can understand, listen actively, observe critically

**Decision Making** Solve problems and make decisions, plan

**Interpersonal** Cooperate with others, advocate and influence, guide others

**Lifelong Learning** Take responsibility for learning, reflect and evaluate, use information and communications technology (*optional*)

## Pre-assessment (*optional*) ◼◼◻

Use the Stand Out Assessment CD-ROM with ExamView® to create a pre-test for Unit 5.

## Warm-up and Review 5–10 mins. ◼◼◻

Ask students to take out a piece of paper and make a list of all the words and phrases they can remember from the vocabulary-building section. When they have written down everything they can think of, have them talk to a partner and try to add one or two more words and phrases to their lists. Make a class list on the board.

## Introduction 5–10 mins. ◼◼◻

Dictation:

1. Stress is a feeling that is created when we react to particular events.
2. The human body responds to stress by activating the nervous system and specific hormones.
3. Stress contributes to high blood pressure, strokes, and other illnesses in many individuals.
4. Stress also affects the immune system, which protects us from many serious diseases.

State the goal: *Today, we will identify ways to promote mental and physical well-being.*

## Presentation 1 10–15 mins. ◼◼◻

### A. Discuss the following questions in a small group.

Have students look at the three pictures in Exercise B. Ask them what they think they will be listening for. Before you play the recording, discuss some possible reasons for stress.

## Practice 1 10–15 mins. ◼◼◻

### B. Listen to the following people talk about how they relieve stress. Take notes.

**Note:** The listening script is on page 125a.

## Evaluation 1
5 mins. ■■■

Go over the answers as a class.

### C. EVALUATE Do you identify with any of these people? If yes, in what ways? If not, why not?

Discuss students' answers as a class.

---

### LISTENING SCRIPT

CD
TR 25

**Cooper:** *My name is Cooper and I work for a mortgage company. My job is very stressful because I work on commission and the only way I get paid is by helping people refinance their homes. If I don't help anyone, I don't make any money. The more people I help, the more money I make. I don't really like my job, so I'm going to school at night to study computer programming. Between work and school, I'm really busy and my work and studies put a lot of stress on me. One of the ways I cope with all this stress is meditation. Every morning before I leave for work, I sit outside on the porch where I can look at the trees and listen to the birds chirping. I close my eyes and breathe deeply, thinking of all the good things in my life. I picture my day at work as a productive, successful day. I picture my evening at school as a fun, eye-opening experience where I learn many new things that will help me change careers. When I open my eyes, I feel refreshed and ready to take on the day.*

**Stephanie:** *My name is Stephanie. I cope with my stress by exercising. I run every night after work. Running gives me time to think and use up all that built-up energy caused by stress. I work three jobs just to make enough money to pay the bills. The jobs aren't stressful, but worrying if I'm going to have enough money each month is. Running seems to be the only thing that calms my nerves.*

**Fletcher:** *I'm Fletcher.*
**Katie:** *And I'm Katie.*
**Fletcher:** *And the only way we can relieve our stress is by talking . . . to each other.*
**Katie:** *My mother is very sick and she lives with us, so I can take care of her.*
**Fletcher:** *And since Katie had to stop working to take care of her mother, I had to start working longer hours to make more money. Both of these things have put a lot of stress on us.*
**Katie:** *So, every night we take a walk around our neighborhood and talk. The fresh air is wonderful and just being able to talk about our days and our future helps us both relax. We know that we're doing the right thing by taking care of Mom, and as long as we have each other we'll be able to survive.*

---

## Presentation 2
5–10 mins. ■■■

### D. Advice columns often appear in newspapers and online. Read the problems. Do you agree with the advice?

---

If students are unfamiliar with the concept of an advice column, explain how it works. Ask students if they have ever read any advice columns and, if so, what kind of advice was given. This is a good opportunity to bring in newspapers as realia.

## Practice 2
10–15 mins. ■■

(Shorter classes can do this exercise for homework.)

### E. SUGGEST Pretend you are Ali and give advice to the following people.

## Evaluation 2
10–15 mins. ■■

Ask volunteers to read their advice letters out loud.

**Extended Practice:** Give each student a note card, or have students use their own sheet of paper. Have them write a short "Dear Ali" letter. Collect the cards and pass them out to students. Make sure no one gets his or her own card. Tell students to spend a few minutes coming up with the advice they would give for the person who wrote the letter. Have each student stand up, read his or her card out loud, and then give the advice that he or she came up with. As a class, discuss if the advice is good or bad. If students think the advice isn't good, have them come up with better advice as a class.

---

### INSTRUCTOR'S NOTES

_____

_____

_____

_____

_____

_____

_____

_____

_____

_____

---

**D.** **Advice columns often appear in newspapers and online. Read the problems. Do you agree with the advice?**

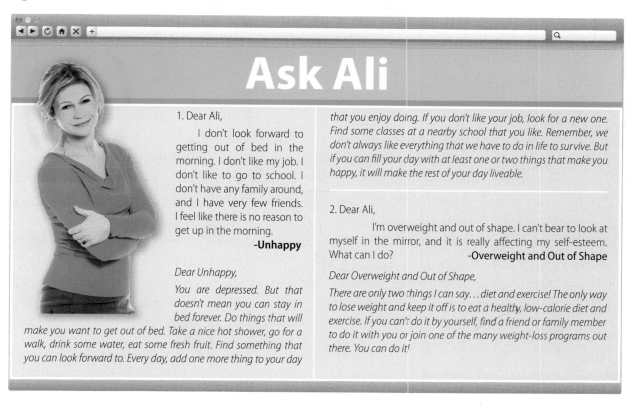

### Ask Ali

1. Dear Ali,

I don't look forward to getting out of bed in the morning. I don't like my job. I don't like to go to school. I don't have any family around, and I have very few friends. I feel like there is no reason to get up in the morning.

**-Unhappy**

*Dear Unhappy,*

*You are depressed. But that doesn't mean you can stay in bed forever. Do things that will make you want to get out of bed. Take a nice hot shower, go for a walk, drink some water, eat some fresh fruit. Find something that you can look forward to. Every day, add one more thing to your day that you enjoy doing. If you don't like your job, look for a new one. Find some classes at a nearby school that you like. Remember, we don't always like everything that we have to do in life to survive. But if you can fill your day with at least one or two things that make you happy, it will make the rest of your day liveable.*

2. Dear Ali,

I'm overweight and out of shape. I can't bear to look at myself in the mirror, and it is really affecting my self-esteem. What can I do? **-Overweight and Out of Shape**

*Dear Overweight and Out of Shape,*

*There are only two things I can say…diet and exercise! The only way to lose weight and keep it off is to eat a healthy, low-calorie diet and exercise. If you can't do it by yourself, find a friend or family member to do it with you or join one of the many weight-loss programs out there. You can do it!*

**E.** **SUGGEST Pretend you are Ali and give advice to the following people.** Answers will vary.

Dear Ali,

My daughter is overweight. All of the kids make fun of her at school, and I think she eats even more because she is unhappy. I try to cook healthy food at home, but that doesn't seem to be helping. What can I do?—*Mother Without a Clue*

Begin an exercise routine with her and make this a family activity.

Show her you are in this effort together. Teach her to cook and prepare her own healthy meals.

Dear Ali,

I have a lot of stress at work. My boss pushes me pretty hard, and I want to do a good job to get ahead, but I never have any time for myself or for my family. The doctor says all the stress is giving me high blood pressure. What should I do?—*Overworked*

You need to take time for yourself and your family or you will lose your health. Exercise together

before or after work. Walk at lunchtime.

WORKPLACE CONNECTION
Exercise G: Complete tasks as assigned.
Exercise H: Combine ideas and information; Interact appropriately with team members.

**F.  Danielle wrote a health-related article for her school paper. Read her article.**

### BACK ON TRACK

I think I take pretty good care of myself. But it wasn't always that way. I used to work really long hours, eat at fast-food restaurants because they were quick and easy, and I barely ever exercised. But I got a wake-up call from the doctor one day. He said I was obese, at risk for diabetes, and that I might not make it to my fortieth birthday. From that day forward, I began to make changes in my life. I started by going for a walk every day. Now I go to the gym three times a week, walk six miles two days a week, and play volleyball with my family on the weekends. The day the doctor gave me that horrible prognosis, I went straight to the market and filled my cart with healthy food. I now make my lunch every day and cook healthy dinners for my family. My purse and my car are always filled with healthy snacks and water. If I ever get a craving for something really unhealthy, I let myself have one bite of it, and then I stick a piece of gum in my mouth. Although the exercise and eating habits really helped to lower my blood pressure and risk for diabetes, I still have quite a bit of stress in my life. To combat that, I make sure I take at least a half an hour a day for myself. Sometimes I meditate, sometimes I call a good friend, and other times I just sit down and read a book for pleasure.

**G.  Answer the following questions.** Answers will vary.

1. What forced Danielle to make changes in her life?

   Her doctor told her she was at risk for diabetes because she was obese.

2. What changes did she make?

   She started exercising, eating healthy foods, and meditating.

3. Do you think her article is inspiring? Why?

   Yes, because diabetes runs in my family. She made good changes.

**H.  CREATE  With your classmates, create a health newsletter. Follow the steps below.**

1. Each student writes a health article that will be inspiring to others who read it.

2. After everyone has finished his or her article, work together to edit the articles.

3. Come up with a title for your newsletter.

4. Put your newsletter together and add artwork and photos.

## Presentation 3

10–15 mins. ■■■

**F.** Danielle wrote a health-related article for her school paper. Read her article.

Have students read the article to themselves. When they finish, read the article out loud to students. Answer any vocabulary questions students might have.

## Practice 3

10–15 mins. ■

(Shorter classes can do this exercise for homework.)

**G. Answer the following questions.**

If you want students to do this exercise individually, have them write their ideas on a piece of paper. If you want students to do this exercise in groups, have them discuss the questions.

## Evaluation 3

5–10 mins. ■

Talk about the word *inspiring* and what it means. Discuss the third question as a class. Discuss what makes something *inspiring*.

## Application

30–45 mins. ■■■

**H. CREATE** With your classmates, create a health newsletter. Follow the steps below.

Let students make this newsletter as simple or as elaborate as they want. The main purpose of this exercise is for students to write an article about their health habits. But, the fact that they are "publishing their writing" gives it more of a purpose and reasons to be inspiring.

If your students need it, help them through the writing process by having them first brainstorm ideas, then narrow down their ideas, write an outline, and create a first draft. (There is a worksheet in the Multilevel Worksheets to guide them through this process.)

**Optional Computer Activity:** Let students type their articles and produce their newsletter on the computer.

### MULTILEVEL WORKSHEETS

Unit 5, Lesson 1, Worksheet 1: Give Advice

Unit 5, Lesson 1, Worksheet 2: Write an Article

Refer students to *Stand Out 5 Workbook,* Unit 5, Lesson 1 for practice with adverbial clauses of place.

Go to the *Activity Bank* online for suggestions on promoting digital literacy and using the Internet to enhance this lesson.

### INSTRUCTOR'S NOTES

**Goal:** Ask about medical bills
**Pronunciation:** Clear speech on the telephone
**Academic Strategy:** Focused listening
**Vocabulary:** *remit to, responsible party, procedure, co-pay, payable, code*

## Agenda

- Listen to two phone conversations between patients and the doctor's office.
- Practice conversations with a partner.
- Write questions you would ask about a medical bill.

## Resources

**Multilevel Worksheets:** Unit 5, Lesson 2, Worksheets 1–2
**Workbook:** Unit 5, Lesson 2
**Audio:** CD Tracks 26–27
**Suggested Realia:** Medical bills

## Pacing

- 1.5 hour classes
- 2.5 hour classes
- 3+ hour classes

## STANDARDS CORRELATIONS

*CCRS:* RI1, RI4, RI7, SL1, SL6
*CASAS:* 3.2.4
*SCANS:* **Information** Acquire and evaluate information, organize and maintain information, interpret and communicate information
**Interpersonal** Participate as a member of a team, teach others, exercise leadership, negotiate to arrive at a decision, work with cultural diversity
**Systems** Monitor and correct performance
**Basic Skills** Reading, writing, arithmetic, listening, speaking
**Thinking Skills** Think creatively, make decisions, solve problems, see things in the mind's eye
**Personal Qualities** Responsibility, sociability, self-management
*EFF:* **Communication** Read with understanding, convey ideas in writing, speak so others can understand, listen actively, observe critically
**Decision Making** Solve problems and make decisions, plan
**Interpersonal** Cooperate with others, advocate and influence, resolve conflict and negotiate, guide others
**Lifelong Learning** Take responsibility for learning

## Warm-up and Review   5–10 mins. ■■■

Have students talk about the process of creating their health newsletter. Ask them if there is any real-world application for an activity like this.

## Introduction   10–20 mins. ■■■

Dictation:

1. After your doctor's appointment, your doctor's office will submit a claim to your insurance company.
2. The insurance company uses the information on the claim to pay the doctor for those services.
3. A statement shows how much your doctor's office billed your insurance company for the services you received.
4. After your insurance company pays your doctor, you may need to pay the doctor any balance due.

State the goal: *Today, you will practice asking questions about medical bills.*

## Presentation 1   10–15 mins. ■■■

**A. Listen to the phone conversation Linda Gregory is having with the receptionist at the doctor's office. Why is Linda confused about the amount she owes?**

## Practice 1   10–15 mins. ■■■

**B. Look at the medical bill and answer the questions.**

### LISTENING SCRIPT   🎧 CD TR 26

**Receptionist:** *Good morning, Dr. Rosenberg's office.*
**Patient:** *Um, yes, this is Linda Gregory. I brought my daughter, Courtney, in a few weeks ago for her six-month checkup. I just received the bill and I have a few questions.*
**Receptionist:** *Yes, Mrs. Gregory. Let me pull up your records. Do you have the date of the statement?*
**Patient:** *Yes, it is October 6.*
**Receptionist:** *OK, I have it right here. How can I help you?*
**Patient:** *Well, I don't see why I owe 20 dollars.*
**Receptionist:** *That is your co-pay.*
**Patient:** *But on the statement it says that I already paid my 20 dollar co-pay.*
**Receptionist:** *Yes, you're right. But when we talked to the insurance company, they told us that your co-pay is 40 dollars. You already paid 20 dollars, so you owe another 20 dollars.*
**Patient:** *40 dollars? When did my co-pay go up to 40 dollars?*
**Receptionist:** *I don't know, ma'am. You'll have to call your insurance company to find out.*
**Patient:** *OK. So all I owe right now is 20 dollars?*
**Receptionist:** *Yes.*
**Patient:** *OK. Thank you for your time.*

# LESSON ② What's this charge for?

GOAL ▪ Ask about medical bills

WORKPLACE CONNECTION
Exercise B: Interpret and communicate information.

🎧 **A.** Listen to the phone conversation Linda Gregory is having with the receptionist at the doctor's office. Why is Linda confused about the amount she owes?

CD TR 26

| DOCTOR | | | |
|---|---|---|---|
| Amy Rosenberg, M.D., Inc. | STATEMENT DATE | STATEMENT # | BALANCE DUE |
| 2880 Chestnut Ave., Ste. 340 | 10/06 | 4689–36 | $20.00 |
| Topeka, KS 66675 | | | |
| Office Phone (785) 555-0012 | | | |

**RESPONSIBLE PARTY**
Mrs. Linda Gregory
56 Plains Ave.
Topeka, KS 66675

**MAKE CHECK PAYABLE AND REMIT TO**
AMY ROSENBERG, M.D., Inc.
2880 Chestnut Ave., Ste. 340
Topeka, KS 66675

**PATIENT NAME:** Gregory, Courtney          **PROVIDER:** Amy Rosenberg, M.D.

| DATE | PROCEDURE | DESCRIPTION OF SERVICE | CO-PAY | AMOUNT PAYABLE |
|---|---|---|---|---|
| 8/23 | 99391 | Well-Child Check | | $100.00 |
| 8/23 | 90700 | DTaP Vaccine | | $40.00 |
| 8/23 | 90465 | Vaccine Admin | | $28.00 |
| 8/23 | 90645 | Hib Vaccine | | $32.00 |
| 8/23 | 90466 | Vaccine Admin | | $28.00 |
| 8/23 | | Patient Co-Pay | −$20.00 | |
| 9/01 | | Primary Insurance Payment | | −$120.00 |
| 9/01 | | Uncollectible | | −$68.00 |

## B. Look at the medical bill and answer the questions.

1. Who is expected to pay this bill?

   *Mrs. Linda Gegory*

2. Why did the patient go to the doctor?

   *for a checkup and vaccines*

3. Why is the name of the responsible party different from the patient's name?

   *She is the mother.*

4. How much is owed?

   *$20*

5. Does anything on the bill confuse you? Write a question to ask your classmates or teacher.

   *Yes. I don't understand what "uncollectible" means. Who is responsible for that? (Answer will vary.)*

CD
TR 27

**C.** **Read and listen to the following conversation between a patient and a receptionist at the doctor's office.**

| | |
|---|---|
| **Receptionist:** | Dr. Brook's office. |
| **Patient:** | Um, yes, this is Cooper Jackson. I came in and saw the doctor a few months ago for the pain I was having in my leg. I just received the bill, and I have a few questions. |
| **Receptionist:** | Of course, Mr. Jackson. Let me pull up your records. Do you have the date of the statement? |
| **Patient:** | Yes, it's June 16th. |
| **Receptionist:** | Ok, I have it here. How can I help you? |
| **Patient:** | Well, I don't understand what this $264 charge is for. |
| **Receptionist:** | That is for the X-rays the technician took of your leg. |
| **Patient:** | OK, but shouldn't my insurance pay for that? |
| **Receptionist:** | Yes, they might pay some. As you can see on the bill, we have billed your insurance company but are still waiting to hear back from them. Once we do, we'll send you an adjusted bill reflecting how much you owe. |
| **Patient:** | Oh, so if I don't have to pay this $264, why did you send me a bill? |
| **Receptionist:** | I know it may seem a bit confusing. Our billing department automatically sends out statements to our current patients every month, whether or not we have heard back from the insurance companies. It usually takes about a month for the bill to reflect what the insurance company has paid, so in general, if you wait two or three months to pay your bill, your statement should show the correct amount due. |
| **Patient:** | I see. That makes sense. So, I don't need to pay this bill now? |
| **Receptionist:** | No. Wait until you see an adjusted amount on there and then pay the bill. |
| **Patient:** | Great! Thanks for your help. |
| **Receptionist:** | Have a nice day, Mr. Jackson. |

**D.** **Practice the conversation with a partner. Switch roles.**

**E.** **VISUALIZE** **Practice the conversation again. This time use the information below to change the patient's questions. The receptionist will have to be creative to come up with a response.**

| Name | Reason for visit | Date of statement | Question |
|---|---|---|---|
| Jenna Lyn | backache | May 25th | Why isn't the payment I made showing up on the statement? |
| Javier Bardo | headaches | December 2nd | Do you offer discounted services? I don't have health insurance. |
| Kim Jensen | skin rash | March 14th | Why do I have to pay more than my co-pay? |
| Young Lee | ingrown toenail | July 7th | Why didn't my insurance pay for the procedure? |

## Practice 1 *(continued)*    10–15 mins. ■■■

Tell the class that insurance forms and medical bills are often difficult to understand. Encourage students to call their doctors' offices or their insurance companies if there is something on a bill they don't understand.

## Evaluation 1    5 mins. ■■■

Go over the answers as a class.

## Presentation 2    5–10 mins. ■■■

> ### LISTENING SCRIPT     CD TR 27
> *The listening script matches the conversation in Exercise C.*

C. **Read and listen to the following conversation between a patient and a receptionist at the doctor's office.**

## Practice 2    10–15 mins. ■■

(Shorter classes can do these exercises for homework.)

D. **Practice the conversation with a partner. Switch roles.**

E. **VISUALIZE  Practice the conversation again. This time use the information below to change the patient's questions. The receptionist will have to be creative to come up with a response.**

Model this activity for students by practicing with a volunteer.

## Evaluation 2    10–15 mins. ■■

Walk around the classroom and listen to students' conversations. When students have finished, ask volunteer pairs to perform their conversations for the class.

### PRONUNCIATION

### Speaking on the phone

Remind students that when speaking on the phone, they need to enunciate clearly. To help them improve this skill, have students stand back-to-back when practicing conversations in pairs.

## Presentation 3

Ask students a few simple questions about the bill in Exercise C. Don't answer any of their questions or give them any information that you think they might need.

## Practice 3
5–10 mins. ■

(Shorter classes can do this exercise for homework.)

F.  **Look at the bill below and write five questions you could ask about it.**

## Evaluation 3
5–10 mins. ■

As a class, go over the questions students wrote and try to answer the questions together.

G.  **Go over the bill with your teacher to make sure you understand everything on it.**

## Application
10–20 mins. ■■■

H.  **Find a partner (receptionist) and have a conversation, asking him or her the questions you wrote in Exercise F. Switch roles.**

### MULTILEVEL WORKSHEETS

Unit 5, Lesson 2, Worksheet 1: Conversations with the Doctor's Office (listening)

Unit 5, Lesson 2, Worksheet 2: Medical Bills

**Refer students to *Stand Out 5 Workbook,* Unit 5, Lesson 2 for practice with adverbial clauses of time.**

**Go to the *Activity Bank* online for suggestions on promoting digital literacy and using the Internet to enhance this lesson.**

### BEST PRACTICE

## Switching roles

The main goal of a conversation exercise is that students practice speaking. When students are engaged in role plays, they can imagine the conversation in a real-world context. Students can also see the relevance of the conversation to real life. Having students switch roles allows them to approach the conversation from another perspective. The additional practice builds speaking skills and increases motivation.

### INSTRUCTOR'S NOTES

WORKPLACE CONNECTION
Exercise F: Combine ideas and information.
Exercise H: Interact appropriately with team members.

**F.** **Look at the bill below and write five questions you could ask about it.**

Answers may vary.

**STATEMENT**

*Skin Care Center*
5948 Atlantic Avenue
Topeka, KS 66675
Office Phone (785) 555-0198

| CLOSING DATE: | 7/15 |
|---|---|
| BALANCE DUE: | $179.90 |
| ACCOUNT #: | 22365-1 |
| AMOUNT ENCLOSED: | _____ |
| PATIENT: | Linda Gregory 7653 |

**Bill to:** Linda Gregory
56 Plains Avenue
Topeka, KS 66675

Any change in the above address should be reported to our office.

*Skin Care Center*
5948 Atlantic Avenue
Topeka, KS 66675

**DETACH AND RETURN UPPER PORTION WITH YOUR PAYMENT**

Keep bottom portion for your records

**PATIENT NAME:** Gregory, Linda          **PROVIDER:** Elton Frank, M.D.

| DATE | CODE | DESCRIPTION | CHARGE | CREDIT |
|---|---|---|---|---|
| 2/05 | 99204 | Office Visit New Patient | $240.00 | |
| | | Paid By Health Care PPO | | $240.00 |
| 6/15 | 11301 | Shave Skin Lesion 0.6-1.0cm | $175.00 | |
| | | Paid By Health Care PPO | | $98.95 |
| 6/15 | 88305 | Tissue Exam by Pathologist | $190.00 | |
| | | Paid By Health Care PPO | | $86.15 |
| 6/15 | A4550 | Surgical Tray | $55.00 | |
| | | Paid By Health Care PPO | | $55.00 |
| | | **DUE FROM PATIENT** | **$179.90** | |

1. When was this bill due? _____

2. Why does the Health Care PPO pay less than the charge? _____

3. Who is the doctor? _____

4. What is a pathologist? _____

5. Can I pay a smaller amount over 3 months? _____

**G.** **Go over the bill with your teacher to make sure you understand everything on it.**

**H.** **Find a partner (receptionist) and have a conversation, asking him or her the questions you wrote in Exercise F. Switch roles.**

LESSON **3** **Health insurance**

GOAL ■ Interpret health insurance information

WORKPLACE CONNECTION
Exercises A, C: Interact appropriately with team members.
Exercise B: Interpret and communicate information.

**A. How much do you know about health insurance? In a small group, try to answer the following questions. If you need help, talk to other groups.** Answers will vary.

1. Is it mandatory in your state to have health insurance?

2. What happens if you see a doctor or go to a hospital without health insurance?

3. What is the difference between an HMO and a PPO?

**B. ANALYZE Look at the chart about insured and uninsured people and answer the questions.**

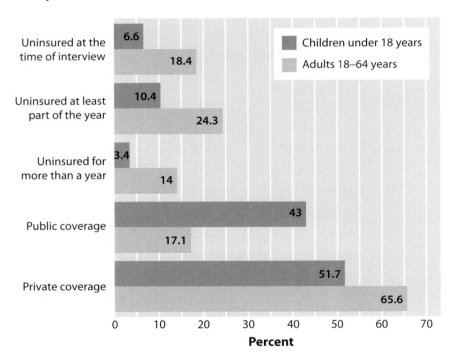

1. What is the percentage of insured adults? _____ 82.7%

2. What is the percentage of children who were uninsured for more than a year? _____ 3.4%

3. What is the percentage of adults who have private insurance? _____ 65.6%

4. What is the percentage of children who have public coverage? _____ 43%

**C. Ask your partner questions about the information presented in the chart in Exercise B. Use the questions from the same exercise as examples.**
Answers will vary.
What percent of adults were uninsured at the time of the interview?
What is the percentage of insured children?

## AT-A-GLANCE PREP

**Goal:** Interpret health insurance information
**Academic Strategy:** Interpreting bar charts and tables
**Vocabulary:** *insured, uninsured, percentage*

### Agenda

☐ Discuss health insurance.
☐ Interpret a bar chart.
☐ Interpret a table.
☐ Recreate a chart.

### Resources

**Multilevel Worksheet:** Unit 5, Lesson 3, PDF and Worksheet 1
**Workbook:** Unit 5, Lesson 3

### Pacing

■ 1.5 hour classes   ■ 2.5 hour classes
■ 3+ hour classes

## STANDARDS CORRELATIONS

*CCRS:* RI1, RI4, RI7, SL1
*CASAS:* 3.2.3
*SCANS:* **Resources** Allocate time, allocate human resources

**Information** Acquire and evaluate information, organize and maintain information, interpret and communicate information, use computers to process information (*optional*)

**Interpersonal** Participate as a member of a team, exercise leadership, negotiate to arrive at a decision, work with cultural diversity

**Systems** Understand systems, monitor and correct performance, improve and design systems

**Technology** Select technology, apply technology to a task (*optional*)

**Basic Skills** Reading, writing, arithmetic, listening, speaking

**Thinking Skills** Think creatively, make decisions, solve problems, see things in the mind's eye

**Personal Qualities** Responsibility, sociability, self-management

*EFF:* **Communication** Read with understanding, convey ideas in writing, speak so others can understand, listen actively, observe critically

**Decision Making** Use math to solve problems and communicate, plan

**Interpersonal** Cooperate with others, advocate and influence, resolve conflict and negotiate, guide others

**Lifelong Learning** Take responsibility for learning, reflect and evaluate, learn through research, use information and communications technology (*optional*)

## Warm-up and Review          5–10 mins. ■■■

Have students repeat the application from the previous lesson, this time with a different partner.

## Introduction          5–10 mins. ■■■

Before beginning the dictation, have students practice writing down large numbers and percentages. Allow students to use numerals in dictation rather than spelling out the numbers.

Dictation:

1. From January to June, 2010, 49.9 million people didn't have health insurance.
2. The percentage of children under age 18 years old who were uninsured in 2010 was 9.8%.
3. The percentage of people covered by private health insurance decreased in 2010 to 64%, or 195.9 million.
4. The percentage of and number of people covered by government health insurance has increased to 31%, or 95 million, in 2010; from 30.06%, or 93.2 million, in 2009.

State the goal: *Today, you will interpret graphs and tables about health insurance coverage.*

## Presentation 1          15–20 mins. ■■■

A. **How much do you know about health insurance? In a small group, try to answer the following questions. If you need help, talk to other groups.**

B. **ANALYZE Look at the chart about insured and uninsured people and answer the questions.**

## Practice 1          10–15 mins. ■■■

C. **Ask your partner questions about the information presented in the chart in Exercise B. Use the questions from the same exercise as examples.**

## Evaluation 1          ■■■

Observe pair work.

The complete PDF file that contains the graphs and tables from this lesson can be found on the Multilevel Worksheet.

(*Source:* Health Insurance Coverage: Early Release of Estimates from the National Health Interview Survey, January–June, 2007, by Robin A. Cohen, Ph.D., and Michael E. Martinez, M.P.H., Division of Health Interview Statistics, National Center for Health Statistics)

## Presentation 2

5–10 mins. ■■■

Go over the chart with students. Make sure they understand how to read it. Ask them a few questions to check for understanding, such as, *What percentage of females aged 45 to 64 don't have health insurance coverage?*

## Practice 2

10–15 mins. ■■

(Shorter classes can do these exercises for homework.)

**D. Look at the chart about people without health insurance and complete the sentences below.**

**E. ANALYZE Write three more sentences about the statistics in the chart in Exercise D.**

## Evaluation 2

5–10 mins. ■■

Ask volunteers to write their sentences on the board. Have students compare the sentences with the information presented in the chart.

### BEST PRACTICE

## Reading a bar chart

Reading a bar chart can initially be challenging for some students because they are unfamiliar with this type of presentation, or erroneously perceive bar charts as puzzling images that are hard to understand. Make it clear to students that bar charts are actually easy-read diagrams that allow us to visualize lots of numerical information in a text. Illustrate that it is sometime easier to read a bar chart than to read a long text. Try using the following analogy to explain how to read a bar chart:

Point out to students that a bar chart looks very much like a city skyline (with short, medium, and tall buildings). Explain that the height of each *building* or bar represents the size or value of the thing being

measured. Demonstrate that the *buildings* may be displayed in colors (usually two or more) and that a legend or guide will indicate what each color stands for. Mention that bar charts are sometimes vertical and sometimes horizontal; however, this doesn't have an effect on the information presented.

### INSTRUCTOR'S NOTES

WORKPLACE CONNECTION
Exercise D: Interpret and communicate information.
Exercise E: Combine ideas and information.

**D.** **Look at the chart about people without health insurance and complete the sentences below.**

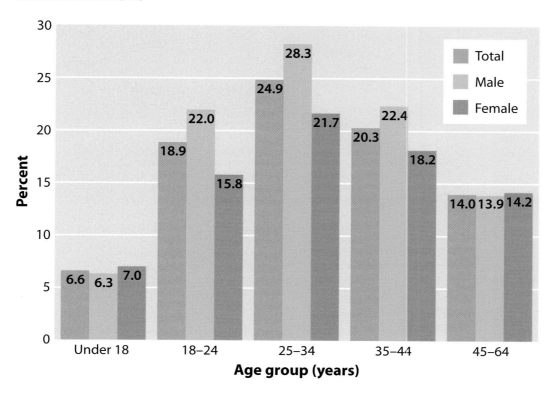

1. Of both sexes, the _____ *males* _____ are the most uninsured.

2. Out of all the age groups, the _____ *25–34* _____ -year-olds are the most uninsured.

3. _____ *6.6%* _____ of children are uninsured.

4. _____ *93.4%* _____ of children are insured.

5. _____ *18.2%* _____ of women aged 35–44 are uninsured.

6. _____ *Answers will vary.* _____ of people in my age group are uninsured.

**E.** **ANALYZE  Write three more sentences about the statistics in the chart in Exercise D.**

*Answers will vary. Sample answers are given.*

1. *24.9% of adults 25–34 are uninsured.* _____

2. *86.1% of men 45–64 are insured.* _____

3. *People 25–34 are the least insured.* _____

WORKPLACE CONNECTION
Exercise G: Interpret and communicate information.
Exercise H: Interact appropriately with team members; Combine ideas and information.

**F.** **Read the chart about insurance coverage and demographics. Then, write six questions based on the data.** Answers will vary. Sample questions are given below.

| Selected characteristic | Uninsured at the time of interview | Public health plan coverage | Private health insurance coverage |
|---|---|---|---|
| | Percent (standard error) | | |
| **Race/Ethnicity** | | | |
| Hispanic or Latino | 34.5 (1.14) | 20.2 (0.87) | 46.0 (1.25) |
| Non-Hispanic: | | | |
| White, single race | 12.3 (0.39) | 14.5 (0.46) | 74.6 (0.60) |
| Black, single race | 18.0 (0.83) | 30.4 (0.99) | 53.0 (1.18) |
| Asian, single race | 13.7 (0.87) | 13.6 (1.31) | 73.4 (1.61) |
| Other races and multiple races | 21.1 (2.36) | 23.8 (2.13) | 56.7 (2.95) |
| **Education** | | | |
| Less than high school | 34.0 (1.23) | 34.6 (1.22) | 32.4 (1.22) |
| High school diploma or GED[4] | 23.2 (0.65) | 21.8 (0.66) | 56.4 (0.80) |
| More than high school | 10.6 (0.38) | 12.2 (0.38) | 78.5 (0.54) |
| **Employment status** | | | |
| Employed | 15.3 (0.42) | 9.4 (0.31) | 75.9 (0.50) |
| Unemployed | 43.1 (1.38) | 28.5 (1.48) | 28.6 (1.39) |
| Not in workforce | 15.9 (0.69) | 41.0 (0.89) | 46.8 (.096) |

1. _What percent of employed people were uninsured at the time of the interview?_

2. _Which ethnic group was least insured at the time of the interview?_

3. _Does education make a difference in how much insurance you have?_

4. _What percent of people with only a GED had insurance at the time of the interview?_

5. _What percent of uninsured were not in the workforce at the time of the interview?_

6. _Which racial/ethnic group was insured 87% at the time of the interview?_

**G.** **Ask three classmates the questions you wrote in Exercise F.**

**H.** **CREATE** In a small group, choose one of the three graphs or charts presented in this lesson. Recreate the data using information from the students in your class.

## Presentation 3
5–10 mins. ■■■

Ask students what data are presented in the table. As a class, come up with some sentences about the data. For example, *43.1% of unemployed people didn't have health insurance at the time of interview.*

On the board, brainstorm some questions students might ask about the data in the table. For example, *What percentage of people with a high school diploma are uninsured?*

## Practice 3
15–20 mins. ■

(Shorter classes can do these exercises for homework.)

F. **Read the chart about insurance coverage and demographics. Then, write six questions based on the data.**

G. **Ask three classmates the questions you wrote in Exercise F.**

## Evaluation 3
5–15 mins. ■

Observe.

## Application
20–30 mins. ■■■

H. **CREATE In a small group, choose one of the three graphs or charts presented in this lesson. Recreate the data using information from the students in your class.**

### MULTILEVEL WORKSHEETS

Unit 5, Lesson 3, PDF: Health Insurance

Unit 5, Lesson 3, Worksheet 1: Doing Research

**Refer students to *Stand Out 5 Workbook*, Unit 5, Lesson 3 for practice with adverbial clauses of reason.**

**Go to the *Activity Bank* online for suggestions on promoting digital literacy and using the Internet to enhance this lesson.**

## INSTRUCTOR'S NOTES

## AT-A-GLANCE PREP

**Goal:** Identify addictions

**Grammar:** Adverb clauses of concession

**Academic Strategies:** Defining words, using a dictionary

**Vocabulary:** *addiction, tolerance, impairment, substance, physiological, psychological, process, detoxification, withdrawal*

### Agenda

- ☐ Define *addiction*.
- ☐ Learn vocabulary related to addictions.
- ☐ Distinguish between substance and process addictions.
- ☐ Work with adverb clauses of concession.
- ☐ Write about an addiction.

### Resources

**Multilevel Worksheets:** Unit 5, Lesson 4, Worksheets 1–2

**Workbook:** Unit 5, Lesson 4

### Pacing

- ■ 1.5 hour classes   ■ 2.5 hour classes
- ■ 3+ hour classes

## STANDARDS CORRELATIONS

*CCRS:* RI4, W3, W4, SL1, SL2, L5

*CASAS:* 3.1.5, 3.5.8, 3.4.5

*SCANS:* **Information** Acquire and evaluate information, organize and maintain information, interpret and communicate information

**Interpersonal** Participate as a member of a team, negotiate to arrive at a decision, work with cultural diversity

**Systems** Monitor and correct performance

**Basic Skills** Reading, writing, arithmetic, listening, speaking

**Thinking Skills** Think creatively, make decisions, solve problems, see things in the mind's eye

**Personal Qualities** Responsibility, sociability, self-management

*EFF:* **Communication** Read with understanding, convey ideas in writing, speak so others can understand, listen actively, observe critically

**Decision Making** Solve problems and make decisions, plan

**Interpersonal** Cooperate with others

**Lifelong Learning** Take responsibility for learning, reflect and evaluate

## Warm-up and Review     10–15 mins. ■■■

Have students take out their graphs from the previous lesson. Ask volunteers from each group to present the graph to the class.

## Introduction     5–10 mins. ■■■

Dictation:

1. She spends over $500 a month on clothes and shoes.
2. He likes to go to the horse races every weekend and place bets.
3. Her brother plays video games with his friends for more than three hours a day.
4. They exercise at least four hours a day, six days a week.

State the goal: *Today, we will identify different addictions and discuss vocabulary associated with addictions.*

## Presentation 1     10–15 mins. ■■■

**A. Look up the word *addiction* in a dictionary. Write the definition and an example sentence that uses the word.**

Have students do this exercise by themselves and then go over the definitions and example sentences as a class.

Ask students to look back at their dictation sentences. Ask them if they think the people described in these sentences have addictions.

**B. Work with a partner and brainstorm a list of addictions.**

Once students have completed their lists, make a comprehensive list on the board.

## Practice 1     10–15 mins. ■■■

**C. FIND OUT  Match the words below to their correct definitions and write the complete sentences on a separate piece of paper. Use a dictionary if you need to.**

# LESSON **4** Addictions

GOAL ■ Identify addictions

WORKPLACE CONNECTION
Exercises A, C: Complete tasks as assigned.
Exercise B: Interact appropriately with team members.

**A. Look up the word *addiction* in a dictionary. Write the definition and an example sentence that uses the word.** Answers will vary.

**addiction** *n.* _the state of being abnormally dependent on something_

_He has an addiction to lying._

**B. Work with a partner and brainstorm a list of addictions.** Answers will vary.
nicotine, alcohol, cocaine, coffee, heroin, chocolate, shopping, food, etc.

**C. FIND OUT** **Match the words below to their correct definitions and write the complete sentences on a separate piece of paper. Use a dictionary if you need to.**

1. Tolerance is _g_.

2. Impairment is _f_.

3. Substance addiction is _b_.

4. Physiological dependence is _j_.

5. A twelve-step program is _c_.

6. Psychological dependence is _d_.

7. Process addiction is _e_.

8. Detoxification is _h_.

9. Withdrawal is _a_.

10. An addict is _i_.

a. the process of giving up a substance or activity to which a person has become addicted

b. a condition in which a person is dependent on some chemical substance

c. a plan for overcoming an addiction by going through twelve stages of personal development

d. a condition in which a person requires certain activities or the intake of some substance in order to maintain mental stability

e. a condition in which a person is dependent on some type of behavior

f. an inability to carry on normal, everyday functions because of an addiction

g. the ability of the body to endure a certain amount of a substance

h. the process of adjusting to the absence of some substance or activity that a person has become addicted to

i. a person physically or emotionally dependent on a substance or an activity

j. a condition in which a person's body requires certain behaviors or the intake of some substance, without which it will become physically ill

WORKPLACE CONNECTION
Exercises D, F: Complete tasks as assigned.
Exercise E: Interact appropriately with team members.

**D.** Look at the list of addictions below. Which ones are substance (*S*) addictions and which ones are process (*P*) addictions? Circle your answers.

| Addictions | | |
|---|---|---|
| alcohol (S) P | food (S) P | shopping  S (P) |
| caffeine (S) P | gambling  S (P) | video games  S (P) |
| prescription medicine (S) P | surfing the Internet  S (P) | work  S (P) |
| illegal drugs (S) P | smoking (nicotine) (S) P | |

**E.** In a small group, discuss the following questions.  Answers will vary.

1. Why do people become addicts?  either physical or psychological dependence

2. What can you do if you are addicted to something?  Seek help from a doctor.

3. What can you do to help a friend or family member who is addicted to something?
Support them. Give them information about recovery programs.

**F.** **ANALYZE** Read the statements below. Do you think each person has an addiction? Circle *yes* or *no* and give a reason for each answer.  Answers will vary.

1. Although my uncle Gerry sold his car to spend more time at casinos in Las Vegas, he says he doesn't have a gambling problem.
**Addiction:** (yes) no  **Reason:** A car is needed to work and live. This is an irresponsible choice.

2. Even though her sister spends thousands of dollars a month on her credit cards, she doesn't think she is a shopaholic.
**Addiction:** (yes) no  **Reason:** If you outspend your budget, you have out-of-control spending.

3. Danielle is convinced she isn't addicted to caffeine although she has to drink two cups of coffee before she can get out of bed in the morning.
**Addiction:** (yes) no  **Reason:** If you need to consume something before you can take action, you are an addict.

4. In spite of the fact that Fletcher plays video games for three hours a night instead of doing his homework, he denies he has a problem.
**Addiction:**  yes (no)  **Reason:** Maybe he has difficulty with schoolwork and he is avoiding it.

Smartphone addiction
can be dangerous.

## Evaluation 1

5 mins. ■■■

Go over the answers as a class.

## Practice 1 *(continued)*

D.  **Look at the list of addictions below. Which ones are substance (*S*) addictions and which ones are process (*P*) addictions? Circle your answers.**

## Presentation 2

5–10 mins. ■■■

E.  **In a small group, discuss the following questions.**

Once students have discussed the questions in groups, discuss them as a class.

## Practice 2

10–15 mins. ■■

(Shorter classes can do this exercise for homework.)

F.  **ANALYZE** **Read the statements below. Do you think each person has an addiction? Circle *yes* or *no* and give a reason for each answer.**

Have students do this exercise by themselves.

## Evaluation 2

10–15 mins. ■■

Put students in small groups and have them discuss their answers. Tell them there are no right or wrong answers, especially since there are not many details given.

### BEST PRACTICE

## Checking homework assignments

The goal of assigning an exercise for homework is to allow students the opportunity to work and think independently. Not all homework has to be collected and graded, but it is good to make sure that students have completed the assignment. If not, students have not met the goal. There are many ways to do this. One suggestion is to ask students to compare their answers in pairs. This gives students the chance to correct and change their work before checking or discussing answers as a class.

### INSTRUCTOR'S NOTES

## Presentation 3

### G. Study the chart with your classmates and teacher.

To help students better understand the meaning of the sentences, have them come up with a few of their own and write them on the board for the class to analyze.

## Practice 3

10–15 mins. ■

(Shorter classes can do this exercise for homework.)

### H. Create sentences with dependent and independent clauses. Use the ideas below and the sentences in the chart in Exercise G as examples.

## Evaluation 3

10–15 mins. ■

Have volunteers write their sentences on the board for the class to see.

## Application

10–20 mins. ■■■

### I. VISUALIZE Imagine a good friend of yours has an addiction to something. Write about his or her addiction. How is it affecting your friend's life? How is it affecting your life? How is your friendship different because of it?

The reason for the imaginary addiction is to raise students' comfort level. You may decide to make this a lighthearted exercise by suggesting they write about something funny, for example, an addiction to chocolate or an addiction to learning English.

Give students an example by talking about one of your own addictions.

Example description of an addiction: *I am addicted to exercise. The first thing I do when I wake up in the morning is go for a run. When I get to work, I park as far away from the building as possible, so I have to walk far to get to my office. Every hour, I take five minutes and do something . . . stretching, jumping jacks, push-ups. During my lunch break, I walk up and down the stairs for 40 minutes. After work, I go for a two-hour bike ride. My family and friends complain that I am too skinny. They also say I never have enough time to spend with them because I am always exercising. My coworkers complain that I never have lunch with them. I really like the way I look and feel. But maybe I need to start exercising less. What do you think?*

MULTILEVEL WORKSHEETS

Unit 5, Lesson 4, Worksheet 1: Substance Abuse and Addiction (reading)

Unit 5, Lesson 4, Worksheet 2: Adverb Clauses of Concession

**Refer students to *Stand Out 5 Workbook,* Unit 5, Lesson 4 for more practice with adverb clauses of concession.**

**Go to the *Activity Bank* online for suggestions on promoting digital literacy and using the Internet to enhance this lesson.**

INSTRUCTOR'S NOTES

_____
_____
_____
_____
_____
_____
_____
_____
_____
_____
_____
_____
_____
_____
_____
_____
_____
_____
_____

WORKPLACE CONNECTION
Exercise H: Complete tasks as assigned.
Exercise I: Combine ideas and information.

**G. Study the chart with your classmates and teacher.**

| Adverb Clauses of Concession | |
|---|---|
| **Dependent clause** | **Independent clause** |
| **Although** he spends a lot of time in Las Vegas, | he says he doesn't have a gambling problem. |
| **Even though** her sister spends thousands of dollars a month, | she doesn't think she is a shopaholic. |
| **Though** she has to drink two cups of coffee before she can get out of bed in the morning, | she is convinced she isn't addicted to caffeine. |
| **In spite of the fact that** he plays video games for three hours a night, | he denies he has a problem. |

**Explanation:** Adverb clauses of concession show a contrast in ideas. The main or independent clauses show the unexpected outcome. The unexpected outcome in the third example is that it is surprising that she thinks she isn't addicted to caffeine.

**Note:** The clauses can be reversed and have the same meaning. Do not use a comma if the independent clause comes first in the sentence.

**Example:** *She doesn't think she is a shopaholic even though she spends thousands of dollars a month.*

**H. Create sentences with dependent and independent clauses. Use the ideas below and the sentences in the chart in Exercise G as examples.** Answers will vary.

    Internet addiction/spends five hours a day online
    shopping addiction/goes to the mall at least once a day
    food addiction/weighs over 300 pounds
    drug addiction/sold all his clothes to buy more drugs

1. Even though she spends 5 hours a day online, she denies an Internet addiction.

2. Although he goes to the mall at least once a day, he is convinced he doesn't have a shopping addiction.

3. In spite of the fact that she weighs over 300 pounds, she denies a food addiction.

4. Though he sold all his clothes to buy more drugs, he doesn't think he has a drug addiction.

**I. VISUALIZE Imagine a good friend of yours has an addiction to something. Write about his or her addiction. How is it affecting your friend's life? How is it affecting your life? How is your friendship different because of it?** Answers will vary.

GOAL ■ Interpret procedures for first aid

WORKPLACE CONNECTION
Exercise A: Complete tasks as assigned.
Exercise B: Interact appropriately with team members.

**A.** **What does a first-aid kit have in it? Use the words in the box to label each item. Write the number.**

| | | |
|---|---|---|
| 1. adhesive bandages | 2. adhesive cloth tape | 3. antibiotic ointment |
| 4. antiseptic wipes | 5. aspirin | 6. cold compress/ice pack |
| 7. compress dressing | 8. first-aid manual | 9. hydrocortisone ointment |
| 10. roller bandage | 11. scissors | 12. sterile gauze pads |
| 13. sterile gloves | 14. thermometer | 15. tweezers |

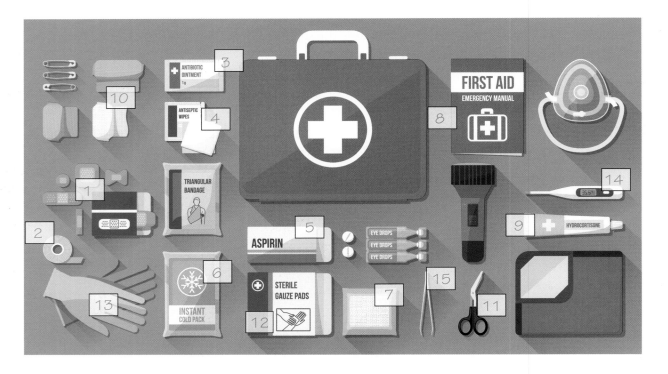

**B.** **Do you have a first-aid kit? Why is each item important? Discuss your ideas with your classmates.** Answers will vary.

## AT-A-GLANCE PREP

**Goal:** Interpret procedures for first aid
**Academic Strategy:** Problem solving
**Vocabulary:** first-aid kit items, *burn, choking, poisoning, open wound, head injury, shock, external bleeding, strike, treat*

### Agenda
- Label items in a first-aid kit.
- Determine appropriate first-aid procedures for various injuries.

### Resources
**Multilevel Worksheet:** Unit 5, Lesson 5, Worksheet 1
**Workbook:** Unit 5, Lesson 5
**Suggested Realia:** First-aid kit, items from a first-aid kit

### Pacing
- 1.5 hour classes
- 2.5 hour classes
- 3+ hour classes

## STANDARDS CORRELATIONS

*CCRS:* RI1, RI2, RI4, SL1

*CASAS:* 3.4.3

*SCANS:* **Resources** Allocate materials and facility resources, allocate human resources

**Information** Acquire and evaluate information, organize and maintain information, interpret and communicate information

**Interpersonal** Participate as a member of a team, teach others, serve clients and customers, exercise leadership, negotiate to arrive at a decision, work with cultural diversity

**Systems** Monitor and correct performance

**Basic Skills** Reading, writing, listening, speaking

**Thinking Skills** Think creatively, make decisions, solve problems, see things in the mind's eye

**Personal Qualities** Responsibility, sociability, self-management

*EFF:* **Communication** Read with understanding, convey ideas in writing, speak so others can understand, listen actively, observe critically

**Decision Making** Solve problems and make decisions, plan

**Interpersonal** Cooperate with others, advocate and influence, resolve conflict and negotiate, guide others

**Lifelong Learning** Take responsibility for learning, reflect and evaluate, learn through research

## Warm-up and Review    5–10 mins. ■■■
Ask students if they have had or been part of a medical emergency. Encourage a class discussion about the nature of the emergency, what they did, what the results were, etc.

## Introduction    5–10 mins. ■■■
Dictation:

1. If someone has been poisoned, you should not give him anything to eat or drink.
2. Do not give a choking victim water.
3. If someone is in shock, you should not raise his or her head.
4. Do not put any creams or grease on burned skin.

State the goal: *Today, we will talk about first-aid kits and interpret first-aid procedures.*

Tell students that the information in this lesson doesn't take the place of a good first-aid class. Encourage students to take a first-aid and/or a CPR (Cardio Pulmonary Resuscitation) class at their local hospital or fire station or community college. Classes are often free or inexpensive to take.

## Presentation 1    10–15 mins. ■■■
With books closed, write *First-Aid Kit* on the board and have students help you brainstorm what they might find in a first-aid kit. Don't give them any answers; just see what they can come up with. If you brought items to class with you, you might show a few of them and see if students know what they are called.

## Practice 1    5–10 mins. ■■■

**A.  What does a first-aid kit have in it? Use the words in the box to label each item.**

Before students begin the exercise, review the vocabulary. Model the correct pronunciation for each word.

## Evaluation 1    10–15 mins. ■■■

**B.  Do you have a first-aid kit? Why is each item important? Discuss your ideas with your classmates.**

## Presentation 2      5–10 mins. ■■■

Pronounce the injuries one at a time and ask if students know what each one is. It is OK to discuss them a bit, but not too much since students will be writing formal definitions in Practice 2.

## Practice 2      15–20 mins. ■■

(Shorter classes can do these exercises for homework.)

### C. Define the following injuries.

Encourage students to use dictionaries to complete this exercise.

### D. APPLY Look at the list of first-aid procedures. Write the appropriate injuries on the line below each procedure.

## Evaluation 2      10–15 mins. ■■

Go over the injuries as a class. Do not go over the answers to Exercise D. Students will do this by themselves in Practice 3.

### BEST PRACTICE

## Reviewing vocabulary

After introducing new vocabulary words, you may have students practice drills. There are several ways to do this. One approach is to engage students in choral repetition. Students simply have to repeat the words after you. This allows them to practice pronunciation immediately after you've modeled it. Divide students into groups and have individual groups repeat certain words after you. Randomize the vocabulary words and try changing the speed and the volume.

### INSTRUCTOR'S NOTES

## C.  Define the following injuries.  Answers will vary.

1. burn: *injury caused by fire or chemicals*

2. choking: *something caught in airway*

3. poisoning: *dangerous chemical, drink, or food ingested*

4. open wound: *injury where layers below skin are exposed*

5. head injury: *injury to head area*

6. shock: *injury to body where blood pressure drops and systems begin to stop functioning*

## D.  APPLY  Look at the list of first-aid procedures. Write the appropriate injuries on the line below each procedure.

1. Call 911.

   **choking, poisoning, head injury, shock**

2. Call Poison Control.

   *poisoning*

3. Control external bleeding.

   *open wound, head injury*

4. Cover with a light gauze dressing.

   *burn*

5. Have the person lie down.

   *shock*

6. Help maintain body temperature.

   *shock*

7. Perform Heimlich maneuver.

   *choking*

8. Stop the bleeding with a piece of sterile gauze.

   *open wound, head injury*

9. Strike the victim's back between the shoulder blades five times.

   *choking*

10. Treat wounds.

    *burn, open wound, head injury*

**E.** **Read the information. Compare it with your answers in Exercise D. Were you right? Make a note of any difficult vocabulary and discuss as a class.**

| First-Aid Procedures* | | |
|---|---|---|
| **Injury** | **Do** | **Don't** |
| burn | Run cold water over burn area for 15 minutes. Cover the burn with a light gauze dressing. If blisters pop, apply a light antibiotic ointment and cover with light gauze dressing. | **Don't** put any creams or greases on the burned area. **Don't** pop any blisters. **Don't** use an ice pack. |
| choking | Call 911. Strike the victim's back between the shoulder blades five times. Perform Heimlich maneuver. | **Don't** give water to the person. |
| poisoning | Call 911 (if person is unconscious or having trouble breathing). Call Poison Control (800-222-1222). | **Don't** induce vomiting. **Don't** give the person anything to eat or drink. |
| open wound | Stop the bleeding with a piece of sterile gauze. Wash with soap and water (if minor), apply a thin layer of antibiotic ointment, and cover with a bandage. | **Don't** remove any object protruding from injury. **Don't** wash or apply ointment to a large, deep wound. |
| head injury | Call 911 if person is unconscious or drowsy. Treat wounds. Ice a small bump. | **Don't** leave the person alone, especially when sleeping. Instead, wake up every two to three hours and have the person answer simple questions. |
| shock | Call 911. Have the person lie down. Control external bleeding. Help maintain body temperature. | **Don't** raise the person's head. **Don't** give the person food or drink. |

\* Not all first-aid procedures for each injury are listed.

**F.** **APPLY** **Divide the class into victims and good citizens. All "victims" should write an injury from Exercise D on a piece of paper and show it to a "good citizen." Good citizens should offer advice.**

EXAMPLE:

**Victim:** (Shows Good Citizen card that reads "Choking.")

**Good Citizen says to Victim:** "I'm going to call 911. Then, I'm going to strike your back five times between your shoulder blades. If that doesn't work, I'm going to perform the Heimlich maneuver. I will not give you water."

## Presentation 3

15–20 mins. ■■■

Go over the chart as a class, discussing each procedure and the *do's* and *don'ts*. Demonstrate some of the procedures if you need to.

Present instructions for Exercise E to students. Show them how to find each procedure from Exercise D in the chart and see if they wrote the correct injuries on the lines.

## Practice 3

10–15 mins. ■

(Shorter classes can do this exercise for homework.)

**E. Read the information. Compare it with your answers in Exercise D. Were you right? Make a note of any difficult vocabulary and discuss as a class.**

## Evaluation 3

10–15 mins. ■

Walk around the classroom and help students as needed.

## Application

10–20 mins. ■■■

**F. APPLY  Divide the class into victims and good citizens. All "victims" should write an injury from Exercise D on a piece of paper and show it to a "good citizen." Good citizens should offer advice.**

Read the directions together. Then, ask a few volunteers to demonstrate this activity before students do it by themselves. Have students switch roles so they have an opportunity to both be a victim and give first aid advice.

### MULTILEVEL WORKSHEET

Unit 5, Lesson 5, Worksheet 1: First-Aid Kit

**Refer students to *Stand Out 5 Workbook,* Unit 5, Lesson 5 for practice with adverbial clauses of purpose and manner.**

**Go to the *Activity Bank* online for suggestions on promoting digital literacy and using the Internet to enhance this lesson.**

### INSTRUCTOR'S NOTES

# LIFESKILLS ▶ I think I might have a problem

## Before You Watch

- Read the title out loud.
- Discuss with students what they think the video will be about.

### A. Look at the picture and answer the questions.

- Ask students to look at the picture.
- Have students answer the questions.
- Discuss the answers as a class.

## While You Watch

### B. Watch the video and complete the dialog.

- Tell students to watch the video and complete the dialog.
- Play the video and ask students to watch and listen carefully.
- Play the video again. Then, ask students to complete the dialog.
- Play the video once more and have students check their answers.

## Check Your Understanding

### C. Circle the correct word in the parentheses to complete each sentence.

- Ask students to complete each sentence.
- Tell students to circle the correct word in parentheses.
- Review answers as a class.

# LIFESKILLS ▶ I think I might have a problem

## Before You Watch

**A. Look at the picture and answer the questions.**

1. What is on the chair next to Naomi?
   *shopping bags*
2. What problem does Hector think Naomi has?
   *a shopping addiction*

## While You Watch

**B. ▶ Watch the video and complete the dialog.**

**Hector:** Can I tell you something? I used to have an (1) _addiction_, too.

**Naomi:** You? (2) _Addicted_?

**Hector:** Yes, believe it or not. I used to be addicted to junk food. I ate it (3) _constantly_, even when I wasn't hungry. At one point, I weighed over 250 pounds.

**Naomi:** You mean—you had an eating (4) _disorder_?

**Hector:** You (5) _could_ say that.

**Naomi:** What did you do about it?

**Hector:** Well, I (6) _got_ help. I went to a counselor, and I joined a support group. I kept track of my eating, and I started working out at the gym. Pretty soon, I was addicted to going to the gym! Now, I feel a lot better.

## Check Your Understanding

**C. Circle the correct word in the parentheses to complete each sentence.**

1. People who buy more things than they can afford are (careful shoppers /(shopaholics)).

2. When people do things they don't want to do, they may have an ((addiction)/ addition).

3. Drug addicts and alcoholics are (depending /(dependent)) on substances.

4. In ((support)/ supporting) groups, people share their experiences.

5. A ((counselor)/ council worker) can also offer help and support.

# Review

**A.  Write one healthy solution for each problem.** Answers may vary.

1. Problem: I eat fast food three times a week because I have no time to cook.

   Solution: *prepare food in advance*

2. Problem: I have high blood pressure, and I am at risk for diabetes.

   Solution: *lose weight, exercise*

3. Problem: I am really stressed at work.

   Solution: *meditate, talk to boss, exercise*

4. Problem: My children are overweight.

   Solution: *family should exercise together*

**B.  Read the bill and write four questions you would ask about it.** Answers will vary. Sample questions are given.

| | PATIENT NAME: Reed, Jacob | | PROVIDER NAME: Robert Wickern, M.D. | | |
|---|---|---|---|---|---|
| **DATE** | **PROCEDURE** | **DESCRIPTION OF SERVICE** | **CO-PAY** | **AMOUNT PAYABLE** | |
| 8/23 | 99391 | Well-Child Check | | $150.00 | |
| 8/23 | 90700 | DTaP Vaccine | | $30.00 | |
| 8/23 | 90465 | Vaccine Admin | | $44.00 | |
| 8/23 | 90645 | Hib Vaccine | | $32.00 | |
| 8/23 | 90466 | Vaccine Admin | | $64.00 | |
| 8/23 | | Patient Co-Pay | −$25.00 | | |
| 9/17 | | Primary Insurance Payment | | −$200.00 | |
| 9/17 | | Uncollectible | | −$75.00 | |
| | | | **AMOUNT DUE** | | |

1. *How much does the patient owe?*

2. *Why is $75 uncollectible?*

3. *Who do I pay?*

4. *When is this bill due?*

**C.  Work with a partner and have a conversation between a patient and a person at the doctor's office with the questions you wrote. Switch roles.**

WORKPLACE CONNECTION
Exercises A, B: Complete tasks as assigned.
Exercise C: Interact appropriately with team members.

## AT-A-GLANCE PREP

**Goal:** All unit goals
**Grammar:** All unit grammar
**Academic Strategy:** Reviewing
**Vocabulary:** All Unit 5 vocabulary

### Agenda

- Discuss unit goals.
- Complete the review.
- Use unit vocabulary.

### Resources

**Stand Out Assessment CD-ROM with ExamView®**

### Pacing

- ■ 1.5 hour classes
- ■ 2.5 hour classes
- ■ 3+ hour classes

## STANDARDS CORRELATIONS

*CCRS:* RI1, RI4, RI7

*CASAS:* 7.2.1

*SCANS:* **Resources** Allocate time

**Information** Acquire and evaluate information

**Interpersonal** Participate as a member of a team, teach others, negotiate to arrive at a decision, work with cultural diversity

**Systems** Monitor and correct performance

**Basic Skills** Reading, writing, arithmetic, listening, speaking

**Thinking Skills** Think creatively, make decisions, solve problems, see things in the mind's eye

**Personal Qualities** Responsibility, sociability, self-management

*EFF:* **Communication** Read with understanding, convey ideas in writing, speak so others can understand, listen actively, observe critically

**Interpersonal** Cooperate with others, guide others

**Lifelong Learning** Take responsibility for learning, reflect and evaluate

## Warm-up and Review          5–10 mins. ■■■

Ask students if they've examined their first-aid kit at home since the previous lesson. Have them name items that are different in their kits at home that weren't discussed in the lesson. Ask them to think about medical emergencies they've experienced and discuss what equipment might have been helpful at that time.

## Introduction          5–10 mins. ■■■

Ask students as a class to try to recall all the goals of this unit without looking back in their books. The goals for this unit include identifying practices that promote mental and physical well-being, asking about medical bills, interpreting health insurance information, identifying addictions, and interpreting procedures for first aid. Write all the goals on the board from Unit 5. Show students the first page of the unit and mention the five goals.

State the goal: *Today, we will be reviewing everything we have learned in this unit and preparing for the team project.*

## Presentation          10–15 mins. ■■■

This presentation will cover the three pages of the review. Quickly go to the first page of each lesson. Discuss the goal of each. Ask simple questions to remind students of what they have learned.

**Note:** Since there is little presentation in the review, you can assign the review exercises that don't require collaboration with a partner or group for homework and go over them in class the following day.

## Practice          20–25 mins. ■■■

**Note:** There are two ways to do the review:

1. Go through the exercises one at a time and, as students complete each one, go over the answers.
2. Quickly go through the instructions of each exercise, let students complete all of the exercises at once, and then go over the answers.

**A. Write one healthy solution for each problem. (Lesson 1)**

**B. Read the bill and write four questions you would ask about it. (Lesson 2)**

**C. Work with a partner and have a conversation between a patient and a person at the doctor's office with the questions you wrote. Switch roles. (Lesson 2)**

## Evaluation          5–15 mins. ■■■

Go around the classroom and check on students' progress. Help individuals when needed. If you see consistent errors among several students, interrupt the class and give a mini-lesson or review to help students feel comfortable with the concept.

## Practice (continued)     25–30 mins. ■■■

D. Read the bar graph about health insurance coverage and answer the questions. (Lesson 3)

E. On a separate piece of paper, write sentences combining the ideas below. (Lesson 4)

F. Write down six injuries you learned about in this unit. In a group, discuss the first-aid procedures for each one. (Lesson 5)

## Evaluation (continued)     15–20 mins. ■■■

Go around the classroom and check on students' progress. Help individuals when needed. If you see consistent errors among several students, interrupt the class and give a mini-lesson or review to help students feel comfortable with the concept.

### BEST PRACTICE

### Recycling/Review

The review exercises, the research activity, and the team project are part of the recycling/review process. Students often need to be reintroduced to concepts to solidify what they have learned. Many concepts are learned and forgotten when students are engaged in learning other new concepts. This is because students learn but are not necessarily ready to acquire language concepts.

Therefore, it becomes very important to review material with students and to show them how to review it on their own. It is also important to recycle the new concepts in different contexts.

### INSTRUCTOR'S NOTES

**Learner Log**

I can interpret health insurance information.    I can identify addictions.    I can interpret procedures for first aid.
■ Yes   ■ No   ■ Maybe     ■ Yes   ■ No   ■ Maybe     ■ Yes   ■ No   ■ Maybe

**D. Read the bar graph about health insurance coverage and answer the questions.**

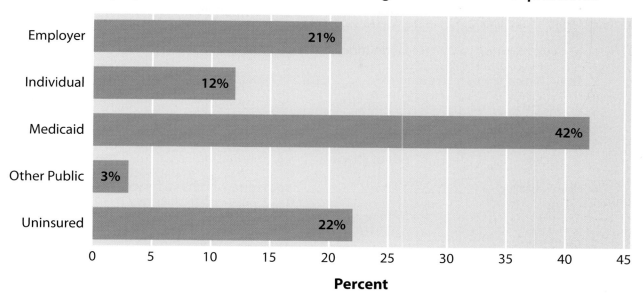

Percent

1. What is the percentage of adults who are uninsured? _____ 22% _____

2. What is the percentage of adults who are insured by their employers? _____ 21% _____

3. What is the percentage of adults who are on Medicaid? _____ 42% _____

4. What is the percentage of adults who have insurance coverage? _____ 78% _____

**E. On a separate piece of paper, write sentences combining the ideas below.**

Answers will vary.

**EXAMPLE:** nicotine addiction/smokes two packs of cigarettes a day

*Even though he smokes two packs of cigarettes a day, he doesn't think he is addicted to nicotine.*

1. exercise addiction/works out 3 times a day     2. sleeping addiction/sleeps 11 hours a night

3. food addiction/eats all day long     4. coffee addiction/drinks 4 cups a day

**F. Write down six injuries you learned about in this unit. In a group, discuss the first-aid procedures for each one.** Answers will vary.

| | | |
|---|---|---|
| burns | shock | poisoning |
| head injury | choking | open wound |

WORKPLACE CONNECTION
Exercise D: Interpret and communicate information.
Exercise E: Combine ideas and information.
Exercise F: Interact appropriately with team members.

# Vocabulary Review

**A. Choose the correct word for each sentence.**

1. _____Meditation_____ helps me relax when I've had a long day at work.

   a. Detoxification    (b.) Meditation    c. Tolerance    d. Depression

2. They think she has a sleeping pill _____addiction_____.

   a. process    b. insurance    c. depression    (d.) addiction

3. If you are with someone who is in _____shock_____, you should call 911.

   (a.) shock    b. out of shape    c. meditation    d. treatment

4. How would you _____treat_____ someone who has a head injury?

   a. affect    (b.) treat    c. impair    d. insure

5. Jared's body has built up a _____tolerance_____ to alcohol since he has been drinking for so long.

   (a.) tolerance    b. substance    c. detoxification    d. withdrawal

**B. Give two examples of each of the following items.** Answers will vary.

1. Substance addictions: _____heroin_____ _____caffeine_____

2. Process addictions: _____shopping_____ _____gambling_____

3. First-aid kit items: _____cold compress_____ _____antibiotic ointment_____

4. Items on a medical bill: _____co-pay_____ _____uncollectible_____

**C. Write sentences using each of the following terms.** Answers will vary.

1. uninsured: _There are many uninsured people 18–24 years old._

2. at risk: _Trying drugs puts you at risk for addiction._

3. self-esteem: _People with high self-esteem often are healthy._

4. responsible party: _The responsible party pays the bills._

5. survive: _Call 911 to survive a bad car accident._

WORKPLACE CONNECTION
Exercises A, B, C: Complete tasks as assigned.

## Practice *(continued)*     25–30 mins. ■■■

### Vocabulary Review

A. Choose the correct word for each sentence.

B. Give two examples of each of the following items.

C. Write sentences using each of the following terms.

### Evaluation *(continued)*     15–20 mins. ■■■
Go around the classroom and check on students' progress. Help individuals when needed. If you see consistent errors among several students, interrupt the class and give a mini-lesson or review to help students feel comfortable with the concept.

### Assessment *(optional)*     20–25 mins. ■■■
Use the Stand Out Assessment CD-ROM with ExamView® to create a post-test for Unit 5.

INSTRUCTOR'S NOTES

*Make decisions and solve problems; Collect and organize information; Combine ideas and information; Exercise leadership roles; Manage time; Complete tasks as assigned; Interact appropriately with team members; Interpret and communicate information.*

## STANDARDS CORRELATIONS

**CCRS:** W2, W8, SL1, SL2, SL4, SL5 SL6

**CASAS:** 4.8.1, 4.8.5, 4.8.6

**SCANS: Resources** Allocate time

**Information** Acquire and evaluate information, organize and maintain information, interpret and communicate information, use computers to process information

**Systems** Understand systems, improve and design systems

**Technology** Select technology, apply technology to exercise

**Basic Skills** Writing

**Thinking Skills** Think creatively, make decisions, solve problems, see things in the mind's eye, use reasoning

**Personal Qualities** Responsibility, self-esteem, self-management, integrity

**EFF: Communication** Read with understanding, convey ideas in writing, speak so others can understand, listen actively, observe critically

**Decision Making** Solve problems and make decisions, plan

**Interpersonal** Cooperate with others, advocate and influence, resolve conflict and negotiate, guide others

**Lifelong Learning** Take responsibility for learning, reflect and evaluate, learn through research, use information and communications technology (*optional*)

## TEAM PROJECT

### Give a presentation on a health-related topic

Each team will prepare a presentation for the class based on one of the topics from the unit. The presentation should include information from the unit as well as from additional research.

The team project is the final application for the unit. It gives students a chance to show that they have mastered all the Unit 5 goals.

(Shorter classes can extend this project over two class meetings.)

### Stage 1
5–10 mins.

**COLLABORATE Form a team with four or five students. Decide which topic your team will work on. (Each team should choose a different topic.)**

### Stage 2
10–15 mins.

**Choose positions for each member of your team.**

Have students decide who will lead each step as described on the student page. Provide well-defined directions on the board for how teams should proceed. Explain that all the students do every step as a team. Teams shouldn't go to the next stage until the previous one is complete.

### Stage 3
15–20 mins.

**Gather information for your presentation from this unit and other sources.**

Tell students to use what they learned in class as well as gather any additional research they can.

### Stage 4
10–15 mins.

**Decide how to present your material creatively. For example, you can use charts, role plays, or encourage class participation.**

As a class, brainstorm different methods of presentation. Try to make the list exhaustive so that every team doesn't use the same presentation format. Briefly discuss how some presentation methods lend themselves better to some material. Encourage the teams to use at least two different presentation methods in their presentations.

### Stage 5
15–20 mins.

**Create any materials needed for your presentation.**

Anticipate materials students might need for the presentation such as health magazines, computer printouts, poster board, glue, and markers.

**Optional Computer Activity:** Students may want to use a computer to create presentation materials.

### Stage 6
20–30 mins.

**Practice your presentation.**

Remind students that each team member must be involved in the presentation.

### Stage 7
15–20 mins.

**Give your presentation to the class.**

# TEAM PROJECT ✔ Health presentation

## Presentation Topics

- Healthy Practices
- Medical Bills
- Health Insurance
- Addictions
- First Aid

1. **COLLABORATE** Form a team with four or five students. Decide which topic your team will work on. (Each team should choose a different topic.)

2. Choose positions for each member of your team.

| Position | Job description | Student name |
|---|---|---|
| Student 1: Project Leader | Check that everyone speaks English. Check that everyone participates. | |
| Student 2: Secretary | Take notes on your team's ideas. | |
| Student 3: Coordinator | Divide presentation into parts. Assign each team member one part of presentation. | |
| Student 4: Director | Organize presentation so that individual parts create a unified whole. | |
| Student 5: Member | Do assigned part of presentation. Supportively critique other members' work as they rehearse their parts of presentation. | |

3. Gather information for your presentation from this unit and other sources.

4. Decide how to present your material creatively. For example, you can use charts, role plays, or encourage class participation.

5. Create any materials needed for your presentation.

6. Practice your presentation.

7. Give your presentation to the class.

## About the Explorer

Grace Gobbo is an ethnobotanist from Tanzania. Grace uses the lush nature of her home continent to help find holistic remedies for people who cannot afford to buy expensive medication. Medication used to help people with a wide range of ailments including chest infections and ulcers is sometimes unaffordable in some countries like Tanzania, so Grace interviewed traditional healers to find out what they used to treat illnesses in their communities. She is working to catalog this information so that it's not lost. She is also teaching people about the environment in which they live and how they can use it to help themselves.

## About the Photo

This photo shows Grace Gobbo. Grace works with the Jane Goodall Institute's Greater Gombe Ecosystem's program. This program helps preserve the chimpanzee habitat in western Tanzania. As Grace becomes more successful in showing people the health benefits of their environment, the institute is able to protect the natural habitat of the primates who depend on the area for survival.

- Introduce the explorer, Grace Gobbo.
- Read the title and ask students what it means.
- Have a volunteer read the quote to the class. Ask students how the quote is related to the title.

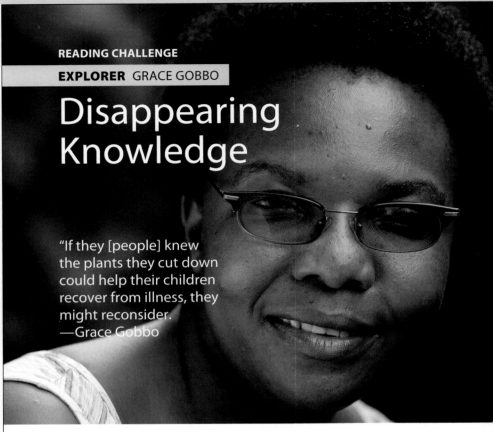

READING CHALLENGE

**EXPLORER** GRACE GOBBO

# Disappearing Knowledge

"If they [people] knew the plants they cut down could help their children recover from illness, they might reconsider."
—Grace Gobbo

**A.** **PREDICT** Plants are a very important part of Grace Gobbo's work. In a group, discuss the different uses of plants.

**B.** Natural remedies are non-manufactured medicines that can cure illnesses. Make a list of natural remedies that you know of. Answers will vary.

| Remedy | Illness it cures |
|---|---|
|  |  |

144   Unit 5

## CCRS FOR READING

RI1, RI2, RI4, RI10

**C. Read about Grace Gobbo, ethnobotanist.**

For many people in Tanzania, imported pharmaceuticals are too expensive. Until recent times, it hasn't been a problem because the east African country has had traditional healers who use locally grown medicinal plants to help treat sick people. Unfortunately, this indigenous medical knowledge is disappearing and so are the plants. Grace Gobbo hopes to change that.

Grace's father was a doctor; therefore, she didn't believe in traditional healing. But once she began studying botany, she learned about plants that had successfully treated coughs and stopped bacterial infections. The evidence was too strong to ignore. Wanting to know more, Grace started interviewing traditional healers who had endless accounts of plants being used to treat skin and chest infections, diabetes, stomach ulcers, heart disease, and even mental illnesses. "Before now, these facts existed only as an oral tradition," she explains. "Nothing was written down. The knowledge is literally dying out with the elders since today's young generation considers natural remedies old-fashioned." Grace hopes that by creating a record of these natural remedies, she can convince other young people of the importance of these plants for use in curing ailments.

In addition to the traditional healers' knowledge dying with them, there is another problem: Medicinal plants are disappearing due to farming, mining, and other development. Plant products are used for fuel by most of the people in Tanzania, and agriculture is a major part of their economy. But Grace still believes people will ultimately do what is right. "I believe in people. I think if they learn and understand the value of the environment, they will make better choices. If they knew the plants they cut down could help their children recover from illness, they might reconsider. Loggers might give healers a chance to collect tree bark at the same time wood is harvested. We're working hard to bring information about sustainable agriculture and forest management to the public, and show them how to apply it."

**D. SUMMARIZE** On a separate piece of paper, complete each sentence with what you learned from the reading.

1. The people of Tanzania don't use imported pharmaceuticals because they are too expensive .

2. Grace wanted to learn more about traditional healing, so she interviewed traditional healers .

3. Secrets of traditional healers are dying with them because young people consider natural remedies old-fashioned .

4. Medical plants in Tanzania are disappearing because of farming, mining, and other development .

5. Grace believes that people will make better choices if they understand the value of the environment .

---

## READING STRATEGIES

### Reading Strategies: 3 – 2 – 1 Strategy

The 3 – 2 – 1 strategy is a good way to motivate reading. After students have finished, ask them to write three things they learned. Then, have students write two things they found interesting. Finally, ask students to write one question they have about the reading.

---

**A. PREDICT** Plants are a very important part of Grace Gobbo's work. In a group, discuss the different uses of plants.

- Point out that plants are a very important part of Grace Gobbo's work.
- Have students form small groups and discuss the different uses of plants.

**B.** Natural remedies are non-manufactured medicines that can cure illnesses. Make a list of natural remedies that you know of.

- Point out that natural remedies are non-manufactured medicines that can cure illnesses.
- Ask students to make a list of natural remedies they know of.
- Have students complete the table with their information.

**C.** Read about Grace Gobbo, ethnobotanist.

- Ask students if they can guess what an *ethnobotanist* is.
- Tell students that Grace Gobbo is an ethnobotanist.
- Have students read the article about Grace Gobbo.

**D. SUMMARIZE** On a separate piece of paper, complete each sentence with what you learned from the reading.

Ask students to complete the sentences with what they have learned from the reading. Have students write their sentences on a separate piece of paper.

# Retail

### About the Photo

Brent Humphreys took this photo. It shows robots in a warehouse collecting orders for an online shoe retailer. Customer orders are received by the robots wirelessly. They then follow barcode stickers on the ground to find the merchandise in different parts of the warehouse. Once collected, the robots bring it to the front of the warehouse where a human employee can pack it for delivery. Many online retailers have started using these robots, but how long will it be until they replace human workers completely?

- Introduce the unit by reading the title out loud.
- Ask students what the title means.
- Have students look at the photo and ask a volunteer to read the caption to the class.
- Ask students how the title is related to the photo.
- Have students answer the questions about the photo and discuss as a class.
- Go over each unit outcome.

UNIT **6**

## Retail

Robots in a warehouse collect orders for an online store.

| UNIT OUTCOMES | GRAMMAR | VOCABULARY | EL CIVICS |
|---|---|---|---|
| • Do product research<br>• Purchase goods and services by phone and online<br>• Interpret product guarantees and warranties<br>• Return a product<br>• Sell a product | • Information questions<br>• Embedded questions<br>• Appositives<br>• Parts of speech: nouns, verbs, adjectives<br>• Conditionals with *would*<br>• Future with *will* | Retail: *convince, exchange, free of charge, guarantee, make, model, policy, product, quality, receipt, refund, research, return, review, transaction, warranty, allege, confirm, fault, malfunction, quality, refund, goods and services, online, Internet* | The skills students learn in this unit can be applied to the following EL Civics competency areas:<br>• Consumer education<br>• Clothes<br>• Common Activities<br>• Shapes and Colors |

## Life Skills Link

In this unit, students will learn how to use purchasing strategies such as comparison shopping, analyzing advertisements, and recognizing marketing to be better-informed consumers. Students will also learn the basic concepts of warranties, and will get information about selling and buying items from online sources.

## Workplace Link

All lessons and units in *Stand Out* include basic communication skills and interpersonal skills important for the workplace. They are not individually identified. Other workplace skills are indicated. They include *collecting and organizing information, making decisions and solving problems*, and *combining ideas and information*.

### UNIT OUTCOMES

- Do product research
- Purchase goods and services by phone and online
- Interpret product guarantees and warranties
- Return a product
- Sell a product

**Look at the photo and answer the questions.**

1. What products do you think the robots are collecting?
2. Which online store do you think owns this warehouse?

| CASAS | SCANS | CCRS |
|---|---|---|
| Vocabulary Builder: 7.4.5<br>Lesson 1: 1.2.4, 1.2.3, 1.2.5, 6.4.1, 6.4.3, 7.4.4<br>Lesson 2: 1.3.1, 1.3.3<br>Lesson 3: 1.6.3, 1.6.4, 1.7.1<br>Lesson 4: 1.3.3<br>Lesson 5: 1.6.3<br>Review: 7.2.1<br>Research: 4.9.3, 7.2.1, 7.4.4, 7.4.5, 7.4.6<br>Team Project: 4.8.1, 4.8.5, 4.8.6 | Many SCANS skills are incorporated in this unit with an emphasis on:<br>• Social interaction<br>• Negotiation<br>• Self-management<br>• Decision making<br>• Writing | RI1, RI2, RI3, RI4, RI7, RI8, W1, W2, W4, W5, W6, W7, W8, W9, SL1, SL2, SL4, SL5 SL6, L1 |

# Vocabulary Builder

WORKPLACE CONNECTION
Exercise A: Interact appropriately with team members.
Exercise B: Complete tasks as assigned.

**A.** **Using the words and phrases in the box, discuss the picture with a partner. Look up any words or phrases you do not know in a dictionary.** *Answers will vary.*

**EXAMPLE:** *The woman is asking the salesperson about the product warranty.*

| | | | |
|---|---|---|---|
| convince | exchange | free of charge | guarantee |
| make | model | policy | quality |
| receipt | refund | research | return |
| review | transaction | warranty | |

**B.** **CLASSIFY** **Look at the unit outcomes. Then, look back at the words and phrases from Exercise A. Decide which words and phrases go with each outcome. (Some words and phrases can be used with more than one outcome.)** *Answers will vary. Sample answers given.*

1. Do product research: _make, review, model, free of charge, policy, research, warranty, guarantee, quality_

2. Purchase goods and services by phone and online: _receipt, transaction, free of charge, policy, model, transaction_

3. Interpret product guarantees and warranties: _receipt, exchange, refund, policy, warranty, guarantee, quality, return_

4. Return a product: _receipt, review, exchange, refund, policy, guarantee, return_

5. Sell a product: _convince, warranty, guarantee, quality, review, free of charge_

**Goal:** Introduce new vocabulary
**Academic Strategies:** Categorizing vocabulary, using a dictionary
**Vocabulary:** See lesson

### Agenda

☐ Discuss store vocabulary.

☐ Relate unit vocabulary to unit goals.

☐ Use synonyms to figure out meanings.

### Resources

**Dictionaries:** It is recommended that each student in class have an ESL learner's dictionary or that there be dictionaries available in the classroom for students to use. Dictionaries that will be referred to in this book are *Heinle's Newbury House Dictionary of American English* and the *Collins Cobuild Intermediate* or *Advanced Dictionary of American English*.

### Pacing

■ 1.5 hour classes   ■ 2.5 hour classes
■ 3+ hour classes

## STANDARDS CORRELATIONS

*CCRS:* RI4

*CASAS:* 7.4.5

*SCANS:* **Information** Acquire and evaluate information, organize and maintain information

**Interpersonal** Participate as a member of a team, negotiate to arrive at a decision, work with cultural diversity

**Systems** Understand systems, monitor and correct performance

**Basic Skills** Reading, writing, listening, speaking

**Thinking Skills** Think creatively, make decisions, see things in the mind's eye

**Personal Qualities** Responsibility, sociability, self-management

*EFF:* **Communication** Read with understanding, convey ideas in writing, speak so others can understand, listen actively

**Decision Making** Use math to solve problems and communicate, solve problems and make decisions, plan

**Interpersonal** Cooperate with others

**Lifelong Learning** Take responsibility for learning, reflect and evaluate, learn through research

## Academic Feature: Vocabulary Builder

Each unit will begin with a vocabulary-building section. The purpose of this two-page section is to introduce students to many of the words they will be using in the unit lessons. Students will have a chance to see how much they already know, and they will get exposure to the new vocabulary found in the unit.

**Note:** All of the exercises on these two pages should be done in class, no matter the class length. Longer classes can do this lesson and then move onto Lesson 1 during the same class meeting; shorter classes may have to devote one whole class meeting to this lesson.

### Introduction                     1 min. ■■■

State the goal: *Today, we will be identifying and working with the vocabulary you will learn in this unit.*

### Presentation 1                   5 mins. ■■■

Talk about the picture as a class. Ask students what they see, what is happening, etc.

### Practice 1                       10–15 mins. ■■■

A. **Using the words and phrases in the box, discuss the picture with a partner. Look up any words or phrases you do not know in a dictionary.**

### Evaluation 1                     10–15 mins. ■■■

Talk about the picture as a class. Have students use the words from the box. Ask students which words they had to look up in a dictionary and make sure they understand the meanings.

### Practice 2                       10–15 mins. ■■■

B. **CLASSIFY Look at the unit outcomes. Then, look back at the words and phrases from Exercise A. Decide which words and phrases go with each outcome. (Some words and phrases can be used with more than one outcome.)**

### Evaluation 2                     5–10 mins. ■■

Go over the answers as a class.

## Presentation 2 5–10 mins. ■■

Go over the instructions to Exercise B with students, briefly discussing each outcome. Do an example or two with students before they complete the exercise on their own. For example, ask *Which outcome or outcomes does* convince *fit into?* (Sell a product or purchase goods and services by phone and online.)

### PRONUNCIATION

### Vocabulary

When teaching students new vocabulary, pronounce each word for them several times and ask them to repeat it. Often, students may be familiar with the words you are introducing but have never seen them spelled out. By pronouncing the words for students, you allow students to make a connection between the words' spellings and their sounds. It is also important that students learn the correct pronunciation of new words so they feel comfortable using their new vocabulary inside and outside of the classroom.

## Practice 3 10–15 mins. ■

**C. Knowing a synonym for an unfamiliar word will often help you better understand its meaning. Find synonyms for the words below in a dictionary or thesaurus.**

Remind students what a synonym is. Ask them to see if they can come up with any on their own before turning to a dictionary or thesaurus.

## Evaluation 3 5–10 mins. ■

Go over the answers as a class.

**C.** **Knowing a synonym for an unfamiliar word will often help you better understand its meaning. Find synonyms for the words below in a dictionary or thesaurus.**

Answers will vary. Sample answers given.

| Word | Synonym | |
|---|---|---|
| allege | claim | |
| conform | comply | |
| convince | persuade | |
| exchange | give back to/take another of same value | |
| fault | error | |
| guarantee | promise | |
| malfunction | break down | |
| model | type | |
| quality | value | |
| refund | money given back | |
| research | investigation | |
| return | give/take back | |
| review | opinion/look over | |

**Window shopping is one way of doing product research.**

Vocabulary Builder 149

# LESSON **1** How much is it?

GOAL ■ Do product research

WORKPLACE CONNECTION
Exercises A, C: Interact appropriately with team members.
Exercise B: Interpret and communicate information.

**A. DETERMINE** Imagine that you are going to buy the following products. In a group, discuss what information you need to research before you make your purchases. Write your ideas on the lines next to each item. *Answers will vary. Sample answers given.*

1. a bed: *price, standards, warranty, quality*

2. a refrigerator: *size, price, features: freezer, ice maker, energy use*

3. a television: *size, price, warranty, installation fee*

4. a cell phone/smartphone: *price, monthly payments, minutes, plan, features*

5. an air conditioner: *price, size, energy usage*

6. a car: *price, style, MPG, gas usage, repair records, review*

**B.** Listen to the conversation Maya is having with the salesperson. What does she want to know about the patio set? Write her questions below.

1. *Could you answer some questions about patio furniture?*

2. *Is it lightweight? Easy to move?*

3. *How can I clean it?*

4. *I wasn't sure if it had to be re-sanded or what.*

5. *How does teak hold up in bad weather?*

6. *How much does this set (with table, umbrella, and 4 chairs) cost?*

7. *Can I use it (this 20% off coupon)?*

8. *Does it come with a warranty?*

**C.** How did the salesperson answer the questions in Exercise B? Discuss the answers with your classmates.

## AT-A-GLANCE PREP

**Goal:** Do product research

**Academic Strategy:** Focused listening, writing a review

**Vocabulary:** *research, review, make, model, quality*

### Agenda

- Listen to a conversation between a salesperson and a customer.
- Read product reviews.
- Research a product.

### Resources

**Multilevel Worksheets:** Unit 6, Lesson 1, Worksheets 1–2

**Workbook:** Unit 6, Lesson 1

**Audio:** CD Track 28

**Suggested Realia:** Consumer magazines, printouts from websites with reviews

**Stand Out Assessment CD-ROM with ExamView®**

### Pacing

- 1.5 hour classes
- 2.5 hour classes
- 3+ hour classes

## STANDARDS CORRELATIONS

*CCRS:* RI1, W2, W4, W8, SL1, SL2

*CASAS:* 1.2.5, 7.4.4

*SCANS:* **Information** Acquire and evaluate information

**Interpersonal** Participate as a member of a team, teach others, work with cultural diversity

**Systems** Understand systems, monitor and correct performance, improve and design systems

**Technology** Select technology, apply technology to a task

**Basic Skills** Reading, writing, listening, speaking

**Thinking Skills** Think creatively, make decisions

**Personal Qualities** Responsibility, sociability, self-management

*EFF:* **Communication** Read with understanding, convey ideas in writing, speak so others can understand, listen actively, observe critically

**Decision Making** Solve problems and make decisions, plan

**Interpersonal** Cooperate with others, advocate and influence, guide others

**Lifelong Learning** Take responsibility for learning, reflect and evaluate, learn through research, use information and communications technology

### Pre-assessment *(optional)* ■■■

Use the Stand Out Assessment CD-ROM with ExamView® to create a pre-test for Unit 6.

### Warm-up and Review  5 mins. ■■■

Ask students to think about big purchases they have made within the last year (car, house, computer, camera, etc.). Ask volunteers to share what they bought and where they bought it.

### Introduction  5–10 mins. ■■■

Dictation:

1. How long will the battery last if I start with a full charge?
2. With this plan, how many minutes do I get per month?
3. Are nights and weekends free and what time do they start?
4. Are calls to my friends and family on the same network free?

After completing the dictation, ask students what these questions pertain to. (cell phones)

State the goal: *Today, we'll be doing product research.*

Ask students how many of them did research before they made the purchase they discussed in the Warm-up and Review. Ask them what kind of research they did and how they did it.

### Presentation 1  10–15 mins. ■■■

Write the word *bed* on the board. Ask students to raise their hands if they have bought a bed before. Ask them what they would want to find out before buying a bed. Write their ideas on the board. (price, comfort, stain-proof, pillow top, etc.)

**A. DETERMINE Imagine that you are going to buy the following products. In a group, discuss what information you need to research before you make your purchases. Write your ideas on the lines next to each item.**

**Note:** Practice 1, listening script, and Evaluation 1 are on page 151a.

## Practice 1 10–15 mins. ■■■

**B. Listen to the conversation Maya is having with the salesperson. What does she want to know about the patio set? Write her questions below.**

### LISTENING SCRIPT 🎧 CD TR 28

**Maya:** *Excuse me, could you answer some questions for me about the patio furniture?*

**Salesperson:** *Sure, which set are you looking at?*

**Maya:** *This teak set.*

**Salesperson:** *One of our best sellers. How can I help?*

**Maya:** *Well, I saw it online and was reading the reviews, so I wanted to see what you thought.*

**Salesperson:** *Sure.*

**Maya:** *I want to know if it's comfortable.*

**Salesperson:** *Well, why don't you sit down and see for yourself?*

**Maya:** *(pause) Yeah, it is pretty comfortable. Is it lightweight, easy to move?*

**Salesperson:** *I think it's pretty lightweight for wood. Why don't you move the table a bit and see what you think?*

**Maya:** *(pause) Not bad. It's definitely lighter than it looks. How can I clean it?*

**Salesperson:** *A damp cloth should do just fine. And when the stain starts to fade, you can just get a brush and some teak oil to brighten it up again.*

**Maya:** *Oh, good. That was the next thing I was going to ask you. I've never owned teak before so I wasn't sure if it had to be re-sanded or what.*

**Salesperson:** *If you keep on top of it with the oil, it shouldn't need re-sanding.*

**Maya:** *Great. So, how does teak hold up in bad weather?*

**Salesperson:** *Just fine. The sun will cause the fading, but we already talked about how to fix that. It's heavy enough that it won't get blown by wind. And it does just fine in the rain.*

**Maya:** *Good to know. So, how much does this set, with the table, umbrella, and four chairs, cost?*

**Salesperson:** *$1,450.*

**Maya:** *And I got this 20-percent-off coupon in the mail. Can I use it?*

**Salesperson:** *Sure. That will bring the price down to around $1,160.*

**Maya:** *OK. Oh, and one more thing. Does it come with a warranty?*

**Salesperson:** *Yep, a 90-day manufacturer's warranty against any product defects.*

**Maya:** *Great. I'll talk it over with my husband and then we'll make a decision. Thanks for your help.*

**Salesperson:** *No problem. That's what I'm here for!*

## Evaluation 1 5 mins. ■■■
Go over the answers as a class.

**C. How did the salesperson answer the questions in Exercise B? Discuss the answers with your classmates.**

## Presentation 2 10–15 mins. ■■■

**D. Look at the list of ways to research a product. Which methods have you used before?**

**E. Maya went online to research the patio furniture she saw in the store. Read the product reviews she found.**

Have students read the reviews to themselves. Then, go over them as a class.

## Practice 2 10–15 mins. ■■
(Shorter classes can do these exercises for homework.)

**F. Based on the reviews in Exercise E, would you buy the patio furniture if it were on sale? Why?**

Have students answer these questions with a partner.

**G. Which review has the biggest impression on you? Why?**

**H. EVALUATE Think of something you have bought recently. Write a review for it on a separate piece of paper.**

## Evaluation 2 10–15 mins. ■■
Ask volunteers to read their reviews out loud.

### INSTRUCTOR'S NOTES

_____

_____

_____

_____

_____

_____

WORKPLACE CONNECTION
Exercises E, F, G: Interpret and communicate information.
Exercise H: Combine ideas and information.

**D. Look at the list of ways to research a product. Which methods have you used before?**
Answers will vary.

- Ask friends and family
- Ask a salesperson
- Go online and read product reviews
- Read a consumer magazine

**E. Maya went online to research the patio furniture she saw in the store. Read the product reviews she found.**

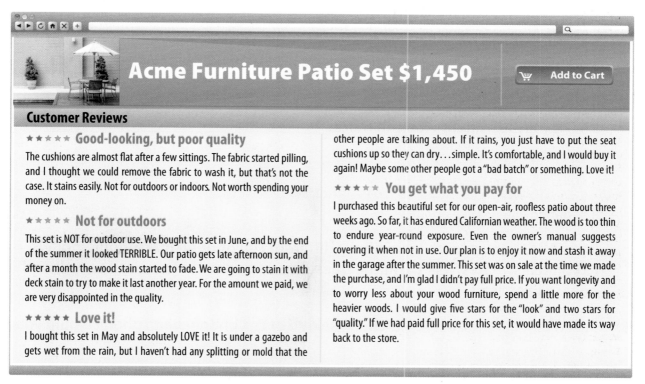

**Acme Furniture Patio Set $1,450** ⛟ Add to Cart

**Customer Reviews**

★ ★ ★ ★ ★ **Good-looking, but poor quality**

The cushions are almost flat after a few sittings. The fabric started pilling, and I thought we could remove the fabric to wash it, but that's not the case. It stains easily. Not for outdoors or indoors. Not worth spending your money on.

★ ★ ★ ★ ★ **Not for outdoors**

This set is NOT for outdoor use. We bought this set in June, and by the end of the summer it looked TERRIBLE. Our patio gets late afternoon sun, and after a month the wood stain started to fade. We are going to stain it with deck stain to try to make it last another year. For the amount we paid, we are very disappointed in the quality.

★ ★ ★ ★ ★ **Love it!**

I bought this set in May and absolutely LOVE it! It is under a gazebo and gets wet from the rain, but I haven't had any splitting or mold that the other people are talking about. If it rains, you just have to put the seat cushions up so they can dry…simple. It's comfortable, and I would buy it again! Maybe some other people got a "bad batch" or something. Love it!

★ ★ ★ ★ ★ **You get what you pay for**

I purchased this beautiful set for our open-air, roofless patio about three weeks ago. So far, it has endured Californian weather. The wood is too thin to endure year-round exposure. Even the owner's manual suggests covering it when not in use. Our plan is to enjoy it now and stash it away in the garage after the summer. This set was on sale at the time we made the purchase, and I'm glad I didn't pay full price. If you want longevity and to worry less about your wood furniture, spend a little more for the heavier woods. I would give five stars for the "look" and two stars for "quality." If we had paid full price for this set, it would have made its way back to the store.

**F. Based on the reviews in Exercise E, would you buy the patio furniture if it were on sale? Why?** Answers will vary.

_____

_____

**G. Which review has the biggest impression on you? Why?** Answers will vary.

_____

_____

**H. EVALUATE Think of something you have bought recently. Write a review for it on a separate piece of paper.** Answers will vary.

WORKPLACE CONNECTION
Exercises I, J: Complete tasks as assigned.
Exercise K: Interact appropriately with team members; Collect and organize information.
Exercise M: Apply technology to a task; Combine ideas and information.

**I.** **Imagine that you are buying a new cell phone/smartphone. What questions would you ask before you made your decision to purchase a particular model?**

Answers will vary. Sample answers given.

1. What are the special features of this phone? _____

2. How is the quality of the camera? _____

3. Can I see a cheaper phone and a more expensive one? _____

**J.** **Think about your current cell phone/smartphone. Answer the following questions.**

Answers will vary.

1. What is the make and model? _____

2. How much did it cost? _____

3. Where did you buy it? _____

4. How is the quality? _____

5. Have you ever had any problems with it? _____

6. Did it come with a warranty? _____

7. What do you like about it? _____

8. What do you not like about it? _____

**K.** **RESEARCH** **In order to learn about different cell phone/smartphone models, talk to your classmates. Ask them the questions you wrote in Exercise I as well as the ones in Exercise J.**

**L.** **Based on your product research, what kind of cell phone/smartphone would you buy?**

Answers will vary.
_____

**M.** **RESEARCH** **Choose one of the items from Exercise A to purchase. Do product research by reading reviews on the Internet or talking to your classmates. What did you find out about this product? Write some of the things you learned below.**

Answers will vary.
_____
_____
_____
_____
_____

## Presentation 3      5–10 mins. ■■■

**I.** **Imagine that you are buying a new cell phone/smartphone. What questions would you ask before you made your decision to purchase a particular model?**

Do this exercise as a class.

**J.** **Think about your current cell phone/smartphone. Answer the following questions.**

Go over each question and have students write their own answers on the lines.

## Practice 3      15–20 mins. ■

**K.** **RESEARCH** **In order to learn about different cell phone/smartphone models, talk to your classmates. Ask them the questions you wrote in Exercise I as well as the ones in Exercise J.**

## Evaluation 3      5–10 mins. ■

**L.** **Based on your product research, what kind of cell phone/smartphone would you buy?**

## Application      10–20 mins. ■■■

**M. RESEARCH** **Choose one of the items from Exercise A to purchase. Do product research by reading reviews on the Internet or talking to your classmates. What did you find out about this product? Write some of the things you learned below.**

Students can do this exercise in pairs or small groups.

### MULTILEVEL WORKSHEETS

Unit 6, Lesson 1, Worksheet 1: Product Reviews

Unit 6, Lesson 1, Worksheet 2: Product Research

**Refer students to *Stand Out 5 Workbook*, Unit 6, Lesson 1 for practice with adjective clauses with subject pronouns.**

**Go to the *Activity Bank* online for suggestions on promoting digital literacy and using the Internet to enhance this lesson.**

**Goal:** Purchase goods and services by phone and online

**Academic Strategies:** Focused listening, critical thinking

**Vocabulary:** *lightweight, withstand the elements, fabric pilling, stain, longevity*

## Agenda

- Read a catalog page.
- Listen to customers order products on the phone.
- Review the process of shopping online.

## Resources

**Multilevel Worksheet:** Unit 6, Lesson 2, Worksheet 1
**Grammar Challenge 5:** Unit 6, Challenge 2
**Audio:** CD Track 29
**Suggested Realia:** Store, mail-order, and online catalog pages

## Pacing

- 1.5 hour classes
- 2.5 hour classes
- 3+ hour classes

---

STANDARDS CORRELATIONS

*CCRS:* RI1, RI7, W7, W8, SL1, SL2

*CASAS:* 1.3.1, 1.3.3

*SCANS:* **Resources** Allocate time, allocate money, allocate materials and facility resources, allocate human resources

**Information** Acquire and evaluate information, organize and maintain information, interpret and communicate information, use computers to process information

**Interpersonal** Participate as a member of a team, teach others, serve clients and customers, exercise leadership, negotiate to arrive at a decision, work with cultural diversity

**Systems** Understand systems, monitor and correct performance, improve and design systems

**Technology** Select technology, apply technology to a task, maintain and troubleshoot technology

**Basic Skills** Reading, writing, arithmetic, listening, speaking

**Thinking Skills** Think creatively, make decisions, solve problems, see things in the mind's eye

**Personal Qualities** Responsibility, sociability, self-management

*EFF:* **Communication** Read with understanding, convey ideas in writing, speak so others can understand, listen actively, observe critically

**Decision Making** Use math to solve problems and communicate, solve problems and make decisions, plan

---

**Interpersonal** Cooperate with others, advocate and influence, resolve conflict and negotiate, guide others

**Lifelong Learning** Take responsibility for learning, reflect and evaluate, learn through research, use information and communications technology

## Warm-up and Review            5–10 mins. ■■■

Have students get in small groups and talk about things they have researched before they purchased something. Ask them to tell their group members how they did their research and what they found.

## Introduction            5–10 mins. ■■■

Dictation:

1. Does the product come with a warranty?
2. Have you ever had any problems with it?
3. Did you shop around for the best price?
4. Would you buy the same product again?

State the goal: *Today, you will practice buying things by phone and online.*

## Presentation 1            10–15 mins. ■■■

A. **Take a class poll. How many of your classmates shop online? How many of your classmates order from catalogs by phone?**

Ask students who raise their hands for either question what catalogs they shop from and what online stores they buy from. Discuss the benefits to buying online or by phone.

B. **Look at the page from a housewares catalog. Underline each of the following pieces of information for each product: item name, item description, item price, and item number.**

## Practice 1            10–15 mins. ■■■

C. **Listen to four telephone conversations between salespeople and customers who are buying items from this catalog page. Complete the table based on what you hear.**

**Note:** The listening script is on page 154a.

## Evaluation 1            5 mins. ■■■

Go over the answers as a class.

For more practice, have students work with a partner to practice ordering items from the catalog.

WORKPLACE CONNECTION
Exercise A: Collect and organize information.
Exercises B, C: Complete tasks as assigned.

GOAL ■ Purchase goods and services by phone and online

**A.** Take a class poll. How many of your classmates shop online? How many of your classmates order from catalogs by phone? *Answers will vary.*

**B.** Look at the page from a housewares catalog. Underline each of the following pieces of information for each product: item name, item description, item price, and item number.

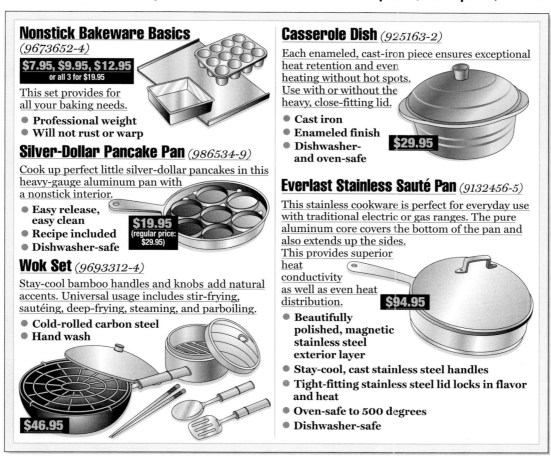

**Nonstick Bakeware Basics** *(9673652-4)*
**$7.95, $9.95, $12.95** or all 3 for $19.95
This set provides for all your baking needs.
● Professional weight
● Will not rust or warp

**Silver-Dollar Pancake Pan** *(986534-9)*
Cook up perfect little silver-dollar pancakes in this heavy-gauge aluminum pan with a nonstick interior.
● Easy release, easy clean
● Recipe included
● Dishwasher-safe
**$19.95** (regular price: $29.95)

**Wok Set** *(9693312-4)*
Stay-cool bamboo handles and knobs add natural accents. Universal usage includes stir-frying, sautéing, deep-frying, steaming, and parboiling.
● Cold-rolled carbon steel
● Hand wash
**$46.95**

**Casserole Dish** *(925163-2)*
Each enameled, cast-iron piece ensures exceptional heat retention and even heating without hot spots. Use with or without the heavy, close-fitting lid.
● Cast iron
● Enameled finish
● Dishwasher- and oven-safe
**$29.95**

**Everlast Stainless Sauté Pan** *(9132456-5)*
This stainless cookware is perfect for everyday use with traditional electric or gas ranges. The pure aluminum core covers the bottom of the pan and also extends up the sides. This provides superior heat conductivity as well as even heat distribution.
**$94.95**
● Beautifully polished, magnetic stainless steel exterior layer
● Stay-cool, cast stainless steel handles
● Tight-fitting stainless steel lid locks in flavor and heat
● Oven-safe to 500 degrees
● Dishwasher-safe

**C.** Listen to four telephone conversations between salespeople and customers who are buying items from the catalog page. Complete the table based on what you hear.

CD TR 29

| | Item | Total cost | Method of payment |
|---|---|---|---|
| **1.** | Casserole Dish | $32.42 | Versa |
| **2.** | Silver-Dollar Pancake Pan | $21.60 | Discovery |
| **3.** | 2 Everlast Stainless Sauté Pans | $205.57 | Discovery |
| **4.** | Nonstick Bakeware Muffin Pan | $14.02 | MisterCard |

**D.** **With your teacher, review the process of making a purchase online. Look for each step in the screen shots below.**

1. Find the website you want to buy something from.

2. Perform a search.

3. Look at the results of your search.

4. Narrow down the results to one item.

5. Make purchase.

**E.** **EVALUATE** **In a group, discuss the pros and cons of buying something online. Make two lists on a separate piece of paper.** *Answers will vary. Sample answers given.*

*Pros: convenient, easy to compare prices, pay by credit card is usually safe*
*Cons: can't see product, may be unreliable website, shipping costs*

## LISTENING SCRIPT

CD
TR 29

**Conversation 1**
**Salesperson:** *Cook-It-Right Catalog Sales. Would you like to order something from our catalog?*
**Customer:** *Yes, I'd like to order item number 925163-2.*
**Salesperson:** *How many?*
**Customer:** *Just one, please.*
**Salesperson:** *OK, your total will be $32.42 with tax. Will you be paying with Versa, MisterCard, or Discovery today?*
**Customer:** *Versa.*
**Salesperson:** *Great. I'll need the number and expiration date whenever you're ready.*

**Conversation 2**
**Salesperson:** *Cook-It-Right Catalog Sales. Would you like to order something from our catalog?*
**Customer:** *Yes, I'd like to order item number 986534-9.*
**Salesperson:** *How many?*
**Customer:** *Just one, please.*
**Salesperson:** *OK, your total will be $21.60. Will you be paying with Versa, MisterCard, or Discovery today?*
**Customer:** *You don't take American Expression?*
**Salesperson:** *Sorry, ma'am. No.*
**Customer:** *OK, I'll pay with Discovery.*
**Salesperson:** *Great. I'll need the number and expiration date whenever you're ready.*

**Conversation 3**
**Salesperson:** *Cook-It-Right Catalog Sales. Would you like to order something from our catalog?*
**Customer:** *Yes, I'd like to order item number 9132456-5.*
**Salesperson:** *How many?*
**Customer:** *Two, please.*
**Salesperson:** *OK, your total will be $205.57 with tax and shipping. Will you be paying with Versa, MisterCard, or Discovery today?*
**Customer:** *Discovery.*
**Salesperson:** *Great. I'll need the number and expiration date whenever you're ready.*

**Conversation 4**
**Salesperson:** *Cook-It-Right Catalog Sales. Would you like to order something from our catalog?*
**Customer:** *Yes, I'd like to order item number 9673652-4.*
**Salesperson:** *All three pieces?*
**Customer:** *Just the muffin pan, please.*
**Salesperson:** *OK, your total will be $14.02 with tax. Will you be paying with Versa, MisterCard, or Discovery today?*
**Customer:** *MisterCard.*
**Salesperson:** *Great. I'll need the number and expiration date whenever you're ready.*

## Presentation 2     5–10 mins. ■■■

**D.  With your teacher, review the process of making a purchase online. Look for each step in the screen shots below.**

## Practice 2     10–15 mins. ■■
(Shorter classes can do this exercise for homework individually.)

**E.  EVALUATE  In a group, discuss the pros and cons of buying something online. Make two lists on a separate piece of paper.**

### INSTRUCTOR'S NOTES

_____
_____
_____
_____
_____
_____
_____
_____
_____
_____
_____
_____
_____
_____
_____
_____
_____
_____
_____
_____

## Practice 2 (continued)

**F. What goods or services do you like to buy online?**

### Evaluation 2      10–15 mins. ■■□
Go over students' ideas as a class, asking volunteers to write pros and cons on the board.

### Presentation 3      1 min. ■■■
Go over the instructions to Exercise G.

### Practice 3      15–20 mins. ■□□
(Shorter classes can do this exercise for homework.)

**G. With a partner, create a list of specific items to sell in a catalog or online.**

### Evaluation 3      10–15 mins. ■□□
Walk around the classroom and help students as needed.

### Application      10–20 mins. ■■■
**Note:** Students will need a catalog page to look at if they didn't create one in Practice 3. If necessary, they can use the catalog page on page 153. If possible, bring in sample catalogs for students to use.

**H. Exchange your page with another pair of students. Have a conversation about purchasing the new items with your partner. One of you should be a sales representative explaining your products. Sit back-to-back to simulate selling and purchasing on the phone.**

Ideally, the student playing the sales representative would have Internet access and could practice searching for something online.

**I. Do an Internet search to find items similar to the ones on the catalog page in Exercise B. Follow the steps in Exercise D to find the items you want. If you don't have computer access, answer the following questions.**

If students don't have computer access, have them complete the alternate questions 1–5 in Exercise I to the best of their ability.

## MULTILEVEL WORKSHEET

Unit 6, Lesson 2, Worksheet 1: Catalog Shopping

**Refer students to *Stand Out 5 Workbook*, Unit 6, Lesson 2 for practice with adjective clauses with object pronouns.**

**Go to the *Activity Bank* online for suggestions on promoting digital literacy and using the Internet to enhance this lesson.**

## INSTRUCTOR'S NOTES

WORKPLACE CONNECTION
Exercise F: Complete tasks as assigned.
Exercises G, H: Interact appropriately with team members.
Exercise I: Apply technology to a task.

**F.** **What goods or services do you like to buy online?** Answers will vary. Sample answers given.

books, DVDs, games, dishware, some clothes

**G.** **With a partner, create a list of specific items to sell in a catalog or online.** Answers will vary.

1. Decide what type of items you could sell.

2. On a separate piece of paper, create art, descriptions, and prices for at least five items.

**H.** **Exchange your page with another pair of students. Have a conversation about purchasing the new items with your partner. One of you should be a sales representative explaining your products. Sit back-to-back to simulate selling and purchasing on the phone.**

**I.** **Do an Internet search to find items similar to the ones on the catalog page in Exercise B. Follow the steps in Exercise D to find the items you want. If you don't have computer access, answer the following questions.** Answers will vary.

1. What would you like to buy online? _____

2. What words will you type in to search for the item? _____

3. Do you know of an online store that sells the item? _____

4. Once you click on the store that sells your item, what information will you look for?

   _____

5. How will you decide if you are going to purchase the item? What information will you consider?

   _____

Be careful which websites you
trust with your card details.

# LESSON ③ Is this under warranty?

GOAL ■ Interpret product guarantees and warranties

WORKPLACE CONNECTION
Exercise A: Interact appropriately with team members.
Exercise C: Complete tasks as assigned.

**A. Discuss the following situations with a partner and make decisions.**

*Answers will vary. Sample answers are given.*

What would you do if . . .

1. you plugged in your new DVD player and it didn't work? *Take it to a technician.*

2. your printer stopped working one week after you bought it? *Take it back to the store.*

3. the speaker on your new cell phone/smartphone didn't work? *Take it back to the store, go online for help with problems.*

4. you washed a new shirt according to the care instructions on the tag and it shrank? *Take it back to the store for a refund.*

**B. A *warranty* or *guarantee* is a written promise by a company to replace or repair a product free of charge within a certain time period after purchase if it has any defects. Read the following warranty for a set of stereo speakers.**

This product is guaranteed against all defects in workmanship and materials for two years following purchase. All it takes to ensure complete coverage is to register your purchase. Once you have warranty-registered your product, the nearest service center can respond quickly and directly to you.

**C. Answer the following questions about the warranty.**

1. Where do you take your product if something goes wrong?

   *the nearest service center*

2. How long is the product guaranteed?

   *2 years*

3. What do you need to do to make sure you receive the warranty for the product?

   *register the product*

4. Does the warranty cover your dropping and breaking the product?

   *probably not: it covers defects, not damage*

# AT-A-GLANCE PREP

**Goal:** Interpret product guarantees and warranties

**Academic Strategy:** Making inferences

**Vocabulary:** *guarantee, warranty, free of charge, faults, defects in workmanship, foregoing, alleging, conform, deems, malfunctions*

## Agenda

- Read and answer questions about a product warranty.
- Work with legal language used in warranties.
- Choose the best answer about a product guarantee.
- Write a guarantee.

## Resources

**Multilevel Worksheets:** Unit 6, Lesson 3, Worksheets 1–2

**Workbook:** Unit 6, Lesson 3

## Pacing

- ◼ 1.5 hour classes   ◼ 2.5 hour classes
- ◼ 3+ hour classes

## STANDARDS CORRELATIONS

*CCRS:* RI1, RI2, W2, W4, SL1

*CASAS:* 1.6.3, 1.6.4

*SCANS:* **Information** Acquire and evaluate information, interpret and communicate information

**Interpersonal** Participate as a member of a team, teach others, negotiate to arrive at a decision, work with cultural diversity

**Systems** Understand systems, monitor and correct performance

**Basic Skills** Reading, writing, listening, speaking

**Thinking Skills** Think creatively, make decisions, solve problems, see things in the mind's eye

**Personal Qualities** Responsibility, sociability, self-management

*EFF:* **Communication** Read with understanding, convey ideas in writing, speak so others can understand, listen actively, observe critically

**Decision Making** Solve problems and make decisions, plan

**Interpersonal** Cooperate with others, advocate and influence, resolve conflict and negotiate, guide others

**Lifelong Learning** Take responsibility for learning, reflect and evaluate

## Warm-up and Review          5–10 mins. ◼◼◼

Repeat the application activity from the previous lesson. Have students work with a different student than they did in the previous lesson.

## Introduction          5–10 mins. ◼◼◼

Dictation:

1. We will not be undersold by our competitors.
2. Our products are backed by our no-hassle warranty.
3. They guarantee their products for two years from purchase date.
4. The warranty covers only defects arising from normal use.

State the goal: *Today, you will be interpreting product warranties and guarantees.*

## Presentation 1          10–15 mins. ◼◼◼

### A. Discuss the following situations with a partner and make decisions.

Once students have had a chance to discuss the situations with a partner, discuss each one as a class.

### B. A *warranty* or *guarantee* is a written promise by a company to replace or repair a product free of charge within a certain time period after purchase if it has any defects. Read the following warranty for a set of stereo speakers.

Point out to students that guarantees and warranties are basically the same. In fact, if you look both words up in the dictionary, the definitions are almost identical.

## Practice 1          5 mins. ◼◼◼

### C. Answer the following questions about the warranty.

## Evaluation 1          5 mins. ◼◼◼

Go over the answers as a class.

## Presentation 2  5–10 mins. ■■■

**D. Warranties are often difficult to understand because they are worded with legal language.**

Go over the example and show students how to arrive at the general meaning of a warranty.

## Practice 2  15–20 mins. ■■
(Shorter classes can do this exercise for homework.)

**E. INTEPRET  With a partner, Restate each sentence below in your own words.**

Tell students they can use dictionaries, but all they need to gather is the general idea of each sentence. Consequently, they don't need to understand every word.

## Evaluation 2  10–15 mins. ■■

Go over students' ideas as a class. If you have time, have volunteers write their restatements on the board. Have the class vote on which ones they think are the most accurate.

### BEST PRACTICE

**Restating a sentence**

When restating a sentence in your own words, it is important to look away and write. Tell students to first read the sentence a few times, making sure that they understand it. Once students feel they can rewrite the original sentence in their own words, they can restate it in their own words.

### INSTRUCTOR'S NOTES

**D. Warranties are often difficult to understand because they are worded with legal language.**

> Seller warrants to the original customers purchasing products from Seller that all such products, under normal use and operation, will be free from defects in materials and workmanship affecting form, fit, and function.

In other words . . .

The seller says that if I use this product under normal conditions, as it was meant to be used, there won't be any problems with it.

**E. INTERPRET With a partner, restate each sentence below in your own words.**

*Answers will vary. Sample answers given.*

1. Any claims alleging failure of products to conform to the foregoing warranty may be made only by the customer who purchased the product.

   *Return or refund requests made because the product didn't function as promised can only be made*

   *by the original purchaser.*

2. The foregoing warranty only applies while the product is being used in the original machine with the original hardware and software configuration.

   *The company promise is only valid while the item is used as intended with the original computer*

   *programs and parts.*

3. Seller, at its option, will repair, replace, or provide a credit or refund of either the original purchase price less a restock fee or current fair market value, whichever is less, for any product Seller deems to be defective.

   *The seller will make the decision to fix, match, give credit or refund at the selling price minus a charge for*

   *taking it back, or the current price depending on which is less if the seller sees that the product is imperfect.*

4. The above warranties cover only defects arising under normal use and do not include malfunctions or failures from misuse, neglect, alteration, abuse, improper installation, or acts of nature.

   *The warranty only covers flaws that show up with normal wear and doesn't consider breakdowns or*

   *errors in function from breakage, accidents, drops, or poor installment.*

5. Removal of the labeling on products will void all warranties.

   *If you remove the original labels from the items, the warranty or promise will not be honored.*

WORKPLACE CONNECTION
Exercise G: Complete tasks as assigned.
Exercise H: Interact appropriately with team members; Combine ideas and information.

**F.** **Read the guarantee from a printer company.**

## OUR NO-HASSLE GUARANTEE

Our products are backed the way they are built—the best in the industry. Our no-hassle printer guarantee gives you excellent product support with no worries. Now, you can enjoy the benefit of a substitute printer if your printer fails during the first year of use.

We will send a replacement printer to you within 48 hours of your request for any printer that fails to meet the factory specifications or fails to power up upon delivery within one year of your invoice date. Upon receipt of your no-hassle replacement printer, you must return your defective printer to us. Your defective printer will be exchanged for the same make and model, or for a printer of equal value. In addition, if your printer has three separate quality issues, which are documented with our technical support team, within one year from the date of your invoice, we will permanently replace your defective printer with a new printer of equal or greater value.

**1 YEAR ✓ GUARANTEE**

**G.** **Choose the best answer.**

1. You can receive a substitute printer if your printer doesn't work during the first . . .

   a. 48 hours.           (b.) year.           c. week.

2. How soon will a replacement printer be sent?

   (a.) within 48 hours       b. within one year       c. within one week

3. When you receive your replacement printer, you must . . .

   (a.) return the defective printer.     b. do nothing.       c. call the company.

4. If you have three problems with your printer during the first year, the company will . . .

   a. fix your printer for free.       b. refund your money.     (c.) permanently replace the printer.

**H.** **CREATE** **With a partner, choose a product from the list below and write your own warranty or guarantee. Use the ideas from the warranties and guarantees you have read in this lesson, but use your own words.** Answers will vary.

digital camera             bicycle             cell phone/smartphone             washing machine

## Presentation 3
5 mins. ■■■

Go over the instructions for the next two exercises.

## Practice 3
10–15 mins. ■

(Shorter classes can do these exercises for homework.)

**F.  Read the guarantee from a printer company.**

**G.  Choose the best answer.**

## Evaluation 3
5–10 mins. ■

Go over the answers as a class.

## Application
10–20 mins. ■■□

**H. CREATE  With a partner, choose a product from the list below and write your own warranty or guarantee. Use the ideas from the warranties and guarantees you have read in this lesson, but use your own words.**

To help students get started, brainstorm some ideas of what should be included in a warranty as a class.

### MULTILEVEL WORKSHEETS

Unit 6, Lesson 3, Worksheet 1: Warranties

Unit 6, Lesson 3, Worksheet 2: Sample Complaint Letter

**Refer students to *Stand Out 5 Workbook*, Unit 6, Lesson 3 for practice with adjective clauses using *when*, *where*, or *why*.**

**Go to the *Activity Bank* online for suggestions on promoting digital literacy and using the Internet to enhance this lesson.**

## AT-A-GLANCE PREP

**Goal:** Return a product

**Academic Strategy:** Focused listening

**Vocabulary:** *return, exchange, refund, valid photo ID, original form of payment, issued, policy*

### Agenda

- Listen to customers returning items.
- Interpret return policies.
- Practice conversations about returning or exchanging a product.

### Resources

**Multilevel Worksheet:** Unit 6, Lesson 4, Worksheet 1

**Workbook:** Unit 6, Lesson 4

**Audio:** CD Tracks 30–32

### Pacing

- ■ 1.5 hour classes   ■ 2.5 hour classes
- ■ 3+ hour classes

## STANDARDS CORRELATIONS

*CCRS:* RI1, SL1, SL2, SL6

*CASAS:* 1.3.3

*SCANS:* **Resources** Allocate human resources

**Information** Acquire and evaluate information, interpret and communicate information

**Interpersonal** Participate as a member of a team, teach others, serve clients and customers, exercise leadership, negotiate to arrive at a decision, work with cultural diversity

**Systems** Monitor and correct performance

**Basic Skills** Reading, writing, listening, speaking

**Thinking Skills** Think creatively, make decisions, solve problems, see things in the mind's eye

**Personal Qualities** Responsibility, sociability, self-management

*EFF:* **Communication** Read with understanding, convey ideas in writing, speak so others can understand, listen actively, observe critically

**Decision Making** Solve problems and make decisions, plan

**Interpersonal** Cooperate with others, advocate and influence, resolve conflict and negotiate, guide others

**Lifelong Learning** Take responsibility for learning, reflect and evaluate

---

### Warm-up and Review            5–10 mins. ■■■

Ask volunteers to take out the warranties they wrote from the previous lesson and share them out loud with the class. If their warranties are short, ask volunteers to write them on the board.

### Introduction            5–10 mins. ■■■

Dictation:

1. An original sales receipt is required for a full refund.
2. If you find a lower price at any of our competitors, we will meet that price.
3. Without a receipt, returns can be made for store credit.
4. Some items cannot be returned if opened.

State the goal: *Today, we will practice returning products.*

### Presentation 1            10–15 mins. ■■■

**A. Think of a product you have returned to the store where you bought it. What did you return and why? Discuss your experience with your classmates.**

**B. Read and listen to the conversation.**

> ## LISTENING SCRIPT             CD TR 30
>
> *The listening script matches the conversation in Exercise B.*

### Practice 1            10–15 mins. ■■■

**C. Listen to each question and write the correct answer.**

Tell students they will be listening to questions about the conversation in Exercise B. Tell them to write short answers to the questions they hear.

> ## LISTENING SCRIPT             CD TR 31
>
> 1. *What is the customer trying to return?*
> 2. *Why is she returning them?*
> 3. *Will the store give the customer her money back?*
> 4. *Why not?*
> 5. *What does the sales associate say the customer can do?*
> 6. *Does the customer seem satisfied?*

### Evaluation 1            5 mins. ■■■

Go over the answers as a class.

GOAL ■ Return a product  WORKPLACE CONNECTION
Exercise A: Interact appropriately with team members.
Exercise C: Interpret and communicate information.

**A.** Think of a product you have returned to the store where you bought it. What did you return and why? Discuss your experience with your classmates.

**B.** Read and listen to the conversation.

CD
TR 30

| | |
|---|---|
| **Sales Associate:** | Can I help you with something? |
| **Customer:** | Yes, I'd like to return these shoes. I wore them around my house on the carpet for a few days and they are still uncomfortable. The salesman who sold them to me insisted they would stretch out and soften up, but they haven't. I'd like to get my money back. |
| **Sales Associate:** | I'm afraid I can't give you your money back. These were on sale and we don't offer refunds for sale items. |
| **Customer:** | Can I exchange them? |
| **Sales Associate:** | Yes, you can exchange them for something of equal value. |
| **Customer:** | OK, I'll do that. Let me look around for a bit. |
| **Sales Associate:** | Take your time. |

**C.** Listen to each question and write the correct answer. Answers will vary. Sample answers given.

CD
TR 31

1. The customer is trying to return some shoes.

2. They are uncomfortable.

3. No, it won't.

4. The shoes were on sale and the store doesn't refund sale items.

5. The customer can exchange them for something of equal value.

6. Yes, she does.

Most goods can usually be returned to a store within a few weeks.

Customer Service

**D.   Read each return policy and the statements below them. Circle *T* (true) or *F* (false).**

> Thank you for shopping at Nico's. Return or exchange for merchandise within two weeks with tags attached and/or in original packaging. Original sales receipt is required for full refund. Final sale on all sale items.

1. You can exchange sale items.                                             T          (F)

2. You need an original sales receipt for a refund.          (T)         F

> Valid photo ID required for all returns (except for credit card purchases), exchanges, and to receive and redeem store credit. With a receipt, a full refund in the original form of payment, except payments made with checks, will be issued for new and unread books and unopened music within four days. For merchandise purchased with a check, a store credit will be issued within the first seven days. Without an original receipt, a store credit issued by mail will be offered at the lowest selling price. With a receipt, returns of new and unread books and unopened music from our website can be made for store credit. Textbooks after 14 days or without a receipt are not returnable. Used books are not returnable.

3. If you pay with a check, you can get cash back.              T          (F)

4. You cannot return used books.                                       (T)         F

5. If you have a receipt, you can get a refund on unopened
   music within four days.                                               (T)         F

6. If you don't have a receipt, you can exchange an item.   T          (F)

> All returns and exchanges must be new, unused, and have original packaging and accessories. Some items cannot be returned if opened. For our full return and exchange policy, visit the store or log onto our website. For a gift receipt, bring this receipt back to any store within 90 days. Ask about receipt look-up.

7. All opened items can be exchanged.                               T          (F)

> We will not be undersold. Guaranteed! If you find a lower price at any of our competitors, we will meet that price.

8. This store will offer you a lower price than its competitors.   T          (F)

**E.   Look back at all the false statements. On a separate piece of paper, rewrite each statement correctly.** *Answers on page 160a.*

## Presentation 2

5–10 mins. ■■■

Discuss return policies. Ask students what they think most stores require in order to return or exchange something. Make a list.

## Practice 2

10–15 mins. ■■

(Shorter classes can do these exercises for homework.)

**D. Read each return policy and the statements below them. Circle *T* (true) or *F* (false).**

**E. Look back at all the false statements. On a separate piece of paper, rewrite each statement correctly.**

## Evaluation 2

10–15 mins. ■■

Go over the answers as a class.

### BEST PRACTICE

## Checking answers

Many students think of checking answers as a boring routine. Some teachers are not too enthusiastic about the task either. However, going over answers is important because it allows both teachers and students to monitor understanding and progress. Below are a few ideas to make the process less monotonous.

1. Ask students to compare their answers first.
2. Go over items in random order instead of linearly.
3. Allow students to choose the questions they answer.
4. Call on individual students and allow for students to volunteer.

Answers to Exercise E:
1. You cannot exchange sale items.
3. You cannot get cash back if you pay by check.
6. You cannot exchange an item if you don't have a receipt.
7. Open items cannot be exchanged.
8. This store will not offer you a lower price than its competitors.

## Presentation 3

5–10 mins. ■■■

Go over the reasons listed in Exercise F for why someone might return something. Ask students what sort of items might be returned for these reasons.

## Practice 3

15–20 mins. ■

(Shorter classes can do this exercise for homework by using the script in the back of their books.)

**F. Listen to six conversations and write the corresponding conversation number. Then, write *returned* or *exchanged*.**

---

### LISTENING SCRIPT

CD
TR 32

**Conversation 1**
**Sales Associate:** *Can I help you with something?*
**Customer:** *Yes, I'd like to exchange this phone for a different one.*
**Sales Associate:** *Is something wrong with it?*
**Customer:** *Well, I can't hear the person on the other end very well when I'm at my house or at work. Basically, that makes the phone useless to me.*
**Sales Associate:** *Yeah, that's not good. Let's get you another one and see if it works better.*
**Customer:** *Thanks.*

**Conversation 2**
**Sales Associate:** *How can I help you?*
**Customer:** *I bought these pants here last week and I didn't have time to try them on. When I got home and put them on, I realized they are too small. Can I try on a larger size?*
**Sales Associate:** *Let me see if we have them in stock. (pause) You're in luck! Here, let me get you a fitting room.*

**Conversation 3**
**Sales Associate:** *Can I help you with something?*
**Customer:** *Yes, I ordered these glasses online and when I received them in the mail, they were broken. I thought it would be easier to return them to the store rather than trying to ship them back.*
**Sales Associate:** *Good idea. Unfortunately, we are all out of this style right now. Would you like me to give you a credit and then we'll call you when they come in?*
**Customer:** *Could I get something different?*
**Sales Associate:** *Certainly. Why don't you look around and I'll hold them up here at the counter for you.*
**Customer:** *Great.*

**Conversation 4**
**Sales Associate:** *What can I do for you today?*
**Customer:** *Well, I got this printer home and realized it doesn't work with my computer. I called tech support and they told me I never should've been sold this printer because it doesn't come with a driver to make it work with my computer.*

**Sales Associate:** *I'm sorry about that. Would you like to shop around for another printer?*
**Customer:** *No, I think I just want my money back.*
**Sales Associate:** *As long as you have your receipt, we can definitely do that.*
**Customer:** *Here it is.*

**Conversation 5**
**Customer:** *Hi. I need to exchange these baby diapers for a larger size. I accidentally bought the wrong ones.*
**Sales Associate:** *No worries. Why don't you go ahead and pick out the size you need. Then, come back and I'll do the exchange for you.*
**Customer:** *Perfect. Thanks!*

**Conversation 6**
**Sales Associate:** *Can I help you with something?*
**Customer:** *Yes, I was given these three books as a gift last week and I actually already have them.*
**Sales Associate:** *Do you have a receipt?*
**Customer:** *I don't.*
**Sales Associate:** *OK, well let me see how much they were and you can pick out something of equal value to exchange with them.*
**Customer:** *Sounds great. Thank you.*

## Evaluation 3

5–10 mins. ■

Go over the answers as a class.

## Application

10–20 mins. ■■■

**G. SUPPOSE  Write two reasons you might return each of the items listed below.**

**H. ROLE-PLAY  Pretend you are in a store, either as a clerk or as a customer.**

Clerks should help each customer with his or her return.

Customers should choose one item from Exercise G to return or exchange. Use one of the reasons you came up with. Have at least three conversations with different clerks or customers and then switch roles.

### MULTILEVEL WORKSHEET

Unit 6, Lesson 4, Worksheet 1: Returns and Exchanges

Refer students to *Stand Out 5 Workbook,* Unit 6, Lesson 4 for practice with the reduction of adjective clauses to adjective phrases.

Go to the *Activity Bank* online for suggestions on promoting digital literacy and using the Internet to enhance this lesson.

WORKPLACE CONNECTION
Exercise F: Interpret and communicate information.
Exercise G: Complete tasks as assigned.
Exercise H: Interact appropriately with team members.

CD
TR 32

**F.** **Listen to six conversations and write the corresponding conversation number. Then, write *returned* or *exchanged*.**

| Conversation # | Reason for returning or exchanging item | Was item returned or exchanged? |
|---|---|---|
| 5 | bought the wrong package | exchanged |
| 6 | already have them | exchanged |
| 1 | bad reception | exchanged |
| 2 | don't fit right | exchanged |
| 3 | broken | exchanged |
| 4 | doesn't work with computer | returned |

**G.** **SUPPOSE** **Write two reasons you might return each of the items listed below.**

Answers will vary. Sample answers given.

1. digital video camera

    a. screen doesn't work    b. not enough features

2. gallon of milk

    a. sour    b. already opened

3. pair of pants

    a. too large/small    b. defective zipper

4. laptop computer

    a. too slow    b. programs crash/don't load/fail

5. sunglasses

    a. not dark enough    b. pinch nose

6. textbook

    a. wrong edition    b. already written in

**H.** **ROLE-PLAY** **Pretend you are in a store, either as a clerk or as a customer.**

Clerks should help each customer with his or her return. Have at least three conversations with different customers.

Customers should choose one item from Exercise G to return or exchange. Use one of the reasons you came up with. Have at least three conversations with different clerks.

# LESSON ⑤ For sale!

GOAL ▶ Sell a product

WORKPLACE CONNECTION
Exercise A: Interact appropriately with team members.
Exercises B, C: Complete tasks as assigned.

**A.** **If you don't go to an actual store to get product information, you might learn about different products by reading ads. Where can you find ads? Brainstorm ideas with a partner.** Answers will vary. Sample answers given.
from a catalog, on the phone, on the Internet

**B.** **If you were going to sell some items you owned, what would they be? Make a list on a separate piece of paper.** Answers will vary. Sample answers given.
books, clothes, dishes, knitting, car

**C.** **ANALYZE** **Read each of the ads below and think about the following questions.**

1. What is for sale?  a car, a bicycle

2. How is the seller trying to convince you to buy it?  Answers will vary.

3. Would you consider buying any of the items in the ads? Why?  Answers will vary.

marketplace | local | cars | for sale

**Rare Red Dino 1973 Ferrari 246 GTS**   REPLY

This car, a sporty red convertible, will make you feel like royalty.
- Right-hand drive
- 50,000 miles before restoration
- 10,500 miles after restoration
- One owner
- Serious inquiries only

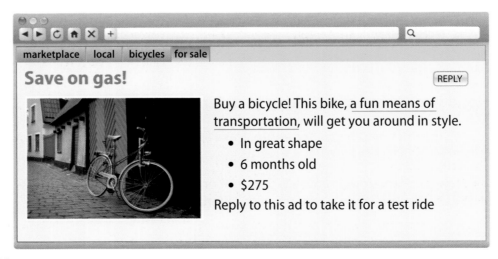

marketplace | local | bicycles | for sale

**Save on gas!**   REPLY

Buy a bicycle! This bike, a fun means of transportation, will get you around in style.
- In great shape
- 6 months old
- $275
Reply to this ad to take it for a test ride

**Goal:** Sell a product
**Grammar:** Appositives
**Vocabulary:** *convince, face value, appositive*

### Agenda

- ▢ Read classified ads.
- ▢ Work with appositives.
- ▢ Write an ad.

### Resources

**Multilevel Worksheets:** Unit 6, Lesson 5,
    Worksheets 1–2
**Workbook:** Unit 6, Lesson 5
**Suggested Realia:** Printouts from websites where
    people sell or auction things, other publications
    (local newspapers, flyers in the mail, etc.)

### Pacing

- ■ 1.5 hour classes  ■ 2.5 hour classes
- ■ 3+ hour classes

## STANDARDS CORRELATIONS

*CCRS:* RI1, W2, W4, SL1, L1
*CASAS:* 1.6.3
*SCANS:* **Information** Acquire and evaluate information, organize and maintain information, interpret and communicate information, use computers to process information *(optional)*
**Interpersonal** Participate as a member of a team, teach others, exercise leadership, negotiate to arrive at a decision, work with cultural diversity
**Systems** Understand systems, monitor and correct performance
**Technology** Select technology, apply technology to a task, maintain and troubleshoot technology *(optional)*
**Basic Skills** Reading, writing, listening, speaking
**Thinking Skills** Think creatively, make decisions, see things in the mind's eye
**Personal Qualities** Responsibility, sociability, self-management
*EFF:* **Communication** Read with understanding, convey ideas in writing, speak so others can understand, listen actively, observe critically
**Decision Making** Solve problems and make decisions, plan
**Interpersonal** Cooperate with others, guide others
**Lifelong Learning** Take responsibility for learning, reflect and evaluate, use information and communications technology *(optional)*

## Warm-up and Review
10–15 mins. ■■▢

Repeat the application in Exercise H from the previous lesson, giving students more practice with returning or exchanging different items.

## Introduction
5–10 mins. ■■▢

Dictation:

1. These tickets, the best seats in the house, are selling for face value.
2. This car, a sporty red convertible, will make you feel like royalty.
3. This brown leather couch, a part of our family for years, will be the most comfortable piece of furniture you have ever sat on.
4. This bike, a great, fun means of transportation, will get you around in style.

State the goal: *Today, we will discuss how to sell a product.*

## Presentation 1
10–15 mins. ■■▢

**A. If you don't go to an actual store to get product information, you might learn about different products by reading ads. Where can you find ads? Brainstorm ideas with a partner.**

Have students come up with places where they could find ads selling products.

**B. If you were going to sell some items you owned, what would they be? Make a list on a separate piece of paper.**

Ask students to share what they might sell.

## Practice 1
10–15 mins. ■■▢

**C. ANALYZE Read each of the ads below and think about the following questions.**

You can do this activity in a variety of ways:

1. Have students do just as the instructions say and then go over the answers in Evaluation 1.
2. Have students work with a partner and ask each other the questions.
3. Have students work in small groups and discuss the questions for each ad.

## Evaluation 1
5 mins. ■■▢

Go over the answers as a class.

## Presentation 2      10–15 mins. ■■■

**D. Read about appositives with your classmates and teacher.**

**E. Find and underline the appositives in both ads in Exercise C.**

Do Exercise E as a class. Ask students to find each appositive by themselves and then ask the entire class for the correct answer. If necessary for more clarification, discuss each appositive and point out what makes it an appositive (as opposed to an adjective clause).

---

**BEST PRACTICE**

### Appositive vs. adjective clause

An appositive renames a noun, usually with a description, but it does not include any verbs and it must include another noun.

For example:

The ad, <u>the one with all the great pictures</u>, makes me want to buy those dishes.

The ad, <u>part of my favorite cooking magazine</u>, makes me want to buy those dishes.

An adjective clause usually includes a relative pronoun and must include a verb.

For example:

The ad <u>that I saw in that magazine</u> makes me want to buy those dishes.

The ad, <u>where the girl is cooking in her new kitchen</u>, makes me want to buy those dishes.

---

## Practice 2      10–15 mins. ■■
(Shorter classes can do this exercise for homework.)

**F. Complete each of the statements below with an appositive.**

## Evaluation 2      10–15 mins. ■■
Ask volunteers to write their sentences on the board. As you go over each statement, ask other volunteers to read what they wrote out loud. This will enable students to see that there is more than one possibility for each sentence.

## D. Read about appositives with your classmates and teacher.

| Appositives | | |
|---|---|---|
| **Noun or Noun Phrase** | **Appositive** | **Remainder of sentence (Predicate)** |
| The ad, | the one with all the great pictures, | makes me want to buy those dishes. |
| That computer, | the fastest machine in the store, | sells for over $2,000. |

**Explanation:**
- An appositive is a noun or noun phrase that renames another noun next to it in a sentence.
- The appositive adds extra descriptive detail, explains, or identifies something about the noun.
- An appositive can come before or after the noun phrase it is modifying.

**Example:** *A helpful gift, money is always appreciated by a newly married couple.*

**Note:** Appositives are usually set off by commas.

## E. Find and underline the appositive in both ads in Exercise C.

## F. Complete each of the statements below with an appositive. Answers will vary. Sample answers given.

1. Her dress, __a really fancy gown__, got the attention of every customer in the room.

2. That used car, __an old, rusty sedan__, will probably be for sale for quite a while.

3. Used pots and pans, __the ones from your mom__, are hard to sell without the matching lids.

4. Two round-trip plane tickets, __the winning prize__, can be used to travel anywhere in the United States.

5. The smartphone, __a convenient source of music__, has 64 GB of storage.

6. Those leather shoes, __imports from Italy__, have many more years of walking in them.

7. This restaurant, __a place for home-cooking__, will make you money as soon as you open the doors.

8. That set of suitcases, __the largest in the store__, will carry enough clothing and accessories for two weeks of traveling.

9. Her website, __an attractive and accessible site__, is an online store with tons of gently worn clothes for sale.

WORKPLACE CONNECTION
Exercises G, I: Complete tasks as assigned.
Exercises: H, K: Interact appropriately with team members.
Exercise J: Combine ideas and information.

**G.** **If you wanted to buy the following things, where would you look?** *Answers will vary. Sample answers given.*

1. car: _Internet, Autotrader, classified ads_____

2. shoes: _Internet, catalog_____

3. CDs (music): _online, magazine_____

4. furniture: _catalog, Internet_____

**H.** **Imagine that you are going to sell something. Answer the questions below and then discuss your ideas with a partner.** *Answers will vary.*

1. What would you sell? _____

2. What would you say to make your product sound appealing?

_____

3. How much would you sell it for? _____

4. Where would you place your ad? _____

5. How would you want people to contact you? _____

**I.** **Write three statements with appositives that you would use in your advertisement.**
*Answers will vary.*

1. _____

2. _____

3. _____

**J.** **CREATE** On a separate piece of paper, write an ad to sell your product. Find an attractive photo to draw attention to your ad. *Answers will vary.*

**K.** Share your ad with your classmates. See if you can find anyone who would buy what you are selling.

Smartphone apps make it easier to sell goods online.

## Presentation 3 5–10 mins. ■■■

**G. If you wanted to buy the following things, where would you look?**

Do this exercise as a class. Make sure you exhaust all the possibilities of places to sell things (Penny Saver, eBay, Craigslist, local newspaper, etc.).

## Practice 3 10–15 mins. ■

(Shorter classes can do these exercises for homework.)

**H. Imagine that you are going to sell something. Answer the questions below and then discuss your ideas with a partner.**

**I. Write three statements with appositives that you would use in your advertisement.**

## Evaluation 3 5–10 mins. ■

Ask volunteers to share their answers with the class.

## Application 10–20 mins. ■■■

**J. CREATE On a separate piece of paper, write an ad to sell your product. Find an attractive photo to draw attention to your ad.**

**Optional Computer Activity:** Have students create their ads on the computer.

**K. Share your ad with your classmates. See if you can find anyone who would buy what you are selling.**

If you have a smaller class, ask each student to read his or her ad out loud. Ask the other students in the class to make a note to themselves if they might be interested in buying the product. When students have finished reading their ads out loud, have them walk around and talk to the students whose products they might be interested in buying.

For a larger class, have students post their ads around the room and let students walk around and read the ads, looking for something they might be interested in buying.

## MULTILEVEL WORKSHEETS

Unit 6, Lesson 5, Worksheet 1: Radio Ads (listening)

Unit 6, Lesson 5, Worksheet 2: Appositives

Refer students to *Stand Out 5 Workbook*, Unit 6, Lesson 5 for more practice with appositives.

Go to the *Activity Bank* online for suggestions on promoting digital literacy and using the Internet to enhance this lesson.

## INSTRUCTOR'S NOTES

# LIFESKILLS ▶ What could go wrong?

## Before You Watch

- Ask students how they think the title of the video relates to what they have learned in the unit.
- Discuss students' ideas as a class.

### A. Look at the picture and answer the questions.

- Have students look at the picture.
- Ask students to read and answer each question.
- Have volunteers share their answers with the class.

## While You Watch

### B. Watch the video and complete the dialog.

- Ask students to watch the video and complete the dialog.
- Play the video and ask students to watch and listen carefully.
- Play the video again. Then, ask students to complete the dialog.
- Play the video once more and have students check their answers.

## Check Your Understanding

### C. What are the steps in making purchases online? Write numbers to show the correct order.

- Ask students to think about the steps a person takes when they buy something online.
- Have students read the steps below.
- Ask students to write the numbers to show the correct order in making an online purchase.
- Review in class by having volunteers write the steps on the board.

INSTRUCTOR'S NOTES

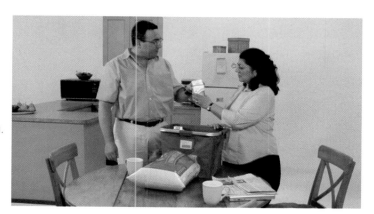 # What could go wrong?

## Before You Watch

**A.  Look at the picture and answer the questions.**

1. Where are Mr. and Mrs. Sanchez?
   *Mr. and Mrs. Sanchez are in their kitchen.*
2. What are they discussing?
   *They are discussing grocery purchases.*

## While You Watch

**B.  ▶ Watch the video and complete the dialog.**

**Mr. Sanchez:**  Miriam, I think you forgot to check the (1) _____*sizes*_____ of all these things.

**Mrs. Sanchez:**  Victor, I think you're right. I just (2) _____*clicked*_____ on the pictures without (3) _____*checking*_____ the sizes.

**Mr. Sanchez:**  Now, do you see why I wanted to be (4) _____*careful*_____?

**Mrs. Sanchez:**  Well, I learned my lesson. (5) _____*Shopping*_____ online isn't as easy as I thought. From now on, I will be more careful.

## Check Your Understanding

**C.  What are the steps in making purchases online? Write numbers to show the correct order.**

1. __4__ Make your selection.
2. __3__ View the products available, comparing quality and prices.
3. __6__ Submit your order.
4. __2__ Search for the product you want to buy.
5. __1__ Log on to the merchant's website.
6. __5__ Enter your payment online.

# Review

Learner Log

I can do product research.
☐ Yes ☐ No ☐ Maybe

I can purchase goods and services by phone and online.
☐ Yes ☐ No ☐ Maybe

**A. Imagine that you are going to buy a used car. Write four questions you would ask car sellers.** Questions will vary. Sample questions given.

1. What repairs have been done?

2. How often do you replace the oil?

3. Did you buy this car new?

4. How old are the tires?

**B. Ask your classmates the questions you wrote in Exercise A. Write some of their responses below. When your classmates ask you their questions, you can talk about your own car or a car you are familiar with.** Answers will vary.

**C. Imagine that you are going to buy a product online. Write a short paragraph about the steps you will need to take to buy the product.** Answers will vary. Sample answer given.

First, I will go online. On the Internet I will go to my favorite website for clothing. Next, I will search for

"hoodies" or sweatshirts. After that, I will choose the look and color I like. Finally, I will choose the one

with the best price and pay for it with my credit card.

**D. Write a conversation between a salesperson and a customer for one of the items on page 153.** Answers will vary. Sample answers given.

**Salesperson:** How can I help you today?

**Customer:** Hi, I'm interested in buying a wok.

**Salesperson:** We have a good one here for $46.95.

**Customer:** Oh, that's expensive. Does it come with a warranty?

**Salesperson:** Yes, it comes with a one-year warranty and a steamer.

**Customer:** That sounds reasonable. I'll take that wok set.

WORKPLACE CONNECTION
Exercises A, D: Complete tasks as assigned.
Exercise B: Interact appropriately with team members.
Exercise C: Combine ideas and information.

## AT-A-GLANCE PREP

**Goals:** All unit goals
**Grammar:** All unit grammar
**Academic Strategy:** Reviewing
**Vocabulary:** All Unit 6 vocabulary

### Agenda

- Discuss unit goals.
- Complete the review.
- Use unit vocabulary.

### Resources

**Stand Out Assessment CD-ROM with ExamView®**

### Pacing

- 1.5 hour classes
- 2.5 hour classes
- 3+ hour classes

## STANDARDS CORRELATIONS

*CCRS:* RI1, RI4

*CASAS:* 7.2.1

*SCANS:* **Resources** Allocate time

**Information** Acquire and evaluate information

**Interpersonal** Participate as a member of a team, teach others, negotiate to arrive at a decision, work with cultural diversity

**Systems** Monitor and correct performance

**Basic Skills** Reading, writing, arithmetic, listening, speaking

**Thinking Skills** Think creatively, make decisions, solve problems, see things in the mind's eye

**Personal Qualities** Responsibility, sociability, self-management

*EFF:* **Communication** Read with understanding, convey ideas in writing, speak so others can understand, listen actively, observe critically

**Interpersonal** Cooperate with others, guide others

**Lifelong Learning** Take responsibility for learning, reflect and evaluate

## Warm-up and Review          5–10 mins. ■■■

Review appositives with students. Have students write a few examples in groups and then share them with the class.

## Introduction          5–10 mins. ■■■

Ask students as a class to try to recall all the goals of this unit without looking back in their books. The goals for this unit include doing product research, purchasing goods and services by phone and online, interpreting product guarantees and warranties,

returning a product, and selling a product. Write all the goals on the board from Unit 6. Show students the first page of the unit and mention the five goals.

State the goal: *Today, we will be reviewing everything we learned in this unit and preparing for the team project.*

## Presentation          10–15 mins. ■■■

This presentation will cover the three pages of the review. Quickly go to the first page of each lesson. Discuss the goal of each. Ask simple questions to remind students of what they have learned.

**Note:** Since there is little presentation in the review, you can assign the review exercises that don't require collaboration with a partner or group for homework and go over them in class the following day.

## Practice          20–25 mins. ■■■

**Note:** There are two ways to do the review:

1. Go through the exercises one at a time and, as students complete each one, go over the answers.
2. Quickly go through the instructions of each exercise, let students complete all of the exercises at once, and then go over the answers.

A. **Imagine that you are going to buy a used car. Write four questions you would ask car sellers. (Lesson 1)**

B. **Ask your classmates the questions you wrote in Exercise A. Write some of their responses below. When your classmates ask you their questions, you can talk about your own car or a car you are familiar with. (Lesson 1)**

C. **Imagine that you are going to buy a product online. Write a short paragraph about the steps you will need to take to buy the product. (Lesson 2)**

D. **Write a conversation between a salesperson and a customer for one of the items on page 153. (Lesson 2)**

## Evaluation          5–15 mins. ■■■

Go around the classroom and check on students' progress. Help individuals when needed. If you see consistent errors among several students, interrupt the class and give a mini-lesson or review to help students feel comfortable with the concept.

## Practice *(continued)*

**E.** Read the following warranty and circle *T* (true) or *F* (false). (Lesson 3)

**F.** Working in pairs, use the return policy and the situations below to practice asking questions about returning items. One student is a customer and one is a clerk. Switch roles. (Lesson 4)

**G.** Write appositives to complete each statement below. (Lesson 5)

**H.** Using one of the statements in Exercise G, write an ad for the product on a separate piece of paper. Include an appositive in the ad. (Lesson 5)

## Evaluation *(continued)*

5–10 mins. ■■■

Go around the classroom and check on students' progress. Help individuals when needed. If you see consistent errors among several students, interrupt the class and give a mini-lesson or review to help students feel comfortable with the concept.

### BEST PRACTICE

## Recycling/Review

The review exercises, the research activity, and the team project are part of the recycling/review process. Students often need to be reintroduced to concepts to solidify what they have learned. Many concepts are learned and forgotten when students are engaged in learning other new concepts. This is because students learn but are not necessarily ready to acquire language concepts.

Therefore, it becomes very important to review material with students and to show them how to review it on their own. It is also important to recycle the new concepts in different contexts.

### INSTRUCTOR'S NOTES

**Learner Log**

| I can interpret product guarantees and warranties. | I can return a product. | I can sell a product. |
|---|---|---|
| ☐ Yes  ☐ No  ☐ Maybe | ☐ Yes  ☐ No  ☐ Maybe | ☐ Yes  ☐ No  ☐ Maybe |

**E.** **Read the following warranty and circle *T* (true) or *F* (false).**

> CLARICO warrants this product against defects in material and workmanship under normal use and service for one year from the original purchase date. CLARICO will repair or replace the defective product covered by this warranty. Please retain the dated sales receipt as evidence of the date of purchase. You will need it for any warranty service. In order to keep this warranty in effect, the product must have been handled and used as described in the instructions accompanying this warranty. This warranty does not cover any damage due to accident, misuse, abuse, or negligence.

1. This warranty is good for two years.                                  T     (F)
2. CLARICO will replace your product if it gets stolen.              T     (F)
3. You need your receipt to get service under this warranty.     (T)     F
4. This warranty covers product defects.                               (T)     F

**F.** **Working in pairs, use the return policy and the situations below to practice asking questions about returning items. One student is a customer and one is a clerk. Switch roles.** *Questions and answers will vary.*

> Valid photo ID required for all returns (except for credit card purchases), exchanges, and to receive and redeem store credit. With a receipt, a full refund in the original form of payment, except payments made with checks, will be issued for new and unread books and unopened music within four days. For merchandise purchased with a check, a store credit will be issued within the first seven days. Without an original receipt, a store credit issued by mail will be offered at the lowest selling price. With a receipt, returns of new and unread books and unopened music from our website can be made for store credit. Textbooks after 14 days or without a receipt are not returnable. Used books are not returnable.

1. return books with the original receipt
2. return textbooks after three weeks
3. return two calendars without a receipt
4. exchange CDs that have not been opened

**G.** **Write appositives to complete each statement below.** *Answers will vary. Sample answers given.*

1. This pre-owned car, _____*a four-door sedan*_____, has been thoroughly inspected and is in tip-top shape.

2. This laptop computer, _____*the lightest on the market*_____, still has a two-year warranty.

3. Two theater tickets, _____*the most expensive in town*_____, can be used any weeknight in the month of August.

4. The bicycle, _____*a red, ten-speed*_____, has barely been ridden.

**H.** **Using one of the statements in Exercise G, write an ad for the product on a separate piece of paper. Include an appositive in the ad.** *Answers will vary.*

WORKPLACE CONNECTION

Exercises E, G: Complete tasks as assigned.

Exercise F: Interact appropriately with team members.

Exercise H: Combine ideas and information.

# Vocabulary Review

**A.  Use the following words in a sentence.** Answers will vary. Sample answers given.

1. allege: _The salesperson alleged that this computer was the best for $ 1,000._

2. guarantee: _The guarantee stated that all parts were covered._

3. quality: _The quality of the product should be guaranteed._

4. convince: _Salespeople convince customers to buy new things._

5. malfunction: _If the computer malfunctions, we will replace it._

6. policy: _Our policy is to refund gifts with store credit._

**B.  Share your sentences with a partner. Write your partner's best sentence below.**

_Answers will vary._

**C.  Match each word to its synonym.**

| Word | Synonym |
|---|---|
| 1. return  _h_ | a.  claim |
| 2. refund  _e_ | b.  promise |
| 3. model  _g_ | c.  match |
| 4. guarantee  _b_ | d.  replace |
| 5. exchange  _d_ | e.  reimburse |
| 6. convince  _f_ | f.  persuade |
| 7. conform  _c_ | g.  type |
| 8. allege  _a_ | h.  take back |

WORKPLACE CONNECTION
Exercises A, C: Complete tasks as assigned.
Exercise B: Interact appropriately with team members.

## Practice *(continued)*

25–30 mins. ■■■

### Vocabulary Review

A. Use the following words in a sentence.

B. Share your sentences with a partner. Write your partner's best sentence below.

C. Match each word to its synonym.

### Evaluation *(continued)* ■■■

Go around the classroom and check on students' progress. Help individuals when needed. If you see consistent errors among several students, interrupt the class and give a mini-lesson or review to help students feel comfortable with the concept.

### Assessment *(optional)* ■■■

Use the Stand Out Assessment CD-ROM with ExamView® to create a post-test for Unit 6.

## STANDARDS CORRELATIONS

*CCRS:* W4, W5, W6, W7, W8, SL1, SL2, SL4, SL5, SL6

*CASAS:* 4.8.1, 4.8.5, 4.8.6

*SCANS:* **Resources** Allocate time

**Information** Acquire and evaluate information, organize and maintain information, interpret and communicate information, use computers to process information

**Systems** Understand systems, improve and design systems

**Technology** Select technology, apply technology to exercise

**Basic Skills** Writing

**Thinking Skills** Think creatively, make decisions, solve problems, see things in the mind's eye, use reasoning

**Personal Qualities** Responsibility, self-esteem, self-management, integrity

*EFF:* **Communication** Read with understanding, convey ideas in writing, speak so others can understand, listen actively, observe critically

**Decision Making** Solve problems and make decisions, plan

**Interpersonal** Cooperate with others, advocate and influence, resolve conflict and negotiate, guide others

**Lifelong Learning** Take responsibility for learning, reflect and evaluate, learn through research, use information and communications technology *(optional)*

## TEAM PROJECT

### Create an online or catalog-only store

Each team will create a store where they will sell things over the Internet or by a catalog. For each store, students must create a catalog page or a web page. Then, they must write a return policy and warranty of the items they carry in their store.

The team project is the final application for the unit. It gives students a chance to show that they have mastered all of the Unit 6 goals.

(Shorter classes can extend this project over two class meetings.)

### Stage 1 — 5 mins.

**COLLABORATE** **Form a team with four or five students. Choose positions for each member of your team.**

Have students decide who will lead each step as described on the student page. Provide well-defined directions on the board for how teams should proceed. Explain that all the students do every step

as a team. Teams shouldn't go to the next stage until the previous one is complete.

### Stage 2 — 5 mins.

**Decide the name of your store and what you will sell. Select a variety of items to sell.**

Ask the spokesperson of each team to report this information to the class.

### Stage 3 — 20–30 mins.

**Create the following items for your store: catalog or web page, the store's return policy, and a warranty/guarantee policy.**

### Stage 4 — 15–20 mins.

**Prepare a poster that contains all of the information in Steps 2 and 3.**

**Optional Computer Activity:** Students may want to use the computer to design their catalog page or web pages.

### Stage 5 — 15–20 mins.

**Present your store's catalog pages or web page to the class.**

Help teams prepare for their presentations. Suggest that each member choose a different part of the project to present to the class.

# TEAM PROJECT  ✓ Create an online or catalog-only store

1. **COLLABORATE** Form a team with four or five students. Choose positions for each member of your team.

| Position | Job description | Student name |
|---|---|---|
| Student 1: Project Leader | Check that everyone speaks English. Check that everyone participates. | |
| Student 2: Secretary | Take notes on your team's ideas. | |
| Student 3: Designer | Design layout of catalog or web page. | |
| Student 4: Director | Assign each team member one part of presentation. Organize presentation so that individual parts create a unified whole. | |
| Student 5: Assistant | Help secretary and designer with their work. | |

2. Decide the name of your store and what you will sell. Select a variety of items to sell.

3. Create the following items for your store: catalog or web page, the store's return policy, and a warranty/guarantee policy.

4. Prepare a poster that contains all of the information in Steps 2 and 3.

5. Present your store's catalog pages or web page to the class.

# READING CHALLENGE

## About the Explorer

Bryan Christy is an investigative reporter. He is the director of special investigations for the *National Geographic* magazine and was named National Geographic Explorer of the Year in 2014 for his work on international wildlife trafficking. Bryan has worked for years covering the illegal ivory trade. According to Christy, "The illegal ivory trade is clearly organized crime. The surprising thing is that it's taken them so long to call it that."

## About the Photo

This photo shows Bryan speaking for National Geographic. Originally a lawyer, Bryan is a frequent public speaker and has appeared on a number of news channels in order to raise awareness of international crime. His work exposing the ivory trade has shown people around the world that organized crime is wiping out elephant populations in Africa. Over 30,000 African elephants are killed every year just for their ivory.

- Introduce the explorer, Bryan Christy.
- Have students look at the pictures.
- Read the title out loud and ask students what they know about the ivory trade.
- Have a volunteer read the quote to the class.
- Ask students how they think Bryan Christy is involved with the ivory trade.
- Discuss as a class.

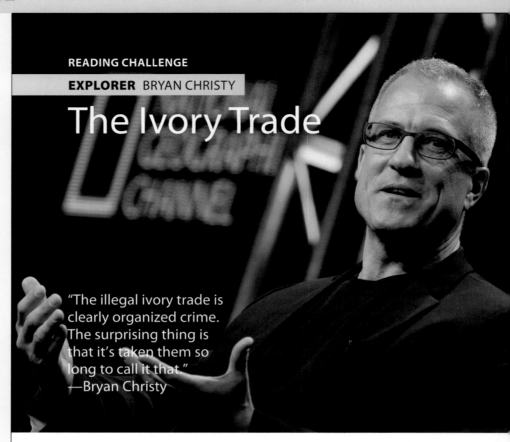

### READING CHALLENGE

### EXPLORER  BRYAN CHRISTY

# The Ivory Trade

"The illegal ivory trade is clearly organized crime. The surprising thing is that it's taken them so long to call it that."
—Bryan Christy

**A.  PREDICT  Look at the small picture and answer the questions.** Answers will vary.

1. What do you see? Do you think this is a good thing or a bad thing? Why?

2. How much do you think an elephant tusk is worth?

3. Does an elephant regrow its tusk if it is removed?

170   Unit 6

### CCRS FOR READING

RI1, RI2, RI3, RI4, RI8, W1, W4, W5, W9

**B.** Read about Bryan Christy and the ivory trade.

Did you know that in China, a pair of ivory chopsticks could cost more than one thousand dollars? And that a carved elephant tusk could sell for hundreds of thousands of dollars? Bryan Christy does. He is an investigative reporter who has worked for years covering the illegal ivory trade. He is also the director of special investigations for *National Geographic* magazine and was named National Geographic Explorer of the Year in 2014 for his work on international wildlife trafficking. According to Christy, "The illegal ivory trade is clearly organized crime. The surprising thing is that it's taken them so long to call it that."

The middle class in China is growing by leaps and bounds, and products made of ivory are popular. On the contrary, poverty is devastating Africa, where most of the ivory comes from. If people in Africa can sell this product, what is the problem? The problem is that in order to get the ivory from an elephant, you must kill it and remove its tusks.

Over 30,000 African elephants are killed every year. In fact, more than 100,000 were slaughtered between 2010 and 2012. How is this happening? Poor villagers and unpaid park rangers are killing these elephants for cash. Even though it's against the law, the money is worth more than the possible punishment. But it has gotten even worse. Now military and terrorist groups, who are partially funded by trading ivory, are traveling from their home countries, hiding out inside national parks, and poaching elephants, too. They're stealing from local communities, enslaving local villagers, and killing park rangers to get to the elephants. They want the ivory to sell so that they can purchase ammunition.

The only way to stop this unlawful killing of elephants is to ban the trading of ivory. In September of 2015, the presidents of the United States and China agreed to work together on banning the import and export of ivory. But the success of these bans may be limited in China because ivory is still an important commodity there.

**C.** Fact or Opinion? Write *F* in front of each fact and *O* in front of each opinion.

1. __F__ Over 30,000 African elephants are killed every year.

2. __O__ Poverty is devastating Africa.

3. __F__ Bryan Christy was named National Geographic Explorer of the Year in 2014.

4. __F__ A pair of chopsticks made out of ivory costs more than one thousand dollars.

5. __O__ The only way to stop this unlawful killing of elephants is to ban the trading of ivory.

**D.** **DEFEND** What is your opinion on the ivory trade? Write a paragraph explaining your point of view.

- Have students look at the smaller picture again.
- Ask students to read and answer the questions.
- Have volunteers share their answers with the class.

**B.  Read about Bryan Christy and the ivory trade.**

Ask students to read about Bryan Christy and the ivory trade.

**C.  Fact or Opinion? Write *F* in front of each fact and *O* in front of each opinion.**

- Ask students about the difference between a fact and an opinion.
- Have students read each statement below.
- Ask students to determine if each one is a fact or an opinion.
- Tell students to write *F* in front of each fact and *O* in front of each opinion.

**D.  DEFEND  What is your opinion on the ivory trade? Write a paragraph explaining your point of view.**

Ask students what their opinion is on the ivory trade. Then, have students write a paragraph explaining their point of view.

READING STRATEGIES

## Identifying Facts and Opinions

An important reading skill is knowing when a writer is being objective with the facts and when he or she is trying to express an opinion. A reading often contains information that can be either fact-based or opinion-based. To distinguish between the two, it is necessary to analyze the way a sentence is written. In general, sentences based on opinion will contain words such as *believe*, *think*, *feel*, *possible* or *possibly*, *perhaps* or *maybe*; whereas, factual sentences will not.

# The Office

## About the Photo

This photo shows the New York office for the Barbarian Group. Designed by Clive Wilkinson architects in Los Angeles, the office features the "superdesk." The desk is 4,400 square feet and stretches around the entire office. At some points, the desk creates archways where employees can gather to work collaboratively. Modern offices around the world are changing. Some offices even feature game rooms! In the Toronto office for Google in Canada, there is a mini golf course on the roof of the building.

- Introduce the unit by reading the title out loud.
- Ask students to look at the photo and have a volunteer read the caption to the class.
- Ask students how this office is the same as and different from traditional offices.
- Go over each unit outcome.
- Have students read and answer the questions. Then, discuss as a class.

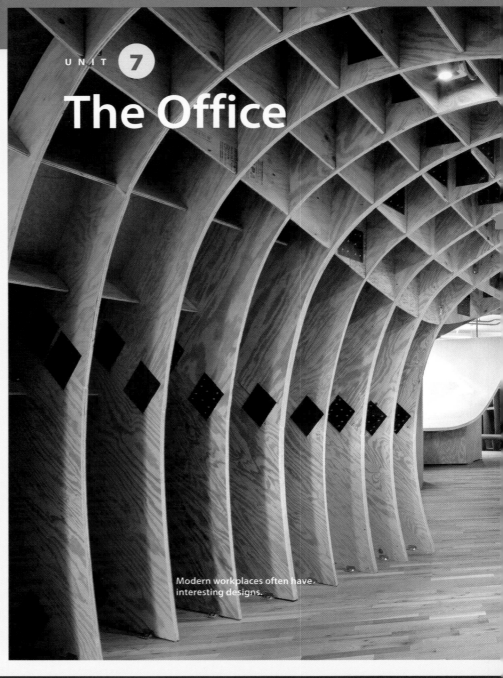

UNIT 7

The Office

Modern workplaces often have interesting designs.

| UNIT OUTCOMES | GRAMMAR | VOCABULARY | EL CIVICS |
|---|---|---|---|
| • Identify and use technology<br>• Resolve technology problems<br>• Establish an organizational system<br>• Identify and resolve problems at work<br>• Report progress | • Comparing parts of speech: verbs, nouns, adjectives<br>• Noun clauses<br>• Noun clauses as objects<br>• Imperatives | • Technology: *outlet, business telephone, computer, external hard drive, MP3 player, fax (machine), flash drive, label maker, LCD projector, paper shredder, photocopier, printer, scanner, fan, toner, power supply (cord), display, firewire (port/cable), handset, cable, (USB) port, memory card, troubleshoot, paper jam, feed*<br>• Organizational resources<br>• Business strategies | The skills students learn in this unit can be applied to all EL Civics competency areas with a particular focus on the following:<br>• Communication<br>• Employment |

## Life Skills Link

In this unit, students will learn about using and maintaining tools and technology commonly at use in office settings. They will get practice with typical alpha-numeric filing systems. Students will also learn about job performance reports as well as different conflict resolution strategies.

## Workplace Link

All lessons and units in *Stand Out* include basic communication skills and interpersonal skills important for the workplace. They are not individually identified. Other workplace skills are indicated. They include *collecting and organizing information, making decisions and solving problems,* and *combining ideas and information.*

**UNIT OUTCOMES**

- Identify and use technology
- Resolve technology problems
- Establish an organizational system
- Identify and resolve problems at work
- Report progress

**Look at the photo and answer the questions.**

1. What technology might you find in an office like this?
2. What do you think the people at the table are discussing?

| CASAS | SCANS | CCRS |
|---|---|---|
| Vocabulary Builder: 4.5.1, 7.4.5 | Many SCANS skills are incorporated in this unit with an emphasis on: | RI1, RI2, RI3, RI4, RI7, RI10, W2, W4, W5, W8, W9, SL1, SL2, L1 |
| Lesson 1: 4.4.8, 4.5.1, 4.5.4, 4.5.6 | • Social interaction | |
| Lesson 2: 4.5.7 | • Problem-solving | |
| Lesson 3: 4.5.3, 4.7.2 | • Visualization | |
| Lesson 4: 4.8.1, 4.8.5, 4.8.6 | • Creative thinking | |
| Lesson 5: 4.6.4 | • Negotiation | |
| Review: 7.2.1 | • Teamwork | |
| Research Project: 4.9.3, 7.2.1, 7.4.4, 7.4.5, 7.4.6 | • Leadership | |
| Team Project: 4.8.1, 4.8.5, 4.8.6 | • Reading | |

# Vocabulary Builder

**A. EXPLAIN** Use the terms in the box below to label each item you might find in an office. Under each item, write a brief description of its purpose. Answers will vary. Sample answers given.

| | | | |
|---|---|---|---|
| business telephone | external hard drive | LCD projector | photocopier |
| ~~laptop computer~~ | USB stick | paper shredder | printer |

laptop computer: process information, create reports, and do Internet research

external hard drive: provides more memory, exchanges information

business telephone: allows hold, transfers calls, conference calls

photocopier: makes copies, collates papers

paper shredder: destroys sensitive personal documents

flash drive: provides extra storage/ memory for computer

printer: prints documents and photos

LCD projector: projects images and slide shows from computer

**Goal:** Introduce new vocabulary

**Academic Strategies:** Identifying and defining vocabulary, finding word families, using a dictionary

**Vocabulary:** See lesson

## Agenda

☐ Label and describe technology.

☐ Illustrate and define vocabulary.

☐ Find nouns and adjectives in word families.

## Resources

**Dictionaries:** It is recommended that each student in class have an ESL learner's dictionary or that there be dictionaries available in the classroom for students to use. Dictionaries that will be referred to in this book are *Heinle's Newbury House Dictionary of American English* and the *Collins Cobuild Intermediate* or *Advanced Dictionary of American English.*

## Pacing

■ 1.5 hour classes    ■ 2.5 hour classes
■ 3+ hour classes

## STANDARDS CORRELATIONS

*CCRS:* RI4, RI7, L4

*CASAS:* 4.5.1, 7.4.5

*SCANS:* **Information** Acquire and evaluate information, organize and maintain information

**Interpersonal** Participate as a member of a team, negotiate to arrive at a decision, work with cultural diversity

**Systems** Understand systems, monitor and correct performance

**Basic Skills** Reading, writing, listening, speaking

**Thinking Skills** Think creatively, make decisions, see things in the mind's eye

**Personal Qualities** Responsibility, sociability, self-management

**EFF: Communication** Read with understanding, convey ideas in writing, speak so others can understand, listen actively

**Decision Making** Use math to solve problems and communicate, solve problems and make decisions, plan

**Interpersonal** Cooperate with others

**Lifelong Learning** Take responsibility for learning, reflect and evaluate, learn through research

## Academic Feature: Vocabulary Builder

Each unit will begin with a vocabulary-building section. The purpose of this two-page section is to introduce students to many of the words they will be using in the unit lessons. Students will have a chance to see how much they already know, and they will get exposure to the new vocabulary found in the unit.

**Note:** All of the exercises on these two pages should be done in class, no matter the class length. Longer classes can do this lesson and then move onto Lesson 1 during the same class meeting; shorter classes may have to devote one whole class meeting to this lesson.

### Introduction                    5–10 mins. ■■■

Ask students what types of technology they have in their homes. Get them started by writing *telephone* on the board.

State the goal: *Today, we will be identifying and working with the vocabulary you will learn in this unit.*

### Presentation 1                  5–10 mins. ■■■

Get students started on Exercise A by reviewing the directions and then describing the purpose of one or two items together. Have them complete Exercise A for Practice 1.

### Practice 1                     10–15 mins. ■■■

**A. EXPLAIN Use the terms in the box below to label each item you might find in an office. Under each item, write a brief description of its purpose.**

### Evaluation 1                    5 mins. ■■■

Go over the answers as a class. Ask students if they see any of these items in the classroom. If so, have them point them out. Also, ask if they have any of these items at home or at work.

## INSTRUCTOR'S NOTES

_____

_____

_____

_____

## Presentation 2

Go over the instructions to Exercises B, C, and D.

### PRONUNCIATION

#### Vocabulary

When teaching students new vocabulary, pronounce each word for them several times and ask them to repeat it. Many times, students may be familiar with the words you are saying but have never seen them spelled out. By pronouncing the words for students, you allow students to make a connection between the words' spellings and their sounds. It is also important that students learn the correct pronunciation of new words so they feel comfortable using their new vocabulary inside and outside of the classroom. Remember to point out which letters are silent when pronounced aloud.

### Practice 2

10–15 mins. ■■

**B. A great way to remember vocabulary is to draw pictures. Draw pictures for the following terms. Use a dictionary to look up any words you don't know, but remember to look for the definition that is related to technology.**

**C. The three following technology terms cannot be drawn easily. Write a definition for each one.**

**D. Look at the verbs in the table below. Find the nouns and adjectives in the verbs' word families.**

### Evaluation 2

10–15 mins. ■■

Go over the answers as a class.

## INSTRUCTOR'S NOTES

WORKPLACE CONNECTION
Exercise B: Combine ideas and information.
Exercises C, D: Complete tasks as assigned.

**B.** **A great way to remember vocabulary is to draw pictures. Draw pictures for the following terms. Use a dictionary to look up any words you don't know, but remember to look for the definition that is related to technology.** Drawings will vary.

| | | | |
|---|---|---|---|
| | | | |
| **headset** | **cable** | **port** | **memory card** |

**C.** **The three following technology terms cannot be drawn easily. Write a definition for each one.** Answers will vary. Sample answers given.

1. troubleshoot: _to search for the solution of a technical problem_

2. paper jam: _paper caught in the workings of a machine_

3. feed: _to put paper into the proper machine area_

**D.** **Look at the verbs in the table below. Find the nouns and adjectives in the verbs' word families.**

| Verb | Noun | Adjective |
|---|---|---|
| compete | competition | competitive |
| collaborate | collaboration | collaborative |
| avoid | avoidance | avoidant |
| accommodate | accommodation | accommodating |
| compromise | compromise | compromising |
| motivate | motivation | motivational |
| resolve | resolution | resolute |

GOAL ■ Identify and use technology

WORKPLACE CONNECTION
Exercise A: Complete tasks as assigned.
Exercise B: Interpret and communicate information.

**A. Read the instructions for connecting a printer to a computer.**

1. Take the **printer** out of the box and set it next to your **computer**.

2. Make sure the printer is **off**.

3. Plug the **power supply cord** into the back of the printer and then plug it into the wall socket.

4. Plug one end of the **USB cable** into the **USB port** on the back of the printer. Plug the other end into the **USB port** on the computer.

**B. SUMMARIZE** Reread the instructions in Exercise A. Then, in your own words, tell a partner how to connect a printer to a computer. (If you have a computer and printer in your classroom, you can explain the steps as you do them.)

## AT-A-GLANCE PREP

**Goal:** Identify and use technology
**Academic Strategy:** Paraphrasing
**Vocabulary:** *power supply, USB, port, firewire, cable, document, feeder*

## Agenda

- Connect a printer.
- Connect a projector.
- Use a fax machine.
- Write instructions.

## Resources

**Multilevel Worksheet:** Unit 7, Lesson 1, Worksheet 1
**Workbook:** Unit 7, Lesson 1
**Suggested Realia:** Computer, hard drive, printer, scanner, technology manuals
**Stand Out Assessment CD-ROM with ExamView®**

## Pacing

- 1.5 hour classes
- 2.5 hour classes
- 3+ hour classes

## STANDARDS CORRELATIONS

*CCRS:* RI1, RI2, RI7, W2, W4, SL1
*CASAS:* 4.4.8, 4.5.1, 4.5.4, 4.5.6
*SCANS:* **Information** Acquire and evaluate information, organize and maintain information, interpret and communicate information
**Interpersonal** Participate as a member of a team, teach others, exercise leadership, work with cultural diversity
**Systems** Understand systems, monitor and correct performance, improve and design systems
**Technology** Select technology, apply technology to a task
**Basic Skills** Reading, writing, listening, speaking
**Thinking Skills** Think creatively, make decisions
**Personal Qualities** Responsibility, sociability, self-management
*EFF:* **Communication** Read with understanding, convey ideas in writing, speak so others can understand, listen actively
**Interpersonal** Cooperate with others, guide others
**Lifelong Learning** Take responsibility for learning, reflect and evaluate, use information and communications technology

## Preassessment (*optional*)

Use the Stand Out Assessment CD-ROM with ExamView® to create a pre-test for Unit 7.

## Warm-up and Review          5–10 mins.

Ask students to write a list of the vocabulary they learned in the vocabulary-building lessons without looking back in their books. Have them share their list with a partner and try to add more words to their list. For extra practice, have them discuss what each word means.

## Introduction          5–10 mins.

Dictation:

1. Make sure it is plugged in and turned on.
2. Put less than 50 sheets of paper in the paper tray.
3. Select the document you want to print.
4. Click on the word *Print* in the print dialog box.

Ask students this question once the dictation is complete: *Two pieces of technological equipment are being discussed in these instructions. What are they?*

State the goal: *Today, we will interpret and follow instructions for connecting and using technology.*

## Presentation 1          10–15 mins.

Ask students what kinds of technology they have in their homes. *Raise your hand if you have a computer. Raise your hand if you have a printer.* Ask the same questions about technology they use at work. Have a discussion about who uses the technology in both of these places. Ask them who set up the technology.

### A. Read the instructions for connecting a printer to a computer.

Go over the instructions as a class.

## Practice 1          10–15 mins.

**B. SUMMARIZE Reread the instructions in Exercise A. Then, in your own words, tell a partner how to connect a printer to a computer. (If you have a computer and printer in your classroom, you can explain the steps as you do them.)**

If you think students need more practice, have them work with several different partners, doing the exercise as many times as necessary.

**Note:** See page 177a for a Best Practice on paraphrasing.

## Evaluation 1          5–10 mins.

Ask a few volunteers to explain the directions to the class without looking at their books.

BEST PRACTICE

## Paraphrasing

Paraphrasing is a great skill for students to develop. Not only will it help them show that they truly understand something they have learned, but it will give them confidence to be able to explain something to someone else. You can draw on this skill for almost any exercise in the book: a reading text, a grammar chart, a conversation, and so on.

### Presentation 2                     5 mins. ■■■
Go over the instructions for Exercise C.

### Practice 2                  10–15 mins. ■■
(Shorter classes can do this exercise for homework.)

**C. Connecting a projector to a computer is similar to connecting a printer. Match the instructions below to the correct picture. Then, label each picture.**

**Extra Practice:** Now that students have completed two exercises related to connecting pieces of hardware, have them close their books and take out a sheet of paper. Have them write and illustrate the instructions for connecting something to a computer, either a printer or a projector.

**Even Better Practice:** Set up a computer somewhere in the classroom where students can practice connecting something to it—a printer, a projector, a scanner, etc. Have students work in pairs to practice connecting the external component to the computer.

### Evaluation 2               10–15 mins. ■■
Go over the answers as a class.

### MULTILEVEL WORKSHEET

Unit 7, Lesson 1, Worksheet 1: Technology Instructions

**Refer students to *Stand Out 5 Workbook*, Unit 7, Lesson 1 for practice with nouns: phrases, pronouns, and clauses.**

**Go to the *Activity Bank* online for suggestions on promoting digital literacy and using the Internet to enhance this lesson.**

BEST PRACTICE

## Hands-on instruction

It is very beneficial to students' learning for them to apply what they have learned about to the real world. This lesson gives you a perfect opportunity to teach students how to do something and then let them put the instructions into practice. Even if your classroom doesn't have the technology, you can perhaps borrow something from your school's resource center or even bring something in from home—in this case, a laptop and a small printer or projector is all you need.

### INSTRUCTOR'S NOTES

_____

_____

_____

_____

_____

_____

_____

_____

_____

_____

_____

_____

_____

_____

_____

_____

_____

_____

**C.** **Connecting a projector to a computer is similar to connecting a printer. Match the instructions below to the correct picture. Then, label each picture.**

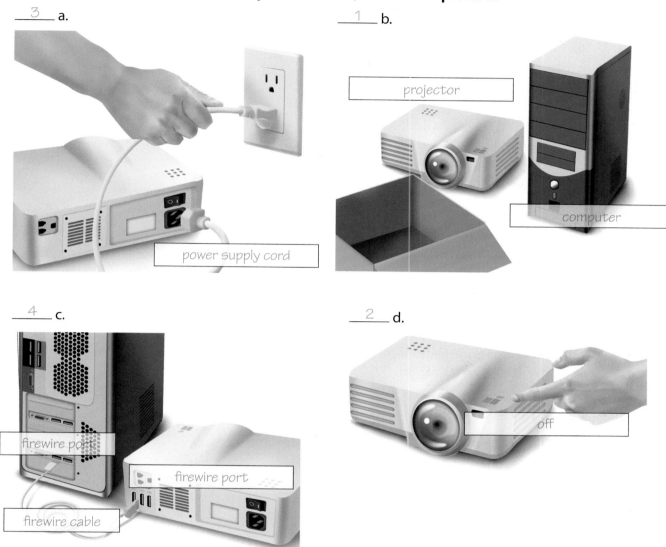

__3__ a.

power supply cord

__1__ b.

projector

computer

__4__ c.

firewire port

firewire port

firewire cable

__2__ d.

off

1. Take the **projector** out of the box and set it next to your **computer**.

2. Make sure the projector is **off**.

3. Plug the **power supply cord** into the back of the projector and then plug it into the wall socket.

4. Plug one end of the **firewire cable** into the **firewire port** on the back of the projector. Plug the other end into the **firewire port** on the computer.

WORKPLACE CONNECTION
Exercise D: Complete tasks as assigned.
Exercise E: Combine ideas and information.

**D.   Read the excerpt from a fax machine manual and answer the questions that follow.**

## How to send a fax

**1** Place the document (up to 15 pages) to be sent in the document feeder.

**2** Enter the fax number in one of the following ways:
- Use the dial pad.
- Select the number from the address book (see *Address Book* on page 15).
- Use the speed dial function (see *Speed Dialing* on page 16).

**3** Press **Start.**

📝 Note ————————————————
To cancel, press **Stop/Exit.**

## How to receive a fax

There are three modes for receiving faxes:
- Fax mode: The machine will automatically answer each call as a fax (See *Fax Mode* on page 21).
- Auto answer mode: The telephone rings for a certain number of rings and then switches to fax (See *Auto Answer Mode* on page 22).
- Manual mode: The telephone will ring. Press **Start** to receive the fax (See *Manual Mode* on page 23).

1. When sending a fax, how many different ways are there to enter a fax number? _____3_____

2. Which method of sending a fax doesn't require pushing the start button? ___They all require it.___

3. How many pages can you fax at once? _____up to 15_____

4. How many modes are there to receive a fax? _____3_____

5. Which mode for receiving a fax requires that you press the start button? _____manual mode_____

**E.   GENERATE  Look back at the list of technology items on pages 174 and 175. Choose one item that you are familiar with and write a list of instructions with illustrations. Review your instructions with a partner.** Answers will vary.

## Presentation 3
5–10 mins. ■■■

Look at the fax machine together and go over all the parts.

## Practice 3
15–20 mins. ■

(Shorter classes can do this exercise for homework.)

**D. Read the excerpt from a fax machine manual and answer the questions that follow.**

## Evaluation 3
5–10 mins. ■

Go over the answers as a class.

## Application
10–20 mins. ■■■

**E. GENERATE Look back at the list of technology items on pages 174 and 175. Choose one item that you are familiar with and write a list of instructions with illustrations. Review your instructions with a partner.**

Have students share their completed instructions with the class.

## BEST PRACTICE

### Instructions - Using imperatives

Instructions are a part of everyday life. Either we are giving and listening to them or reading and writing them. Mastering instructions is an important language goal to have.

Instructions require that students be familiar with the *imperative form*. The imperative form is very easy to learn and use. Explain to students that we make the imperative by using the infinitive form of the verb without "to." Point out that to make a negative imperative we simply place "do not" or "don't" in front of the verb.

## INSTRUCTOR'S NOTES

**Goal:** Resolve technology problems

**Academic Strategies:** Solving problems and making decisions

**Vocabulary:** *paper jam, feed, fan, humidity, obstructions, force, faded, splotchy, cartridge, toner, LCD screen, resolution, display, compartment*

## Agenda

▢ Troubleshoot fax machine problems.

▢ Listen to employees.

▢ Troubleshoot problems with a digital camera.

▢ Troubleshoot problems with a label maker.

▢ Ask classmates for help.

## Resources

**Multilevel Worksheet:** Unit 7, Lesson 2, Worksheet 1

**Workbook:** Unit 7, Lesson 2

**Audio:** CD Track 33

**Suggested Realia:** Technology manuals

## Pacing

■ 1.5 hour classes ■ 2.5 hour classes
■ 3+ hour classes

### STANDARDS CORRELATIONS

*CCRS:* RI1, SL1, SL2

*CASAS:* 4.5.7

*SCANS:* **Information** Acquire and evaluate information, interpret and communicate information

**Interpersonal** Participate as a member of a team, teach others, exercise leadership, negotiate to arrive at a decision, work with cultural diversity

**Systems** Understand systems, monitor and correct performance

**Technology** Maintain and troubleshoot technology

**Basic Skills** Reading, writing, listening, speaking

**Thinking Skills** Think creatively, make decisions, solve problems, see things in the mind's eye

**Personal Qualities** Responsibility, sociability, self-management

*EFF:* **Communication** Read with understanding, convey ideas in writing, speak so others can understand, listen actively, observe critically

**Decision Making** Solve problems and make decisions

**Interpersonal** Cooperate with others, advocate and influence, resolve conflict and negotiate, guide others

**Lifelong Learning** Take responsibility for learning, reflect and evaluate, learn through research

## Warm-up and Review  5–10 mins.

Ask volunteers to stand up and give the class instructions on using technology.

## Introduction  5–10 mins.

Dictation:

1. When loading the paper, do not force the paper down into the printer.
2. If you are using batteries, check that they are inserted correctly.
3. Make sure the tape compartment cover has been closed.
4. If the paper tears while you are removing it, make sure that no small pieces are left inside the machine.

State the goal: *Today, we will learn how to resolve technology problems.*

## Presentation 1  10–15 mins.

A. **Think of some problems you have had in the past with technology. In a small group, discuss what the problems were and how you fixed them.**

B. **Carla is having trouble with her printer. No paper comes out when she tries to receive a fax. Read what she found in her manual about *troubleshooting*.**

Go over the manual excerpt as a class.

## Practice 1  10–15 mins.

C. **Answer the questions based on the troubleshooting guide in Exercise B.**

Have students do this exercise by themselves.

D. **SUGGEST** **Read Carla's problem in Exercise B again. What are three suggestions you might give her?**

## Evaluation 1  5 mins.

Go over the answers as a class.

# LESSON ② How do you fix it?

GOAL ▪ Resolve technology problems

WORKPLACE CONNECTION
Exercise A: Interact appropriately with team members.
Exercise C: Complete tasks as assigned.
Exercise D: Interpret and communicate information.

**A.** **Think of some problems you have had in the past with technology. In a small group, discuss what the problems were and how you fixed them.**

*Answers will vary. Sample problems: jammed paper, no ink, computer slow, lost documents*

**B.** **Carla is having trouble with her printer. No paper comes out when she tries to receive a fax. Read what she found in her manual about *troubleshooting*.**

| Problem | Solution | |
|---|---|---|
| Paper jams during printing. | Remove the jammed paper by pulling it out gently. If the paper tears while you are removing it, make sure that no small pieces are left inside the machine. | |
| Paper sticks together. | Make sure you do not have more than 40 sheets in the paper tray. Take the paper out, fan the pages, and put them back in. Note: Humidity can cause pages to stick together. | |
| Paper will not feed. | Remove any obstructions from inside the printer. | |
| Multiple sheets of paper feed at the same time. | When loading the paper, do not force the paper down into the printer. If multiple sheets have caused a paper jam, clear it. | |

**C.** **Answer the questions based on the troubleshooting guide in Exercise B.**

1. What should you do if paper tears while you are removing it from the printer?

   *Make sure there are no small pieces left in the machine.*

2. How many sheets can the paper tray hold? *no more than 40*

3. What causes pages to stick together? *humidity*

4. What should you do if the paper won't feed? *Remove obstructions*
   *from inside the printer.*

5. What should you do if there is a paper jam? *Remove the paper by pulling gently*

**D.** **SUGGEST Read Carla's problem in Exercise B again. What are three suggestions you might give her?** *Answers will vary. Sample answers given.*

1. *Check to see if the paper is jammed.*

2. *Check if the paper is stuck together; fan the pages.*

3. *Look to see if multiple pages fed at one time; remove.*

WORKPLACE CONNECTION
Exercise E: Interpret and communicate information.
Exercise F: Complete tasks as assigned.

**E.** Listen to the conversations between employees at a small printing company. Write the problems and suggestions for fixing them in the table below.

CD TR 33

| Problem | Suggestions |
|---|---|
| Pages are faded and splotchy from printer. | 1. Take out toner and shake.<br>2. Replace the cartridge. |
| Computer won't turn on. | 1. Check that power cord is plugged in. |
| Photocopier isn't working. | 1. Plug in.<br>2. Make sure there is paper in tray.<br>3. Check the toner. |

**F.** Maya has to take pictures for her job as a home appraiser. She is having some problems with her digital camera. Match each problem to its possible solution.

1. Camera will not operate. __b__

2. Camera won't take any more pictures or video. __d__

3. Only a few pictures will fit on the memory card. __e__

4. Battery loses its charge quickly. __c__

5. Pictures won't display on the LCD screen. __a__

a. Turn LCD screen on.

b. Turn camera on.

c. Replace battery.

d. Clear memory card.

e. Take pictures at a lower resolution.

**G.** Read the troubleshooting guide for a label maker.

| Problem | Solution |
|---|---|
| 1. The display stays blank after you have turned on the machine. | Check that the AC adaptor is connected correctly. If you are using batteries, check that they are inserted correctly. If the batteries are low on power, replace them. |
| 2. The machine doesn't print or the printed characters are blurred. | Check that the tape cassette has been inserted properly. If the tape cassette is empty, replace it. Make sure the tape compartment cover has been closed. |
| 3. The text files that you stored in the memory are no longer there. | Replace the batteries. |
| 4. A blank horizontal line appears through the printed label. | Clean the printhead. |
| 5. Striped tape appears. | You have reached the end of the tape. Replace the tape cassette with a new one. |

## Presentation 2       5–10 mins. ■■■

Go over the instructions for Exercises E and F (separately).

## Practice 2       10–15 mins. ■■

**E.** **Listen to the conversations between employees at a small printing company. Write the problems and suggestions for fixing them in the table below.**

---

### LISTENING SCRIPT
CD
TR 33

**Conversation 1**
**Aaron:** *Hey, Linda, could you help me for a second?*
**Linda:** *Sure. What do you need?*
**Aaron:** *Something is wrong with my printer. The pages are coming out faded and splotchy.*
**Linda:** *Hmm. Sounds like a problem with your toner. Did you take it out and shake it?*
**Aaron:** *I tried that. It didn't help.*
**Linda:** *Well, then you probably need to replace the cartridge. When is the last time you changed it?*
**Aaron:** *I have no idea. Maybe six months ago?*
**Linda:** *Yep, that's probably the issue. Put another one in and see if that helps.*
**Aaron:** *Thanks, Linda.*

**Conversation 2**
**Preston:** *Oh, Mark, I'm so glad you were walking by.*
**Mark:** *What's up?*
**Preston:** *For some reason, my computer won't turn on.*
**Mark:** *That's strange.*
**Preston:** *I know. It was working just fine before lunch.*
**Mark:** *Did you check to make sure the power cord is plugged in?*
**Preston:** *No. Let me check. (pause) Boy, do I feel stupid. I must have knocked it out with my foot.*
**Mark:** *Happens to the best of us.*
**Preston:** *Thanks.*

**Conversation 3**
**Kim:** *Claudia, do you know anything about this photocopier?*
**Claudia:** *I know a bit. Try me.*
**Kim:** *Well, it's just not working. When I push the green button, nothing happens.*
**Claudia:** *Is it plugged in?*
**Kim:** *Yep.*
**Claudia:** *Did you check to make sure there is paper in the paper tray?*
**Kim:** *Yep, it has plenty.*
**Claudia:** *What about the toner?*
**Kim:** *I didn't check the toner. How do I do that?*
**Claudia:** *Well, you can see on the display right here how much toner is left in the cartridge. Yep, it looks like it's low. This copier won't even try to make copies if the toner is too low. If you put a new toner cartridge in, that should solve your problem.*
**Kim:** *Thanks, Claudia.*

---

**F.** **Maya has to take pictures for her job as a home appraiser. She is having some problems with her digital camera. Match each problem to its possible solution.**

## Evaluation 2       10–15 mins. ■■

Go over the answers as a class.

## Presentation 3       1 min. ■■■

Go over the instructions for Exercise G.

## Practice 3       15–20 mins. ■

(Shorter classes can do these exercises for homework.)

**G.** **Read the troubleshooting guide for the label maker.**

### INSTRUCTOR'S NOTES

_____
_____
_____
_____
_____
_____
_____
_____
_____
_____
_____
_____
_____
_____
_____
_____
_____

## Practice 3 (continued)          15–20 mins. ■

**H.** Read the troubleshooting guide for the label maker in Exercise G again. Check (✓) the best answer.

## Evaluation 3          5–10 mins. ■
Go over the answers to Exercise G as a class.

## Application          10–20 mins. ■■■

**I.  SUGGEST**  In a small group, ask for help with the technology problems below. Write suggestions in the table.

Prepare students for this activity by having them look at the conversations from Practice 2. (The listening script can be found in the back of their books.) You can also create a sample conversation on the board. Encourage students to have a complete conversation, not just one that starts right off with the problem. Offer this example below if needed.

**Student 1:** _____, *can you help me with something?*
**Student 2:** *Sure.*
**Student 1:** *I can't get my fax machine to send a fax.*
**Student 2:** *Hmm, that's strange. Is there paper in the tray?*
**Student 1:** *Yes, that's the first thing I checked.*
**Student 2:** *Maybe there's a paper jam.*
**Student 1:** *I didn't even think to open up the machine. (pause) Yep, it looks like a small piece of paper is stuck in there. That should fix the problem. Thanks, _____.*

**J.  JUDGE**  Share the suggestions you received from your classmates for the problems in Exercise I. Which suggestions are the best?

### MULTILEVEL WORKSHEET

Unit 7, Lesson 2, Worksheet 1: Troubleshoot Technology (listening)

**Refer students to *Stand Out 5 Workbook,* Unit 7, Lesson 2 for practice with noun clauses as objects of prepositions.**

**Go to the *Activity Bank* online for suggestions on promoting digital literacy and using the Internet to enhance this lesson.**

### INSTRUCTOR'S NOTES

_____
_____
_____
_____
_____
_____
_____
_____
_____
_____
_____
_____
_____
_____
_____
_____
_____
_____
_____
_____
_____
_____
_____
_____
_____
_____

WORKPLACE CONNECTION
Exercise H: Complete tasks as assigned.
Exercises I, J: Interact appropriately with team members.

**H. Read the troubleshooting guide for the label maker in Exercise G again. Check (✓) the best answers.**

1. You should clean the printhead when . . .
   - ☐ a. striped tape appears.
   - ☑ b. a horizontal line appears.
   - ☐ c. the display is blank.

2. When your files from memory are no longer there, you should . . .
   - ☐ a. connect the AC adaptor.
   - ☐ b. clean the printhead.
   - ☑ c. replace the batteries.

3. If the printed characters are blurred, you should . . .
   - ☑ a. make sure the tape compartment cover has been closed.
   - ☐ b. replace the batteries.
   - ☐ c. clean the printhead.

4. What does it mean when striped tape appears?
   - ☐ a. The printhead is dirty.
   - ☑ b. The tape cassette needs to be replaced.
   - ☐ c. The tape compartment needs to be closed.

**I. SUGGEST In a small group, ask for help with the technology problems below. Write suggestions in the table.** Answers will vary. Sample answers are given.

| Problem | Suggestions |
| --- | --- |
| My fax machine won't send a fax. | Check the phone connection.<br>Check the power switch. |
| There is no dial tone on my telephone. | Check the phone jack.<br>Press the receiver button again. |
| My printer won't print. | Check the toner.<br>Check the plug. |
| My paper shredder won't shred. | Check the electric cord. |
| The copier keeps jamming. | Fan the paper.<br>Look for small pieces stuck in copier. |

**J. JUDGE Share the suggestions you received from your classmates for the problems in Exercise I. Which suggestions are the best?** Answers will vary.

GOAL ■ Establish an organizational system

WORKPLACE CONNECTION
Exercise A: Interact appropriately with team members.
Exercise B: Complete tasks as assigned.

**A. CLASSIFY** One way of organizing things is by putting similar items in groups. How would you organize this supply closet? Discuss your solutions with your classmates.

Cleaning supplies/Bathroom supplies/Office supplies

**B.** On a separate piece of paper, reorganize the supply closet. Do a simple drawing of the closet and show where you would keep each item.

Answers will vary. Sample answers given.

| Cleaning supplies | Office supplies | Bathroom supplies |
|---|---|---|
| Paper towels | HR forms | Hand soap |
| Cleaning liquid | File folders | Toilet paper |
| Sponges | Toner | Cleaning liquid |
| Rags | Colored card stock | (also in cleaning supplies) |
| Bucket | Color print cartridges | Paper towels |
| Broom | Pens | (also in cleaning supplies) |
| Mop | Paper | |
| | Paper clips | |

**Goal:** Establish an organizational system
**Academic Strategy:** Organizing paperwork
**Vocabulary:** *organize, reorganize, purchase orders, alphabetical order, hanging files, liabilities*

## Agenda

- Group items.
- Organize files.
- Describe organizational problems and solutions.

## Resources

**Multilevel Worksheet:** Unit 7, Lesson 3, Worksheet 1
**Workbook:** Unit 7, Lesson 3
**Suggested Realia:** Hanging file folders, file folders, labels, label maker (anything used for organizing)

## Pacing

■ 1.5 hour classes   ■ 2.5 hour classes
■ 3+ hour classes

## STANDARDS CORRELATIONS

*CCRS:* RI1, W2, W4
*CASAS:* 4.5.3, 4.7.2
*SCANS:* **Resources** Allocate materials and facility resources
**Information** Acquire and evaluate information, organize and maintain information
**Interpersonal** Participate as a member of a team, teach others, exercise leadership, negotiate to arrive at a decision, work with cultural diversity
**Systems** Understand systems, monitor and correct performance, improve and design system
**Basic Skills** Reading, writing, arithmetic, listening, speaking
**Thinking Skills** Think creatively, make decisions, solve problems, see things in the mind's eye
**Personal Qualities** Responsibility, sociability, self-management
*EFF:* **Communication** Read with understanding, convey ideas in writing, speak so others can understand, listen actively, observe critically
**Decision Making** Solve problems and make decisions, plan
**Interpersonal** Cooperate with others, advocate and influence, resolve conflict and negotiate, guide others
**Lifelong Learning** Take responsibility for learning, reflect and evaluate

## Warm-up and Review     5–10 mins. ■■■

Ask students to share something new they learned in Lesson 2. Make a comprehensive list on the board as students are sharing.

## Introduction     5–10 mins. ■■■

Dictation: Read all or as many of the tips below as you want.

Tips for Staying Organized

1. Put each item away after each use so you won't waste time searching for it when you really need it.
2. Set up a box in each room and use it for your clutter. Before it overflows, clean it out so it's ready to start collecting more stuff.
3. Use clear containers to store stuff. Seeing what's inside will save you a lot of time.
4. Keep a small container in a convenient place to hold keys, glasses, and wallets.
5. Schedule weekly bill-paying and paperwork sessions.
6. Keep files well categorized, alphabetized, and up-to-date.

State the goal: *Today, we will practice establishing organizational systems.*

## Presentation 1     10–15 mins. ■■■

A. **CLASSIFY** **One way of organizing things is by putting similar items in groups. How would you organize this supply closet? Discuss your solutions with your classmates.**

## Practice 1     10–15 mins. ■■■

B. **On a separate piece of paper, reorganize the supply closet. Do a simple drawing of the closet and show where you would keep each item.**

## Evaluation 1     5–10 mins. ■■■

Go over students' ideas as a class.

## Presentation 2 5–10 mins. ■■■

**C. Each folder represents a place to file certain documents. Look at the list and match each document with its folder. Write the letters on the folders.**

Help students get started on this exercise and then let them finish by themselves.

## Practice 2 10–15 mins. ■■

(Shorter classes can do these exercises for homework.)

**D. One way of organizing things is by putting them in alphabetical order. Rewrite the list of folders in Exercise C in alphabetical order.**

**E. CLASSIFY Organize the purchase orders and returns in Exercise C in numerical order.**

## Evaluation 2 10–15 mins. ■■

Go over the answers as a class. Ask students what things they have at home that are filed or could be filed. Ask students to share some specific examples.

### BEST PRACTICE

### Classification

The skill of classification is sorting or grouping items into categories based on particular traits or features. Classification is a normal human activity. Everyone practices classification by putting items that are similar into groups. It is an important skill because it helps us to organize. It also demonstrates a clear understanding of the relationship between things.

### INSTRUCTOR'S NOTES

**C.** Each folder represents a place to file certain documents. Look at the list and match each document with its folder. Write the letters on the folders.

a. Bank of the East Statement for March

b. Canyon i867 User Guide

c. City National Bank Statement for April

d. Claire's Order #7654

e. Delpi Photo Plus Manual

f. Dresses 'n' More Order #7625

g. Fancy Pants Return #7986

h. HL Printer 5000 User Guide

i. Jimbo's Return #7893

j. Leapin' Lizards Return #5678

k. Pink Lady Order #6879

l. Sunshine Girls Order #9864

**Purchase Orders**
d/f/k/l

**Bank Statements**
*a*/c

**Returns**
g/i/j

**Manuals**
b/e/h

**D.** One way of organizing things is by putting them in alphabetical order. Rewrite the list of folders in Exercise C in alphabetical order.

1. Bank Statements

2. Manuals

3. Purchase Orders

4. Returns

**E. CLASSIFY** Organize the purchase orders and returns in Exercise C in numerical order.

| Purchase Orders | Returns |
|---|---|
| 1. #6879 (Pink Lady) | 1. #5678 (Leapin' Lizards) |
| 2. #7625 (Dresses n' More) | 2. #7893 (Jimbo's) |
| 3. #7654 (Claire's) | 3. #7986 (Fancy Pants) |
| 4. #9864 (Sunshine Girls) | |

WORKPLACE CONNECTION
Exercise G: Interact appropriately with team members.
Exercise H: Combine ideas and information.

**F.** **Lars needs to get organized in his home office. Read about his problem and solution.**

**Problem:** My financial papers are very disorganized. They are in huge piles on my desk and in my desk drawers.

**Solution:** I'm going to buy hanging files and file folders. The tabs on my hanging files will be labeled as follows: *Bank Accounts, Credit Cards, Income, Investments, Retirement Accounts, Liabilities, Insurance, Real Estate,* and *Tax Returns*. Each hanging folder will be a different color and inside there will be file folders of that same color. For example, in my *Bank Account* file, there will be a file folder for each of the three banks where I have accounts. Inside those folders, I will keep my bank statements and any papers related to those accounts.

**G.** **SOLVE In a small group, come up with organizing solutions for the problems below.** Answers will vary. Sample answers given.

1. **Problem:** There are over 300 books scattered about the office—in bookcases, on people's desks, and on the floor next to desks.

   **Solution:** Set up an office library in a hallway or spare room where everyone can have access to it.
   _____

2. **Problem:** The supply closet has supplies everywhere; nothing can be found.

   **Solution:** Organize the supply closet with clear labels and categories.
   _____

3. **Problem:** My papers are very disorganized; there are stacks of papers everywhere.

   **Solution:** Sort papers into active, inactive, and throw out piles. Sort into separate files.

   Maintain files daily.

**H.** **Think of an organizational problem you have at home. Describe the problem below and write out a detailed solution.**

Answers will vary. See Exercise F for an example.
_____
_____
_____
_____

## Presentation 3

10–15 mins. ■■■

**F. Lars needs to get organized in his home office. Read about his problem and solution.**

Read about Lars as a class. Discuss his problem and solution. Ask: *Do you think it's a good solution? Why or why not? Is there one solution that is best? Or do different solutions work for different people?*

## Practice 3

15–20 mins. ■

(Shorter classes can do this exercise for homework.)

**G. SOLVE  In a small group, come up with organizing solutions for the problems below.**

## Evaluation 3

10–15 mins. ■

Have groups share their solutions. See how many people came up with the same solution. Vote on which solutions are the most creative.

## Application

10–20 mins. ■■■

**H. Think of an organizational problem you have at home. Describe the problem below and write out a detailed solution.**

### MULTILEVEL WORKSHEET

Unit 7, Lesson 3, Worksheet 1: Organize it!

**Refer students to *Stand Out 5 Workbook,* Unit 7, Lesson 3 for practice with noun clauses as complements.**

**Go to the *Activity Bank* online for suggestions on promoting digital literacy and using the Internet to enhance this lesson.**

### INSTRUCTOR'S NOTES

**Goal:** Identify and resolve problems at work
**Academic Strategies:** Analyzing reading, defining vocabulary, writing a summary
**Vocabulary:** See the article.

## Agenda

- Discuss and read about conflict resolution.
- Define new vocabulary.
- Write a summary.

## Resources

**Multilevel Worksheets:** Unit 7, Lesson 4, Worksheets 1–4
**Workbook:** Unit 7, Lesson 4

## Pacing

- 1.5 hour classes
- 2.5 hour classes
- 3+ hour classes

## STANDARDS CORRELATIONS

*CCRS:* RI1, RI2, RI4, RI10, W2, W4, W5
*CASAS:* 4.8.1, 4.8.5, 4.8.6
*SCANS:* **Information** Acquire and evaluate information, organize and maintain information, interpret and communicate information
**Interpersonal** Teach others, work with cultural diversity
**Systems** Monitor and correct performance
**Basic Skills** Reading, writing, listening, speaking
**Thinking Skills** Think creatively, make decisions, see things in the mind's eye
**Personal Qualities** Responsibility, sociability, self-management
*EFF:* **Communication** Read with understanding, convey ideas in writing, speak so others can understand, listen actively, observe critically
**Decision Making** Plan
**Interpersonal** Cooperate with others, advocate and influence, resolve conflict and negotiate, guide others
**Lifelong Learning** Take responsibility for learning, reflect and evaluate, learn through research

## Warm-up and Review          5–10 mins. ■■■

Have students form small groups and discuss the organizational problems they wrote about in the previous lesson. Have them ask their classmates for suggestions on how to better organize.

## Introduction          1 min. ■■■

**Note:** No dictation is included due to the length of the reading in this lesson. However, if you choose to do a dictation, choose a few sentences from the reading. Additionally, there are only two presentations in this lesson.

State the goal: *Today, we will read and analyze an article on resolving conflicts.*

## Presentation 1          10–15 mins. ■■■

### A. Answer the following questions with a partner.

After students complete Exercise A, go over the questions in Exercise B with students to help prepare them for the reading.

## Practice 1          20–30 mins. ■■■

**B. PREDICT Read the questions before each section of the article. Think about them as you read and answer them after you finish reading.**

Have students read the article silently.

**Note:** The article takes up all three pages of the lesson, not leaving much room for activities. See suggestions on the next page for activities you might want to do to help students better understand the reading. Also, there are more comprehension and vocabulary-building activities on the Multilevel Worksheets CD-ROM.

## Evaluation 1          10–15 mins. ■■■

Once students have read the article, make sure they come back to the questions in Exercise B. Go over the answers as a class.

Sample answers:

1. increased understanding, increased group cohesion, and improved self-knowledge
2. Conflicting goals can turn into personal dislike. Teamwork can break down. Talent can be wasted if people disengage from their work. Increasing negativity and recrimination in the workplace may result.
3. competitive, collaborative, compromising, accommodating, avoiding
4. The steps are: 1. Set the scene. 2. Gather information. 3. Agree on the problem. 4. Brainstorm possible solutions. 5. Negotiate a solution.

# LESSON 4 What's the problem?

WORKPLACE CONNECTION
Exercise A: Interact appropriately with team members.
Exercise B: Complete tasks as assigned.

**A. Answer the following questions with a partner.** Answers will vary.

1. What is *conflict resolution*? resolving a problem or argument

2. Where are some places that conflicts might occur? the office, between businesses and relatives

3. Who are some people that you might have conflicts with? boss, coworkers, roommates

4. Think about the ways you handle conflicts with people. What would you say your personal style of behavior is when speaking to people in a conflict? not very aggressive

**B. PREDICT Read the questions before each section of the article. Think about them as you read and answer them after you finish reading.** Answers will vary. See sample answers on LP page 185a.

1. What are the three benefits of resolving conflict?

2. What can happen if conflict is not handled effectively?

## Conflict Resolution: Resolving Conflict Rationally and Effectively

In many cases, conflict in the workplace just seems to be a fact of life. The good news is that by resolving conflict successfully, you can solve many of the problems that it has brought to the surface, as well as get benefits that you might not at first expect:

1. **Increased understanding:** The discussion needed to resolve conflict expands people's awareness of the situation, giving them an insight into how they can achieve their own goals without undermining those of other people.

2. **Increased group cohesion:** When conflict is resolved effectively, team members can develop stronger mutual respect and a renewed faith in their ability to work together.

3. **Improved self-knowledge:** Conflict pushes individuals to examine their goals in close detail, helping them understand the things that are most important to them, sharpening their focus, and enhancing their effectiveness.

However, if conflict is not handled effectively, the results can be damaging. Conflicting goals can quickly turn into personal dislike. Teamwork breaks down. Talent is wasted as people disengage from their work. And it's easy to end up in a vicious downward spiral of negativity and recrimination.

3. What are the five different conflict styles in Thomas and Kilmann's theory?

## Understanding the Theory: *Conflict Styles*

In the 1970s, Kenneth Thomas and Ralph Kilmann identified five main styles of dealing with conflict that vary in their degrees of cooperativeness and assertiveness:

**Competitive:** People who tend towards a competitive style take a firm stand and know what they want. They usually operate from a position of power, drawn from things like title, rank, expertise, or persuasive ability.

**Collaborative:** People tending towards a collaborative style try to meet the needs of all people involved.

**Compromising:** People who prefer a compromising style try to find a solution that will at least partially satisfy everyone.

**Accommodating:** This style indicates a willingness to meet the needs of others at the expense of the person's own needs.

**Avoiding:** People tending towards this style seek to evade the conflict entirely.

People tending towards a collaborative style try to meet the needs of all people involved.

Unit 7, Lesson 4, Worksheet 1: Conflict Resolution: Resolving Conflict Rationally and Effectively (complete article)

## BEST PRACTICE

### Highlighting or taking notes while reading

The article in this lesson is long and complicated, but it is very similar to something students might read in a textbook in their college classes. The entire article is available on the Multilevel Worksheets CD-ROM, so you can print it out for students. A way to make the material easier to digest is to break it up into smaller pieces, having students read and analyze one piece at a time before moving on to the next. Show students how to go through the article by starting with the first part and reading it out loud. Tell them what you would highlight or take notes on. Once they have seen an example, have them do it themselves for the next section.

## BEST PRACTICE

### Jigsaw

One way to turn the reading into a cooperative learning activity would be to break up the pieces and assign each group one part. Each group will then be responsible for understanding its part and teaching it to the rest of the class.

## INSTRUCTOR'S NOTES

## Presentation 2 10–15 mins. ■■□

Ask students to make a list of all the vocabulary words in the article from Exercise B that are unfamiliar to them. When they have finished, have them call out the words and make a comprehensive list on the board.

## Practice 2 15–20 mins. ■■

Have students take out a sheet of paper and choose ten words that are the most important to them for understanding the article. Ask students to define the words and write example sentences.

## Evaluation 2 15–20 mins. ■■

Call on students to write their original sentences on the board. If some students are still unsure of a word's meaning, even after they have seen a student's example sentence, ask the sentence creator to define the word for the class.

## Application 10–20 mins. ■■■

C. SUMMARIZE **Choose one of the following topics and write a one-paragraph summary.**

Before students begin the exercise, discuss the tips for writing a good summary.

BEST PRACTICE

### Writing a summary

1. Make a brief outline of the important points you want to include in your summary.
2. Identify the main idea and write it first.
3. Identify only the most important supporting points and omit unnecessary details.
4. Use your own words, but don't include your own ideas or comments.
5. Present the ideas in the order in which they were discussed in the article.
6. Remind the reader that you are summarizing someone else's ideas by using citation expressions. (The author . . . says that, states that, explains that, points out that, mentions that, emphasizes that, argues that, maintains that, highlights the fact that, concludes that . . . .)

MULTILEVEL WORKSHEETS

Unit 7, Lesson 4, Worksheet 2: Conflict Resolution—Vocabulary

Unit 7, Lesson 4, Worksheet 3: Conflict Resolution—Scenarios

**Refer students to *Stand Out 5 Workbook,* Unit 7, Lesson 4 for practice with noun clauses as subjects.**

**Go to the *Activity Bank* online for suggestions on promoting digital literacy and using the Internet to enhance this lesson.**

INSTRUCTOR'S NOTES

4. What are the five steps for resolving conflict?

## Using the Tool: *A Conflict-Resolution Process*

**Step One: Set the scene.**

Make sure that people understand that the conflict may be a mutual problem, which may be best resolved through discussion and negotiation rather than through raw aggression.

**Step Two: Gather information.**

Here, you are trying to get to the underlying interests, needs, and concerns of the other people involved. Ask for the other people's viewpoints and confirm that you respect their opinions and need their cooperation to solve the problem.

**Step Three: Agree on the problem.**

This sounds like an obvious step, but often different underlying needs, interests, and goals can cause people to perceive problems very differently. You'll need to agree on the problems that you are trying to solve before you'll find a mutually acceptable solution.

**Step Four: Brainstorm possible solutions.**

If everyone is going to feel satisfied with the resolution, it will help if everyone has had fair input in generating solutions. Brainstorm possible solutions and be open to all ideas, including ones you never considered before.

**Step Five: Negotiate a solution.**

By this stage, the conflict may be resolved—both sides may better understand the position of the other, and a mutually satisfactory solution may be clear to all.

**C. SUMMARIZE Choose one of the following topics and write a one-paragraph summary.** Answers will vary.

1. The benefits of conflict resolution

2. Thomas and Kilmann's five conflict styles

3. The five steps of the conflict-resolution process

_____

_____

_____

_____

_____

_____

# LESSON ⑤ What did you do?

WORKPLACE CONNECTION
Exercises B, C: Interpret and communicate information.

**A.** Maria's supervisor has asked her to write a progress report about a long-term project she is working on. Read the guidelines he gave her.

## Progress Report Guidelines

You write a progress report to inform a supervisor, associate, or customer about progress you've made on a project over a certain period of time. In the progress report, you explain all of the following:

- what the project is
- how much of the work is complete
- which part of the work is currently in progress
- what work remains to be done
- what problems or unexpected issues have arisen

**B. ANALYZE** Read part of Maria's report. Is she following the guidelines so far?

**To:** Henry Kim, Human Resources Director
**From:** Maria Avalos
**Date:** April 14th
**Subject:** Program for Employee Training

It seems that many problems have arisen from the employees working such long hours and not being able to communicate effectively with one another. It was proposed that I put together a training program for our employees on conflict resolution.

So far, I have been conducting research on whether it is better to bring in an outside training organization or do the training ourselves. I have concluded that it would be more cost-effective for us to do the training ourselves. So, I am currently working on putting together a training manual that can be used for the conflict-resolution training. I foresee that it will take me another two weeks to complete the manual. Once it has been completed, we will need to choose several people to conduct the training and train them to be effective leaders.

**C.** Is anything missing from Maria's report? If so, include details of what is missing below.

Answers will vary, but may mention that Maria has neglected to say how much of the project is complete

or that the report is missing an explanation about what problems have arisen to delay her progress.

**Goal:** Report progress
**Grammar:** Noun clauses as objects
**Academic Strategy:** Writing a progress report
**Vocabulary:** *long-term, in progress, cost-effective, effective*

## Agenda

Read guidelines for writing a progress report.
Read Maria's report.
Work with noun clauses.
Write a paragraph.
Write a progress report.

## Resources

**Multilevel Worksheets:** Unit 7, Lesson 5, Worksheets 1–2
**Workbook:** Unit 7, Lesson 5

## Pacing

■ 1.5 hour classes   ■ 2.5 hour classes
■ 3+ hour classes

### STANDARDS CORRELATIONS

*CCRS:* RI1, W2, W4, L1
*CASAS:* 4.6.4
*SCANS:* **Resources** *(optional)* Allocate time, allocate money, allocate materials and facility resources, allocate human resources
**Information** Acquire and evaluate information, organize and maintain information, interpret and communicate information, use computers to process information
**Interpersonal** Participate as a member of a team, teach others, serve clients and customers, exercise leadership, negotiate to arrive at a decision, work with cultural diversity
**Systems** Understand systems, monitor and correct performance, improve and design systems
**Technology** Select technology, apply technology to a task, maintain and troubleshoot technology
**Basic Skills** Reading, writing, arithmetic, listening, speaking
**Thinking Skills** Think creatively, make decisions, solve problems, see things in the mind's eye
**Personal Qualities** Responsibility, sociability, self-management
*EFF:* **Communication** Read with understanding, convey ideas in writing
**Decision Making** Solve problems and make decisions, plan
**Lifelong Learning** Take responsibility for learning, reflect and evaluate, use information and communications technology *(optional)*

## Warm-up and Review          5–10 mins. ■■■

Discuss the article from the previous lesson. Ask students to write down three things they learned and then share them with the class.

## Introduction          5–10 mins. ■■■

Dictation:

1. He has started on the project and will have it completed by June.
2. She put a team together to help her prepare the presentation by the end of the week.
3. They delegated the tasks to three teams of employees.
4. His supervisor asked him to head the new research project.

State the goal: *Today, you will learn how to write a progress report.*

## Presentation 1          10–15 mins. ■■■

**A. Maria's supervisor has asked her to write a progress report about a long-term project she is working on. Read the guidelines he gave her.**

Go over the guidelines as a class.

**B. ANALYZE Read part of Maria's report. Is she following the guidelines so far?**

## Practice 1          5 mins. ■■■

**C. Is anything missing from Maria's report? If so, include details of what is missing below.**

## Evaluation 1          5 mins. ■■■

Go over the answers as a class.

### INSTRUCTOR'S NOTES

_____
_____
_____
_____
_____

## Presentation 2

**D. Study the chart with your classmates and teacher.**

5–10 mins. ■■■

## Practice 2

15–20 mins. ■■

(Shorter classes can do these exercises for homework.)

**E. Complete each of the sentences below with an appropriate noun clause from the list. More than one noun clause may be appropriate.**

**F. Complete each sentence with a noun clause of your own.**

## Evaluation 2

10–15 mins. ■■

Go over the answers to Exercise E as a class by asking volunteers to read each sentence out loud. Discuss if there is more than one appropriate answer. Then, ask volunteers to read their sentences from Exercise F.

### MULTILEVEL WORKSHEET

Unit 7, Lesson 5, Worksheet 1: Noun Clauses

**Refer students to *Stand Out 5 Workbook,* Unit 7, Lesson 5 for practice with noun clauses as objects of verbs.**

**Go to the *Activity Bank* online for suggestions on promoting digital literacy and using the Internet to enhance this lesson.**

### BEST PRACTICE

### Noun clauses

It is very common for English speakers to use noun clauses in everyday speech. Noun clauses are important because they add key information to sentences. Because noun clauses come in a variety of forms, it is challenging for students to master them in regular speech. However, exposure to noun clauses and regular practice will make students more confident about using them.

### INSTRUCTOR'S NOTES

**D.** Study the chart with your classmates and teacher.

| Noun Clauses as Objects | | |
| --- | --- | --- |
| **Subject + Verb** | **Noun clause** | **Explanation** |
| I did | *what* I was asked. | |
| She knows | *how* the computer works. | • A noun clause starts with a question word or *that* and is followed by a subject and verb. |
| They decided | *where* the location would be. | |
| My boss asked | *who* would be best for the job. | • In these examples, the noun clauses are the objects of the sentences. |
| I hope | *that* they work as a team. | |

**E.** Complete each of the sentences below with an appropriate noun clause from the list. More than one noun clause may be appropriate. *Answers will vary. Sample answers given.*

| | |
| --- | --- |
| how the filing system worked | where the files were stored |
| ~~what she told me to~~ | who got to receive the training |
| that they would be promoted | how to complete the progress report |
| that we knew what we were doing | who wanted to be the team leader |

1. I did _what she told me to_ .

2. She found _where the files were stored_ .

3. The supervisor asked _how the filing system worked_ .

4. He explained _how to complete the progress report_ .

5. Our team showed _that we knew what we were doing_ .

6. Sari asked _who wanted to be the team leader_ .

7. Jared and Giulia hoped _that they would be promoted_ .

8. The representative chose _who got to receive the training_ .

**F.** Complete each sentence with a noun clause of your own. *Answers will vary. Sample answers given.*

1. I asked _when lunch would be served_ .

2. I hoped _that the report was well written_ .

3. I decided _who would assist me on the oral report_ .

4. I explained _where the files were stored_ .

**G.** **SUGGEST**  Maria reports that she has encountered problems. Read the problems and write a paragraph from Maria's perspective. Include what she might suggest as solutions.  Answers will vary. Sample answer is given.

- The employees do not want this training.

- None of the supervisors who could be trainers want to lead the training.

In doing my research, I discovered two more problems. First, I know that the employees do not want this training. They feel that they are overworked as it is. Second, I hoped that supervisors would lead the training. The supervisors have decided that none of them want to lead the training. I suggest that both the employees and the supervisors be offered an incentive for doing the training.

_____

_____

_____

_____

**H.** Write a progress report using the guidelines in Exercise A. Use the format of Maria's report in Exercise B and the information below. Using the examples in Exercises D and E, include noun clauses in your report.  Answers will vary.

**Project:** Change the way scheduling of staff is handled.

**Work completed:** Servers and bartenders have been interviewed.

**Doing now:** Interviewing the kitchen staff.

**To do:** Take information from interviews and come up with a better way to handle scheduling in the future.

**Problems:** Last-minute shift switching without manager approval; some shifts are too short.

## Presentation 3
5 mins. ■■□

Go over the instructions for Exercise G.

## Practice 3
15–20 mins. ■□□

(Shorter classes can do this exercise for homework.)

**G. SUGGEST** **Maria reports that she has encountered problems. Read the problems and write a paragraph from Maria's perspective. Include what she might suggest as solutions.**

## Evaluation 3
5–10 mins. ■□□

Walk around the classroom and help students as needed. Make suggestions for how to improve their paragraphs. Ask a few students whom you think have written good paragraphs to read them out loud.

## Application
10–20 mins. ■■□

**H. Write a progress report using the guidelines in Exercise A. Use the format of Maria's report in Exercise B and the information below. Using the examples in Exercises D and E, include noun clauses in your report.**

### MULTILEVEL WORKSHEET

Unit 7, Lesson 5, Worksheet 2: Progress Reports

### BEST PRACTICE

## Teacher positioning

Teaching does not always have to occur at the front of the classroom. Make walking around the classroom and presenting lessons from different places a habitual routine. When teachers walk around, student sometimes see it as an opportunity for the teacher to criticize their work, which may make them feel uneasy. If students are familiar with your moving about, they accept it as a part of regular instruction.

## INSTRUCTOR'S NOTES

# You seem to be doing a very good job

## Before You Watch

- Read the video title out loud.
- Ask students in what situations they might hear this statement.

### A. Look at the picture and answer the questions.

- Ask students to look at the picture. Then, have them answer the questions.
- Ask volunteers to share their answers with the class. Then, discuss.

## While You Watch

### B. Watch the video and complete the dialog.

- Ask students to watch the video and complete the dialog.
- Play the video and ask students to watch and listen carefully.
- Play the video again. Then, ask students to complete the dialog.
- Play the video one more time and have students check their answers.
- Have student practice the conversation with partners.

## Check Your Understanding

### C. Watch the video. Read the statements and write *T* for true and *F* for false.

- Ask students to write *T* for true and *F* for false for each statement below.
- Have students read the statements and write their answers.
- Ask volunteers to share their answers with the class.

INSTRUCTOR'S NOTES

 # You seem to be doing a very good job

## Before You Watch

**A. Look at the picture and answer the questions.**

1. Where are Hector and Mr. Patel?
   *Hector and Mr. Patel are in the clothing store.*
2. What are they discussing?
   *They are discussing Hector's performance.*

## While You Watch

**B. ▶ Watch the video and complete the dialog.**

**Mr. Patel:** This stick on the side is called a (1) ___*stylus*___. You can use it to operate the functions on the screen. There's a keypad on the bottom.

**Hector:** That's really cool. The (2) ___*screen*___ is so clear, and it's really big.

**Mr. Patel:** And there are (3) ___*ports*___ on both sides for things like charging the battery, inserting the flash memory card, etc. With a USB cable, you can directly download things from your computer.

**Hector:** That's great! This is a really useful little (4) ___*tool*___.

**Mr. Patel:** Yes, it is. You can send e-mails from this, you can receive calls, and you can store all sorts of (5) ___*data*___.

## Check Your Understanding

**C. Watch the video. Read the statements and write *T* for true and *F* for false.**

1. __T__ Mr. Patel says that Mateo has been doing a good job.
2. __F__ Hector is going to manage the women's department.
3. __T__ Hector can send e-mails from his PDA.
4. __T__ Hector can connect the PDA to his computer.
5. __T__ Other employees can reach Hector on his PDA at any time.
6. __T__ The stick on the side is a pen.

# Review

**A.** Read the instructions for setting up an MP3 player and answer the questions that follow.

> **Setting Up Your MP3 Player**
>
> Step 1: Charge the battery.
> Step 2: Install the software.
> Step 3: Import music to your computer.
> Step 4: Connect the MP3 player to your computer and transfer music.
> Step 5: Play music.

1. What do you need to do before you import music to your computer?

   *Charge the battery and install the software.*

2. What can you do after you have transferred music?

   *Play music.*

3. What is the first thing you must do?

   *Charge the battery.*

4. What must you do in order to be able to transfer music?

   *Connect the MP3 player to your computer.*

**B.** Read the tips and troubleshooting advice for an MP3 player. Then, choose the best answers.

> Most problems can be resolved by resetting your MP3 player.
>    To reset your MP3 player:
>    1. Connect it to a power outlet using the power adaptor.
>    2. Toggle the **Hold** switch on and off.
>    3. Press and hold the **Menu** button for at least 10 seconds.
> If your player won't turn on or respond:
>    • Make sure the **Hold** switch is off.
>    • If you're using the remote, make sure the remote's **Hold** switch is off.
>    • Recharge your battery.

1. You can solve most problems with your MP3 player by . . .

   a. recharging the battery.      b. turning it on and off.      (c.) resetting it.

2. Which button do you hold down when resetting the player?

   a. Hold                          (b.) Menu                          c. Power Adaptor

3. What's the first thing you should do to reset your player?

   a. Make sure the *Hold* switch is off.

   (b.) Connect it to a power outlet.

   c. Hold down the *Menu* button.

WORKPLACE CONNECTION
Exercises A, B: Complete tasks as assigned.

## AT-A-GLANCE PREP

**Goals:** All unit goals
**Grammar:** All unit grammar
**Academic Strategy:** Reviewing
**Vocabulary:** All Unit 7 vocabulary

### Agenda

▪ Discuss unit goals.
▪ Complete the review.
▪ Use unit vocabulary.

### Resources

**Stand Out Assessment CD-ROM with ExamView®**

### Pacing

■ 1.5 hour classes   ■ 2.5 hour classes
■ 3+ hour classes

## STANDARDS CORRELATIONS

*CCRS:* RI1, RI4, W2, W4
*CASAS:* 7.2.1
*SCANS:* **Resources** Allocate time
**Information** Acquire and evaluate information
**Interpersonal** Participate as a member of a team, teach others, negotiate to arrive at a decision, work with cultural diversity
**Systems** Monitor and correct performance
**Basic Skills** Reading, writing, arithmetic, listening, speaking
**Thinking Skills** Think creatively, make decisions, solve problems, see things in the mind's eye
**Personal Qualities** Responsibility, sociability, self-management
*EFF:* **Communication** Read with understanding, convey ideas in writing, speak so others can understand, listen actively, observe critically
**Interpersonal** Cooperate with others, guide others
**Lifelong Learning** Take responsibility for learning, reflect and evaluate

## Warm-up and Review                5–10 mins. ■ ■ ■

Talk about progress reports. Ask students how many of them have written one before or might be asked to write one in the future. For students who don't work, ask them for some other situations in their lives where they might write a progress report.

## Introduction                5–10 mins. ■ ■ ■

Ask students as a class to try to recall all the goals of this unit without looking back in their books. The goals for this unit include identifying and using technology, resolving technology, establishing an organizational system, identifying and resolving problems at work, and reporting progress. Write all the goals on the board from Unit 7. Show students the first page of the unit and mention the five goals.

State the goal: *Today, we will be reviewing everything we have learned in this unit and preparing for the team project.*

## Presentation                10–15 mins. ■ ■ ■

This presentation will cover the three pages of the review. Quickly go to the first page of each lesson. Discuss the goal of each. Ask simple questions to remind students of what they have learned.

**Note:** Since there is little presentation in the review, you can assign the review exercises that don't require collaboration with a partner or group for homework and go over them in class the following day.

## Practice                20–25 mins. ■ ■ ■

**Note:** There are two ways to do the review:

1. Go through the exercises one at a time and, as students complete each one, go over the answers.

2. Quickly go through the instructions of each exercise, let students complete all of the exercises at once, and then go over the answers.

**A. Read the instructions for setting up an MP3 player and answer the questions that follow. (Lesson 1)**

**B. Read the tips and troubleshooting advice for an MP3 player. Then, choose the best answers. (Lesson 2)**

## Evaluation                10–15 mins. ■ ■ ■

Go around the classroom and check on students' progress. Help individuals when needed. If you see consistent errors among several students, interrupt the class and give a mini-lesson or review to help students feel comfortable with the concept.

## Practice *(continued)* 15–20 mins. ■■■

C. Alphabetize the following items on a separate piece of paper. (Lesson 3)

D. How would you organize the items in Exercise C in an office?

E. Answer the following questions about the conflict-resolution article on pages 185–187. (Lesson 4)

F. Write the five things a progress report should include. (Lesson 5)

## Evaluation *(continued)* 10–15 mins. ■■■

Go around the classroom and check on students' progress. Help individuals when needed. If you see consistent errors among several students, interrupt the class and give a mini-lesson or review to help students feel comfortable with the concept.

### BEST PRACTICE

#### Recycling/Review

The review exercises, the research activity, and the team project are part of the recycling/review process. Students often need to be reintroduced to concepts to solidify what they have learned. Many concepts are learned and forgotten when students are engaged in learning other new concepts. This is because students learn but are not necessarily ready to acquire language concepts.

Therefore, it becomes very important to review material with students and to show them how to review it on their own. It is also important to recycle the new concepts in different contexts.

### INSTRUCTOR'S NOTES

**Learner Log**

I can establish an organizational system.   I can identify and resolve problems at work.   I can report progress.
☐ Yes ☐ No ☐ Maybe                       ☐ Yes ☐ No ☐ Maybe                         ☐ Yes ☐ No ☐ Maybe

## C. Alphabetize the following items on a separate piece of paper.

5 paper shredder

11 USB stick

2 computer

4 fax machine

10 telephone

3 external hard drive

7 printer

6 power adaptor

9 scanner

8 projector

1 cable

## D. How would you organize the items in Exercise C in an office? Answers will vary. Sample answer given.

Each employee should have a business telephone and a computer. A paper shredder,

fax machine, scanner, printer, and label maker should be kept in a central location.

Extra flash drives (USB sticks), cables, external hard drives, and power adapters should be kept

with the LCD projector in a locked technology cabinet.

## E. Answer the following questions about the conflict-resolution article on pages 185–187.

1. What are the three benefits to resolving conflict?

   a. Increased understanding

   b. Increased group cohesion

   c. Improved self-knowledge

2. What are the five different conflict styles in Thomas and Kilmann's theory?

   a. Competitive

   b. Collaborative

   c. Compromising

   d. Accommodating

   e. Avoiding

3. What are the five steps for resolving conflict?

   a. Set the scene.

   b. Gather information

   c. Agree on the problem.

   d. Brainstorm possible solutiuons.

   e. Negotiate a solution.

## F. Write the five things a progress report should include.

   a. what the project is

   b. how much of the work is complete

   c. which part of the work is currently in progress

   d. what work remains to be done

   e. what problems or unexpected issues have arisen

WORKPLACE CONNECTION
Exercises C, E, F: Complete tasks as assigned.
Exercise D: Collect and organize information.

Review   193

# Vocabulary Review

**A.** Put each word below in the correct column according to its part of speech: *noun,* *verb,* or *adjective.*

| cost-effective | reorganize | organize | hanging files | fan |
| feed | effective | splotchy | paper jam | long-term |
| obstructions | force | faded | toner | power supply |

**Noun**

1. obstructions
2. hanging files
3. paper jam
4. toner
5. power supply

**Verb**

1. feed
2. reorganize
3. force
4. organize
5. fan

**Adjective**

1. cost-effective
2. effective
3. splotchy
4. faded
5. long-term

**B.** Use words from Exercise A to complete the sentences. Not all the words are used.

1. Did you get a chance to put the _____ hanging files _____ in alphabetical order?

2. The computer wasn't working because the _____ power supply _____ wasn't plugged in.

3. If you _____ fan _____ out the paper, it shouldn't stick together so much.

4. It doesn't seem _____ cost-effective _____ to have so many computers running at the same time. That wastes a lot of energy.

5. Tim, can you _____ reorganize _____ these files? They seem to have gotten out of order.

6. If you _____ force _____ the paper into the feeder, it will probably cause a _____ paper jam _____.

7. When I opened up the fax machine, I couldn't see any _____ obstructions _____.

8. We need a/an _____ effective _____ solution to this disorganized supply closet.

9. Is there any more _____ toner _____ in the supply closet? These copies are _____ splotchy _____ and _____ faded _____.

10. I wonder why the paper won't _____ feed _____ through the printer correctly?

WORKPLACE CONNECTION
Exercises A, B: Complete tasks as assigned.

## Practice *(continued)*  25–30 mins. ■■■

### Vocabulary Review

A. Put each word below in the correct column according to its part of speech: *noun, verb,* or *adjective.*

B. Use words from Exercise A to complete the sentences. Not all the words are used.

### Evaluation *(continued)*  5–15 mins. ■■■
Go around the classroom and check on students' progress. Help individuals when needed. If you see consistent errors among several students, interrupt the class and give a mini-lesson or review to help students feel comfortable with the concept.

### Assessment *(optional)*  ■■■
Use the Stand Out Assessment CD-ROM with ExamView® to create a post-test for Unit 7.

## INSTRUCTOR'S NOTES

## AT-A-GLANCE PREP

**Goal:** Research careers
**Academic Strategy:** Research
**Vocabulary:** *earnings, related occupations*

### Agenda

- Research jobs.
- Research salary, training/qualifications, and related occupations.

### Resources

**Multilevel Worksheets CD-ROM:** Research: PDF files on retail and office careers
**Internet access**

## STANDARDS CORRELATIONS

*CCRS:* W7, W8, W9

*CASAS:* 4.9.3, 7.2.1, 7.4.4, 7.4.5, 7.4.6

*SCANS:* **Information** Acquire and evaluate information, organize and maintain information, interpret and communicate information, use computers to process information *(optional)*

**Interpersonal** Participate as a member of a team, teach others, negotiate to arrive at a decision, work with cultural diversity

**Systems** Understand systems

**Technology** Select technology, apply technology to a task, maintain and troubleshoot technology *(optional)*

**Basic Skills** Reading, writing

**Thinking Skills** Think creatively, make decisions, see things in the mind's eye

**Personal Qualities** Responsibility, sociability, self-management

*EFF:* **Communication** Read with understanding, convey ideas in writing, observe critically

**Decision Making** Solve problems and make decisions, plan

**Lifelong Learning** Take responsibility for learning, reflect and evaluate, learn through research, use information and communications technology *(optional)*

## Academic Feature: Research

Each unit will have a research or team project page where students are required to collaborate to complete a task or conduct research. Options will be given for students to use the Internet as well as printed resource materials. The printed resource materials can be found on the Multilevel Worksheets CD-ROM.

## Introduction
5–10 mins.

Ask students to raise their hands if they work in a retail store. Ask students to raise their hands if they work in an office. Ask students who didn't raise their hands what type of environment they work in.

State the goal: *Today, you will research different careers associated with the retail world and the office world.*

## Presentation
10–15 mins.

A. **In the past two units, you have learned about two different areas of work: the retail setting and the office. In a group, brainstorm a list of jobs that might be found in each of these areas.**

B. **Look back at your two lists. Circle the jobs that you think earn the most money.**

## Practice
10–15 mins.

C. **Using the Internet or printed materials from your teacher, research jobs and see if you can add to your lists in Exercise A.**

D. **Choose two or three jobs that seem the most interesting to you and find out the following information.**

## Evaluation
5–10 mins.

Have students share their research with the class.

### MULTILEVEL WORKSHEET

Unit 7, Research: PDF Files on Retail and Office Careers

### INSTRUCTOR'S NOTES

_____

_____

_____

_____

_____

_____

✓ **Looking for a job**

**A.** In the past two units, you have learned about two different areas of work: the retail setting and the office. In a group, brainstorm a list of jobs that might be found in each of these areas. *Answers will vary.*

| Retail jobs | Office jobs |
|---|---|
| clerk | supervisor |
| supervisor | office manager |
| manager | facilities manager |
| stock assistant | administrative assistant |
| owner | information systems manager |
| buyer | vice president |
| assistant buyer | receptionist |

**B.** Look back at your two lists. Circle the jobs that you think earn the most money. *Answers will vary.*

**C.** Using the Internet or printed materials from your teacher, research jobs and see if you can add to your lists in Exercise A. *Answers will vary.*

**D.** Choose two or three jobs that seem the most interesting to you and find out the following information. *Answers will vary.*

| Job title | Salary | Training/Qualifications required | Related occupations |
|---|---|---|---|
|  |  |  |  |
|  |  |  |  |
|  |  |  |  |

# READING CHALLENGE

## About the Explorer

Patrick Meier is a crisis mapper. He maps important information that is posted in real time from social media. The maps are full of information and available for free to humanitarian organizations and their volunteers so that they can provide help to those in need. As disaster strikes, whether it be an earthquake, a tsunami, a fire, or a hurricane, people start e-mailing, texting, tweeting, and posting on Facebook and Instagram. As this information pours in, it is inputted on the map. Volunteer organizations can then access the map to see where help is most needed.

## About the Photo

This photo shows Patrick giving a presentation on crisis mapping. Mapping is not something Patrick does alone. He has built a network of volunteers who come from 80 different countries so they can input information around the clock. More than 800 volunteers are trained, tech-savvy, and ready to work at a moment's notice. They gather the messages, photos, video, and high-resolution satellite images, and integrate them into maps.

- Introduce the explorer, Patrick Meier. Have students look at the photo.
- Read the title out loud and ask students what they think it means.

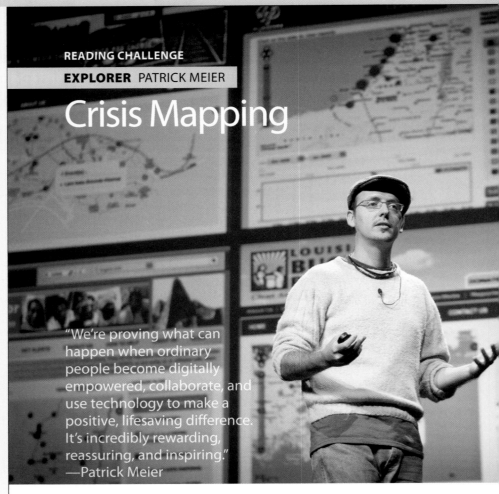

**READING CHALLENGE**

**EXPLORER** PATRICK MEIER

# Crisis Mapping

"We're proving what can happen when ordinary people become digitally empowered, collaborate, and use technology to make a positive, lifesaving difference. It's incredibly rewarding, reassuring, and inspiring."
—Patrick Meier

**A. PREDICT** Read the title and the quote. What do you think the relationship between the two is?

**B.** Discuss the social media terms and websites with a partner. Which are you familiar with? Which do you use? Are there other websites you use that are not listed?

| | | | |
|---|---|---|---|
| crowdsourcing | Facebook | texting | Instagram |
| e-mailing | Snapchat | tweeting | Twitter |

---

**CCRS FOR READING**

RI1, RI2, RI3, RI4, RI10, SL1, SL2

**C. Read about Patrick Meier.**

Patrick Meier has come up with a way to use technology to help save lives. But not in a hospital, like you might think. He is leading the way in the field of crisis mapping. Patrick maps important information that is posted in real time from social media. The maps are full of information and available for free to humanitarian organizations and their volunteers so that they can provide help to those in need.

Patrick is the director of crisis mapping at a nonprofit technology company formed in 2008 called Ushahidi, which means *witness* in Swahili. Ushahidi provides a place for anyone to gather information and create live multimedia maps using crowdsourced information. He's also the co-founder of the Standby Task Force (SBTF). This company and task force together have changed and strengthened relief efforts around the world. Organizations such as the United Nations, U.S. Marines and Coast Guard, the World Health Organization, and Amnesty International can access these crisis maps.

So how does it work? As disaster strikes, whether it be an earthquake, a tsunami, a fire, or a hurricane, people start e-mailing, texting, tweeting, and posting on Facebook and Instagram. As this information pours in, it is inputted on the map. Volunteer organizations can then access the map to see where help is most needed. "Situational awareness is key to allocating resources and coordinating logistics," says Patrick. "These dynamic, ever-changing maps are like having your own helicopter. They provide a bird's-eye view as events unfold across time and space. Gaining information like this straight from crisis zones is a game changer; these technologies didn't exist just a few years ago."

Who inputs the information as it comes in? The SBTF is a network of people involved in crisis mapping who come from 80 different countries so they can input the information around the clock. More than 800 volunteers are trained, tech-savvy, and ready to work at a moment's notice. They gather the messages, photos, video, and high-resolution satellite images, and integrate them into the Ushahidi map. "These people are passionate about helping and making a difference."

Patrick has figured out how to resolve a problem. By establishing an organizational system that can take incoming information in real time and put it on a map that relief organizations can access, he has figured out a way to get help to the people who need it most.

**D.  SUMMARIZE   Explain to a partner how crisis mapping works.**

Answers will vary.

Reading Challenge   197

---

**READING STRATEGIES**

## Summarizing

Summarizing teaches students how to reduce texts to their bare essentials. In other words, students learn how to focus on the most important parts of a text, ignore information that is trivial or unimportant, and express the main ideas in a meaningful way. Having students regularly summarize improves their memory skills and builds comprehension by making ideas clearer. It also improves writing and vocabulary skills.

---

**A.  PREDICT  Read the title and the quote. What do you think the relationship between the two is?**

- Have a volunteer read the quote to the class. Then, ask students how they think the quote relates to the title.
- Ask students if they can guess how people might already work together, using widespread technology, to respond to emergencies.
- Have students share their opinions as a class.

**B.  Discuss the social media terms and websites with a partner. Which are you familiar with? Which do you use? Are there other websites you use that are not listed?**

- Review the social media terms and websites as a class.
- Ask students which social media websites they use.
- Ask students if there are other apps they use that aren't listed.

**C.  Read about Patrick Meier.**

Ask students to read about Patrick Meier. Tell students that he is the creator of crisis mapping.

**D.  SUMMARIZE  Explain to a partner how crisis mapping works.**

Have students explain to a partner how crisis mapping works.

# Civic Responsibility

## About the Photo

This photo shows a man holding a banner that contains the preamble to the U.S. Constitution. The Constitution is the supreme law of the United States of America. It sets out the rules by which the country is run. The document was signed in 1787 and presided over by George Washington. It was written in the same state house in Philadelphia as the Declaration of Independence. More than 11,000 amendments have been introduced in Congress, but only 27 of those have actually received approval.

- Introduce the unit by reading the title out loud.
- Have students look at the photo. Then, ask a volunteer to read the caption to the class.
- Ask students what they think the *preamble to the U.S. Constitution* is.
- Have students read and answer the questions.
- Ask volunteers to share and discuss their opinions with the class.
- Go over the unit outcomes.

UNIT **8**

# Civic Responsibility

A man holds a banner that contains the preamble to the U.S. Constitution.

| UNIT OUTCOMES | GRAMMAR | VOCABULARY | EL CIVICS |
|---|---|---|---|
| • Identify requirements for establishing residency and citizenship<br>• Understand your rights<br>• Identify local civic organizations<br>• Interpret information about environmental issues<br>• Communicate your opinion | • Transitional expressions<br>• Opinion expressions<br>• Future with *will*<br>• Imperatives<br>• Modals with *should*<br>• Simple past<br>• Modals with *must, can, may, should* | • Residency: *citizen, nonresident, permanent, alien, foreigner, status, eligible, naturalization, refugee*<br>• Rights: *amendment, Constitution, Bill of Rights, slavery, impartial, punishment, jury, capital crime, verdict, trial, bear arms, beliefs, opinion, peaceably assemble, protect*<br>• Civic Organizations: *civic, charitable, community, dues, members, social welfare*<br>• Environmental Issues: *carpooling, sustainable, environment, conserve, commuter, resource, reusable, recyclable* | The skills students learn in this unit can be applied to all EL Civics competency areas with a particular focus on the following:<br>• U.S. Constitution<br>• Citizenship/Immigration<br>• Civic involvement<br>• Democracy<br>• Political issues and speed<br>• Rights and freedoms |

## UNIT OUTCOMES

- ☐ Identify requirements for establishing residency and citizenship
- ☐ Understand your rights
- ☐ Identify local civic organizations
- ☐ Interpret information about environmental issues
- ☐ Communicate your opinion

**Look at the photo and answer the questions.**

1. What is the U.S. Constitution?
2. Why do you think the man is displaying the banner?

## Life Skills Link

In this unit, students will learn about the requirements and process of becoming a United States citizen. Students will examine types of opportunities for civic participation, beginning at the local level, with attention focused on the rights and freedoms that make political involvement possible. The concept of freedom of speech is expanded to include presentation of a step-by-step exploration of crafting persuasive political communication in support of an important issue.

## Workplace Link

All lessons and units in *Stand Out* include basic communication skills and interpersonal skills important for the workplace. They are not individually identified. Other workplace skills are indicated. They include *collecting and organizing information, making decisions and solving problems,* and *combining ideas and information*

| CASAS | SCANS | CCRS |
|---|---|---|
| Vocabulary Builder: 7.4.5<br>Lesson 1: 1.5.1, 5.3.6<br>Lesson 2: 1.6.2, 5.2.2, 5.3.2, 5.7.1,<br>Lesson 3: 5.6.2 , 5.3.8, 7.4.2<br>Lesson 4: 1.3.2, 5.3.7, 5.7.1, 7.4.2<br>Lesson 5: 5.1.6, 5.7.1, 7.4.2<br>Review: 7.2.1<br>Research Project: 4.9.3, 7.2.1,<br>             7.4.4, 7.4.5, 7.4.6<br>Individual Project: 4.8.1, 4.8.5, 4.8.6 | Many SCANS skills are incorporated in this unit with an emphasis on:<br><br>• Reading<br>• Speaking<br>• Responsibility<br>• Cultural diversity<br>• Decision making | RI1, RI2, RI3, RI4, RI5, RI8, RI10, W1, W3, W4, W5, SL1, SL2, SL3, SL4, SL6, L5 |

# Vocabulary Builder

**A.** **INFER** Guessing the meaning of a word from the context of a sentence is called *making an inference*. Read each sentence and infer the meaning of the italicized word and its part of speech. Then, look each word up in a dictionary. *Answers will vary. Sample answers given.*

1. The judge gave an *impartial* verdict that did not favor either side.

   Part of speech: _____ adj. _____ Meaning: _____ doesn't favor one side or the other _____

   Dictionary definition: _____ not partial; unprejudiced _____

2. There are so many *commuters* on the roads today that there is always a lot of pollution and noise.

   Part of speech: _____ n.(pl.) _____ Meaning: _____ people who drive back and forth _____

   Dictionary definition: _____ a person who travels regularly from one place to another _____

3. We all must *conserve* energy so that we can protect the environment for our kids.

   Part of speech: _____ v. _____ Meaning: _____ retain or keep _____

   Dictionary definition: _____ to protect from loss or depletion _____

4. During the war, many *refugees* went to safer countries to live better lives.

   Part of speech: _____ n.(pl.) _____ Meaning: _____ people who leave a country because of problems _____

   Dictionary definition: _____ a person who flees to find refuge or safety _____

5. She runs a *charitable* organization that gives food to homeless people.

   Part of speech: _____ adj. _____ Meaning: _____ giving of things to the poor _____

   Dictionary definition: _____ generous in giving money or other help _____

**Goal:** Introduce new vocabulary
**Academic Strategies:** Making inferences, categorizing vocabulary, using a dictionary
**Vocabulary:** See lesson

## Agenda

- Make inferences.
- Guess lesson themes.
- Categorize vocabulary.
- Write sentences.

## Resources

**Dictionaries:** It is recommended that each student in class have an ESL learner's dictionary or that there be dictionaries available in the classroom for students to use. Dictionaries that will be referred to in this book are *Heinle's Newbury House Dictionary of American English* and the *Collins Cobuild Intermediate* or *Advanced Dictionary of American English*.

## Pacing

- 1.5 hour classes
- 2.5 hour classes
- 3+ hour classes

# STANDARDS CORRELATIONS

*CCRS:* RI4, L3, L4

*CASAS:* 7.4.5

*SCANS:* **Information** Acquire and evaluate information, organize and maintain information

**Interpersonal** Participate as a member of a team, negotiate to arrive at a decision, work with cultural diversity

**Systems** Understand systems, monitor and correct performance

**Basic Skills** Reading, writing, listening, speaking

**Thinking Skills** Think creatively, make decisions, see things in the mind's eye

**Personal Qualities** Responsibility, sociability, self-management

*EFF:* **Communication** Read with understanding, convey ideas in writing, speak so others can understand, listen actively

**Decision Making** Use math to solve problems and communicate, solve problems and make decisions, plan

**Interpersonal** Cooperate with others

**Lifelong Learning** Take responsibility for learning, reflect and evaluate, learn through research

## Academic Feature: Vocabulary Builder

Each unit will begin with a vocabulary-building section. The purpose of this two-page section is to introduce students to many of the words they will be using in the unit lessons. Students will have a chance to see how much they already know, and they will get exposure to the new vocabulary found in the unit.

**Note:** All of the exercises on these two pages should be done in class, no matter the class length. Longer classes can do this lesson and then move onto Lesson 1 during the same class meeting; shorter classes may have to devote one whole class meeting to this lesson.

## Introduction                          5–10 mins. ■■■

State the goal: *Today, we will be identifying and working with the vocabulary you will learn in this unit.*

## Presentation 1                        10–15 mins. ■■■

Write this sentence on the board: *Born and raised in Hong Kong, she moved to the U.S. and was naturalized is 2002.* Ask students what part of speech *naturalized* is (verb). Then, ask them what they think the word means. Write all their ideas on the board. Then, ask a volunteer to look it up in a dictionary and read the definition out loud. Explain that this process of guessing what a word means is also called making an inference.

## Practice 1                            10–15 mins. ■■■

**A. INFER** Guessing the meaning of a word from the context of its sentence is called *making an inference*. Read each sentence and infer the meaning of the italicized word and its part of speech. Then, look up each word in a dictionary.

**B.** Each sentence in Exercise A reflects the topic of a lesson in this unit. Look at the sentences and guess what you think each lesson will be about.

**Evaluation 1**            10–15 mins. ■■■

Go over the answers as a class.

**Presentation 2**            5–10 mins. ■■■

Go over the instructions for Exercises C and D. Do a few examples if necessary. Tell students that they can use a dictionary for both exercises if they need to.

### PRONUNCIATION

## Vocabulary

When teaching students new vocabulary, pronounce each word for them several times and ask them to repeat it. Often, students may be familiar with the words you are introducing, but have never seen them spelled out. By pronouncing the words for students, you allow students to make a connection between the words' spellings and their sounds. It is also important that students learn the correct pronunciation of new words so they feel comfortable using their new vocabulary inside and outside of the classroom.

**Practice 2**            10–15 mins. ■■

**C.** **CLASSIFY** Look at the list of terms. Categorize each term by writing it under the correct lesson title.

**D.** Write your own sentence for each of the words below.

**Evaluation 2**            10–15 mins. ■■

Go over the answers to Exercise C as a class. Although there is a suggested answer key, some words may fit under more than one lesson title.

Ask volunteers to write their original sentences from Exercise D on the board. As a class, analyze the sentences to make sure the words have been used correctly.

WORKPLACE CONNECTION
Exercise B: Interpret and communicate information.
Exercises C, D: Complete tasks as assigned.

**B.** **Each sentence in Exercise A reflects the topic of a lesson in this unit. Look at the sentences and guess what you think each lesson will be about.** Answers will vary. Sample answers given.

1. Rights _____

2. Environmental issues _____

3. Environmental issues/Communicate opinion _____

4. Requirements for establishing residency _____

5. Civic organizations _____

**C.** **CLASSIFY** **Look at the list of terms. Categorize each term by writing it under the correct lesson title.** Answers may vary.

| alien | conserve | punishment | reusable |
|-------|----------|------------|----------|
| bear arms | eligible | refugee | slavery |
| believe | naturalization | peaceably assemble | social welfare |
| capital crime | opinion | resource | status |
| civic | protect | | |

| Identify requirements for establishing residency and citizenship | Understand your rights | Identify local civic organizations | Interpret information about environmental issues | Communicate your opinion |
|---|---|---|---|---|
| alien<br>eligible<br>naturalization<br>refugee<br>status | bear arms<br>capital crime/believe<br>protect<br>punishment<br>peaceably assemble<br>slavery | civic<br>social welfare | conserve<br>resource<br>reusable | believe<br>opinion |

**D.** **Write your own sentence for each of the words below.** Answers will vary. Sample answers given.

1. naturalization: He went through the naturalization process to become a citizen.

2. punishment: Her punishment was to pay a fine.

3. civic: His civic duty was to vote in every election.

4. reusable: I think some garbage is reusable.

5. resource: Water is an important resource in all countries.

GOAL ▪ Identify requirements for establishing residency and citizenship

WORKPLACE CONNECTION
Exercises A, B: Complete tasks as assigned.

**A. How can an immigrant become a permanent resident of the United States? Make a list of your ideas below.** Answers will vary. Sample answers are given.

1. Live in the U.S. a long time on a visa and then apply.

2. Marry a U.S. citizen.

3. Get a job in the United States with a work visa.

4. Join a family member who is already a citizen.

**B. PREDICT** Several students in Mrs. Morgan's class want to become permanent residents of the United States. Read about each nonresident below and decide if you think he or she is eligible to become a permanent resident. Write *yes* or *no*.

 Answers will vary.

1. Hanh has been living in the U.S. since 1995. She recently became engaged to a U.S. citizen. Is she eligible? _____

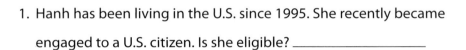

2. Sadiq is a refugee from Iraq who has been here for six months. Is he eligible? _____

3. Ella is 35 and her mother just became a permanent resident. Is she eligible? _____

4. Phillipe has lived in the U.S. since 1965. Is he eligible?

_____

5. Enrique's wife just became a permanent resident. Is he eligible?

_____

# AT-A-GLANCE PREP

**Goal:** Identify requirements for establishing residency and citizenship

**Academic Strategies:** Active reading, evaluating situations

**Vocabulary:** *permanent resident, eligible, petition, alien, admitted, asylee, refugee, naturalization*

## Agenda

▢ Read and discuss resident status requirements.

▢ Listen to an immigration officer talk about citizenship requirements.

▢ Discuss naturalization.

## Resources

**Multilevel Worksheets:** Unit 8, Lesson 1, Worksheet 1 and Citizenship PDF

**Workbook:** Unit 8, Lesson 1

**Audio:** CD Track 34

**Stand Out Assessment CD-ROM with ExamView®**

## Pacing

■ 1.5 hour classes   ■ 2.5 hour classes
■ 3+ hour classes

## STANDARDS CORRELATIONS

*CCRS:* RI1, RI4, RI10, W3, SL1, SL2

*CASAS:* 5.3.6

*SCANS:* **Information** Acquire and evaluate information, organize and maintain information, interpret and communicate information

**Interpersonal** Participate as a member of a team, teach others, serve clients and customers, exercise leadership, negotiate to arrive at a decision, work with cultural diversity

**Systems** Monitor and correct performance

**Technology** Select technology, apply technology to a task (optional)

**Basic Skills** Reading, writing, listening, speaking

**Thinking Skills** Make decisions, see things in the mind's eye

**Personal Qualities** Responsibility, sociability, self-management

*EFF:* **Communication** Read with understanding, convey ideas in writing, speak so others can understand, listen actively, observe critically

**Decision Making** Solve problems and make decisions

**Interpersonal** Cooperate with others, advocate and influence, resolve conflict and negotiate, guide others

**Lifelong Learning** Take responsibility for learning, reflect and evaluate, learn through research, use information and communications technology (optional)

## Pre-assessment (optional)   ■■■

Use the Stand Out Assessment CD-ROM with ExamView® to create a pre-test for Unit 8.

## Warm-up and Review   5–10 mins. ■■■

Write the goal of this lesson on the board: *Identify requirements for establishing residency and citizenship.* Ask students to come up with a list of vocabulary from the previous lesson that would fit into this goal. Have them work with a small group to define each word on their lists.

## Introduction   10–15 mins. ■■■

Dictation:

1. Their entire family applied to become permanent residents three years ago.
2. His employer likes him so much that he filed a visa petition so Joe could stay here to work.
3. We are still waiting to hear if our application has been approved.
4. Now that he has been a resident for five years, he is applying for citizenship.

State the goal: *Today, we will be identifying requirements for establishing residency and citizenship.*

## Presentation 1   10–15 mins. ■■■

**A. How can an immigrant become a permanent resident of the United States? Make a list of your ideas below.**

Have students work in small groups to discuss the questions and then write all their ideas on the board. Don't comment on students' discussions at this stage.

## Practice 1   5–10 mins. ■■■

**B. PREDICT Several students in Mrs. Morgan's class want to become permanent residents of the United States. Read about each nonresident below and decide if you think he or she is eligible to become a permanent resident. Write *yes* or *no*.**

Tell students they will just be making guesses based on what they think they know.

## Evaluation 1   5–10 mins. ■■■

Have students discuss their answers with a partner and see if they can come to a consensus. The real answers will be revealed in the next practice.

## Presentation 2
15–20 mins. ■■■

**C. Read the following information found on the U.S. Citizenship and Immigration Services website (www.uscis.gov).**

Have students read silently to themselves. Then, go over each section together, making sure students completely understand the eligibility requirements.

**Note:** If you have Internet access in your classroom and students want to get more detailed information, have them go to the USCIS website.

## Practice 2
10–15 mins. ■■

**Note:** Shorter classes may want to do this exercise for homework. Students may work individually.

**D. EVALUATE Look back at each of the nonresidents in Exercise B. Do you need to change some of your answers? Discuss each situation with a partner and decide what specific details would make each person eligible for permanent resident status.**

Do the first one together as a class.

## Evaluation 2
10–15 mins. ■■

Discuss each person. As a class, decide if he or she is eligible. If not, ask what would make him or her eligible.

**BEST PRACTICE**

### Internet searches

Most students are already familiar with how to do general searches on the Internet. If required to do a specific search where the website URL is provided, point out that students have two options. Students may type the website address, for example, *www. uscis.gov* directly into the address bar. In another way, students may type the name (institution or organization), for instance, *U.S. Citizenship and Immigration Services* in the search engine window.

**INSTRUCTOR'S NOTES**

**C.** **Read the following information found on the U.S. Citizenship and Immigration Services website (www.uscis.gov).**

You may be *eligible* to apply for adjustment to permanent resident status if you are already in the United States *and* if one or more of the following categories apply to you.

**Family Member** 1. You are the spouse, parent, unmarried child under age 21, the unmarried son or daughter over age 21, the married son or daughter, or the brother or sister of a United States citizen and have a visa petition approved on your behalf. 2. You are the spouse or unmarried son or daughter of any age of a lawful permanent resident and you have a family-based visa petition approved on your behalf.

**Employment** You are an alien who has an approved visa petition filed on your behalf by a United States employer.

**Fiancé** You were a fiancé who was admitted to the United States on a K-1 visa and then married the U.S. citizen *who applied for the K-1 visa for you*. Your unmarried, minor children are also eligible for adjustment of status. If you did not marry the U.S. citizen who filed the K-1 petition on your behalf, or if you married another U.S. citizen or lawful permanent resident, you are not eligible to adjust status in the United States.

**Asylee** You are an asylee or refugee who has been in the United States for at least a year after being given asylum or refugee status and still qualify for asylum or refugee status.

**Diversity Visa** You received notice from the Department of State that you have won a visa in the Diversity Visa Lottery.

**U.S. Resident Since Before 01/01/72** You have been a continuous resident of the United States since before January 1, 1972.

**Parent's Lawful Permanent Resident (LPR) Status** Your parent became a lawful permanent resident after you were born. You may be eligible to receive following-to-join benefits if you are the unmarried child under age 21 of the lawful permanent resident. In these cases, you may apply to adjust to permanent resident status at the same time that your parent applies for following-to-join benefits for you.

**Spouse's LPR Status** Your spouse became a lawful permanent resident after you were married. You may be eligible to receive following-to-join benefits. In these cases, you may apply to adjust to permanent resident status at the same time that your spouse applies for following-to-join benefits for you.

**D.** **EVALUATE** **Look back at each of the nonresidents in Exercise B. Do you need to change some of your answers? Discuss each situation with a partner and decide what specific details would make each person eligible for permanent resident status.**

Answers may vary. Sample answers given.

1. No, if her fiancé did not apply for a K-1 visa for her.
2. No, he needs to have been here for at least one year.
3. Yes, if she is unmarried. She is the daughter of a permanent resident.
4. Yes, he has been a continuous U.S. resident since before 01/01/72.
5. Yes, he may be eligible to receive "following-to-join" benefits.

WORKPLACE CONNECTION
Exercise E: Complete tasks as assigned.
Exercise F: Interact appropriately with team members.
Exercise G: Combine ideas and information.

**E.** **Listen to the talk about how to become a citizen. Fill in the missing words.**

CD
TR 34

United States (U.S.) citizenship carries many _____responsibilities_____ with it. The decision to become a U.S. citizen is a very important one. Being granted U.S. citizenship is known as _____naturalization_____. In most cases, a person who wants to naturalize must first be a _____permanent_____ resident. By becoming a U.S. citizen, you gain many _____rights_____ that permanent residents or others do not have, including the _____right to vote_____. To be eligible for naturalization, you must first meet certain _____requirements_____ set by U.S. law.

**What are the basic requirements to apply for naturalization?**

Generally, to be eligible for naturalization you must:

• Be age _____18_____ or older; and
• Be a permanent resident for a certain amount of time (usually five years); and
• Be a person of good _____moral_____ character; and
• Have a basic knowledge of U.S. _____history_____ and government; and
• Have a period of _____continuous_____ residence and physical presence in the U.S.; and
• Be able to read, _____write_____, and speak basic English. There are exceptions to this rule for someone who:
  – Is _____55_____ years old and has been a permanent resident for at least 15 years; or
  – Is _____50_____ years old and has been a permanent resident for at least 20 years; or
  – Has a physical or mental impairment that makes them unable to _____fulfill_____ these requirements.

**When can I apply for naturalization?**

You may be able to apply for naturalization if you are at least 18 years of age and have been a permanent resident of the U.S.:

• For at least _____5_____ years; or
• For at least _____3_____ years during which time you have been, and continue to be, married to and living in marriage with your U.S. citizen husband or wife; or
• Have honorable service in the U.S. military. Certain _____spouses_____ of U.S. citizens and members of the military may be able to file for naturalization sooner than noted above previously.

**F.** **ANALYZE How many requirements are there to apply for naturalization? What are they? Discuss with a partner.** Six main requirements with three exceptions. (See document in Exercise E.)

**G.** **Do you know people who have become permanent residents or citizens? Write short paragraphs about them on a separate piece of paper.**

## Presentation 3

5–10 mins. ■ ■ ■

Have students briefly read through the information in Exercise E. Have them guess at the missing words.

## Practice 3

15–20 mins. ■

### E. Listen to the talk about how to become a citizen. Fill in the missing words.

Play the recording once. Have students share their answers with a partner. If students are able to come up with most of the answers in pairs, go on to the evaluation. If you think your students need to hear the recording one more time, play it again and have them continue to share with their partners until they have most of the blanks filled in.

---

### LISTENING SCRIPT

CD
TR 34

*United States (U.S.) citizenship carries many responsibilities with it. The decision to become a U.S. citizen is a very important one. Being granted U.S. citizenship is known as naturalization. In most cases, a person who wants to naturalize must first be a permanent resident. By becoming a U.S. citizen, you gain many rights that permanent residents or others do not have, including the right to vote. To be eligible for naturalization, you must first meet certain requirements set by U.S. law.*

*What are the basic requirements to apply for naturalization?*

*Generally, to be eligible for naturalization you must:*

- *Be age 18 or older; and*
- *Be a permanent resident for a certain amount of time (usually 5 years); and*
- *Be a person of good moral character; and*
- *Have a basic knowledge of U.S. history and government; and*
- *Have a period of continuous residence and physical presence in the U.S.; and*
- *Be able to read, write, and speak basic English. There are exceptions to this rule for someone who:*
  - *Is 55 years old and has been a permanent resident for at least 15 years; or*
  - *Is 50 years old and has been a permanent resident for at least 20 years; or*
  - *Has a physical or mental impairment that makes them unable to fulfill these requirements.*

---

*When can I apply for naturalization?*
*You may be able to apply for naturalization if you are at least 18 years of age and have been a permanent resident of the U.S.:*

- *For at least 5 years; or*
- *For at least 3 years during which time you have been, and continue to be, married to and living in marriage with your U.S. citizen husband or wife; or*
- *Have honorable service in the U.S. military. Certain spouses of U.S. citizens and members of the military may be able to file for naturalization sooner than noted above previously.*

## Evaluation 3

5–10 mins. ■

Go over the answers as a class.

### F. ANALYZE How many requirements are there to apply for naturalization? What are they? Discuss with a partner.

## Application

10–20 mins. ■ ■ ■

### G. Do you know people who have become permanent residents or citizens? Write short paragraphs about them on a separate piece of paper.

If students are comfortable sharing, ask volunteers to read their short paragraphs out loud.

### MULTILEVEL WORKSHEETS

Unit 8, Lesson 1, Worksheet 1: Can you become a resident? (listening)
**PDF Documents**
Citizenship Flash Cards
Citizenship Answers
Citizenship Questions

**Refer students to *Stand Out 5 Workbook*, Unit 8, Lesson 1 for practice with articles: *a, an,* and *the*.**

**Go to the *Activity Bank* online for suggestions on promoting digital literacy and using the Internet to enhance this lesson.**

**Goal:** Understand your rights
**Academic Strategy:** Paraphrasing
**Vocabulary:** *entitled, just, establishment, abridge, peaceably assemble, bear arms, quartered, seizure, capital crime, indictment, impartial, trial by jury, bail, fines, excessive, cruel, punishment, slavery, involuntary servitude*

## Agenda

- Read the Bill of Rights.
- Paraphrase amendments.
- Create a Bill of Rights for a school or classroom.

## Resources

**Multilevel Worksheets:** Unit 8, Lesson 2, Worksheets 1–2
**Workbook:** Unit 8, Lesson 2

## Pacing

- 1.5 hour classes
- 2.5 hour classes
- 3+ hour classes

## STANDARDS CORRELATIONS

*CCRS:* RI1, RI2, RI4, RI10, SL1

*CASAS:* 5.2.2, 5.3.2

*SCANS:* **Information** Acquire and evaluate information, organize and maintain information, interpret and communicate information, use computers to process information (optional)

**Interpersonal** Participate as a member of a team, teach others, exercise leadership, negotiate to arrive at a decision, work with cultural diversity

**Systems** Monitor and correct performance, improve and design systems

**Technology** Apply technology to a task (optional)

**Basic Skills** Reading, writing, listening, speaking

**Thinking Skills** Think creatively, make decisions, solve problems, see things in the mind's eye

**Personal Qualities** Responsibility, sociability, self-management

*EFF:* **Communication** Read with understanding, convey ideas in writing, speak so others can understand, listen actively, observe critically

**Decision Making** Solve problems and make decisions, plan

**Interpersonal** Cooperate with others, advocate and influence, resolve conflict and negotiate, guide others

**Lifelong Learning** Take responsibility for learning, reflect and evaluate, learn through research

## Warm-up and Review          10–15 mins. ■■■

Ask students to write down what they can remember about becoming a resident or a citizen without looking back in their books. When they have finished, ask students to pair up with one or two students who wrote about the same topic. See if they can add anything to their notes. Then, have them look back in their books for more clarification.

## Introduction          15–20 mins. ■■■

Dictation: Quotes about civil rights by famous Americans

1. It was we, the people; not we, the white male citizens; nor yet we, the male citizens; but we, the whole people, who formed the Union. (Susan B. Anthony)
2. Freedom and the power to choose should not be the privilege of wealth. They are the birthright of every American. (George Herbert Walker Bush)
3. If we don't believe in freedom of expression for people we despise, we don't believe in it at all. (Noam Chomsky)
4. Honest difference of views and honest debate are not disunity. They are the vital process of policy among free men. (Herbert Hoover)

State the goal: *Today, we will identify the rights of U.S. citizens by interpreting some of the amendments of the Constitution.*

## Presentation 1          10–15 mins. ■■■

Write *Bill of Rights* on the board and draw students' attention to the amendments listed in Exercise A. Explain that the Bill of Rights is the name for the first ten amendments to the United States Constitution. In other words, it is a list of the highest laws in the country that everyone must obey.

## Practice 1          15–25 mins. ■■■

A. **SUMMARIZE** **In 1791, the Bill of Rights was added to the United States Constitution. Read and paraphrase the first 10 amendments.**

Explain to students that this exercise may be very difficult. The wording of each amendment is from the original document so encourage students to look for key words rather than to try to understand every word.

## Evaluation 1          10–15 mins. ■■■

Go over the answers as a class.

# LESSON ② Rights

GOAL ■ Understand your rights

**A. SUMMARIZE** In 1791, the Bill of Rights was added to the United States Constitution. Read and paraphrase the first 10 amendments.

**Amendment I** Congress shall make no law respecting an establishment of religion, or prohibiting the free exercise thereof; or abridging the freedom of speech, or of the press; or the right of the people peaceably to assemble, and to petition the government for a redress of grievances.

**Amendment II** A well regulated militia, being necessary to the security of a free state, the right of the people to keep and bear arms, shall not be infringed.

**Amendment III** No soldier shall, in time of peace be quartered in any house, without the consent of the owner, nor in time of war, but in a manner to be prescribed by law.

**Amendment IV** The right of the people to be secure in their persons, houses, papers, and effects, against unreasonable searches and seizures, shall not be violated, and no warrants shall issue, but upon probable cause, supported by oath or affirmation, and particularly describing the place to be searched, and the persons or things to be seized.

**Amendment V** No person shall be held to answer for a capital, or otherwise infamous crime, unless on a presentment or indictment of a grand jury, except in cases arising in the land or naval forces, or in the militia, when in actual service in time of war or public danger; nor shall any person be subject for the same offense to be twice put in jeopardy of life or limb; nor shall be compelled in any criminal case to be a witness against himself, nor be deprived of life, liberty, or property, without due process of law; nor shall private property be taken for public use, without just compensation.

**Amendment VI** In all criminal prosecutions, the accused shall enjoy the right to a speedy and public trial, by an impartial jury of the state and district wherein the crime shall have been committed, which district shall have been previously ascertained by law, and to be informed of the nature and cause of the accusation; to be confronted with the witnesses against him; to have compulsory process for obtaining witnesses in his favor, and to have the assistance of counsel for his defense.

**Amendment VII** In suits at common law, where the value in controversy shall exceed twenty dollars, the right of trial by jury shall be preserved, and no fact tried by a jury, shall be otherwise reexamined in any court of the United States, than according to the rules of the common law.

**Amendment VIII** Excessive bail shall not be required, nor excessive fines imposed, nor cruel and unusual punishments inflicted.

**Amendment IX** The enumeration in the Constitution, of certain rights, shall not be construed to deny or disparage others retained by the people.

**Amendment X** The powers not delegated to the United States by the Constitution, nor prohibited by it to the states, are reserved to the states respectively, or to the people.

**B. Match each amendment with the right it guarantees.**

1. The first amendment guarantees ___d___.

2. The second amendment guarantees ___f___.

3. The third amendment guarantees ___h___.

4. The fourth amendment guarantees ___e___.

5. The fifth amendment guarantees ___b___.

6. The sixth amendment guarantees ___a___.

7. The seventh amendment guarantees ___i___.

8. The eighth amendment guarantees ___j___.

9. The ninth amendment guarantees ___c___.

10. The tenth amendment guarantees ___g___.

a. a speedy and public trial by an impartial jury

b. the right to be charged by a grand jury if accused of a serious crime

c. people have other rights not listed in the Bill of Rights

d. freedom of religion

e. people, homes, and belongings are protected from unreasonable search and seizure

f. right to keep and bear arms

g. people have all the rights not given to the government by the Constitution

h. that government cannot force people to house soldiers during times of peace

i. a trial by jury in civil cases (dispute between private parties or between the government and a private party)

j. no excessive bail or fines will be imposed and that punishment will not be cruel and unusual

**C. DETERMINE Read each situation. Then, decide which amendment describes your rights. Write the amendment numbers on the lines.**

1. Your friend is Christian and celebrates Easter, but you are Jewish. ___First (I)___

2. You have a registered gun in your house, locked up in a safe. ___Second (II)___

3. The police can't come into your home without a warrant. ___Fourth (IV)___

4. If you are convicted of a crime, your punishment will not be cruel. ___Eighth (VIII)___

5. If you are accused of a crime, you will get a fair trial. ___Fifth (V)___

## Presentation 2      10–15 mins. ■■■

**B. Match each amendment with the right it guarantees.**

If you think students can do this exercise by themselves, have them try it first before you do it together. This is another opportunity for you to explain the amendments in the Bill of Rights.

## Practice 2      5–10 mins. ■■

**Note:** Shorter classes can do this exercise for homework.

**C. DETERMINE** **Read each situation. Then, decide which amendment describes your rights. Write the amendment numbers on the lines.**

## Evaluation 2      5 mins. ■■

Go over the answers as a class.

### BEST PRACTICE

## The Bill of Rights (simplified)

As mentioned before, the wording of the amendments in the Bill of Rights may be challenging to read and comprehend. Provide a simplified version and/or explain each amendment if necessary.

1. You are guaranteed freedom of religion, speech, press, and the right to gather peacefully to ask the government to change something.
2. You have the right to have and carry weapons.
3. You don't have to let soldiers live in your home, except in time of war, and the government has to pass a law requesting this beforehand.
4. No one can search you or your home unless they can prove to a judge that there is good reason.
5. You are guaranteed a fair trial for any crime.
6. If arrested for a crime, you have the right to know what you are accused of and will be judged publicly.
7. You have a right to a jury.
8. The government can only make you pay reasonable fines or bail and the government can not punish you in a cruel or unusual way.
9. You have rights other than those listed in the Constitution.
10. What is not stated in the Constitution is left in the hands of the state and the people.

### INSTRUCTOR'S NOTES

## Presentation 3

Go over the amendments together and then have students answer the questions by themselves.

## Practice 3

15–20 mins. ■

**Note:** Shorter classes can do this exercise for homework.

**D. INTERPRET There is currently a total of 27 amendments to the Constitution. Read about four of the amendments and answer the questions that follow.**

## Evaluation 3

5–10 mins. ■

Go over the answers as a class.

**E. ANALYZE Discuss the following in a small group.**

Do any of the rights identified in this lesson affect your life? Which ones? In what ways?

## Application

10–20 mins. ■■■

**F. Create a Bill of Rights for your classroom or school.**

Put students in small groups or have students work as one large group. You may need to help students get started by brainstorming one or two ideas.

**Optional Computer Activity:** Have students create their Bill of Rights on the computer.

### MULTILEVEL WORKSHEETS

Unit 8, Lesson 2, Worksheet 1: Quotes from Famous People

Unit 8, Lesson 2, Worksheet 2: Thomas Jefferson and the Bill of Rights

**Refer students to *Stand Out 5 Workbook*, Unit 8, Lesson 2 for practice with using definite articles vs. nothing.**

**Go to the *Activity Bank* online for suggestions on promoting digital literacy and using the Internet to enhance this lesson.**

### INSTRUCTOR'S NOTES

WORKPLACE CONNECTION
Exercise D: Interpret and communicate information.
Exercise E: Interact appropriately with team members.
Exercise F: Combine ideas and information.

**D. INTERPRET** There is currently a total of 27 amendments to the Constitution. Read about four of the amendments and answer the questions that follow.

*Answers will vary. Sample answers given.*

**Amendment XIII (1865)**

Neither slavery nor involuntary servitude, except as a punishment for crime whereof the party shall have been duly convicted, shall exist within the United States, or any place subject to their jurisdiction.

**Amendment XV (1870)**

The right of citizens of the United States to vote shall not be denied or abridged by the United States or by any state on account of race, color, or previous condition of servitude.

**Amendment XIX (1920)**

The right of citizens of the United States to vote shall not be denied or abridged by the United States or by any state on account of sex.

**Amendment XXVI (1971)**

The right of citizens of the United States, who are 18 years of age or older, to vote, shall not be denied or abridged by the United States or any state on account of age.

1. What does the thirteenth amendment guarantee? *Slavery is illegal.*

2. The fifteenth, nineteenth, and twenty-sixth amendments are all about the same right.

   What is it? *the right to vote*

3. What is the difference between these three amendments?

   *The 15ᵗʰ prevents discrimination in voting because of race, the 19ᵗʰ prevents voting discrimination based on gender, and the 26ᵗʰ gives the voting right to citizens 18 years old and older.*

4. In the original Constitution, why do you think so many groups of people were not given the

   right to vote? *Women and people of color were not allowed to vote formerly because they weren't considered legally responsible people.*

**E. ANALYZE** Discuss the following in a small group. *Answers will vary.*

Do any of the rights identified in this lesson affect your life? Which ones? In what ways?

**F. Create a Bill of Rights for your classroom or school.** *Answers will vary.*

# LESSON ③ Getting involved

WORKPLACE CONNECTION
Exercise C: Interact appropriately with team members;
Interpret and communicate information.

## A. Read about civic organizations.

A civic organization is a group of people who come together for educational or charitable purposes, including the promotion of community welfare. The money generated by these clubs is devoted exclusively to charitable, educational, recreational, or social welfare purposes.

## B. Read about a civic organization.

### The Mothers' Club of Northville, Michigan

The Mothers' Club is a group of 35 dynamic women working to help Northville school children excel by providing enrichment materials and opportunities.

**History**

In 1935, a group of 12 women decided to meet regularly for enlightenment and social activities. During the Depression of the 1930s, the Mothers' Club held a fundraiser to purchase milk for schoolchildren to drink with their lunches. The Club's fundraising has now grown to three events each year, enabling the Club to donate approximately $30,000 annually to student enrichment programs and activities.

**Fundraising**

A. Fall: The Mothers' Club hosts a booth during Northville's Victorian Festival.

B. Winter: *All Aglow* is an opportunity to honor or remember someone by purchasing a light on the community Christmas tree, located in front of the bandshell in downtown Northville.

C. Spring: *Hands to the Future*, a dinner and auction held annually in March, alternates every other year with *The Community Telephone Directory*, distributed biannually to every household in the Northville School District.

**Community Service**

The Mothers' Club performs service projects at the public school buildings on a rotating cycle, working at two or three schools each year.

**Social**

1. Book club
2. Lunch and movie afternoons
3. Evening socials
4. Weekend getaways

## C. Answer the following questions with a partner. Share your answers with others in your class. Answers will vary. Sample answers are given.

1. What makes the Mothers' Club a civic organization? They perform charitable tasks in the community.

2. What civic organizations are there in your community? Boy and Girl Scouts, Rotary Clubs, Lions, Elks, Odd Fellow, Knights of Columbus Clubs

# AT-A-GLANCE PREP

**Goal:** Identify local civic organizations
**Vocabulary:** *civic, charitable, social welfare*

## Agenda

- Read about the Mothers' Club of Northville, MI.
- Read about and discuss civic organizations.
- Create a civic organization.

## Resources

**Multilevel Worksheet:** Unit 8, Lesson 3, Worksheet 1
**Workbook:** Unit 8, Lesson 3

## Pacing

- 1.5 hour classes
- 2.5 hour classes
- 3+ hour classes

## STANDARDS CORRELATIONS

*CCRS:* RI1, SL1

*CASAS:* 5.6.2

*SCANS:* **Resources** Allocate time, allocate materials and facility resources, allocate human resources

**Information** Acquire and evaluate information, organize and maintain information, interpret and communicate information

**Interpersonal** Participate as a member of a team, teach others, exercise leadership, negotiate to arrive at a decision, work with cultural diversity

**Systems** Monitor and correct performance

**Basic Skills** Reading, writing, arithmetic, listening, speaking

**Thinking Skills** Think creatively, make decisions, solve problems, see things in the mind's eye

**Personal Qualities** Responsibility, sociability, self-management

*EFF:* **Communication** Read with understanding, speak so others can understand, listen actively, observe critically

**Decision Making** Solve problems and make decisions, plan

**Interpersonal** Cooperate with others, advocate and influence, resolve conflict and negotiate, guide others

**Lifelong Learning** Take responsibility for learning

## Warm-up and Review    10–20 mins.

Ask students to take out a piece of paper and number it from 1 to 10. Ask them to write down the ten amendments from the Bill of Rights in their own words. Give them about ten minutes before letting them look in their books.

## Introduction    5–10 mins.

Dictation:

1. We raise money to help low-income schools continue their music and arts programs.
2. Our group conducts environmental awareness seminars in the community.
3. She started a group that brings hot meals to families who have loved ones in the hospital.
4. Every year, we have a live and silent auction to raise scholarship money for high school students.

State the goal: *Today, we will talk about local civic organizations and, by the end of class, you will have created your own organization.*

## Presentation 1    10–15 mins.

### A. Read about civic organizations.

### B. Read about a civic organization.

Have students read about the Mothers' Club. Then, ask them the following questions: What is the name of the organization? What is their purpose? What do they do for community service? How much money do they donate per year? Go over the definition of a civic organization.

## Practice 1    5–10 mins.

### C. Answer the following questions with a partner. Share your answers with others in your class.

## Evaluation 1    5–10 mins.

Go over the answers as a class. Ask pairs to share about civic organizations in their community.

## Presentation 2

5–10 mins. ■■■

Go over the different organizations in Exercise D.

## Practice 2

10–15 mins. ■■

**Note:** Shorter classes can do this exercise for homework.

**D. Read about the civic organizations and answer the questions on the next page.**

## Evaluation 2

10–15 mins. ■■

Go over the answers as a class. Ask a number of students to share their answers to the fifth question on page 210.

**BEST PRACTICE**

### Benefits of joining a civic organization

Joining a civic organization is a good way to become more involved in your community. Some personal benefits are listed below:

1. You will learn more about your own personal goals, strengths, and weaknesses.
2. You will develop your communication skills.
3. You will put into good use anything you have learned in class.
4. You will learn more about team or group work.
5. You will meet people from varied backgrounds.
6. You will have something interesting to add to your resume.
7. You will be able to help your own community.
8. You will probably enjoy the experience.

**INSTRUCTOR'S NOTES**

**D. Read about the civic organizations and answer the questions on the next page.**

 **American Legion**

**Purpose:** To provide care for veterans and their families at hospitals and homes in the community
**Members:** Relatives of veterans
**Annual Dues:** Amounts vary

 **Boy Scouts**

**Purpose:** To promote self-confidence, service to others, citizenship, and outdoor skills
**Members:** Boys only, at least 11 years old
**Volunteer Scoutmasters:** Male and female scoutmasters needed
**Annual Dues:** $24

 **Friends of the Library**

**Purpose:** To promote and support the local public library
**Members:** All welcome
**Annual Dues:** $15

 **Hiking Club**

**Purpose:** To enjoy the outdoors and also help raise public awareness of issues that face the present-day outdoors
**Members:** Anyone who enjoys hiking
**Annual Dues:** $10

 **Garden Club**

**Purpose:** To share experiences in gardening
**Members:** Anyone who enjoys gardening
**Annual Dues:** $15
**Special Events:** Plant sale

 **Rotary Club**

**Purpose:** To provide humanitarian service, encourage high ethical standards in all vocations, and help build goodwill and peace in the world
**Members:** To become a Rotarian, you must be invited to join a Rotary Club by a member of that club. A qualified candidate for Rotary Club membership is an adult of good character and good business, professional, or community reputation.
**Annual Dues:** Amounts vary

WORKPLACE CONNECTION
Exercise E: Interpret and communicate information.
Exercise F: Interact appropriately with team members; Combine ideas and information.

1. Which clubs would you join if you liked nature? _Hiking Club/Garden Club_

2. Which clubs can you join if you are a woman? _All of the clubs. Of special interest might be_
   _American Legion and Garden Clubs._

3. Of those which have them, which club has the highest dues? _Boy Scouts_
   The lowest? _Hiking Club_

4. Which clubs provide community service? _All of them, but Boy Scouts and Rotary Club in particular._

5. If you could join one club, which one would it be? _Answers will vary._
   Why? _____

**E.** **Some of the students from Mrs. Morgan's class want to create a civic organization. They have come together because they have common interests. Read about the students below and then come up with ideas for their organization.** _Answers will vary._

> Hanh, Sadiq, Ella, Phillipe, and Enrique have just found out that many students at their school can't afford to buy books. There are over 100 students a year who attend class without textbooks. Hanh, Sadiq, Ella, Phillipe, and Enrique have one thing in common—they are all very creative. Sadiq takes beautiful photographs, Hanh and Ella both knit; they can make anything from hats to sweaters and blankets, Phillipe is an accomplished musician and songwriter, and Enrique paints oil paintings of flowers and animals.

Name of civic organization: _____

Purpose: _____

Members: _____

Annual dues: _____

Special events: _____

**F.** **CREATE** **Follow the directions for creating a civic organization.**

**Step 1.** Get together with a few students from your class and create a new civic organization. Complete the information about your organization below.

- Name of civic organization
- Purpose
- Members
- Annual dues
- Special events

**Step 2.** Recruit members for your organization. You need at least ten members to be a true organization.

## Presentation 3       5–10 mins. ■■■

Go over the instructions and scenario in Exercise E with the class. Then, put them into groups or have them select their own groups to complete the exercise.

## Practice 3       15–20 mins. ■

**Note:** Shorter classes can do this exercise for homework.

**E.** **Some of the students from Mrs. Morgan's class want to create a civic organization. They have come together because they have common interests. Read about the students below and then come up with ideas for their organization.**

## Evaluation 3       10–15 mins. ■

Ask each group to present its organization to the class.

## Application       10–20 mins. ■■■

**F.** **CREATE** **Follow the directions for creating a civic organization.**

**Step 1. Get together with a few students from your class and create a new civic organization. Complete the information about your organization below.**

**Step 2. Recruit members for your organization. You need at least ten members to be a true organization.**

Have students walk around the classroom and tell other students about their organization. Then, have them write down any students that want to join. Tell them they can be seated when they have at least ten members.

### MULTILEVEL WORKSHEET

Unit 8, Lesson 3, Worksheet 1: Civic Organizations

**Refer students to _Stand Out 5 Workbook_, Unit 8, Lesson 3 for more practice with _the_ and demonstrative determiners.**

**Go to the _Activity Bank_ online for suggestions on promoting digital literacy and using the Internet to enhance this lesson.**

### INSTRUCTOR'S NOTES

**Goal:** Interpret information about environmental issues

**Academic Strategies:** Reading for understanding, brainstorming

**Vocabulary:** *sufficient, reusable, commuters, auto emissions*

## Agenda

- Find out how to create less trash.
- Interview a partner about conserving energy.
- Read about SEQL's action item.
- Brainstorm community programs.
- Develop a program.

## Resources

**Multilevel Worksheet:** Unit 8, Lesson 4, Worksheet 1 and PDFs

**Workbook:** Unit 8, Lesson 4

## Pacing

- 1.5 hour classes
- 2.5 hour classes
- 3+ hour classes

## STANDARDS CORRELATIONS

*CCRS:* RI1, RI4, SL1

*CASAS:* 5.7.1

*SCANS:* **Resources** Allocate time, allocate money, allocate materials and facility resources, allocate human resources

**Information** Acquire and evaluate information, organize and maintain information, interpret and communicate information

**Interpersonal** Participate as a member of a team, teach others, exercise leadership, negotiate to arrive at a decision, work with cultural diversity

**Systems** Understand systems, monitor and correct performance, improve and design systems

**Basic Skills** Reading, writing, arithmetic, listening, speaking

**Thinking Skills** Think creatively, make decisions, solve problems, see things in the mind's eye

**Personal Qualities** Responsibility, sociability, self-management

*EFF:* **Communication** Read with understanding, convey ideas in writing, speak so others can understand, listen actively, observe critically

**Decision Making** Solve problems and make decisions, plan

**Interpersonal** Cooperate with others, advocate and influence, resolve conflict and negotiate, guide others

**Lifelong Learning** Take responsibility for learning, reflect and evaluate, learn through research

## Warm-up and Review          10–15 mins. ■■■

Ask volunteers to present their civic organization to the class and list the ten members who they recruited in the previous lesson.

## Introduction          5–10 mins. ■■■

Dictation:

1. Learn about alternatives to household cleaning items that do not use hazardous chemicals.
2. Take your car to a car wash instead of washing it in the driveway.
3. Use an electric-powered lawn mower instead of a gas-powered one.
4. Turn off lights, computers, and other appliances when not in use.

When you have finished the dictation, ask students how following each of these suggestions would help the environment.

State the goal: *Today, we will talk about ways to save the environment and create an action plan for something you can do in this community.*

## Presentation 1          10–15 mins. ■■■

A. **EVALUATE  Look at the list of ways to create less trash. Which ones do you do? Put a check (✓) next to them.**

Go over each item as a class and have students put checks next to the ones they do. If there are certain items that most students don't do, ask them why. Try to come up with some ways that would make it easier to follow some of the suggestions.

## Practice 1          10–15 mins. ■■■

B. **Interview your partner to find out how he or she conserves energy at home. Put a check (✓) next to the ones he or she does.**

## Evaluation 1          5–10 mins. ■■■

Have each pair sit down once they've finished their interview and discuss the ways that they conserve energy. Have them come up with some suggestions on how to do more of the items on the list.

There is a list of one hundred ways to save the environment on the Multilevel Worksheets CD-ROM.

GOAL ■ Interpret information about environmental issues

WORKPLACE CONNECTION
Exercise A: Complete tasks as assigned.
Exercise B: Interact appropriately with team members.

**A. EVALUATE** **Look at the list of ways to create less trash. Which ones do you do? Put a check (✓) next to them.** Answers will vary.

- ☐ Buy items in bulk from loose bins when possible to reduce the packaging wasted.
- ☐ Avoid products with several layers of packaging when only one is sufficient.
- ☐ Buy products that you can reuse.
- ☐ Maintain and repair durable products instead of buying new ones.
- ☐ Check reports for products that are easily repaired and have low breakdown rates.
- ☐ Reuse items like bags and containers when possible.
- ☐ Use cloth napkins instead of paper ones.
- ☐ Use reusable plates and utensils instead of disposable ones.
- ☐ Use reusable containers to store food instead of aluminum foil and cling wrap.
- ☐ Shop with a canvas bag instead of using paper and plastic bags.
- ☐ Buy rechargeable batteries for devices used frequently.
- ☐ Reuse packaging cartons and shipping materials. Old newspapers make great packaging material.
- ☐ Buy used furniture—there is a surplus of it, and it is much cheaper than new furniture.

**B.** **Interview your partner to find out how he or she conserves energy at home. Put a check (✓) next to the ones he or she does.** Answers will vary.

- ☐ Clean or replace air filters on your air-conditioning unit at least once a month.
- ☐ Lower the thermostat on your water heater to 120°F.
- ☐ Wrap your water heater in an insulated blanket.
- ☐ Turn down or shut off your water heater when you will be away for extended periods.
- ☐ Turn off unneeded lights even when leaving a room for a short time.
- ☐ Set your refrigerator temperature at 36 to 38°F and your freezer at 0 to 5°F.
- ☐ When using an oven, minimize door opening while it is in use.
- ☐ Clean the lint filter in your dryer after every load so that it uses less energy.
- ☐ Unplug seldom-used appliances.
- ☐ Use a microwave whenever you can instead of a conventional oven or stove.
- ☐ Wash clothes with warm or cold water instead of hot.
- ☐ Turn off lights, computers, and other appliances when not in use.
- ☐ Use compact fluorescent lightbulbs to save money and energy.
- ☐ Keep your thermostat at 68°F in winter and 78°F in summer.
- ☐ Use cold water instead of warm or hot water when possible.
- ☐ Connect your outdoor lights to a timer.

**C.** Sustainable Environment for Quality of Life (SEQL) has put together several action items that they would like to see accomplished in their communities in North and South Carolina. Read their plan for carpooling.

### Carpooling: What is it?

Vanpooling/carpooling is an arrangement by a group of commuters to ride together from home or a prearranged meeting place in a van or a car to their destinations in a single round trip, with the driver as a fellow commuter. Vanpools/carpools usually consist of individuals who live near each other and are employees of the same company, or are employees of different companies located only a short distance apart, and have the same work hours. The great advantage of vanpools and carpools is that it reduces vehicle trips, reduces vehicle miles traveled, and therefore reduces auto emissions that result in poor air quality.

#### Shared Impact and Benefits

- Car- and vanpooling reduce overall auto emissions by reducing vehicle miles traveled, and by doing so, improve air quality.
- Peak-hour traffic congestion (and resulting gasoline consumption) are reduced. Nine billion gallons of fuel are wasted in traffic congestion each year.
- Employers will be able to offer employees a value-added benefit and take a tax write-off.
- Eight of ten U.S. workers believe commuter benefits are valuable to employees.
- Furthermore, employers that pay for employee parking costs can save money.
- Vanpool/carpool participants save money by sharing commuting costs.
- Vanpool/carpool riders have less stressful commutes to work. Employers will also have more productive employees with higher morale.

#### Costs

Usually vanpoolers/carpoolers will share the costs of gasoline, maintenance, and/or leasing the vehicles.

#### How long does this take to implement?

A vanpooling/carpooling program can be implemented within a few months. Once the program is established, individual pools can be set up in less than a few weeks.

#### The Bottom Line

Carpooling and vanpooling commuters get to work in ways that reduce air pollution and traffic congestion, save employers and employees money, reduce the environmental impacts associated with driving single-passenger vehicles, reduce parking space demand and expenses, and relieve commuter stress.

#### Who needs to be involved?

- Governing board and/or management (to endorse a vanpool/carpool policy and support a program that provides incentives for employees who participate in a vanpool or carpool)
- Businesses and their human resource or fiscal office staff
- Transit providers and/or private vanpool leasing companies
- Private parking deck and lot owners
- Employees willing to start up their own vanpool or carpool

## Presentation 2

5–10 mins. ■■■

Write the word *carpooling* on the board and ask the following questions:

1. What is carpooling?
2. What are some examples of places you can carpool to?
3. Are there special lanes on the highways here for people who carpool?
4. Are there special parking places for people who carpool?
5. Do you think carpooling is a good idea? Why or why not?

Go over the instructions for Exercise C.

## Practice 2

10–15 mins. ■■

**Note:** Shorter classes can do this exercise for homework.

C. **Sustainable Environment for Quality of Life (SEQL) has put together several action items that they would like to see accomplished in their communities in North and South Carolina. Read their plan for carpooling.**

## Evaluation 2

10–15 mins. ■■

In the Multilevel Worksheets, there is a worksheet related to this reading that you can give students to see if they have understood what they've read. You can also do an oral evaluation by asking the following questions:

1. *Why is carpooling good?* (reduces vehicle trips and miles traveled, which, in turn, reduces auto emissions)
2. *How can people who carpool save money?* (spend less on gas, auto maintenance, and parking)
3. *How long would it take to implement a carpooling program?* (a few months)
4. *Name two groups of people who need to be involved in the carpooling plan.* (businesses, transit providers, private parking lot owners, employees)

### MULTILEVEL WORKSHEET

Unit 8, Lesson 4, Worksheet 1: Carpooling

### BEST PRACTICE

## Oral evaluation

A quick way to see if students have understood something they have read is to ask questions and have students answer. The only problem with this method is that your more vocal students will answer all the questions. A quick way to see if everyone has understood the text is to ask students to take out a sheet of paper and number it for the number of questions you will ask. Then, ask questions and have students write their answers. Then, collect students' papers, have students check their own answers, or have them exchange their papers with a partner.

### INSTRUCTOR'S NOTES

## Presentation 3

5 mins. ■■■

Go over the instructions for Exercise D and put students in pairs.

**Definitions of Topics:**

*Improving air quality:* making the air we breathe healthier

*Protecting water resources:* making sure we don't use up so much water that we have a water shortage

*Creating sustainable development:* making sure we're not taking too many resources from the earth while allowing people to meet basic needs and enjoy a good quality of life without compromising the quality of life for future generations (should be socially desirable, ecologically viable, economically feasible).

## Practice 3

15–20 mins. ■

**Note:** Shorter classes can do this exercise individually for homework.

D. **Working with a partner, choose one of the following three environmental topics. Come up with a list of programs that might work to improve the environment in your community.**

## Evaluation 3

5–10 mins. ■

Write each of the three topics on the board. Ask students to share some of the ideas they came up with.

## Application

10–20 mins. ■■■

Help students get into teams of four and explain what they will be doing. Point out that they will be coming up with information similar to that found on page 212. If possible, allow students to do research. If not, tell them to come up with information that they think is accurate.

E. **DETERMINE Find another pair of students who chose the same topic as you. Work together and share your ideas. Then, choose one program to develop. Think about and decide on the following items.**

Have each team present its program to the class.

### MULTILEVEL WORKSHEETS

Unit 8, Lesson 4, PDFs:

100 Ways to Save the Environment (PDF)

*Kids Can Do* Bookmark

Refer students to *Stand Out 5 Workbook,* **Unit 8, Lesson 4 for practice with demonstrative determiners and pronouns.**

**Go to the *Activity Bank* online for suggestions on promoting digital literacy and using the Internet to enhance this lesson.**

### INSTRUCTOR'S NOTES

WORKPLACE CONNECTION
Exercises D, E: Interact appropriately with team members.
Exercise E: Combine ideas and information.

**D.** Working with a partner, choose one of the following three environmental topics. Come up with a list of programs that might work to improve the environment in your community.

air quality                water resources                sustainable development

Answers will vary.

**Topic:** _____

**Possible programs:** _____

_____

_____

_____

**E.** DETERMINE  Find another pair of students who chose the same topic as you. Work together and share your ideas. Then, choose one program to develop. Think about and decide on the following items.  Answers will vary.

Topic: _____

Name of program: _____

Brief description of how the program works: _____

_____

_____

_____

Impact on and benefit to the environment: _____

_____

_____

Length of time to implement: _____

Cost: _____

People involved: _____

# LESSON (5) Expressing yourself

WORKPLACE CONNECTION
Exercise A: Complete tasks as assigned.
Exercises A, B: Interact appropriately with team members.

**A.** **BRAINSTORM** Everyone has an opinion when it comes to the environment. In a small group, brainstorm some *yes* and *no* opinions for each of the suggestions below.

Answers will vary. Sample answers are given.

**EXAMPLE:** People should not be permitted to buy large cars that create a lot of pollution.

**Yes:** *If everyone bought smaller cars, pollution would be significantly reduced.*

**No:** *Many people need large cars for their families. Large cars are safer and hold more people and more groceries.*

1. Our city should build more carpool lanes.

| **Yes** | **No** |
|---|---|
| a. This will reduce pollution in the air. | a. These lanes are wasted space. |
| b. _____ | b. _____ |
| c. _____ | c. _____ |

2. Everyone should take their own recyclable items to a recycling center.

| **Yes** | **No** |
|---|---|
| a. All individuals and families should recycle. | a. The government should provide pick-up service. |
| b. _____ | b. _____ |
| c. _____ | c. _____ |

3. Each home should only be allowed to have a certain amount of water each month.

| **Yes** | **No** |
|---|---|
| a. People should be aware of their water use. | a. There should be no limits on water use. |
| b. _____ | b. _____ |
| c. _____ | c. _____ |

**B.** **Practice communicating your opinion to a partner. Use the phrases below.**

| I think . . . | I believe . . . | In my opinion, . . . | I agree. | I disagree. |
|---|---|---|---|---|

**EXAMPLE:** **Student A:** *I think our city should build more carpool lanes.*

**Student B:** *I disagree. In my opinion, it is a waste of money because it won't make more people carpool.*

**Goal:** Communicate your opinion
**Pronunciation:** Express an opinion
**Academic Strategy:** Writing an opinion paragraph
**Vocabulary:** *opinion, protect, conserve, resource*

## Agenda

- Brainstorm opinions.
- Communicate your opinion.
- Read and answer questions about Ella's paragraph on water conservation.
- Use transitional expressions.
- Write a paragraph.

## Resources

**Multilevel Worksheets:** Unit 8, Lesson 5, Worksheets 1–2
**Workbook:** Unit 8, Lesson 5

## Pacing

- 1.5 hour classes
- 2.5 hour classes
- 3+ hour classes

### STANDARDS CORRELATIONS

*CCRS:* RI1, RI5, W1, W4, W5, SL1, L5
*CASAS:* 5.1.6, 5.7.1
*SCANS:* **Information** Acquire and evaluate information, organize and maintain information, interpret and communicate information
**Interpersonal** Participate as a member of a team, teach others, exercise leadership, negotiate to arrive at a decision, work with cultural diversity
**Systems** Understand systems, monitor and correct performance
**Basic Skills** Reading, writing, listening, speaking
**Thinking Skills** Think creatively, make decisions, solve problems, see things in the mind's eye
**Personal Qualities** Responsibility, sociability, self-management
*EFF:* **Communication** Read with understanding, convey ideas in writing, speak so others can understand, listen actively, observe critically
**Decision Making** Solve problems and make decisions, plan
**Interpersonal** Cooperate with others, advocate and influence, resolve conflict and negotiate, guide others
**Lifelong Learning** Take responsibility for learning, reflect and evaluate

## Warm-up and Review     5–10 mins. ■■■

Quickly review each program that students came up with in the previous lesson. Write them on the board. Ask the class to discuss which programs they think are most possible. Vote as a class on the best program.

## Introduction     5–10 mins. ■■■

Dictation:

1. Recycling means taking a product at the end of its useful life and turning it into a usable raw material to make another product.
2. Curbside recycling is the most convenient means for households to recycle a variety of materials.
3. The most commonly recycled items are aluminum cans, glass bottles, paper, plastic, and steel/tin cans.
4. Not all things are recyclable in all areas of the country.

(*Source:* Excerpted from www.earth911.org)

State the goal: *Today, you will practice communicating opinions, verbally and on paper.*

## Presentation 1     10–15 mins. ■■■

Write this on the board: *People shouldn't be allowed to turn on lights from 8 a.m. to 4 p.m.* Ask students if they think this would be a good way to conserve energy. Ask: *Is it realistic? Why or why not?*

Go over the instructions for Exercises A and B.

## Practice 1     10–15 mins. ■■■

A. **BRAINSTORM** **Everyone has an opinion when it comes to the environment. In a small group, brainstorm some *yes* and *no* opinions for each of the suggestions below.**

Review the example together and present the different opinions.

B. **Practice communicating your opinion to a partner. Use the phrases below.**

## Evaluation 1     5 mins. ■■■

Walk around the classroom and help students come up with ideas if necessary.

## Presentation 2
10–15 mins. ■■■

### C. Ella wrote a paragraph communicating her opinion on the environment. Read.

Have students read Ella's paragraph silently and then read it out loud. Tell them this is an opinion paragraph. Ask students what makes it an opinion paragraph. Ask them if they agree with Ella.

## Practice 2
10–15 mins. ■■

**Note:** Shorter classes can do this exercise for homework.

### D. Answer the questions about the sentence types in Ella's paragraph.

## Evaluation 2
10–15 mins. ■■

Go over the answers as a class.

### BEST PRACTICE

## Stating your opinion

Being able to express your opinion is important in any language. It is sometimes challenging for students to come up with the vocabulary to state how they think or feel about something. Some helpful words and expressions to use when expressing opinions are:

I feel . . .
I know . . .
Everyone should . . .
You should . . .
The best _____ is . . .
The worst _____ is . . .
The best part about . . .
_____ is my favorite because . . .
_____ is my least favorite because . . .
Here are my reasons why . . .

### INSTRUCTOR'S NOTES

**C.** **Ella wrote a paragraph communicating her opinion on the environment. Read.**

### Our Most Precious Resource

There are many things we should do to protect our environment, but I think one of the most important things we can do is to conserve water. Why? Water is our most precious resource. I believe this for many reasons. One reason is that the human body is made up of 75% water. We can only live for one week without water; therefore, we need to drink water to survive. Another reason that water is so important is that we need it to clean. We need water to clean our bodies, wash our dishes, flush our toilets, and launder our clothes. Can you imagine not being able to do any of these things? Still another reason is that plants and trees need water to grow and survive. Without plants and trees, humans wouldn't survive because plants give off the oxygen we need in order to breathe. For these reasons, I believe that we need to conserve our most precious resource—water.

**D.** **Answer the questions about the sentence types in Ella's paragraph.**

1. What is Ella's topic sentence?

   Water is our most precious resource.

2. What is Ella's concluding sentence?

   For these reasons, I believe that we need to conserve our most precious resource—water.

3. Ella gives three reasons to support her main idea. For each idea, she gives a supporting detail. What are her reasons and details?

   a. Reason: The human body is 75% water.

   Detail: We can only live one week without water.

   b. Reason: We need water to clean.

   Detail: We clean our bodies, wash dishes, do laundry, and flush toilets.

   c. Reason: Plants and trees need water to grow.

   Detail: We need the oxygen given off by plants to breathe.

WORKPLACE CONNECTION
Exercise F: Collect and organize information.
Exercise G: Complete tasks as assigned.
Exercise H: Combine ideas and information.

**E.** **ANALYZE** Study these transitional expressions with your teacher. Which ones did Ella use in her paragraph?

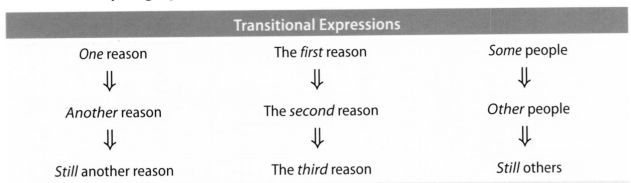

| Transitional Expressions | | |
| --- | --- | --- |
| *One* reason ⇩ *Another* reason ⇩ *Still* another reason | The *first* reason ⇩ The *second* reason ⇩ The *third* reason | *Some* people ⇩ *Other* people ⇩ *Still* others |

- Use these phrases to connect your ideas.
- Choose the set of phrases that works best for your topic.
- Don't shift back and forth among sets of phrases.

**F.** Choose an environmental issue you feel strongly about. Brainstorm ways to resolve the issue by creating a cluster diagram on a separate piece of paper. Answers will vary.

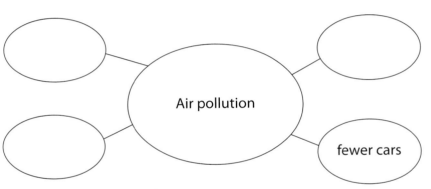

Air pollution

fewer cars

**G.** Look at your cluster diagram. Write complete sentences for the ways in which your chosen environmental issue can be resolved. Answers will vary.

Reason 1: _____

_____

Reason 2: _____

_____

Reason 3: _____

_____

**H.** **COMPOSE** On a separate piece of paper, write a paragraph communicating your opinion about the environmental issue you chose in Exercise F.

## Presentation 3 5–10 mins. ■■■

**E. ANALYZE** Study these transitional expressions with your teacher. Which ones did Ella use in her paragraph?

## Practice 3 15–20 mins. ■

**Note:** Shorter classes can do these exercises for homework.

**F.** Choose an environmental issue you feel strongly about. Brainstorm ways to resolve the issue by creating a cluster diagram on a separate piece of paper.

**G.** Look at your cluster diagram. Write complete sentences for the ways in which your chosen environmental issue can be resolved.

## Evaluation 3 5–10 mins. ■

Walk around the classroom and help students as needed.

## Application 20–30 mins. ■■■

**H. COMPOSE** On a separate piece of paper, write a paragraph communicating your opinion about the environmental issue you chose in Exercise F.

You can give these guidelines to students when they are writing the first draft of their opinion paragraphs:

1. Begin with a topic sentence that includes your opinion.
2. Write about three reasons, no more.
3. Use enumeration signals to connect your ideas for the reader.
4. Add supporting details to each reason to make it clearer and more interesting.
5. End with a concluding sentence that restates your opinion.

### MULTILEVEL WORKSHEET

Unit 8, Lesson 5, Worksheet 1: Opinions
                         Opinion Paragraphs

Refer students to *Stand Out 5 Workbook*, Unit 8, Lesson 5 for practice with *such* and demonstrative determiners.

Go to the *Activity Bank* online for suggestions on promoting digital literacy and using the Internet to enhance this lesson.

### INSTRUCTOR'S NOTES

# LIFESKILLS ▶ Mom, I'm so proud of you

## Before You Watch

- Read the title of the video to the class.
- Ask students if and when they have been proud of someone.
- Have volunteers share their experiences with the class.

### A. Look at the picture and answer the questions.

- Ask students to look at the picture and answer the questions.
- Have volunteers share their answers with the class.

## While You Watch

### B. Watch the video and complete the dialog.

- Ask students to watch the video and complete the dialog.
- Play the video and ask students to watch and listen carefully.
- Play the video again. Then, ask students to complete the dialog.
- Play the video once more and have students check their answers.
- Ask students to practice the dialog with partners.

## Check Your Understanding

### C. What are the steps in the Immigration process? Write numbers to show the order.

- Ask students what the steps in the Immigration process are.
- Have students read the statements and then write numbers to show the correct order.
- Check answers as a class.

**INSTRUCTOR'S NOTES**

# LIFESKILLS ▶ Mom, I'm so proud of you

## Before You Watch

**A. Look at the picture and answer the questions.**

1. Where are Hector, Mateo, Naomi, and Mr. and Mrs. Sanchez?
   *Hector, Mateo, Naomi, and Mr. and Mrs. Sanchez are in the Sanchezes' living room.*

2. Why are there drinks on the table?
   *The Sanchez family is celebrating.*

## While You Watch

**B. ▶ Watch the video and complete the dialog.**

**Naomi:** You mean you've kept your Turkish (1) *citizenship* this whole time?

**Mrs. Sanchez:** Yes. I've been a legal permanent (2) *resident* until now. Victor was a U.S. citizen, and so is my son. I was busy with my family and my job. The years passed, and I just never took the time to change my status.

**Naomi:** What made you (3) *change* your mind?

**Mrs. Sanchez:** Well, now I have more time, and I've been thinking it's more important to get (4) *involved*.

**Mr. Sanchez:** The next presidential (5) *election* is coming up in a couple of years, as you know, and I convinced Miriam that it's important to vote.

## Check Your Understanding

**C. What are the steps in the immigration process? Write numbers to show the order.**

a. _6_ Take an oath at the immigration ceremony.

b. _2_ Wait while officials review your application.

c. _1_ File an immigration application.

d. _3_ Meet with an immigration official.

e. _4_ When the application is approved, schedule a citizenship test.

f. _5_ Take the citizenship test.

# Review

**A. List four ways a person can become a permanent resident of the United States.**
Answers will vary. Sample answers given.

1. You are the spouse of an LPR who filed a family-based petition.

2. Have a visa petition filed by a U.S. employer.

3. Be an asylee or refugee for at least one year.

4. You have been a continuous resident since before 1/1/72.

**B. List four requirements for becoming a U.S. citizen.** Answers will vary. Sample answers given.

1. Be 18 years old or older.

2. Be a permanent resident for five years.

3. Be a person of good moral character.

4. Be able to read, write, and speak basic English.

**C. Write the correct amendment number in front of each description.**

1. The ___13th___ amendment is about the abolishment of slavery.

2. The ___19th___ amendment is about the right for women to vote.

3. The ___5th___ amendment is about the right to be charged by a grand jury if accused of a serious crime.

4. The ___4th___ amendment is about protection from unreasonable search and seizure.

5. The ___7th___ amendment is about a trial by jury in civil cases (dispute between private parties or between the government and a private party).

6. The ___6th___ amendment is about a speedy and public trial by an impartial jury.

7. The ___1st___ amendment is about freedom of religion.

8. The ___2nd___ amendment is about the right to keep and bear arms.

9. The ___15th___ amendment is about the right for people of all races to vote.

10. The ___3rd___ amendment is about protection from forced housing of soldiers.

WORKPLACE CONNECTION
Exercises A, B, C: Complete tasks as assigned.

**Goals:** All unit goals
**Grammar:** All unit grammar
**Academic Strategy:** Reviewing
**Vocabulary:** All Unit 8 vocabulary

## Agenda

☐ Discuss unit goals.

☐ Complete the review.

☐ Use unit vocabulary.

## Resources

**Stand Out Assessment CD-ROM with ExamView®**

## Pacing

■ 1.5 hour classes   ■ 2.5 hour classes
■ 3+ hour classes

### STANDARDS CORRELATIONS

*CCRS:* RI4, SL1, SL2

*CASAS:* 7.2.1

*SCANS:* **Resources** Allocate time

**Information** Acquire and evaluate information

**Interpersonal** Participate as a member of a team, teach others, negotiate to arrive at a decision, work with cultural diversity

**Systems** Monitor and correct performance

**Basic Skills** Reading, writing, arithmetic, listening, speaking

**Thinking Skills** Think creatively, make decisions, solve problems, see things in the mind's eye

**Personal Qualities** Responsibility, sociability, self-management

*EFF:* **Communication** Read with understanding, convey ideas in writing, speak so others can understand, listen actively, observe critically

**Interpersonal** Cooperate with others, guide others

**Lifelong Learning** Take responsibility for learning, reflect and evaluate

## Warm-up and Review        5–10 mins. ■■■

Have students summarize their paragraph about the environment for the class. Encourage students to ask questions to clarify each others' opinions.

## Introduction        5–10 mins. ■■■

Ask students as a class to try to recall all the goals of this unit without looking back in their books. The goals for this unit include identifying requirements for establishing residency and citizenship, identifying your rights, identifying local civic organizations, interpreting information about environmental issues, and communicating your opinion. Write all the goals on the board from Unit 8. Show students the first page of the unit and mention the five goals.

State the goal: *Today, we will be reviewing everything we have learned in this unit and preparing for the individual project.*

## Presentation        10–15 mins. ■■■

This presentation will cover the three pages of the review. Quickly go to the first page of each lesson. Discuss the goal of each. Ask simple questions to remind students of what they have learned.

**Note:** Since there is little presentation in the review, you can assign the review exercises that don't require collaboration with a partner or group for homework and go over them in class the following day.

## Practice        20–25 mins. ■■■

**Note:** There are two ways to do the review:

1. Go through the exercises one at a time and, as students complete each one, go over the answers.
2. Quickly go through the instructions of each exercise, let students complete all of the exercises at once, and then go over the answers.

**A. List four ways a person can become a permanent resident of the United States. (Lesson 1)**

**B. List four requirements for becoming a U.S. citizen. (Lesson 1)**

**C. Write the correct amendment number in front of each description. (Lesson 2)**

## Evaluation        5–15 mins. ■■■

Go around the classroom and check on students' progress. Help individuals when needed. If you see consistent errors among several students, interrupt the class and give a mini-lesson or review to help students feel comfortable with the concept.

## Practice (continued)    25–30 mins. ■■■

D.  Create a civic organization for the following group's problem. (Lesson 3)

E.  Work with a partner and list five ways you can help protect and preserve the environment. (Lesson 4)

F.  Choose one of the ways you can help protect and preserve the environment in Exercise E and write a paragraph about why it is important. (Lesson 5)

## Evaluation (continued)    5–15 mins. ■■■

Go around the classroom and check on students' progress. Help individuals when needed. If you see consistent errors among several students, interrupt the class and give a mini-lesson or review to help students feel comfortable with the concept.

### BEST PRACTICE

## Recycling/Review

The review exercises, the research activity, and the individual project are part of the recycling/review process. Students often need to be reintroduced to concepts to solidify what they have learned. Many concepts are learned and forgotten when students are engaged in learning other new concepts. This is because students learn but are not necessarily ready to acquire language concepts.

Therefore, it becomes very important to review material with students and to show them how to review it on their own. It is also important to recycle the new concepts in different contexts.

### INSTRUCTOR'S NOTES

**Learner Log**

I can identify local civic organizations.
■ Yes  ■ No  ■ Maybe

I can interpret information about environmental issues.
■ Yes  ■ No  ■ Maybe

I can communicate my opinion.
■ Yes  ■ No  ■ Maybe

**D.  Create a civic organization for the following group's problem.**

*A group of children who live in a shelter for homeless families goes to a nearby elementary school. However, the parents of the children don't have any money to buy the required school uniform—blue pants and a white shirt. The volunteers at the shelter want to find a way to raise money for these kids.* Answers will vary.

Name of organization: _____

Purpose: _____

Members: _____

Annual dues: _____

Special events: _____

**E.  Work with a partner and list five ways you can help protect and preserve the environment.** Answers will vary. Sample answers are given.

1. Drive my car less. _____

2. Use less paper. _____

3. Support alternative energies. _____

4. Recycle my plastic. _____

5. Compost my vegetable waste. _____

**F.  Choose one of the ways you can help protect and preserve the environment in Exercise E and write a paragraph about why it is important.** Answers will vary.

_____

_____

_____

_____

_____

_____

_____

_____

WORKPLACE CONNECTION
Exercise D: Complete tasks as assigned.
Exercise E: Interact appropriately with team members.
Exercise F: Combine ideas and information.

# Vocabulary Review

**A.** Choose five words from the vocabulary list. Use each word in a meaningful sentence that reviews an important point or piece of information that you have learned in this unit. *Answers will vary. Sample answer is given.*

| | | | |
|---|---|---|---|
| alien | conserve | protect | reusable |
| bear arms | eligible | punishment | slavery |
| believe | naturalization | refugee | social welfare |
| capital crime | opinion | resource | status |
| civic | peaceably assemble | | |

1. *Slavery is illegal in the U.S.* _____

2. _____

3. _____

4. _____

5. _____

**B.** Use five different words from the list above to write five different opinions you have.

*Answers will vary. Sample answer is given.*

1. *I believe I have the right to criticize the government.* _____

2. _____

3. _____

4. _____

5. _____

**C.** Write the correct word in front of each definition below.

1. _____ *Alien* _____ means resident foreigner.

2. _____ *Eligible* _____ means having the right to do or be chosen for something.

3. _____ *Punishment* _____ means a payment for doing something wrong.

4. _____ *Resource* _____ means useful things.

5. _____ *Status* _____ means a legal condition.

WORKPLACE CONNECTION
Exercises A, B, C: Complete tasks as assigned.

220   Unit 8

## Practice *(continued)*

25–30 mins. ■■■

### Vocabulary Review

A. Choose five words from the vocabulary list. Use each word in a meaningful sentence that reviews an important point or piece of information that you have learned in this unit.

B. Use five different words from the list above to write five different opinions you have.

C. Write the correct word in front of each definition below.

### Evaluation *(continued)*

5–15 mins. ■■■

Go around the classroom and check on students' progress. Help individuals when needed. If you see consistent errors among several students, interrupt the class and give a mini-lesson or review to help students feel comfortable with the concept.

### Assessment *(optional)*

■■■

Use the Stand Out Assessment CD-ROM with ExamView® to create a post-test for Unit 8.

**INSTRUCTOR'S NOTES**

## STANDARDS CORRELATIONS

**CCRS:** RI8, W1, W4, W5, SL3, SL4, SL6

**CASAS:** 4.8.1, 4.8.5, 4.8.6.

**SCANS: Resources** Allocate time

**Information** Acquire and evaluate information, organize and maintain information, interpret and communicate information, use computers to process information

**Systems** Understand systems, improve and design systems

**Technology** Select technology, apply technology to exercise

**Basic Skills** Writing

**Thinking Skills** Think creatively, make decisions, solve problems, see things in the mind's eye, use reasoning

**Personal Qualities** Responsibility, self-esteem, self-management, integrity

**EFF: Communication** Read with understanding, convey ideas in writing, speak so others can understand, listen actively, observe critically

**Decision Making** Solve problems and make decisions, plan

**Interpersonal** Cooperate with others, advocate and influence, resolve conflict and negotiate, guide others

**Lifelong Learning** Take responsibility for learning, reflect and evaluate, learn through research, use information and communications technology (optional)

## INDIVIDUAL PROJECT

### Give an opinion speech

In this project, you will work individually to develop an opinion speech supported with details.

**Note:** Shorter classes can extend this project over two class meetings.

### Stage 1
10 mins.
**Look back at everything you have learned in this unit and choose one topic to give a speech about. Remember, this speech should be persuasive. You should not just present facts without giving your opinion. However, you can support your opinion with facts. First, write one sentence that states your opinion.**

Tell students *Opinions are rooted in people's attitudes, beliefs, and values.* Explain that as they consider ways to draft their speeches, they should think about how to tap into the audience's likely values as a persuasive strategy. If a speech is about the environment, for example, the student might describe the hazards of air pollution to children if the audience contains a high number of parents and grandparents.

Go over the examples from the book and give a few more if you think students need some ideas. Tell them they must come up with their own opinion, not use one from the examples in the book.

### Stage 2
10–15 mins.
**Read your opinion out loud to the class.**

Have each student read his or her opinion out loud. Make sure that it is an opinion. If it is not, help the student reword the sentence. Ask the class to help.

### Stage 3
20–30 mins.
**Come up with reasons to support your opinion and write a speech. Prepare to speak for at least two minutes.**

Walk around the classroom and help students as they are writing their speeches.

### Stage 4
10 mins.
**Practice your speech. Remember the following tips:**
- **Enunciate (speak clearly).**
- **Make eye contact with your audience.**
- **Practice so you recall your major points without notes.**
- **Thank your audience for listening and/or for their time.**

Some students will benefit from having their practice videotaped. If this is possible, have students record themselves (with the help of other students, if necessary) giving their speeches. Students can take notes as they replay their speeches.

### Stage 5
10 mins.
**Give your two-minute opinion speech. At the end of your speech, ask your classmates if they have any questions.**

# Give an opinion speech

**In this project, you will work individually to develop an opinion speech supported with details.**

1. Look back at everything you have learned in this unit and choose one topic to give a speech about. Remember, this speech should be persuasive. You should not just present facts without giving your opinion. However, you can support your opinion with facts. First, write one sentence that states your opinion.

   Some examples:

   - *I think that someone should be able to become a citizen anytime he or she wants.*

   - *I don't think Americans should have the right to bear arms.*

   - *I think every citizen should have to be a part of a civic organization.*

2. Read your opinion out loud to the class.

3. Come up with reasons to support your opinion and write a speech. Prepare to speak for at least two minutes.

4. Practice your speech. Remember the following tips:

   - Enunciate (speak clearly).

   - Make eye contact with your audience.

   - Practice so you recall your major points without notes.

   - Thank your audience for listening and/or for their time.

5. Give your two-minute opinion speech. At the end of your speech, ask your classmates if they have any questions.

A woman takes a selfie after becoming a citizen of the United States.

# READING CHALLENGE

## About the Explorer

Roshini Thinakaran is a filmmaker. She studied at George Mason University in Virginia, where she received a bachelor's degree in communication and minored in journalism. As a filmmaker, Roshini's work currently involves profiling women in war-torn countries. Her goal is to raise awareness of women who are making real strides, and to eventually build schools for both girls and boys in these countries. She believes that if people are not empowered with education, societies will break down.

## About the Photo

This photo shows Roshini. A frequent public speaker, Roshini hopes to raise awareness of the issues that women face living in war-torn countries. One of Roshini's film projects, *Women at the Forefront*, has been turned into a series for television. She focuses on a particular theme for each country, but the overall picture she reveals is a strong women's movement—born out of oppression and hardship—happening all around the world. Unlike other movements where women have striven for equal rights, these women strive for basic rights.

- Introduce the explorer, Roshini Thinakaran.
- Read the title and ask students what they think it means.
- Have a volunteer read the quote out loud.
- Ask students how the quote relates to the title and discuss as a class.

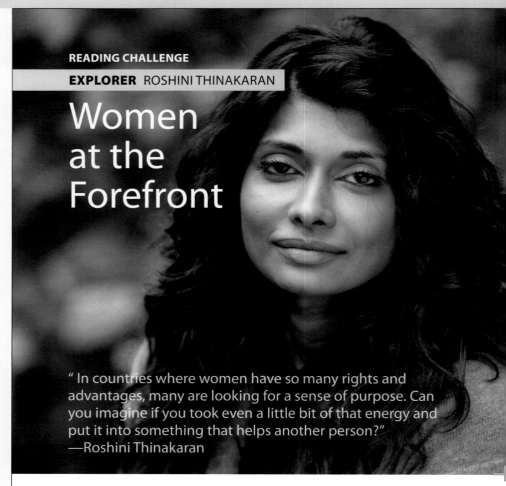

# Women at the Forefront

" In countries where women have so many rights and advantages, many are looking for a sense of purpose. Can you imagine if you took even a little bit of that energy and put it into something that helps another person?"
—Roshini Thinakaran

**A. PREDICT** What do these women have in common?

1. A widow worked as a housekeeper to provide for her family. She then went back to school to get a higher-paying job.

2. A woman was forced to leave school and work as a carpet weaver. She is now working as an editor for a women's magazine and finishing school.

3. Women are fighting to escape being servants.

4. A woman helped start a center that provides medical, psychological, and legal aid to victims of torture and violence.

222  Unit 8

## CCRS FOR READING

RI1, RI2, RI3, RI4, W3, W4, W5

**B.** Read about Roshini Thinakaran.

Roshini Thinakaran was born in Sri Lanka, but she was raised in the United States. She studied at George Mason University in Virginia, where she received a bachelor's in communication and minored in journalism. As a filmmaker, Roshini's work currently involves profiling women in war-torn countries. I had a chance to sit down with her and to talk about the impact she is making on the lives of others.

**Interviewer:** Roshini, your work takes you to different countries affected by war. Where have you traveled to do your research?

**Roshini:** My research has taken me to Sri Lanka, Iraq, Liberia, Afghanistan, and Sudan.

**Interviewer:** Tell us about the women you have met.

**Roshini:** Often without electricity or water, women go on with their lives. They get groceries, cook dinner, and take their kids to school. But an element of danger is always with them. They're always in survival mode.

**Interviewer:** Are these women unique?

**Roshini:** No. Aspirations are universal. They all want their kids to get an education, have enough to eat, be safe, and enjoy a happy life. Just because they were born in a war zone or refugee camp, they still fall in love, care about their families, and have dreams.

**Interviewer:** So you are using these women's stories in your film project?

**Roshini:** Yes. My film project is called Women at the Forefront. This film project is now turning into a television series. I've focused on a particular theme for each country, but the overall picture I reveal is a strong women's movement—born of oppression and hardship—happening all around the world. Unlike movements where women were striving for equal rights, these women strive for basic rights.

**Interviewer:** What is your goal?

**Roshini:** My goal is to bring awareness of women who are making real strides and to eventually build schools in these countries, for both girls and boys. If you don't empower people with education, societies will break down.

**Interviewer:** Do you hope to achieve something more than just awareness with this project?

**Roshini:** I want this project to connect women who have more economic and educational opportunities with women who are struggling to reshape war-torn nations. In countries where women have so many rights and advantages, many are looking for a sense of purpose. Can you imagine if you took even a little bit of that energy and put it into something that helps another person?

**C.** CREATE The women you read about in Exercise A are women that Roshini highlights in her film series. Choose one of the women and write her story as you imagine it. Be creative!

Reading Challenge  223

**A.** PREDICT  What do these women have in common?

- Have students read the statements about the women.
- Tell students to think about what Roshini Thinakaran said in her quote.
- Ask students what the women all have in common.

**B.** Read about Roshini Thinakaran.

**C.** CREATE  The women you read about in Exercise A are women that Roshini highlights in her film series. Choose one of the women and write her story as you imagine it. Be creative!

- Make it clear to students that the women they read about in Exercise A are women that Roshini highlights in her film series.
- Have students choose one of the women and write her story as they imagine.
- Ask students to be creative with their writing.

## READING STRATEGIES

### Visualization

Visualization is simply creating pictures in your mind as you read. It is an important skill for comprehension because the reader often relies on the five senses to bring the text to life. This makes it much easier to recall specific details. Visualization also makes the reader feel more connected, which personalizes the text and enriches the overall reading experience.

### About the Photo

This photo shows the Yamuna River in northern India. The river is 855 miles long and stretches from the Himalayas to Allahabad in Uttar Pradesh, where it insects with the Ganges River. One of India's most iconic landmarks, the Taj Mahal, is situated along the banks of the Yamuna River. Heavy pollution of the river means that some parts of it, especially around New Delhi, can look like a science experiment. A foam gathers on the surface of the river because of the industrial waste that is poured into it. This is especially dangerous for those people who bathe in the river. Their health is at risk because of unclean water.

▶ VIDEO CHALLENGE

# One Village Makes a Difference

**Sometimes the Yamuna River looks like a science project.**

In the last four units, you have learned about health and environmental issues. You have also explored the ways you can help. For people who live along the Yamuna River in northern India, their health is at risk from unclean water. You will now learn about what some individuals are doing to help change that.

224   One Village Makes a Difference

## Before You Watch

**A. Read the sentences. Then, match each word with the correct meaning.**

1. The Yamuna is the longest river in northern India.
2. Even though it is very hot, many people live in the Thar Desert.
3. The visibility in New Delhi is very poor because the smog is so bad.
4. The villagers built a dam to bring more water to the fields.
5. The villagers get their drinking water from a well.

| | | | |
|---|---|---|---|
| _b_ | desert | a. | huge cloud of dirty air |
| _e_ | river | b. | area of very hot, dry land |
| _c_ | dam | c. | barrier to stop a river from moving |
| _d_ | pit | d. | deep hole in the ground to hold water |
| _a_ | smog | e. | large amount of moving water |

**B. Circle the caption that best describes each picture. Then, compare your answers with a partner.**

1. New Delhi has many restaurants and shopping centers.
2. Sometimes there isn't enough water for everyone.
3. Heavy smog fills the sky above the city.

1. Industrial waste is thrown into the river every day.
2. Wells help villagers water their farms.
3. Temperatures frequently reach 100° F.

1. Villagers walk for miles to get water.
2. Water trucks deliver water to surrounding towns.
3. New Delhi is a large city in northern India.

Video Challenge 225

## Before You Watch

**A. Read the sentences. Then, match each word with the correct meaning.**

- Have students read the sentences.
- Remind students to look for other words in the sentence that give clues to an unfamiliar word's meaning.
- Ask students to match each word with the correct meaning.
- Have students read each sentence again to check their matches.

**B. Circle the caption that best describes each picture. Then, compare your answers with a partner.**

- Have students look at the pictures and then read each caption.
- Ask students to circle the caption that best describes each picture.
- Have students compare their answers with a partner.

APPLICABLE STRATEGIES

## Visual-detailing

Visual-detailing refers to identifying and listing individual or minute images in a video. Since we generally use both sight and hearing as we watch videos, we balance the two depending on our focus or concentration. When using visual-detailing, we make a conscious decision to allow our eyes to do the work to pick out key details from the video.

# ▶ VIDEO CHALLENGE

## While You Watch

As a class, review the vocabulary items in the Word Focus box.

**A. Watch the video and circle the items you see.**

While they watch the video, have students circle the items they see.

**B. Read the sentences. Circle *T* if sentences are true or *F* if they are false. Correct the false sentences in your notebook.**

- Play the video again and have students read the sentences.
- Ask students to circle *T* if the sentences are true and *F* if they are false.
- Have students correct the false sentences and write them in their notebooks.

**C. Watch the video again. Choose the correct word to complete each sentence.**

---

### While You Watch

> **WORD FOCUS**
>
> *Industrial waste* is the unwanted material that factories produce when manufacturing something. This can be oil, chemicals, plastic, glass, paper, metal, etc.

**A. Watch the video and circle the items you see.**

| | | | |
|---|---|---|---|
| hospital | (river) | (farms) | (dam) |
| (water truck) | (animals) | classroom | (desert) |
| car accident | cooking | (shopping center) | people playing soccer |

**B. Read the sentences. Circle *T* if sentences are true or *F* if they are false. Correct the false sentences in your notebook.**

1. The people of New Delhi need around eight billion gallons of water each day. T (F)
2. Even expensive restaurants in New Delhi depend on trucks to bring them water. (T) F
3. Villagers often have to share their drinking water with animals. (T) F
4. Some people believe that India's large dams have dried up the rivers. (T) F
5. Rajendra Singh encourages villagers to use modern technology to find water. T (F)

**C. Watch the video again. Choose the correct word to complete each sentence.**

| | | |
|---|---|---|
| environmentalist | one billion | 14 million |
| monsoon | science experiment | |

1. New Delhi residents need _____ one billion _____ gallons of water each day.
2. The Yamuna River sometimes looks like a _____ science experiment _____.
3. About _____ 14 million _____ people live in and around New Delhi.
4. A heavy rain that comes once a year is called a _____ monsoon _____.
5. Rajendra Singh is a(n) _____ environmentalist _____.

226   One Village Makes a Difference

226   Unit 8

## After You Watch

**A. How do the villagers make small earthen dams? Put the steps in the correct order.**

____4____ Wait for rain to raise the water levels.

____2____ Dig a small hole or pit.

____5____ Save the water in wells or reservoirs.

____6____ Water the plants in the fields.

____3____ Make a layer of rocks and stones.

____1____ Collect rocks and stones.

**B. How do you use water? Complete the table with your own information. Then, share your answers in small groups.** Answers will vary.

| Activity | Sunday | Monday | Tuesday | Wednesday | Thursday | Friday | Saturday |
|---|---|---|---|---|---|---|---|
| Taking a shower | ✓ | ✓ | ✓ | ✓ | ✓ | ✓ | ✓ |
| | | | | | | | |
| | | | | | | | |
| | | | | | | | |
| | | | | | | | |

**C. Discuss the questions with a partner and share your answers with the class.**
Answers will vary.

EXAMPLE   Do you ever use more water than you should?
*I take very long showers in the morning. I probably use a lot of water.*

1. Where does your drinking water come from?
2. What would you do if you had no running water?
3. How could you reduce the amount of water that you use?
4. When do you see people wasting water in your community? Can you think of any examples?

## After You Watch

**A. How do the villagers make small earthen dams? Put the steps in the correct order.**

- Ask students how villagers make small earthen dams.
- Have students read each step below.
- Ask students to put the steps in the correct order.

**B. How do you use water? Complete the table with your own information. Then, share your answers in small groups.**

- Ask students how they use water.
- Draw students' attention to the table below.
- Ask students to complete the table with their own information.
- Have students form small groups and share their answers.

**C. Discuss the questions with a partner and share your answers with the class.**

# PHOTO CREDITS

**Cover:** Seth Joel/Getty Images, **Bottom Images** (Left to Right) Jay B Sauceda/Getty Images; Tripod/Getty Images; Portra Images/Getty Images; Portra Images/Getty Images; Mark Edward Atkinson/Tracey Lee/Getty Images; Hero Images/Getty Images; Jade/Getty Images; James Porter/Getty Images; LWA/Larry Williams/Getty Images; Dimitri Otis/Getty Images, **2** (tl) (tc) Portra Images/Getty Images, (tr) Mark Edward Atkinson/Tracey Lee/Getty Images, (cl) Hero Images/Getty Images, (c) Jade/Getty Images, (cr) Seth Joel/Getty Images, **6** (tl) SINITAR/Shutterstock.com, (tc) Comet/Corbis, (tr) Yasser Chalid/Moment Open/Getty Images, **11** kupicoo/iStock/Getty Images, **12–13** Jianan Yu/Reuters, **14** (tl) StockLite/Shutterstock.com, (tr) Juanmonino/E+/Getty Images, (bl) en Pipe Photography/Cultura RM/Getty Images, (br) michaeljung/Shutterstock.com, **18** Yang Liu/Corbis, **25** phipatbig/Shutterstock.com, **28** (tl) StockLite/Shutterstock.com, (tr) Nadino/Shutterstock.com, (cl) Photography/Cultura RM/Getty Images, (cr) Juanmonino/E+/Getty Images, (br) michaeljung/Shutterstock.com, (bl) Fotoluminate LLC/Shutterstock.com, **31** © Cengage Learning, **36** Marco Grob/National Geographic Creative, **38–39** © Kyle Damon Parr, **40** David Molina G/Shutterstock.com, **45** Lightspring/Shutterstock.com, **54** (tl) jason cox/Shutterstock.com, (tc) Jose Luis Pelaez Inc/Getty Images, (tr) maxuser/Shutterstock.com, (b) Image Source/Corbis, **57** © Cengage Learning, **62** Matthew Muspratt/National Geographic Creative, **64–65** Alexander Koerner/Getty Images, **66** kokandr/Shutterstock.com, **68** kokandr/Shutterstock.com, **71** Rawpixel.com/Shutterstock.com, **73** Comet/Corbis, **80** (tl to br) Federal Highway Administration-MUTCD/

Wikimedia Commons; Manual on Uniform Traffic Control Devices for Streets and Highways-2003 Edition/Wikimedia Commons; Wikimedia Commons; MUTCD/Wikimedia Commons; Yield_sign.svg/Wikimedia Commons; Wikimedia Commons; Government of Ontario/Wikimedia Commons; Federal Highway Administration-MUTCD/http://mutcd.fhwa.dot.gov/pdfs/2009r1r2/part2c.pdf/Wikimedia Commons; Road-sign-no-entry.svg: Peeperman/derivative work/Wikipedia Commons; MUTCD/Wikimedia Commons, Fry1989/Wikipedia Commons, **83** © Cengage Learning, **86** Rawpixel.com/Shutterstock.com, **88** Jin-Song Hu/National Geographic Creative, **90–91** Peter Stewart/500px, **94** Forestpath/Dreamstime.com, **102** (tl) Valery Sidelnykov/Shutterstock.com, (tc) Banner/Shutterstock.com, (tr) Stefan90/Getty Images, (cl) ilbusca/Getty Images, (c) Stephen Dalton/ Minden Pictures/Getty Images, (cr) Blend/Corbis, **106** Jon Bilous/Shutterstock.com, **107** sdecoret/Shutterstock.com, **108** SweetBabeeJay/Thinkstock, **109** © Cengage Learning, **114** (t) NASA/Adams Constance/National Geographic Creative, (br) Education Images/Universal Images Group/Getty Images, **116** Tim Laman/National Geographic Creative, **120–121** © Petravb, **124** (cl) Noel Hendrickson/Getty Images, (c) lightpoet/Shutterstock.com, (cr) MSRPhoto/ iStock/Getty Images Plus/Getty Images, **125** Yeko Photo Studio/Shutterstock.com, **134** Dragon Images/Shutterstock.com, **136** elenabsl/Shutterstock.com, **139** © Cengage Learning, **144** Rebecca Hale/National Geographic Creative, **146–147** Brent Humphreys/Redux, **149** Monkey Business Images/Shutterstock.com, **151** Everything/Shutterstock.

com, **154** Seth Joel/Getty Images, **155** LDprod/Shutterstock.com, **159** Felix Mizioznikov/Shutterstock.com, **162** (cl) Encyclopedia/Corbis, (bl) Encyclopedia/Corbis, **164** XiXinXing/Shutterstock.com, **165** © Cengage Learning, **170** (t) AP Images/Richard Shotwell/Invision, (br) Beverly Joubert/National Geographic Creative, **172–173** Clive Wilkinson, **174** (tl) Africa Studio/Shutterstock.com, (tc) IOvE IOvE/Shutterstock.com, (tr) Spiderstock/Getty Images, (cl) Sylvie Bouchard/Shutterstock.com, (c) andres balcazar/Getty Images, (cr) Merydolla/Shutterstock.com, (bl) MSPhotographic/Shutterstock.com, (bc) Goygel-Sokol Dmitry/Shutterstock.com, **176–177** ©Cengage Learning, **178** FabrikaSimf/Shutterstock.com, **186** Konstantin Chagin/Shutterstock.com, **191** © Cengage Learning, **196** © Kris Krug, **198–199** Luis Sinco/Los Angeles Times/Getty Images, **202** (tl) DragonImages/Getty Images, (cl1) Jetta Productions/Blend Images/Getty Images, (cl2) StockLite/Shutterstock.com, (cl3)Monkey Business Images/Shutterstock.com, (bl) Daniel Ernst/Getty Images, **209** (tl) Bob Kreisel/Alamy Stock Photo, (tr) Terra/Corbis, (cl) seyomedo/Shutterstock.com, (cr) Mojca Odar/Shutterstock.com, (bl) MGP/DigitalVision/Getty Images, (br) Esa Hiltula/Alamy Stock Photo, **213** (tl) Vadim Petrakov/Shutterstock.com, (tc) chaoss/Shutterstock.com, (tr) AVN Photo Lab/Shutterstock.com, **217** © Cengage Learning, **221** Mike Segar/Reuters, **222** Mark Thiessen/National Geographic Creative, **224** Hindustan Times/Getty Images, **225** (t) (c) (b) © National Geographic, **237** Rainer Lesniewski/Shutterstock.com.

# STAND OUT VOCABULARY LIST

To access the Vocabulary List, refer to pages 229–230 of *Stand Out 5* student book.

# STAND OUT GRAMMAR REFERENCE

To access the Grammar Reference, refer to pages 230–232 of *Stand Out 5* student book.

# STAND OUT SKILLS INDEX

To access the Skills Index, refer to pages 236–237 of *Stand Out 5* student book.

# TEXT CREDITS

**20** "Educational Attainment and Earning Power for Men and Women 18 and Over" chart. **Source:** Current Population Survey, U.S. Department of Labor, U.S. Bureau of Labor Statistics **Website:** http://www.bls.gov/emp/ep_table_001.htm; **51** "The Four Keys to Great Credit" **Source:** MSN Money **Website:** money.msn.com; **81** "Seat Belt Use in the States, U.S. Territories, and Nationwide, 2006–2013" **Source:** Seat Belt Use in 2013—Use Rates in the States and Territories, National Highway Traffic Safety Administration **Website:** http://www-nrd.nhtsa.dot.gov/Pubs/812030.pdf; **82** "Facts on alcohol-related accidents" Source: Centers for Disease Control and Prevention **Website:** http://www.cdc.gov/motorvehiclesafety/index.html; **107** "Theft prevention newsletter" Source: Burglary Prevention, Jefferson County Sherriff's Department, MO **Website:** http://www.jcsd.org/burglary_prevention.htm; **130** "Percentage of persons without health insurance, by age group using three measures of non-coverage, and percentage of persons with health insurance at the time of interview, by coverage type and age group: United States, January–March 2014" **Source:** Health Insurance Coverage: Early Release of Estimates From the National Health Interview Survey, January–March 2014 **Website:** http://www.cdc.gov/nchs/data/nhis/earlyrelease/insur201409.pdf; **131** "Percentage of persons under age 65 without health insurance coverage at the time of interview, by age group and sex: United States, January–March 2014" **Source:** Health Insurance Coverage: Early Release of Estimates From the National Health Interview Survey, January–March 2014 **Website:** http://www.cdc.gov/nchs/data/nhis/earlyrelease/insur201409.pdf; **132** "Percentage of persons aged 18–64 who lacked health insurance coverage, had public health coverage, and had private health insurance coverage at the time of interview, by selected demographic characteristics: United States, January—March 2014" **Source:** Health Insurance Coverage: Early Release of Estimates From the National Health Interview Survey, January–March 2014 **Website:** http://www.cdc.gov/nchs/data/nhis/earlyrelease/insur201409.pdf; **141** "Health Insurance Coverage of Low Income Adults 19–64" (2013) **Source:** Kaiser Family Foundation estimates based on the Census Bureau's March 2014 Current Population Survey (CPS: Annual Social and Economic Supplements). **Website:** http://kff.org/other/state-indicator/low-income-adults/?state=NY; **185** "Conflict Resolution: Resolving Conflict Rationally and Effectively" **Source:** Mind Tools **Website:** http://mindtools.com; **203–204** "U.S. Citizenship and Immigration Services" **Source:** USCIS **Website:** http://uscis.com; **208** "The Mothers' Club of Northville" **Source:** City of Northville, MI **Website:** http://ci.northville.mi.us; **211** "Create Less Trash" **Source:** Sustainable Environment for Quality of Life **Website:** http://www.centralina.org/; **212** "Carpooling—What is it?" **Source:** Sustainable Environment for Quality of Life **Website:** http://www.centralina.org/

# STAND OUT VIDEO SCRIPTS

**UNIT 1: Lifeskills Video: The presentation is due in two weeks**

**Naomi:** Any ideas?

**Hector:** Nope. My brain is empty.

**Mateo:** Mine too.

**Naomi:** Come on, you guys. We have to do this presentation in two weeks. Two weeks! That's barely enough time.

**Hector:** OK, let's focus. The assignment was to do a presentation on jobs and careers.

**Mateo:** The teacher gave a lecture about the relationship between education and income. Remember? So maybe we could do something about that.

**Naomi:** Good idea. Let's do a presentation showing how an advanced degree can increase your earning potential.

**Hector:** I like it. There have got to be some good statistics on that.

**Mateo:** I think it would be good to show some of those statistics in the form of a graph or a chart.

**Hector:** Definitely. It won't be as interesting if we just talk. We have to have something for the class to look at.

**Naomi:** I can tell this is going to be good. Let's get going. Somebody should take notes.

**Hector:** Who, me?

**Naomi:** Well you are going to be a journalist, aren't you? Listen, if you take notes and write a report, then I'll make the chart. I'm really good with designing graphics.

**Mateo:** I'll present it to the class. I'll use Hector's report to write a short speech.

**Naomi:** This is great! We all have our roles. Hector will write the report. I'll design the graphics, and Mateo will present it to the class.

**Mateo:** When do you think you'll have finished the report, Hector?

**Hector:** I'll need at least a week.

**Mateo:** That's good. That'll give me a week to practice my presentation.

**Naomi:** I will have finished the graphics by then, too. Why don't we get together next Saturday? This room will be empty, so we can meet here.

**Naomi:** Here's the chart I made. I took me a couple of hours to make it. The first page shows the title: Educational Attainment and Earning Power.

**Hector:** That was a good idea to make a title page. I didn't think of that.

**Naomi:** And here is a bar graph that shows all the statistics. I used the information from Hector's report to make the graph.

**Mateo:** Wow. A high school graduate only makes about $21,000 dollars a year.

**Naomi:** With an associate's degree, you can earn $30,000 per year, and with a bachelor's degree you can make more than $40,000. A college graduate with a master's or PhD can make anywhere from $50,000 and up. In other words, with each degree you earn, you can make about ten thousand dollars more per year.

**Hector:** In three years, a high school graduate will have made the same amount of money that a college graduate makes in one year. It really pays off.

**Mateo:** I'll make that point in my speech. Do you have another copy of your report, Hector?

**Hector:** Yeah, here it is. So, do you have everything you need for your speech?

**Mateo:** Naomi made the bar graph, you wrote the report, so I think I've got everything I need. Basically, I'll just summarize your report for the class. When I give my speech, I'll use Naomi's chart as a visual aid.

**Hector:** Good job, everybody.

**Naomi:** It goes to show what you can do with a little teamwork.

**UNIT 2: Lifeskills Video: It's called identity theft**

**Mateo:** Thanks, Naomi. That was good.

**Naomi:** I can see you enjoyed it. Would you like anything else?

**Mateo:** No, that's enough. I'd better get back to work.

**Naomi:** OK, then. Here's your check.

**Mateo:** Wait a second. Where's my wallet? I can't find it.

**Naomi:** Oh, no. Did you leave it at home?

**Mateo:** Let me think. I had it this morning on the bus. I definitely remember that. I must have lost it.

**Naomi:** You'd better notify the bank right away. You have an account at Glendale Bank, don't you?

**Mateo:** I do.

**Naomi:** There's a branch right around the corner. In fact, that's where Mr. Sanchez works.

**Mateo:** That's right. I'd better go over there right now.

**Naomi:** Don't worry about the bill. Good luck!

**Mateo:** And that's what happened.

**Mr. Sanchez:** I'm sorry to hear that, Mateo. When did you lose your wallet?

**Mateo:** Last night or this morning, I'm not sure. I think I left it on the bus.

**Mr. Sanchez:** Uh-oh. Was there a lot of money in it?

**Mateo:** About twenty dollars, I guess. But my ATM card was in it, too. That's why I came in to see you. I need a new ATM card.

**Mr. Sanchez:** Well, sure. I can get a new ATM card for you. But first, I think we should check on your account.

**Mr. Sanchez:** Mateo, did you withdraw some cash this morning?

**Mateo:** No, I haven't withdrawn any money for a couple of days.

**Mr. Sanchez:** Well, somebody withdrew 500 dollars from your account earlier today.

**Mateo:** How could they do that? Don't they need to know my password?

**Mr. Sanchez:** Not necessarily. Does your wallet contain any personal information?

**Mateo:** Such as?

**Mr. Sanchez:** Such as your driver's license or social security number?

**Mateo:** I keep my driver's license and my social security card in my wallet.

**Mr. Sanchez:** That's all they needed. With that information, they can get into your bank account and take out all your money. They can even start a new account and take out a loan in your name. It's called identity theft.

**Mateo:** What should I do?

**Mr. Sanchez:** Well, the first thing you need to do is freeze your checking account. That will prevent the thieves from taking any more money out of your account.

**Mateo:** Am I liable for the 500 dollars that was taken out of my account this morning?

**Mr. Sanchez:** Probably not. I'll fill out a dispute claim. You can probably get the money back, although it may take a couple of weeks.

**Mateo:** Wow! That's a relief. What else should I do?

**Mr. Sanchez:** You should definitely file a police report. Did you have any credit cards in your wallet?

**Mateo:** Yeah, just one.

**Mr. Sanchez:** Then you should call the credit card company right away. Notify the company that your card has been stolen and cancel the card.

**Mateo:** Thanks, Mr. Sanchez. You've been a big help. If you'll excuse me, I have a few calls I have to make.

**Mr. Sanchez:** Yes, you'd better get going. Take care, Mateo. And be careful.

### UNIT 3: Lifeskills Video: I wish I had a car

**Hector:** The bus is late again.

**Naomi:** I wish I had a car. We could have been at school an hour ago.

**Mateo:** Yeah, I wish I had a car, too; a convertible, a silver convertible, like that one over there.

**Hector:** Yeah, that is nice.

**Naomi:** How much would a convertible like that cost, do you think?

**Hector:** A car like that could easily cost $20,000, wouldn't you say, Mateo?

**Mateo:** Yeah, and if I had that much money, I wouldn't hesitate to buy it.

**Naomi:** I can't imagine what the insurance for a car like that would cost. But I guess you wouldn't pay that much for gas. Convertibles get good mileage.

**Mateo:** Who cares about insurance or mileage? The important thing is that you would look good.

**Hector:** Personally, I would rather have something more practical, like that pick-up.

**Mateo:** A pick-up? Are you serious?

**Hector:** Think about it. If you got a pick-up you would have lots of space in the back.

**Mateo:** What would you need so much space for?

**Hector:** I don't know. I'm just saying that you would have the space if you needed it. But I do know one thing. On a day like today, I would be driving down Highway 1, headed for the beach.

**Naomi:** That's what I would get.

**Mateo:** An SUV? Why would you get an SUV?

**Naomi:** If I had an SUV there would be plenty of room for other people. I could give rides to all my friends.

**Hector:** Yeah, but you would spend a fortune on gas. The mileage on an SUV is terrible.

**Naomi:** You wouldn't have to spend that much if you got a hybrid. I've heard hybrids barely use any gas. They mostly use electricity. Oh, look. Here comes the bus.

**Hector:** One second ago I was driving my pick-up down Highway 1. Now here I am, back at the bus stop with you two.

**Mateo:** Life is tough.

**Naomi:** Come on, you guys. Let's go.

### UNIT 4: Lifeskills Video: I'll have my handyman fix it

**Naomi:** I can't concentrate anymore. That dripping sound is driving me crazy!

**Mateo:** Me too.

**Naomi:** Did you call the landlord again?

**Mateo:** Yeah, I called him this morning for the third time.

**Hector:** Did you actually speak to him, or did you leave a message?

**Mateo:** I left a message.

**Hector:** That landlord! He never answers the phone.

**Mateo:** But he did call back.

**Naomi:** Really? What did he say?

**Mateo:** He said he would be here at 7 o'clock.

**Hector:** Well it's already 7:30. Maybe he forgot.

**Naomi:** Oh! The next time I see that landlord I'm going to—

**Landlord:** Hello, hello. I got your phone message this morning.

**Mateo:** You mean our messages.

**Landlord:** Evidently there's some sort of repair you want me to make?

**Naomi:** After all the rain we had this weekend, the roof started to leak. I think a pool of water may still be on the roof.

**Hector:** Yeah, the ceiling is still dripping even though the rain has stopped.

**Landlord:** I see. Has the water damaged the floor?

**Naomi:** No, we caught it right away and put a bucket down to collect all the drips.

**Hector:** But we can't keep emptying out this bucket day and night. And the damage to the ceiling is getting worse.

**Mateo:** That's right. And we can't be responsible for any damage if the water spills over.

**Landlord:** I'll have my handyman come by tomorrow morning. Can one of you be here to let him in?

**Naomi:** Yeah, I can let him in.

**Landlord:** Are there any other repairs that need to be made?

**Naomi:** No, just the leak.

**Landlord:** OK, then. The handyman will be here around 10 a.m.

**All:** Thank you.

**Mateo:** Wow, I can't believe it was that easy. I was expecting the landlord to give us a hard time.

**Naomi:** I guess he isn't such a bad guy after all.

### Video Challenge 1: Enduring Voices

**Narrator:** David Harrison and Greg Anderson work for the Living Tongues Institute. Chris Rainier is a photographer for the National Geographic Society. The three men were traveling in Northern Australia, where they interviewed a man. He may be the last speaker of a language that most people thought was extinct.

**Greg Anderson:** My father.

**Narrator:** There are seven thousand known languages in the world, but more than half of them are expected to disappear in the next fifty years. And when a language disappears, we lose the information about the world that its speakers had. That's why the three men helped create National Geographic's Enduring Voices Project.

**Chris Rainier:** Every two weeks around the planet, a language disappears; completely disappears forever and ever. So, what we're doing with the Enduring Voices Project is really kind of trying to bring awareness to this whole issue of language loss around the planet.

**Narrator:** After Australia, the team travels on. This time, they travel to the extreme northeast of India, a remote area near Bhutan, Myanmar, and China. It's a region where there are many different languages. Many of

them are in danger of becoming extinct. For the team, there are other problems. For example, the equipment isn't working.

**David Harrison:** Say something.

**Greg Anderson:** Something. Something that I'm really getting annoyed with this equipment, making it my life hassle.

**David Harrison:** Go, go a little louder.

**Greg Anderson:** Hey!

**David Harrison:** Ok that works. Good enough.

**Narrator:** Most of these local languages are not written anywhere, so the researchers want to record as much of the languages as possible. The team arrives in a large village called Hong. Many of the older people speak the local language, called Apatani. But the language cannot survive, if the younger people don't speak it.

**David Harrison:** It's very easy in these communities to find young people who are speaking English and Hindi, and not speaking the traditional languages, they're neglecting them, they're perhaps even abandoning them.

**Narrator:** The team spends time trying to find some younger people who speak the language.

**Greg Anderson:** We definitely want to find younger speakers because they're the ones that will be showing the shift. The older speakers of course will have the language. It'll be interesting to see people who have been schooled in modern times, if they've still kept it.

**Narrator:** The team meets a young man named Vijay, who speaks English, and Apatani. Vijay invites them in to his home. A local Indian, called Ganesh Mahmood, helps the researchers while they record basic words of the local language.

**Ganesh Mahmood:** How you count 1, 2, 3 per one.

**Vijay:** One per one, we count [speaks Apatani].

**Narrator:** Each member of the family says some more words. As well as doing their own research, the team trains local people to use special language technology kits. These technology kits have a laptop computer, video cameras, and basic recording equipment, so the local community can record the last speakers of old languages, using modern technology.

**David Harrison:** Not only are these languages very small with just a few thousand speakers in some cases, but their numbers may be decreasing as people shift over to global languages.

**Narrator:** The Enduring Voices team must leave, but with the technology kits, they hope that the local community can record this important part of their local culture. They hope that the people will listen to the words of their elders, and want to keep the language alive and speak it themselves.

## UNIT 5: Lifeskills Video: I think I might have a problem

**Hector:** Hey Naomi. What are you doing?

**Naomi:** Oh, nothing much. Just surfing the net.

**Hector:** Are you doing research for a paper?

**Naomi:** No. Nothing like that. I was just shopping for a pair of shoes.

**Hector:** Shopping for shoes, again? Isn't that a pair of shoes in that bag?

**Naomi:** I couldn't resist them. Aren't they great? I got this fantastic belt, too. I couldn't really afford it, but how could I say no?

**Hector:** Naomi, you've been spending a lot of money lately.

**Naomi:** I know, but I just can't stop myself. I'm a shopaholic.

**Hector:** Are you joking, or are you being serious?

**Naomi:** OK, I admit that I have a problem. I feel like I'm not in control.

**Hector:** Maybe you are losing control. Do you spend money even when you don't want to?

**Naomi:** Well, yeah. I do.

**Hector:** Naomi, I hate to tell you this, but I think you might have an addiction to shopping. Really, I mean it.

**Naomi:** I think you're right, Hector. I used to think I was just doing it for fun. But it isn't fun anymore. I spend all my money on things I don't need or even want.

**Hector:** Can I tell you something? I used to have an addiction too.

**Naomi:** You? Addicted?

**Hector:** Yes, believe it or not, I used to be addicted to junk food. I ate it constantly, even when I wasn't hungry. At one point, I weighed over 250 pounds.

**Naomi:** You mean, you had an eating disorder?

**Hector:** You could say that.

**Naomi:** What did you do about it?

**Hector:** Well, I got help. I went to a counselor and I joined a support group. I kept track of my eating, and I started working out at the gym. Pretty soon, I was addicted to going to the gym! Now, I feel a lot better.

**Naomi:** I want to get myself under control too, Hector. What should I do?

**Hector:** All I can tell you is what worked for me. First, I made the decision to stop overeating, and then I got the help I needed.

**Naomi:** Thank you for being honest with me, Hector. I really appreciate your honesty. Can I ask you for a favor?

**Hector:** Sure. Anything you want.

**Naomi:** Can you help me return these things?

**Hector:** Absolutely.

## UNIT 6: Lifeskills Video: What could go wrong?

**Mrs. Sanchez:** Oh, I'm so excited. I've never ordered anything online before. And groceries? Can you imagine how much time we'll save? We won't ever have to go to the grocery store again!

**Mr. Sanchez:** For the first time, let's just order a couple of things—to make sure it works.

**Mrs. Sanchez:** But what could go wrong? Come on, Victor. Everybody uses the internet to buy things. We have to keep up with the times, dear.

**Mr. Sanchez:** I know, I know. I just want to make sure it works. Later, when we're used to it, we can try it again.

**Mrs. Sanchez:** Alright, if it makes you feel better. Let's get started! Look in the refrigerator and tell me what we need.

**Mr. Sanchez:** We need some milk.

**Mrs. Sanchez:** How much?

**Mr. Sanchez:** A gallon.

**Mrs. Sanchez:** What else?

**Mr. Sanchez:** How about a gallon of juice?

**Mrs. Sanchez:** Oh, good idea. Hector likes to drink juice every morning. What about eggs and butter?

**Mr. Sanchez:** Miriam, let's not buy too many things. Like I said, I just want to buy a few things this first time.

**Mrs. Sanchez:** But Victor, we have to spend at least twenty dollars. That's the minimum amount. So far we've only spent three dollars.

**Mr. Sanchez:** You mean a gallon of juice and a gallon of milk is only three dollars?

**Mrs. Sanchez:** I guess everything is cheaper on the internet. Look in the cupboard.

**Mr. Sanchez:** Alright, alright. Do you think we need more tomato sauce?

**Mrs. Sanchez:** Yes, I always need tomato sauce. I'll get two cans. What about rice? Do we have any rice?

**Mr. Sanchez:** No, we're almost out of rice.

**Mrs. Sanchez:** OK, one bag of rice. That's it. We've spent twenty dollars.

**Mr. Sanchez:** Wait a second. A gallon of juice and a gallon of milk came to three dollars. You mean that two cans of tomato sauce and a bag of rice came to seventeen dollars?

**Mrs. Sanchez:** Oh, who knows how these things work, Victor? Prices are different on the Internet.

**Mr. Sanchez:** I guess you're right. Just submit the order.

**Mrs. Sanchez:** Your order has been submitted, sir. Your groceries will be delivered by 5 p.m. How exciting! We just made our first online purchase! Now all we have to do is sit back and wait.

**Mr. Sanchez:** I have a funny feeling about this.

**Mrs. Sanchez:** Just relax, honey. Everything will be fine.

**Mrs. Sanchez:** Oh! That must be the delivery person. Go get our groceries, dear!

**Mr. Sanchez:** Well, here's your rice. Do you think we have enough rice?

**Mrs. Sanchez:** What happened? I did not order that much rice.

**Mr. Sanchez:** Well, that's what they brought. Maybe it was a mistake. Let's see what else we got. Here's the milk. I thought we ordered a gallon of milk?

**Mrs. Sanchez:** So did I. I did not order a pint of milk. I ordered a gallon of milk.

**Mr. Sanchez:** We didn't order a pint of juice, either. We ordered a gallon of juice. And look at this. Two cans of tomato sauce. Two very large cans of tomato sauce. Miriam, what happened?

**Mrs. Sanchez:** Well, I clicked on the picture of the milk and I clicked on the picture of the juice. And then I clicked on the picture of the rice, and then I clicked twice on the picture of the tomato sauce.

**Mr. Sanchez:** Miriam, I think you forgot to check the sizes of all these things.

**Mrs. Sanchez:** Oh Victor, I think you're right. I just clicked on the pictures without checking the sizes.

**Mr. Sanchez:** Now do you see why I wanted to be careful?

**Mrs. Sanchez:** Well, I learned my lesson. Shopping online isn't as easy as I thought. From now on, I will be more careful. Oh, but what am I going to do with all this tomato sauce?

**UNIT 7: Lifeskills Video: You seem to be doing a very good job**

**Hector:** Excuse me… Mr. Patel, you wanted to see me.

**Mr. Patel:** Yes, Hector. Please, have a seat.

**Mr. Patel:** I guess you know why I asked to see you today.

**Hector:** Well…um…yes, no. Yes. I hope I do.

**Mr. Patel:** Well, I asked to see you because I have some good news for you. Since you joined us a few months back, I have been looking over your progress reports. You seem to be doing a very good job. You are always on time, you're cooperative, and you're very hard-working.

**Hector:** Thank you, sir. I've been trying really hard.

**Mr. Patel:** I can see that. And in recognition of your hard work and dedication, I would like to give you a promotion. Starting next week, you'll manage the men's department. What do you think of that?

**Hector:** I think that's great! Thank you, Mr. Patel. I'll try my best to be a good manager.

**Mr. Patel:** I'm glad to hear you say that. Oh, and there is one more thing. I have a little present for you.

Something that will help you communicate with the other employees. Here you are, a personal digital assistant!

**Hector:** A PDA. Wow! I've always wanted one of these.

**Mr. Patel:** Now Hector, this is strictly for work.

**Hector:** Oh, Mr. Patel. I understand.

**Mr. Patel:** You can do all sorts of things with this little piece of technology, so I hope you will use it well.

**Hector:** I've never had one of these. Um, how do you use it?

**Mr. Patel:** It's not all that difficult. I'll go over the basics, but you really have to read the manual to understand all the features. Go ahead, turn it on. The battery is charged and I'll try to explain a few things.

**Hector:** Great.

**Mr. Patel:** The stick on the side is called a stylus. You can use it to operate the functions on the screen. There's a keypad on the bottom.

**Hector:** That's really cool. The screen is so clear and it's really big.

**Mr. Patel:** And there are ports on both sides for things like charging the battery, inserting the flash memory card, etc. With the USB cable, you can directly download things from your computer.

**Hector:** That's great. This is a really useful little tool.

**Mr. Patel:** Yes, it is. You can send emails from this, you can receive calls and you can store all sorts of data.

**Hector:** Really? Like what?

**Mr. Patel:** Well, like addresses, names, schedules, things like that.

**Hector:** What! This is like a portable office right here in my hand.

**Mr. Patel:** Yes it is. And just like an office, the information inside is very important, so you should keep it with you all the time and never lose it.

**Hector:** Oh, Mr. Patel, I won't lose it. I'll keep it safe and with me all the time.

**Mr. Patel:** That's good. I hope so. It's important that you keep it with you all the time. I gave it to you so that the other employees could contact you any time, in case they are sick or if they want to change their schedules, things like that.

**Hector:** Oh? You mean, all the people from the store can contact me on this at anytime?

**Mr. Patel:** Well, yes. Like I said, you're a manager now! Congratulations! Now back to work.

**UNIT 8: Lifeskills Video: Mom, I'm so proud of you!**

**Mateo:** Hector, you OK? You seem a little nervous.

**Hector:** Yes, I'm fine. It's just. . . wait one second.

**Naomi:** Hi, Mateo. How are you guys?

**Mateo:** I'm fine. But I'm not sure about Hector.

**Hector:** I'm fine. Just . . . relax, get comfortable.

**Naomi:** OK . . . I haven't been to your parents' house in a long time. Where are they, by the way?

**Hector:** Well, that's why I asked you to come over. They said they had a big announcement. I asked what it was about, and they said they wanted it to be a surprise, and they asked me to come home for dinner. They said it was OK for you and Mateo to come, too. So I guess can't be bad news.

**Naomi:** Wow, I'm curious. What could it be?

**Mateo:** Maybe they won the lottery?

**Naomi:** Or maybe they're going to have a baby!

**Hector:** Oh, please.

**Mateo:** Having Hector is enough, don't you think?

**Mrs. Sanchez:** Hi Naomi! How nice to see you. Oh, and Mateo, I've missed you so much. You never come over anymore!

**Mateo:** I've been bad, I know.

**Mrs. Sanchez:** Well anyway, I'm so glad you both could come over.

**Naomi:** Thanks for inviting us. It's good to be here again.

**Mr. Sanchez:** Hello, everybody. What a nice surprise! We haven't had this many people in our house since Hector moved in with you.

**Hector:** Speaking of surprises, I was just telling Naomi and Mateo that you have some important news?

**Mrs. Sanchez:** Well, yes we do. Oh, but don't worry. It's good news. It's a big change, but it's good.

**Hector:** OK, Ma. Get to the point. What is this about?

**Mrs. Sanchez:** Let me explain in my own way, dear. Mateo and Naomi, did Hector ever tell you where I'm from?

**Naomi:** Oh yes, I remember that day that I came over and you were showing me the family photo album. You said you were from Turkey, right?

**Mateo:** And first you moved to New York, and then you moved to California. That's when you met Mr. Sanchez. I know them like I know my own family.

**Mrs. Sanchez:** That's right, Mateo. Hector's father is from Mexico. He became a U.S. citizen and then we got married.

**Mr. Sanchez:** Yes, it wasn't easy becoming a citizen back then. It was expensive, and it took a long time. But it was worth it.

**Hector:** Mom, Dad, you're talking about things that happened 25 years ago. What does this got to do with now?

**Mrs. Sanchez:** Hector always wants to get straight to the point.

**Mr. Sanchez:** What your mother is trying to say is—

**Mrs. Sanchez:** What I'm trying to say is, I have finally decided to become a U.S. citizen.

**Hector:** What?

**Mrs. Sanchez:** Yes, I'm going to be an American, just like my husband and my son.

**Hector:** Mom, are you kidding?

**Mrs. Sanchez:** No, no. I am completely serious.

**Naomi:** You mean you've kept your Turkish citizenship this whole time?

**Mrs. Sanchez:** Yes, I've been a legal permanent resident until now. Victor was a U.S. citizen, and so was my son. I was busy with my family and my job. The years passed, and I just never took the time to change my status.

**Naomi:** What made you change your mind?

**Mrs. Sanchez:** Well now I have more time, and I've been thinking it's more important to get involved.

**Mr. Sanchez:** The next presidential election is coming up in a couple of years, as you know, and I convinced Miriam that it's important to vote. If we start the application process now, she might get her citizenship in time for the election.

**Mrs. Sanchez:** I've accepted the fact that I will never move back to Turkey. So, I might as well start taking my rights and responsibilities here in the U.S. more seriously.

**Hector:** Mom, I'm so proud of you!

**Mrs. Sanchez:** Oh, there are so many things to do. I have to start the application process, and then I have to have an interview with the immigration service.

**Mr. Sanchez:** And don't forget the citizenship test. That's not going to be easy, dear.

**Mrs. Sanchez:** I know, but you're going to help me, right?

**Mr. Sanchez:** I'll be your personal tutor.

**Mateo:** Well, that calls for a toast. Congratulations, Mrs. Sanchez. Here's to new beginnings!

**Mrs. Sanchez: Thank you.**

**All:** Cheers!

**Video Challenge 2: One Village Makes a Difference**

**Narrator:** New Delhi is a large city in northern India. The heavy smog that usually fills the sky is so unclean that it's difficult to see the city. The water supply doesn't look much better. The Yamuna river is the city's main source of drinking water. 50 million gallons of industrial waste are thrown into the river every day. At times, this makes it look more like a science experiment than a proper water supply. The 14 million people in and around New Delhi must get their water from community water tankers. These trucks deliver water to the towns where people live. Sometimes there's enough water for everyone. And sometimes there isn't. The people of New Delhi need about 1 billion gallons of water a day. They're surviving on 25% of that. Even in the richer areas, you'll find busy shopping centers, well dressed shoppers, expensive restaurants, and the same community water tankers. Outside of the city in the desert of Rajasthan, getting water is even harder. The temperatures frequently reach 120 degrees Fahrenheit. Villagers walk for miles to get water. When they reach a well, they often have to drink next to their animals. An annual season of heavy rain, called the monsoon season, does provide relief, but it doesn't replace the water that's used every year. So the question remains: Is there an answer to India's water problem? Some leaders think that the answer lies in a series of new dams. However, many people disagree with this proposal. They believe that India's existing dams have contributed to the water shortage by drying up riverbeds, fields, and wells.

**Rajendra Singh:** Thousands of millions of rupees have already been invested in water policy and big dams. How do you explain villages with no water? Who's responsible for all of this? Well, the blame lies on the very system which advocates the construction of bigger dams.

**Narrator:** The answer to India's water shortage may be found in a group of villages in the Alwar area of Rajasthan. Here, Rajendra Singh has started a non-governmental organization that works with villagers to make clean water easily available. Singh encourages villagers to use an ancient method, one that uses small dams to store water and change the land. Under Singh's direction, villagers decided to try the method. They began collecting stone and rock to make small urban dams. They then made small pits or holes near them and laid a porous layer of stone, earth, and clay. This stopped rainwater from running off and raised the level of the water under the ground. With every rain shower, the ground water level rose higher. Eventually, people were able to create wells to irrigate their farms. Soon, water reached every part of the village. Today, a village that was dry and lifeless is green and healthy. Because of two urban dams, farmers who couldn't grow enough food for their families can now produce food for them, and the idea has spread.

**Villager:** We are building water reservoirs and dams to save rainwater. We want our village, Rosda, to be green and prosperous like [unclear].

**Narrator:** At present, more than 4,000 urban dams collect rainwater across western India. They provide water for more than 800 communities. The small scale methods of Alwar aren't practical for New Delhi. They wouldn't be enough. Experts say that new water supplies and efforts to conserve water may slow the water shortage there, but only for about ten years. Perhaps the big cities can learn something from Alwar. Certainly things here have changed for the better. People no longer walk a long way for water. A well is just down the road. It seems that in the region of Alwar, one village really can make a difference.

# STAND OUT WORKBOOK ANSWER KEY

**PRE-UNIT: GETTING TO KNOW YOU**
**Lesson 1: Classroom community**
**D.** Answers will vary.
**F.** 1. is 2. lives 3. will move 4. came 5. has been 6. will study 7. was 8. has moved 8. likes 9. will stop
**G.** Answers will vary.

**Lesson 2: What are your hobbies?**
**A.** Answers will vary.
**D.** 1. I like to go to the movies. 2. Reading books and fixing up old cars. 3. Playing soccer and cooking. 4. I like to train for bike races. 5. I'm going to a family reunion.
**E.** 1. a 2. c 3. d 4. b
**F.** Answers will vary.

**Lesson 3: Dear friend**
**A.** Answers will vary.
**B.**
I am so anxious to see you. I can't wait for your visit in July. We are going ~~having~~ to have a great time. I want to show you my new school. We are learning a lot of interesting things right now. My English is improving. This ~~school private~~ private school is great! I'm preparing for work in the business field. I will meet you at the bus stop at four o'clock on Monday.
**D.** 1. July: Capitalization 2. to have: Verbs 3. We: Capitalization 4. are: Verb 5. English: Capitalization 6. private school: Word order 7. field: Spelling 8. Monday: Capitalization
**E.** 1. Underline the first sentence. Capitalization. 2. Underline the second sentence. Spelling 3. Underline the second sentence. Punctuation. 4. Underline the second sentence. Word order. 5. Underline the first sentence. Spelling. 6. Underline the second sentence. Nouns.
**F.** 1. Chinh looked at many school (schools) before she chose the best one for nursing. 2. she was looking for one with the best teachers? She was looking for one with the best teachers. 3. She got great recomenations (recommendations) from the teachers at her previous school. 4. She hope (hopes) to complete her degree in three yeas (years). 5. She is going to moves (move) so she can be closer to her new school. (punctuation) 6. chinh (Chinh) will have to work at night so she can pays (pay) for school. 7. She have (has) a time-part (part-time) job as a server food (food server) in a restaurant.
**G.** Answers will vary.

**UNIT 1: BALANCING YOUR LIFE**
**Lesson 1: Learning styles**
**A.** 1. Logical/mathematical 2. musical/rhythmic 3. visual/spatial 4. verbal/linguistic 5. body/kinesthetic

**B.** Answers will vary.
**D.** 1. learns, taking 2. struggle, solving 3. are, remembering 4. excels, explaining 5. practices, repeating 6. learn, participating 7. is, relating 8. learn, working 9. succeeds, creating
**E.** 1. by 2. in 3. with 4. by 5. at 6. by 7. at
**F.** Sample answers: 1. Marion practices by putting things in categories. 2. Neda thinks in rhymes and singing. 3. Mario learns by visualizing problems and solutions. 4. Cynthia memorizes information by repeating what she hears. 5. Jim and John understand things better by acting them out.
**G.** Answers will vary.

**Lesson 2: Career planning**
**A.** Sample answers:
High school diploma or GED certificate – high school degree, 4 years
Associate of Arts degree – undergraduate degree, 2 years
Bachelor's degree – undergraduate degree, 4 years
Master's degree – postgraduate degree, 1-2 years
Doctorate – highest level of education, timeline varies (about 8 years)
**B.** Sample answers:
architect: Bachelor's
farmer: High School/GED
firefighter: High School/GED
computer engineer: Bachelor's
soccer player: High School/GED
teacher: Bachelor's
musician: High School/GED
salesperson: Associate of Arts
small business owner: Associate of Arts
food server: High School/GED
lawyer: MA/MS
dentist: PhD
journalist: BA/BS
**D.** 1. I will go (if I save) 2. (If she passes) she will practice 3. I will look (if I get) 4. (If Emil doesn't get) he will go 5. (If she wants) she will have to go 6. He will have to look (if he wants to start) 7. (If Sasha gets) they will pay
**E.** 1. If Maya **goes** to technical school, she will get a better job. 2. Mario will have to get another job if he **wants** to pay for college. 3 If Elias moves out of the city, he will **find** better job opportunities. 4. If we **finish** our degrees in three years, we can start working sooner. 5. Kendra will **apply** to several more schools if she doesn't get into her first choice. 6. She will ask her boss to change her hours if she **gets** accepted at the technical school. 7. Will you apply for scholarships if you **go** to the university?

**F.** Answers will vary.
**G.** Answers will vary.

**Lesson 3: Achieving Balance**
**A.** Answers will vary.
**C.** Sample answers: 1. Andre's family is most important. His family thinks he works too much. 2. No, he will not work fewer hours. He likes to work. He will go on to new dreams.
**E.** 1. will study 2. studied 3. studies 4. will study 5. studies 6. studied 7. will study
**F.** 1. work 2. worked 3. worked 4. will work 5. will work 6. works
**G.** 1. am 2. was 3. is 4. will be 5. are 6. were
**H.**
Right now I <u>am</u> a student. I study history and political science. One day I <u>want</u> <u>to be</u> a teacher and teach in high school so I <u>need</u> to get my special subjects teaching credentials. My classes <u>are</u> really hard and I <u>have</u> to study for at least three hours every night. Last year, I <u>had</u> easier classes so I <u>was</u> able to work and go to school at the same time. But this year, I <u>am</u> only going to school. I <u>will get</u> my bachelor's degree at the end of next year and then I <u>need</u> to take classes for my credentials. That <u>will take</u> about a year. Hopefully, I <u>will be</u> able to pass the credential exams and then I <u>will</u> <u>look</u> for a job as a teacher.

**Lesson 4: Setting priorities**
**A.** Number as follows: 2, 7, 6, 1, 9, 5, 3, 4, 8
**B.** 1. True 2. True 3. True 4. False
**E.** 1. <u>I had studied computer science</u> 2. <u>Gabe had worked as a mechanic</u> 3. <u>Teaching for five years</u> 4. <u>he had graduated from high school</u> 5. <u>they had studied English</u>
**F.** 1. had started, went 2. finished, had worked 3. studied, applied 4. found, began 5. had, picked, registered
**G.** Sample answers: 1. I had ridden four days a week before I competed in a bicycle race. 2. I had worked for the postal service before I applied for a job with a shipping company. 3. I met with a counselor before the kids were born. 4. I had saved money for college before I chose a college major.
**H.** Answers will vary.
**I.** Answers will vary.

**Lesson 5: Motivation**
**B.** Sample answers: 1. Filipe doesn't have a job. 2. Felipe doesn't have ambition. 3. Felipe needs to search for a new house.
**C.** Answers will vary
**E.** 1. b 2. d 3. a 4. c

**F.** 1. starts, will have chosen 2. will have given, begins 3. will have bought, is 4. completes, will have run 5. turns, will have been married 6. will have looked, choose 7. will have gotten, graduates
**G.** Answers will vary.

**Unit 1 Practice Test**
1. b 2. b 3. b 4. c

**UNIT 2: PERSONAL FINANCE**
**Lesson 1: Getting organized**
**B.** Answers will vary.
**C.** Answers will vary.
**E.** 1. A. FP B. FPP 2. A. FP B. FPP 3. A. FPP B. FP 4. A. FPP B. FP
**F.** 1. will have finished 2. will have paid 3. will have started 4. will have been planning 5. will have been looking 6. will have spent 7. will have had
**G.** Answers will vary.
**H.** Answers will vary.

**Lesson 2: Managing money**
**A.** Answers will vary.
**B.** Improved: bought designer clothes, spent every penny they made; Gotten worse: made coffee at home, bought in bulk
**C.** Answers will vary.
**E.** 1. <u>had been spending her tips</u> / she decided to save up for a computer 2. <u>had been paying cash</u> / …got credit cards 3. had a bank account <u>/ …had been saving</u> 4. <u>had been paying</u> / started online banking <u>5. had been spending</u> / …start saving
**F.** 1. Before she decided to save up for a computer, she had been spending her tips. 2. Until we got credit cards, we had been paying cash for everything. 3. He had been saving his money in a drawer before he had a bank account. 4. Until she started banking online, Lisa had been paying her bills by check every month. 5. Until I started saving for retirement, I had been spending my whole paycheck.
**G.** 1. had been living 2. had been driving 3. had been eating 4. had been doing 5. had been making 6. had been hiring 7. had been meeting
**H.** Answers will vary.
**I.** Answers will vary.

**Lesson 3: Investing wisely**
**A.** 1. f 2. e 3. a 4. g 5. b 6. h 7. d 8. c
**B.** Answers will vary.
**C.** Answers will vary.
**D.** Answers will vary.
**F.** 1. can 2. could 3. could 4. can 5. can 6. could 7. can 8. could 9. can

**G.** 1. can look 2. can use 3. could invest 4. could give 5. Can … help 6. Could … tell 7. could pool 8. could increase 9. can afford
**H.** Answers will vary.

**Lesson 4: Credit**
**A.** 1. open 2. get 3. fix 4. add 5. establish 6. use
**B.** Number as follows: 1, 2, 3, 7, 5, 4, 6, 8
**D.** 1. You should have ordered your credit reports. 2. You should have checked your statement. 3. He ought to have called the bank. 4. They should have found a lower interest rate. 5. I should have started banking online. 6. We ought to have consolidated our credit cards. 7. I should have put money into an IRA.
**E.** 1. You should look for an account with no fee. 2. He should get his credit report. 3. We shouldn't ignore the creditors. 4. They ought to cancel their high-interest credit cards. 5. I should contribute more to my 401K.
**F.** Answers will vary.
**G.** Answers will vary.
**H.** Answers will vary.

**Lesson 5: Identity theft**
**A.** Sample answers: 1. Identity theft. Police report. 2. Incorrect information. Advise credit reporting agencies. 3. Bank error. Audit accounts. 4. Phone company charged twice. Call phone company to check billing.
**B.** Answers will vary.
**C.** Answers will vary.
**E.** 1. It could have been a bank error. 2. You might have left your credit card at the hotel. 3. He could have gotten your number from an online site. 4. They may have checked your credit report. 5. They might have seen your social security number. 6. Someone might have seen your pin number. 7. She could have left her wallet at the restaurant.
**F.** 1. might have forgotten 2. may have given 3. could have found 4. could have taken 5. could be
**G.** Answers will vary.

**Unit 2 Practice Test**
1. d 2. c 3. b 4. a

**UNIT 3: AUTOMOTIVE KNOW-HOW**
**Lesson 1: Buying a car**
**A.** 1. Black SUV Pros: seats 8 people, has GPS, anti-theft device, and new tires; Cons: high mileage, upholstery in fair condition 2. Gray SUV Pros: low mileage, good MPG, leather in good condition
**B.** Answers will vary.
**D.** 1. be, been 2. replace, replaced 3. takes, take 4. taken, took 5. do, does 6. allowing, allow 7. is, are 8. Are, Is

**E.** Answers will vary.
**F.** Answers will vary.

**Lesson 2: Maintenance and repair**
**A.** Sample answers: 1. replace 2. check 3. change 4. check 5. top off 6. check, top off 7. inspect, replace 8. top off 9. inspect
**B.** Answers will vary.
**C.** 1. Who, name of a person 2. Where, location 3. How, an explanation 4. When, a time 5. How, an explanation 6. Why, a reason 7. Whose, name of a person 8. Which, a specific item
**E.** 1. f 2. h 3. a 4. g 5. b 6. c 7. e 8. d
**F.** Answers will vary.
**G.** Answers will vary.

**Lesson 3: Car insurance**
**B.** Answers will vary.
**C.** The questions on the left are negative questions used to assume that something is true.
**E.** 1. Aren't, They are both on the insurance policy. 2. Didn't, She has an insurance policy. 3. Weren't, You were the one who bought the car. 4. Didn't, He called the police officer after the accident. 5. Wasn't, Luisa was the one who wanted the high deductible.
**F.** 1. Isn't she covered by her husband's policy? 2. Isn't the insurance company paying for the accident? 3. Doesn't he have a policy that covers anyone who drives his car? 4. Didn't she call the insurance company five days ago? 5. Didn't they say they would look over the policy and get back to us? 6. Didn't Amar rent a car while his was being fixed?
**G.** Answers will vary.

**Lesson 4: Gas and mileage**
**A.** Trip 1: 1. 2. 4.8 3. 66,245 4. $4.75 Trip 2: 1. 66,245 2. $.16 3. 29 4. 155 Trip 3: 1. 310 2. 11 3. $4.73 4. 66,710
**B.** 609 miles; 21 gallons; $99.63 (*(4.8 x $4.75) $22.80 + (5.2 x $4.77) $24.80 + (11 x $4.73) 52.03 = $99.63); 66,101 miles; 200 miles; $.16; 28.6 MPG; 66,710 miles
**C.** Sample answers: 1. f 2. c 3. a 4. h 5. d 6. b 7. e 8. g
**D.** Answers will vary.
**E.** 1. Q. How much gas do you put in each week? A. 16 gallons 2. Q. How many miles do you drive per week? A. about 230 3. Q. What is your odometer reading right now? A. about 35,000 miles 4. Q. What is your MPG? A. about 19 5. Q. What is your average cost per mile? A. 15 cents 6. Q. How much do you spend on gas per week? A. about $60
**F.** *1/15 – 21 mpg, $.19; 1/26 – 48,189, 22 mpg, $.18; 2/11 – 48,489, 21 mpg, $.19; 2/23 – 48,767, 21 mpg, $.19; Average – 286, 13.3, 21.3 mpg, $4.02, $.19*

**Lesson 5: Traffic laws**
**A.** 1. True 2. False 3. True 4. False 5. True 6. False
**B.** 1. Teenagers 2. No one. Men and women drive about the same. 3. Elderly drivers have a higher accident rate than middle-aged drivers. 4. The can handle alcohol better but that doesn't mean they should drink and drive. 5. Warming up a car before driving is considered to be a good practice. 6. Rain, if it doesn't involve a tornado or a hurricane.
**C.** 1. don't they? 2. aren't they? 3. don't they? 4. can't they? 5. shouldn't you? 6. won't you?
**E.** 1. won't he 2. is she 3. do they 4. hasn't it 5. do I 6. haven't they
**F.** 1. don't we 2. did she 3. didn't they 4. didn't you 5. will we 6. are you 7. had you 8. don't you 9. don't I 10. was she
**G.** Answers will vary.

**Unit 3 Practice Test**
1. a 2. b 3. d 4. a

**UNIT 4: HOUSING**
**Lesson 1: I have a problem**
**A.** Painter; Handyman; Plumber; Handyman; Electrician; Building cleaner and maintenance company; Building cleaner and maintenance company; Building cleaner and maintenance company; Pest control; Handyman; Handyman; Handyman
**B.** Answers will vary.
**D.** 1. The handyman had them leave a key under the mat. 2. The tenants let him put a For Sale sign out front. 3. My landlord made me patch the holes in the wall. 4. I will get the landlord to give us free rent for a month. 5. She let her boyfriend decide which couch to buy. 6. My aunt helped me pay rent for a few months.
**E.** Sample answers: 1. Her parents were helping their neighbors move in. 2. His cousin got us to pay for the party. 3. I have my mom pay on half the utilities. 4. The landlord made his tenants pay an extra security deposit for the dog. 5. The renters will let their friends sleep on the couch for a few days.
**F.** Answers will vary.

**Lesson 2: Understand the fine print**
**A.** *See:* dirt, insects, holes in walls, uncollected garbage. *Hear:* insects in walls, neighbors playing loud music, leaky pipes. *Smell:* strange odor from carpet, uncollected garbage
**B.** Answers will vary.
**D.** Sample answers: 1. the fire 2. the football game 3. the concert 4. the strange smell 5. the parade 6. a large monkey 7. the itchy sweater 8. the squirrels

**E.** Sample answers: 1. is listening to 2. will have been watching 3. heard 4. will look 5. has been looking 6. I hear 7. had smelled 8. saw 9. have been noticing 10. will have arrived
**F.** Answers will vary.

**Lesson 3: Your rights**
**B.** 1. the plumbing 2. termites 3. carpets need to be replaced
**D.** 1. that 2. when 3. where 4. that 5. who 6. where 7. who 8. where
**E.** 1. c 2. a 3. f 4. e 5. b 6. d
**F.** 1. I'm ~~wiriting~~ writing this letter on behalf of all of the ~~resident~~ residents at Crystal ~~cove~~ Cove. 2. Sometimes at night, the guard ~~isn't~~ is not in the booth where he is ~~suppose~~ supposed to be. 3. At times, I have ~~see~~ seen him let people in who don't ~~lived~~ live here and aren't ~~visit~~ visiting anyone who ~~live~~ lives here. 4. A friend who visited me said he ~~give~~ gave them the gate code so they could get in any time they wanted. 5. In ~~adition~~ addition to all of these problems, he is not very ~~freindly~~ friendly to the residents who live here. 6. These are issues that need a response, so please let us know what you ~~plans~~ plan to do.
**G.**
I'm writing this letter on behalf of all of the residents at Crystal Cove. Sometimes at night, the guard is not in the booth where he is supposed to be. At times, I have seen him let people in who don't live here and aren't visiting anyone who lives here. A friend who visited me said he gave them the gate code so they could get in any time they wanted. In addition to all of these problems, he is not very friendly to the residents who live here. These are issues that need a response, so please let us know what you plan to do.
**H.** Answers will vary.

**Lesson 4: Insuring your home**
**A.** 1. #1 2. #2 3. #2 4. Answers will vary.
**B.** Answers will vary.
**D.** 1. His deductible is the highest. 2. This estimate is cheaper than the first one we got. 3. That company has more reputable service than our current one. 4. Her rate is lower than mine. 5. Your quote is the most expensive. 6. My insurance company has the best online service.
**E.** 1. I have the most spacious apartment in my building. 2. Before getting renter's insurance you should compare the lowest quotes you can find. 3. She is using an insurance agency that charges the highest fee of all the agencies. 4. I plan to negotiate with the agent more motivated than the other agents. 5. We found the most decent insurance company in the business.
**F.** Answers will vary.

**Lesson 5: Protecting your home**
**A.** Burglar: breaks into property to steal something
Thief: steals something without the owner's knowledge
**B.** Answers will vary.
**C.** Answers will vary.
**D.** Answers will vary.
**F.** 1. are built 2. was found 3. can be found 4. was sold
5. was broken into 6. will be repaired 7. are being paid
8. can be leased
**G.** 1. Renter's insurance will be added to our policy.
2. All of our tools were taken from the garage by the
thieves. 3. Our home was appraised by the appraiser
last week. 4. Our loan was funded by the loan officer
before escrow closed. 5. The damage from the fire will
be repaired by the handyman. 6. He thinks his truck was
stolen from in front of his house by a local gang.
**H.** Answers will vary.

**Unit 4 Practice Test**
1. b 2. d 3. d 4. b

**UNIT 5: HEALTH**
Lesson   1 : Mind and body
**B.** Answers will vary.
**C.** Answers will vary.
**D.** 1. where I can go running every day 2. wherever
the mountains are 3. anywhere they can see the ocean
4. anywhere there is no pollution 5. where the sun
shines 6. somewhere I can grow my own food 7. wherever my friends live 8. where it is not too hot
**F.** 1. where I can exercise outside every day 2. anywhere
they can see the ocean 3. anywhere there is no pollution 4. wherever the sun shines 5. somewhere I can
grow my own food 6. wherever my friends live
**G.** 1. wherever the air is clean 2. wherever the food is
organic and fresh 3. where I can feel a cool breeze on
my face 4. anywhere she thinks is safe 5. wherever there
is a lot of light 6. anywhere the offices are sanitary
**H.** Answers will vary.
**I.** Answers will vary.

**Lesson 2: What's this charge for?**
**B.** Answers will vary.
**D.** 1. When the nurse called her name 2. as soon as
he left 3. While her sister was waiting 4. after I got the
hospital bill 5. before his next patient arrived 6. Once
the insurance company fixed the mistake 7. When the
insurance representative called
**E.** Answers will vary.
**F.** 1. After I called the office, they sent me an itemized
bill. 2. After she got a call from the insurance company, she filled out the application. 3. He discussed the

charges with his wife after the nurse explained them to
him. 4. Once Liza called the doctor's office, they sent her
a duplicate bill. 5. Once she recovered from surgery, she
went back to work. 6. After Dinuka received her diagno-
sis, she called her family and friends. 7. As soon as Brent
got laid off from work, he started looking for private
insurance.
**G.** Answers will vary.

**Lesson 3: Health insurance**
**B.** Answers will vary.
**C.** Answers will vary.
**D.** Answers will vary.
**E.** Answers will vary.
**G.** 1. e 2. i 3. a 4. j 5. b 6. c 7. d 8. h 9. f 10. g
**H.** Answers will vary.
**I.** Answers will vary.
**J.** Answers will vary.
**K.** Answers will vary.

**Lesson 4: Addictions**
**A.** Answers will vary.
**B.** addict – fanatic; dependence – obsession;
detoxification – purification; impairment – deterioration;
tolerance – endurance; withdraw - removal
**C.** Answers will vary.
**E.** 1. (in spite of the fact) it rains three days a week
2. (even though) she only has one glass per week 3.
(although) he does it three times a week 4. (in spite of
the fact) that I don't like swallowing pills 5. (even if)
they don't feel like it
**F.** Answers will vary.
**G.** Answers will vary.

**Lesson 5: First aid**
**A.** 1. d 2. e 3. c 4. a 5. f 6. b
**B.** Answers will vary.
**C.** Answers will vary.
**E.** 1. Call the doctor so that she can be there when her
contractions get stronger. 2. She is holding her head
as if she has a headache. 3. He wants to call the phar-
macist so that he can get his prescription filled. 4. He
should call another doctor in order that he can get a
second opinion. 5. She needs to rest as she will need
her strength to make it through her physical therapy.
6. She is talking as though she has never gotten a shot
before.
**F.** 1. You call a poison control center because treatment
for poison is different for different substances. 2. You
apply pressure to a wound to stop the bleeding. 3. You
cover someone who is shivering because he or she
may be in shock. 4. You keep a wound clean to avoid

infection. 5. You give someone with chest pains an aspirin because he or she may be having a heart attack and it could save a life. 6. You keep a person who has a head injury from sleep because he may have a concussion.
**G.** Answers will vary.

**Unit 5 Practice Test**
1. c 2. d 3. c 4. a

**UNIT 6: GETTING HIRED**
Lesson 1: How much is it?
**A.** Answers will vary.
**B.** Answers will vary.
**D.** 1. that/which 2. who 3. that/which 4. who 5. who 6. that/which 7. that/which
**E.** 1. I like that store best. The store is far from my house. 2. The manager runs that store. He says he'll match that price. 3. I wanted a warranty. That product didn't come with that warranty. 4. The woman was nice. She convinced me to buy it. 5. The salesman was helping me. I couldn't find him. 6. He bought an item. It was the most expensive. 7. The speakers came with a warranty. The speakers were $700.
**F.** Answers will vary.
**G.** Answers will vary.

**Lesson 2: Shopping from home**
**A.** Answers will vary.
**B.** Answers will vary.
**D.** 1. whom I will contact 2. whom she met in class 3. that she is going to buy 4. that our friends bought 5. whom you like 6. which he sold me 7. whom he called 8. that you are going to eat 9. which they have at home 10. whom we commissioned
**E.** Sample answers: 1. whom I will contact 2. that she is going to buy 3. which he sold me 4. whom she met in class 5. whom he called 6. which they have at home 7. that you are going to eat 8. whom we commissioned 9. that our friends bought 10. whom you like
**F.** Answers will vary.
**G.** Answers will vary.

**Lesson 3: Is this under warranty?**
**A.** *warranty – a guarantee that a product will work, with the promise of compensation if it does not*
**B.** Answers will vary.
**C.** Answers will vary.
**E.** 1. where they sell reusable bags 2. why I never shop 3. where the salespeople work 4. when the mall is quiet 5. where they only grow vegetables 6. when it was raining 7. why that television didn't come with a warranty 8. where they used to serve Mexican food

**F.** 1. I bought the fabric when the store was having a sale. 2. We never go to the store on Sundays when it is crowded. 3. She bought her washing machine at the store when the store promised three years of free service. 4. I don't buy fish in the summer when the fish is not fresh. 5. We went on vacation to Mexico where it is hot.
**G.** Answers will vary.
**H.** Answers will vary

**Lesson 4: Returns and exchanges**
**B.** Sample answers: 1. No return or refund 2. Ask the Manager 3. Refund
**D.** 1. The warranty ~~that is~~ offered by that store is the best one I have seen. 2. The salesperson ~~whom~~ he bought it from doesn't work there anymore. 3. Did you see the customer ~~who was~~ standing here a few minutes ago? 4. The stereo system ~~that is~~ playing right now is too big for Monica's new place. 5. The receipt ~~that~~ she has is too old. 6. I saw the patio furniture ~~that was~~ advertised in the paper. 7. Did they look for a house ~~that was~~ in their price range? 8. We never buy electronics ~~that~~ don't come with a warranty. 9. The new store ~~that~~ opened near our house is having a grand opening sale. 10. The couch ~~that~~ you sold me has fallen apart.
**E.** 1. they sell 2. he couldn't pass up 3. he bought it from 4. that comes with 5. she could find 6. she has been wanting 7. that comes with a free vacuum cleaner 8. on sale
**F.** Answers will vary.

**Lesson 5: For sale**
**B.** 1. We want to sell our old English textbooks for a discounted price. 2. The used TVs in our restaurant will be available this Saturday only. 3. Our plan is coming together. 4. That warehouse will open to the public at 8 a.m.
**C.** Answers will vary.
**E.** 1. the one with the red cover noun 2. to put ads in all the local papers infinitive 3. the website giving medical advice noun 4. happening every Wednesday gerund 5. the brown one with the tiled roof noun 6. to sell all of his furniture infinitive 7. the jeweled one with the pink lace noun 8. the one with artist's drawing noun 9. the one on State Street noun 10. to move all of the sale items into the window infinitive
**F.** Answers will vary.
**G.** Answers will vary.
**H.** Answers will vary.

**Unit 6 Practice Test**
1. b 2. c 3. d 4.a

**UNIT 7: THE OFFICE**
**Lesson 1: How do you turn it on?**
**A.** 1. The job is unique because it keeps important and essential information in the office. 2. The employees are required to use the fax machines, computers, shredders, and copy machines every day, and avoid using any of the equipment for personal use.
**B.**
We would like to welcome you to the field services offices of Plano Distribution Center. The office is the hub of our company. Your job is unique because we keep important and essential information in the office. This information is confidential and cannot be replaced. You are required to use the fax machines, computers, shredders, and copy machines every day, and you are to avoid using any of this equipment for personal use. We are a company of integrity, so if our personal files on clients were to reach our competitors, it would be devastating to our business. You have signed a letter of agreement stipulating your willingness to work under these conditions. The company has invested millions of dollars in the equipment you will use. This handbook will provide you with an orientation on using it. You will also receive training, and we will provide technical support when necessary.
**C.** Person: We, you, clients, competitors; Place: offices, Plano Distribution Center, office; Thing: company, job, information, machines, computers, shredders, day, equipment, company, files, business, letter, conditions, dollars, handbook, orientation, training, support
**E.** 1. Your job, important and essential information, the office 2. field service offices, Plano Distribution Center 3. The office, the hub, our company 4. a letter 5. a company, our personal files, our competitors, our company
**F.** 1. You 2. We, you 3. you, it 4. yourself, it 5. You, we
**G.** 1. What you see 2. what I was supposed to do 3. What she found 4. What she learned 5. what she likes to do
**H.** Answers will vary.
**I.** Answers will vary.

**Lesson 2: How do you fix it?**
**A.** 1. Because the secretary was concerned about the copy machine continually breaking down, the manager asked her to buy a new one. 2. Since the manager sometimes treats the employees inappropriately, he spoke to the secretary in private to understand her point of view and resolve the problem. 3. Because the secretary is interested in learning about the new available software and wants to hear what another employee has to say about it, the manager set up a time for the employees to work together. 4. Because the

several employees who are on a committee to a hire a new supervisor can't decide whom to hire, the manager will make the decision. 5. When the secretary went to the supply closet and discovered the computer paper wasn't there, the manager asked the secretary to complete a supply requisition.
**C.** Sample answers: 1. *what he learned.* 2. where the meeting was held 3. what we can do to help 4. how to solve the problem 5. who make a good leader 6. where the conference is 7. who is giving the seminar 8. what he learned
**D.** Answers will vary.
**E.** Answers will vary.
**F.** Answers will vary

**Lesson 3: Files and folders**
**B.** Answers will vary.
**C.**
Sarah is a good worker in the office. She is what I consider a model employee. I am particularly impressed by her organizational skills. She can find anything almost immediately; however, I am concerned that no one else may be able to understand her system. It seems that she works well in a team and people respect her. It seems that she can teach others. She has complained in the past about how we do certain things. I feel what she has to say has merit.
**E.** Sample answers: 1. She seems to be what I consider an example of a poor employee. 2. It seems she isn't adapted to teamwork and that people don't have much respect for her. 3. It seems she has nothing to say of merit. 4. It appears she can't teach anyone anything. 5. I do not feel particularly impressed by her organizational skills. 6. She has not seemed to complain in the past about how we do certain things.
**F.** 1. that she likes her job 2. what I like to see 3. what they never would hope for 4. what he paid for 5. that she could work harder 6. that they don't like to work very hard
**G.** Sample answers: 1. It seems that she likes her job. 2. It seems that they don't like to work very hard. 3. She has become what they would never hope for. 4. That is what I like to see. 5. We all feel that she could work harder. 6. He got what he paid for.
**H.** Answers will vary.

**Lesson 4: What's the problem?**
**B.** 1. First, set ground rules, show mutual respect and be willing to listen to all sides. This is called setting the scene. 2. Gather information about the problem. 3. Identify and agree upon the problem. 4. Brainstorm how

to resolve the problem. 5. Come to a mutual agreement beneficial to all parties, but especially to the company.
**C.** Answers will vary.
**E.** 1. <u>Where you begin</u> is 2. <u>Where they start</u> is 3. <u>That everyone understands</u> makes 4. <u>What is next</u> seems 5. <u>What's important</u> is 6. <u>How you brainstorm</u> can help 7. <u>That everyone comes to a mutual agreement</u> is 8. <u>What is important</u> is
**F.** Answers will vary.
**G.** Answers will vary.
**H.** Answers will vary.

## Lesson 5: What did you do?
**B.** 80%; re-keying; will complete a security scan of all employees, will train employees on keyless entry procedures and confidentiality; contractor wants more money than he contracted for; fair
**D.** Sample answers: 1. I did what she wanted me to. 2. She hopes she will get some time off for all her hard work. 3. She asked how to complete the application form. 4. We will organize what parts should go where. 5. I know where the human resources office is. 6. They are going to decide how to divide the teams. 7. I decided what office I would work best in. 8. She planned who would lead each part of the presentation.
**E.** Answers will vary.
**F.** Answers will vary.

## Unit 7 Practice Test
1. b 2. c 3. d 4. c

## UNIT 8: CIVIC RESPONSIBILITY
Lesson 1: Investigating Citizenship
**A.** 1. A naturalized citizen is one who becomes a citizen in this country. 2. Dual citizenship is citizenship held in two different countries. 3. Becoming a citizen requires establishing oneself in this country, learning English, and following the law. 4. The oath states willingness to obey the laws and support the country.
**B.**
Many <u>people</u> consider being a <u>citizen</u> of the <u>United States</u> a <u>privilege</u>. Certainly, <u>citizens</u> have specific <u>rights</u>. An <u>immigrant</u> who wants to become a <u>citizen</u> must establish <u>himself</u> or <u>herself</u> in the <u>United States</u>, learn <u>English</u>, and follow all the <u>laws</u> of the <u>land</u>. Since the <u>laws</u> for <u>citizenship</u> for other <u>countries</u> may be different from those of the <u>United States</u>, some <u>people</u> can have dual <u>citizenship</u>, meaning they can be <u>citizens</u> of the <u>United States</u> and another <u>country</u> at the same <u>time</u>. When a <u>person</u> takes the <u>steps</u> necessary to become a <u>citizen</u> and when all <u>requirements</u> are met, <u>he</u> or <u>she</u> takes an <u>oath</u> stating a

<u>willingness</u> to obey the <u>laws</u> and support the <u>country</u>. This <u>person</u> is then known as a naturalized <u>citizen</u> and has all the <u>rights</u> of <u>someone</u> born in the <u>country</u>.
**D.** Answers will vary.
**E.** Sample answers: 1. <u>The</u> green card I have been waiting for finally came in <u>the</u> mail. 2. Salwa is <u>a</u> refugee from the Middle East. <u>The</u> country she comes from doesn't allow emigration. 3. Ella is 35 and her mother just became <u>a</u> permanent resident. 4. Marna just got <u>a</u> green card. <u>The</u> card came in the mail yesterday. 5. Have you taken <u>a</u> citizenship test? 6. <u>The</u> citizenship class they offer at my school starts at <u>the</u> beginning of <u>the</u> month. 7. He took <u>an</u> oath last week and is now <u>a</u> naturalized citizen. 8. She wants to apply to become <u>a</u> citizen but doesn't know what steps to take. 9. Her daughter was born in <u>the</u> United States so she is a citizen. But her father is still waiting to become <u>a</u> permanent resident. 10. Jared and his brother are trying to come to <u>the</u> United States for <u>a</u> job. They are hoping <u>a</u> company that wants to hire them will sponsor them.
**F.** Answers will vary.
**G.** Answers will vary.

## Lesson 2: Rights
**B.** 1. Amendment 7 2. Amendment 2 3. Amendment 1
**D.** 1. The <u>residents</u> of her <u>town</u> called several town hall <u>meetings</u>. 2. <u>People</u> want to change the <u>immigration</u> system. 3. <u>Candidates</u> always promise more than they can deliver. 4. Do you think <u>fairness</u> was involved in his decision? 5. <u>Dr. Stevens</u> presented his <u>paper</u> on <u>global warming</u>. 6. The <u>classes</u> that we took prepared us to pass the <u>interview</u>.
<u>The</u> designates a specific subject.
**E.** 1. The citizens 2. Happiness 3. Refugees 4. problems 5. Crimes 6. the documents 7. belongings 8. Soldiers 9. justice 10. Senator Lyons
**F.** 1. The Bill of Rights guarantees the freedom of religion, speech, press, assembly, and petition 2. The Bill of Rights guarantees the freedom to bear arms 3. The Bill of Rights guarantees freedom from unlawful imprisonment 4. The Bill of Rights guarantees the right to a speedy and public trial 5. The Bill of Rights guarantees powers to be reserved to the states.

## Lesson 3: *Getting involved*
**B.**
The <u>Hamilton Club</u> was established in 1965. It is <u>a service organization</u> with 3200 members worldwide. The club helps provide food to underprivileged families.

This <u>organization</u> is proud of the efforts made over the past forty years. To become a member of <u>Hamilton,</u> you must…
1) be willing to contribute to underprivileged families.
2) attend monthly meetings.
3) take leadership roles in the <u>club.</u>
**C.** Answers will vary.
**D.** Answers will vary.
**F.** 1. The club 2. It 3. Organization 4. the group 5. Organization 6. It
**G.** 1. The Mother's Club 2. the group 3. the organization 4. The Club's 5. The Mother's Club 6. The Club
**H.** Answers will vary.
**I.** Answers will vary.

**Lesson 4: Saving the environment**
**A.** Answers will vary.
**B.** Answers will vary.

**D.** 1. near 2. far 3. near 4. far 5. near 6. far 7. near 8. near 9. far 10. far
**E.** 1. Those 2. this 3. that 4. these 5. this 6. this 7. That 8. these 9. That 10. those
**Exercise F.** Answers will vary.
**Exercise G.** Answers will vary.

**Lesson 5: Express yourself**
**B.** Answers will vary.
**D.** 1. A. this B. such a 2. A. These B. Such 3. A. these B. such
**E.** Answers will vary.
**F.** Answers will vary.

**Unit 8 Practice Test**
1. b 2. d 3. a 4. b

# LESSON PLANNER METHODOLOGY

**The Stand Out Lesson Planner methodology ensures success!**

**Stand Out** ensures student success through good lesson planning and instruction. Each of the five Lessons in every Unit has a lesson plan. Unlike most textbooks, the Lesson Planner was written before the student book materials. A lot of learning occurs with the student books closed so by writing the lesson plans first, we could ensure that each objective was clearly achieved. Each lesson plan follows a systematic and proven format:

| | |
|---|---|
| **W** | Warm-up and/or review |
| **I** | Introduction |
| **P** | Presentation |
| **P** | Practice |
| **E** | Evaluation |
| **A** | Application |

### Warm-up and/or review

The warm-up activities establish a context and purpose to the lesson. Exercises use previously learned content and materials that are familiar to students from previous lessons.

### Introduction

In the introduction step, exercises focus the students' attention on the goals of the lesson by asking questions, showing visuals, telling a story, etc. Instructors should state the objective of the lesson and tell students what they will be doing. The objective should address what students are expected to be able to do by the end of the lesson.

### Presentation

The presentation activities provide students with the building blocks and skills they need to achieve the objectives set in the introduction. The exercises introduce new information to the students through visuals, realia, description, listenings, explanation, or written text. This is the time to check students' comprehension.

### Practice

Practice activities provide meaningful tasks for students to practice what they have just learned through different activities. These activities can be done as a class, in small groups, pairs, or individually. All of these activities are student centered and involve cooperative learning. Instructors should model each activity, monitor progress, and provide feedback.

### Evaluation

Evaluation ensures that students are successful. Instructors should evaluate students on attainment of the objective set at the start of the lesson. This can be done by oral, written, or demonstrated performance. At this point, if students need more practice, instructors can go back and do additional practice activities before moving onto the application.

### Application

Application activities help students apply new knowledge to their own lives or new situations. This is one of the most important steps of the lesson plan. If students can accomplish the application task, it will build their confidence to be able to sue what they've learned out in the community. The Team Projects are an application of unit objectives that involves task-based activities with a product.

In addition to each lesson plan following the WIPPEA model, each Unit in **Stand Out** follows this same approach. The first lesson is always in Introduction to the Unit, introducing new vocabulary and the basic concepts that will be expanded upon in the unit. The following four lessons are the Presentations and Practices for the unit topic. Following the five lessons is a Review lesson, which allows students to do more practice with everything they already learned. The final lesson is an Application for everything they learned in the unit, a team project.